THE
GOSPELS
INTERWOVEN

The GOSPELS

A chronological narrative of the life of Jesus
interweaving details from the four Gospels in the words
of the *New International Version* of the Bible

REFERENCE EDITION
with Harmonization Endnotes:
Help in Understanding Gospel Differences

Compiled and written by
KERMIT ZARLEY

INTERWOVEN

Wipf and Stock Publishers
EUGENE, OREGON

:

Wipf and Stock Publishers
199 West 8th Avenue, Suite 3
Eugene, Oregon 97401

The Gospels Interwoven
A chronological story of Jesus blending the four Gospels in the words of the NIV. Plus solutions to apparent Gospel differences.
By Zarley, Kermit
Copyright©1987 Zarley, Kermit
ISBN: 1-57910-775-3
Publication date: October, 2001
Previously published by Victor Books, 1987.

Contents.

List of Maps.

Note: These maps are intended to acquaint the reader with the area involved and suggest travel routes that Jesus might have taken. However, there is uncertainty as to the exact chronology of these travels and the routes taken. In addition, it is likely that Jesus made other journeys not recorded in the Gospels (see John 21:25).

A circular route indicates itinerant ministry in that region. Numbers refer to sections in the narrative where the travel is indicated. A question mark following a number, town, or other site signifies considerable uncertainty of location.

Foreword.

Some of us, given at one time or another to chasing a small white ball over a large plot of real estate and depositing it eventually in eighteen small holes, know Kermit Zarley as a member of the PGA Tour and winner of the Canadian Open Championship and three other tournaments. I also know Kermit as a diligent student of the Bible, and remember his visiting seminary libraries and reading and studying, even during tournaments.

For some time Kermit gave himself to producing this single-narrative harmony of the Gospels. The idea is not new, for it reaches back as far as Tatian, a second-century apologist and pupil of Justin Martyr. Tatian authored the *Diatessaron* (lit., *through four*), which was for a long time popular among Syriac-speaking Christians. In the early stages of his project, I encouraged Kermit to pursue this narrative harmony, especially since he wanted to produce it in the words of the *New International Version*, which had not been done.

There are different ways to read the Gospels. To read them separately is to read them exposing oneself to the special themes and emphases that each Gospel author sought to stress. To read them in a parallel, four-column harmony is to study the areas of similarities and differences. To read them in such a book as Zarley's *The Gospels Interwoven* is to expose oneself in an admirable way to an immediate, uninterrupted, and straightforward personal encounter with our Lord and Savior, Jesus Christ. That cannot fail to help any reader of God's Word.

Dr. S. Lewis Johnson, Jr., *Minister, Believers Chapel, Dallas, Texas; former Professor of New Testament, Dallas Theological Seminary, and of Biblical and Systematic Theology, Trinity Evangelical Divinity School*

Preface.
The Story behind This Book

Golf was the center of my life from the age of ten, when I learned to play, until I was a student at the University of Houston. In 1960 I was invited to a weekend retreat conducted by Campus Crusade for Christ. There I heard Hal Lindsey, known today for *The Late Great Planet Earth* and other books, speak on Bible prophecy. Four years earlier I had made a commitment to Jesus Christ in prayer with my Sunday School teacher, but I hadn't grown as a Christian. Bible prophecy was a new subject to me. Lindsey piqued my interest as he explained the relevance of Bible prophecy to current world events. This inspired me for the first time to read and study the Bible. My constant prayer became that God would give me a desire to read and study the Scriptures diligently and that He would teach me His truth as revealed in them.

After graduation from the University of Houston in 1963, and following a six-month active duty stint in the Army, I joined the ranks of the Professional Golfers' Association (PGA) Tour. In order to help us follow Christ, my best friend, Babe Hiskey, and I started the PGA Tour Bible Study in 1965, which continues to thrive today. Through the Tour Bible Study I have enjoyed meeting and being taught by many outstanding Christian teachers, pastors, evangelists, and seminary professors. As a result, my interest in Bible study continued to grow. Often, as soon as I finished a round of golf in a tournament, I would search out the best theological library and study into the night.

In time I developed a desire to write. Eventually I began working on a book about biblical prophecies. Then in the early 1980s I hit on the idea of joining all the material of the Gospels together into a single chronological narrative, including all the details but deleting all repetition. What motivated me most about this idea was that, if successful, it could be used as a tool for evangelism.

To my surprise, my research revealed that the idea was not new, but had enjoyed much success throughout church history until the last two centuries. Most of these harmonies, however, had weaknesses in composition. I felt I could improve the integrity of the single-narrative harmony. I decided to base my work on the *New International Version,* since it was becoming the most popular English translation of the Bible. I was delighted when my friend and mentor in biblical study, Dr. S. Lewis Johnson, Jr., encouraged me to go ahead with the project. I laid aside my writing on prophecy and launched into the complex and tedious task of joining together the Gospels of Matthew, Mark, Luke, and John.

To aid my project, I bought a personal computer with some of my earnings from winning the 1984 Tallahassee Open. It enabled me, with the help of my wife, Marilyn, to complete *The Gospels Interwoven* in less than two years. She not only constantly encouraged me but served as collaborator, editor, and proofreader of my work. Her background as a proofreader and a high school English teacher made her contribution to the project extremely valuable. We were both ever-conscious of the awesome responsibility of working with the words of Scripture. We doggedly adhered to the "Principles of Composition" (see page 25) I had established to maintain the integrity of the work.

I am grateful for the encouragement of others, especially my close friend Jim Hiskey, and, of course, Dr. Johnson, who offered suggestions for improvement of the first draft. I am thankful for the confidence that Victor Books had in my manuscript and in me, a professional golfer who has dared to enter the field of theological writing. Today, I still like to play occasional tournament golf, but I am even more excited to write about Jesus Christ.

Kermit Zarley
Friendswood, Texas

Excerpts from the Preface to the New International Version.

THE NEW INTERNATIONAL VERSION is a completely new translation of the Holy Bible made by over a hundred scholars working directly from the best available Hebrew, Aramaic and Greek texts. It had its beginning in 1965 when . . . a group of scholars met . . . and concurred in the need for a new translation of the Bible in contemporary English. This group, though not made up of official church representatives, was transdenominational. Its conclusion was endorsed by a large number of leaders from many denominations. . . .

Responsibility for the new version was delegated . . . to a self-governing body of fifteen, the Committee on Bible Translation, composed for the most part of biblical scholars from colleges, universities and seminaries. . . . That they were from many denominations . . . helped safeguard the translation from sectarian bias. . . .

. . . It may well be that no other translation has been made by a more thorough process of review and revision from committee to committee than this one.

From the beginning of the project, the Committee on Bible Translation held to certain goals for the *New International Version:* that it would be an accurate translation and one that would have clarity and literary quality and so prove suitable for public and private reading, teaching, preaching, memorizing and liturgical use. The Committee also sought to preserve some measure of continuity with the long tradition of translating the Scriptures into English.

In working toward these goals, the translators were united in their commitment to the authority and infallibility of the Bible as God's Word in written form. . . .

The Greek text used in translating the New Testament was an eclectic one. No other piece of ancient literature has such an abun-

13

dance of manuscript witnesses as does the New Testament. Where existing manuscripts differ, the translators made their choice of readings according to accepted principles of New Testament textual criticism. Footnotes call attention to places where there was uncertainty about what the original text was. The best current printed texts of the Greek New Testament were used. . . .

As in other ancient documents, the precise meaning of the biblical texts is sometimes uncertain. . . . The more significant of these have been called to the reader's attention in the footnotes. . . .

To achieve clarity the translators sometimes supplied words not in the original texts but required by the context. If there was uncertainty about such material, it is enclosed in brackets. . . .

As an aid to the reader . . . sectional headings are inserted in most of the books. They are not to be regarded as part of the NIV text. . . .

The footnotes in this version are of several kinds, most of which need no explanation. Those giving alternative translations begin with "Or" and generally introduce the alternative with the last word preceding it in the text, except when it is a single-word alternative; in poetry quoted in a footnote a slant mark indicates a line division. Footnotes introduced by "Or" do not have uniform significance. In some cases two possible translations were considered to have about equal validity. In other cases, though the translators were convinced that the translation in the text was correct, they judged that another interpretation was possible and of sufficient importance to be represented in a footnote.

In the New Testament, footnotes that refer to uncertainty regarding the original text are introduced by "Some manuscripts" or similar expressions. . . .

The Committee on Bible Translation

June 1978
(Revised August 1983)

In Defense of the
Single-Narrative Harmony.

No book has ever been published more than the Bible. No literature has ever been subjected to more scrutinizing examination than the four Gospels of the New Testament (NT). Many books have been written to show the similarities and differences of these four Gospels. This is one of those books, called a *harmony* of the Gospels of Matthew, Mark, Luke, and John. These four men, three of them eyewitnesses,[1] wrote of the life of that greatest Person who ever lived—Jesus Christ.

---

1. All four Gospels of the NT are anonymous. This writer, however, accepts the church tradition that the four Gospel titles, appended after the fact, correctly identify their authors. For the past two centuries, NT scholars have devoted much attention to the authorship of the four NT Gospels. Many contemporary scholars distinguish between "author" and "writer" (though not so distinguished herein). It is possible that the author of one or more of the canonical Gospels used an amanuensis, or secretary, as the actual writer, much like the Apostle Paul did in some of his letters (e.g., Gal. 6:11; Col. 4:18; 2 Thes. 3:17; Phile. 19). This may be the case with the Gospel of John, as indicated by the writings of certain early church fathers and by the difference of its Greek from that of *The Revelation*, assuming that the exiled Apostle John is its writer. In addition, there exists fairly reliable patristic evidence that Matthew first penned a Gospel in Hebrew or Aramaic, which may have been translated into Greek, perhaps by someone else. A number of church fathers allege that the Gospel of Mark was written by John Mark, who, as a companion of the Apostle Peter on preaching tours in and near Rome, compiled his Gospel from the preaching and reminiscing of Peter. Such evidence later assured that Gospel's entrance into the canon.

In some cases there exists internal evidence in the Gospels to substantiate the claim of the Gospel's title, as well as of the author's being an eyewitness. E.g., in the Gospel of Mark, the *young man* (Mark 14:51) appears to be the author (see EN 15:1), making Mark an eyewitness to at least some of the events of Passion Week. Such expressions in the Gospel of John as *the other disciple* (John 1:35-40; 18:15-16; 20:2) and *the disciple whom Jesus loved* (20:2; 13:23; 19:25; 21:7, 20) suggest the identity of the author while John 21:24 compared with v. 20 solidifies it (see EN 15:2), making him a frequent eyewitness of the incidents in his Gospel (John 21:24). The author often associates himself with the Apostle Peter, almost

What Is a Harmony of the Gospels?

The phrase *harmony of the Gospels* refers to a joining together of the four Gospels of the NT in primarily one of two forms. One is called a composite, interwoven, or single-narrative harmony, as is this volume. In harmonies of this kind, most or all of the material of the four Gospels is interwoven in a continuous reading that excludes all repetition. This type is primarily for reading. The other type is known as the parallel-column harmony.[2] In it the four Gospels (or sometimes only Matthew, Mark, and Luke) are arranged in vertical, parallel columns with the same incidents appearing on the same horizontal lines. This type is for study. To analyze variations in the Gospel accounts, one must turn to a parallel-column harmony. But to obtain a comprehensive view of the life of Christ, a continuous-narrative harmony is of considerable value.

History of Harmonies

At various times in history either the composite type or some form of column harmony has led in popularity. About A.D. 160, Tatian wrote the first known harmony of the four Gospels. His composite was called the *Diatessaron,*[3] meaning "by four." It enjoyed widespread popularity in the following centuries, especially in the Syrian church. Syria was a primary region of early missionary outreach. Antioch, capital of Syria and third largest city in the Roman empire, soon became the center of the Christian church, which shifted early from Jerusalem following persecution there. In Syria,

---

certainly being one of the inner circle of three apostles: Peter and the two brothers, James and John. Since James was early martyred, the internal evidence of the fourth Gospel corroborates patristic evidence identifying the author as the Apostle John.

Luke, who later accompanied the Apostle Paul on missionary journeys, distinguishes himself from eyewitnesses of the Lord. He writes that the events of Jesus' life *were handed down to us by those who from the first were eyewitnesses* (Luke 1:2), which suggests that Luke may have appealed to some of these writings in authoring his Gospel.

2. The term "harmony" was first applied by the German theologian A. Osiander in his harmony entitled *Harmonia Evangelourum,* published in 1537. German biblical scholars, and some others, refer to the composite type as a "harmony," and the parallel-column arrangement as a "synopsis." This volume follows English-speaking writers, who generally refer to both types as "harmonies."

3. Due to its antiquity, Tatian's *Diatessaron* has in modern times become increasingly significant as evidence for determining the Greek text for the Gospels.

the *Diatessaron* must have been for the churches long the service-book in the Gospels, while the translations of the separate Gospels were used in the studies of the theologians, a condition which prevailed at least till about A.D. 370.[4]

This is remarkable, since the official church canonization of the NT books did not actually occur until two African synods were held in A.D. 393 and A.D. 397.[5] It therefore appears that use of the *Diatessaron* in the Syrian church superseded that of the separated Gospels for perhaps 200 years or more before official church canonization of the NT.

After three centuries, a movement began in the Catholic Church to abolish the use of Tatian's *Diatessaron*. R.V. Tasker reports that this was provoked because the *Diatessaron*

was the only form in which the Gospels were read in the Syriac-speaking church, until it was replaced by what our oldest authorities for the Syriac version call the "separated" Gospels.[6]

This was carried out by Syrian bishop Theodoret in the fifth century, who gives us the following account:

I have met with above two hundred of these books (the *Diatessaron*), which were in use in our churches—all which I took away and laid aside in a parcel, placing in their room the Gospels of the four Evangelists.[7]

Theodoret demonstrated an aversion to the *Diatessaron* because he thought it appeared to *supplant* the canonical Gospels. Leading authorities now contend that Tatian's intention was to *supplement* the Gospels. Bruce M. Metzger quotes eminent NT scholar F.C. Burkitt about the *Diatessaron*:

---

4. Philip Schaff and Johann Jacob Herzog, eds. *The New Schaff-Herzog Encyclopedia of Religious Knowledge* (New York: Funk & Wagnalls, 1908; Grand Rapids: Baker, 1977), 152.
5. Philip Schaff, *History of the Christian Church*, 8 vols. (New York: Scribner's, 1910; Grand Rapids: Eerdmans, 1985), 2:519.
6. R.V.G. Tasker, *Tyndale New Testament Commentaries: The Gospel According to St. John* (Grand Rapids: Eerdmans, 1960), 22.
7. Jamieson, Fausset & Brown, *A Commentary, Critical, Experimental and Practical*, 3 vols., rev. ed. (Grand Rapids: Eerdmans, 1978), 1:xiii.

I see no reason to withdraw my conjecture about the origin of this famous Harmony, that it was not a rival to the Gospels themselves, but rather the first of the versions.[8]

Nevertheless, Tatian's harmony exceeded all others in influence. "In the Middle Ages the Latin Tatian [*Diatessaron*] was much used, and there are extant commentaries on it. . . . Other [composite] harmonies were circulated in the latter half of the Middle Ages."[9] These harmonies in other languages appear to be revisions of the *Diatessaron*. G. Quispel traced the translation and use of the *Diatessaron*, finding that it was translated into many Euro-Asian languages, such as Arabic, Armenian, Latin, German, Dutch, French, and English. English writer J. Hamlyn Hill comments on the considerable impact of the *Diatessaron* in the spread of the Gospel:

> Its intrinsic merit and the need of such a work made it a great success for centuries in its own country, and led to its use at a later period in a modified form in other countries and in other languages, so that even in this country our Anglo-Saxon forefathers derived their conceptions of Jesus and His life on earth to a large extent from their poetical version of it.[10]

From Augustine until J. Clericus' (Le Clerc) *Harmonia Evangelica* (Amsterdam, 1699), "the material of the Gospels was treated preponderatingly from the viewpoint of the interwoven narrative."[11]

Only two other harmonies are noteworthy during the early centuries of the church. Ammonius, teacher of Origen, was the next to publish a harmony, ca. A.D. 220. He took Matthew as his text, placing in the margin on parallel lines comparable portions from the other Gospels. Church historian Eusebius followed with a more complex harmony, useful for study, consisting of "ten canons" in different colored ink to identify material common to two or more Gospels.

The Protestant Reformation produced an abundance of both

8. Bruce M. Metzger, comp., *Annotated Bibliography of the Textual Criticism of the New Testament 1914-1939* (Copenhagen: Ejnar Munksgaard, 1955), 76.
9. Schaff-Herzog, *Religious Encyclopedia*, 153.
10. J. Hamlyn Hill, *The Earliest Life of Christ Being the Diatessaron of Tatian* (Edinburgh: T. & T. Clark, 1893), 38.
11. Schaff-Herzog, *Religious Encyclopedia*, 154.

types of harmonies. From the mid-sixteenth century through the mid-nineteenth century, at least fifty-one harmonies of both types are accounted for by the *Cyclopaedia of Biblical, Theological, and Ecclesiastical Literature.*[12] Many of these were by leading scholars such as Calvin, Lightfoot, Bengel, and Tishchendorf. John Lightfoot was the first to design a four-column harmony. J. Clericus (1699) actually carried it out and included a composite at the foot of each page as well. But it was J.J. Greisbach (1776) who authored the first modern parallel-column harmony. He not only had the four Gospels in four columns on each page like that of Clericus, but he placed the same portions in the Gospels along the same horizontal lines. His format for study harmonies was adopted in the following years.

From the mid-nineteenth century to the present, at least forty-two harmonies have appeared in English, evenly divided between both types of harmonies.[13] The composite harmony has not received the attention of biblical scholars that it enjoyed in former times. Aided by the rise of biblical criticism in the last century, the parallel-column type of harmony surged ahead of the composite type in popularity. Today, almost all Christians familiar with harmonies know only of the parallel-column type.

For more than a century and a half, the application of literary criticism to the Gospels has influenced many NT scholars to study the individual characteristics of these writings. While benefit has been derived from this approach, these scholars have tended to ignore comparison of the Gospels between themselves and repudiate attempts at their harmonization, leading to radically liberal views of inspiration. John Wenham observes,

> The tendency today, however, is . . . to force the New Testament writings into disharmony, in order to emphasize their individuality. The current analytical approach to the Gospels often has the effect of making scholars more and more uncertain at more and more points, till eventually their view of Jesus and his teaching is lost in haze. The harmonistic approach, on

12. John M'Clintock and James Strong, *Cyclopaedia of Biblical, Theological, and Ecclesiastical Literature* [1871], 10 vols. in 5 (New York: Arno Press, 1969), 3-4:79-81.
13. Robert L. Thomas, ed., and Stanley N. Gundry, assoc. ed., *A Harmony of the Gospels with Explanations and Essays* (Chicago: Moody, 1978), 271-72. The authors admit to a partial listing.

the other hand, enables one to ponder . . . how one account illuminates and modifies another. Gradually (without fudging) people and events take shape and grow in solidity, and the scenes come to life in one's mind. Such study is beautifully constructive.[14]

Objections to a Composite Harmony

Some biblical scholars express an aversion to the idea of a composite harmony. They frequently object that it is impossible to arrange a correct chronology of events, an argument that correctly presupposes that all the Gospels are not written in a thoroughly chronological order. This objection must be readily admitted, but such reasoning also nullifies most parallel-column harmonies, which also rearrange the order of some events in the Gospels to achieve a more correct chronology. In presenting a history of harmonies, J.H.A. Ebrard concludes:

> When, at length, after so many attempts to settle the order of sequence, all interest in the matter had ceased, the thought of its possibility was entirely given up. It was assumed that the Evangelists had no intention of writing in chronological order, and therefore that it was impossible to discover the order in which the events occurred. Hence [composite] *harmonies* became more rare, and [parallel-column] *synopses* took their place.[15]

The difficulty encountered, however, in achieving a correct chronological order of events, should not deter the production of either type of harmony. It did not prevent Matthew from penning his sometimes unchronological Gospel. (See Introduction to Harmonization Endnotes: "The Gospel of Matthew.") Calvin has well said concerning the chronological sequence of events in the Gospels, "I have not wished to be overprecise in calculating times, as I have seen them disregarded by the Spirit of God."

---

14. John Wenham, *Easter Enigma* (Grand Rapids: Academie Books, Zondervan, 1984), 128.
15. J.H.A. Ebrard, *The Gospel History: A Compendium of Critical Investigation in Support of the Historical Character of the Four Gospels*, tr. James Martin, rev. and ed. Alexander B. Bruce (Edinburgh: T. & T. Clark, 1876), 53.

Some writers allege that in a composite harmony "the distinctive purposes of each Evangelist are almost hopelessly obscured."[16] This will be readily admitted by composite harmonists, who do well to direct the reader to a parallel-column harmony for studying such differences. However, most Christians will never investigate a parallel-column harmony, nor the individual Gospels themselves, to consider the "distinctive purposes of each Evangelist." This is mostly due to a lack of interest on the part of most readers of the Scriptures to enter into an in-depth, comparative study of the Gospels. In contrast, any reader can appreciate the beauty and simplicity of the uninterrupted, natural flow of a single-narrative harmony.

Many scholars understandably dismiss single-narrative harmonies due to their careless and arbitrary composition. Thomas and Gundry conclude:

> Unfortunately, the care with which many of these have been executed leaves much to be desired, and results are mixed. This is especially true of the diatessaron type. . . . If done carefully, this method can communicate a sense of the course of development of Christ's life and ministry.[17]

Leading harmonist A.T. Robertson writes: "There is a superficial advantage in such an effort in the freedom from variations in the accounts, but the loss is too great for such an arbitrary gain."[18]

In this volume the author seeks to overcome some of these objections by use of guidelines outlined in "Principles of Composition." In addition, rather than avoided, significant Gospel variations are discussed in appended endnotes. It is believed that many readers will find this combination of a single complete account of Jesus' life with appended extensive discussion of apparent discrepancies in the Gospels a refreshing help rather than an "arbitrary gain."

In regard to a composite harmony, consider the example of a court of law. Several witnesses are called to testify. Their independent testimonies are gathered into a single, interwoven narrative in an effort to discover the whole truth. Even more applicable to the composite harmony is A.T. Robertson's claim about harmonies in

---

16. Thomas and Gundry, *A Harmony,* 271.
17. Ibid., 270-72.
18. A.T. Robertson, *A Harmony of the Gospels for the Students of the Life of Christ* (New York: Harper & Row, 1922), 253.

general: "The whole is infinitely richer than the picture given by any one of the Four Gospels."[19] In fact, one reason the Gospel of Matthew became more popular than the Gospels of Mark and Luke, and was placed first in the canon, is that it includes more events than the others, therefore presenting a fuller picture of the life of Christ.

Opposition to the interwoven harmony is not restricted to the scholarly community. The popular assertion is frequently voiced, "If God had wanted a composite of the Gospels, He would have made one from the beginning." If fully applied, the basis for this argument would disallow all paraphrase; a composite is very similar to a paraphrase, though translated words are used maintaining more faithfulness to the text. If Kenneth Taylor's best-selling *The Living Bible* has proven the usefulness of a good paraphrase of the Bible, then why not a carefully written composite of the Gospels, using a trustworthy translation? In his introduction, Kenneth Taylor defends his paraphrase by referring to the many paraphrased quotations of OT passages in the NT (some of them quite loose), most of these from the Septuagint (Greek translation of the OT). Regardless of the merits of a paraphrase of the Bible, many excellent commentators frequently use paraphrase throughout their writings for purposes of clarification, sometimes even to explain their interpretations.

Most leading contemporary biblical scholars accept that the three Synoptic Gospels (Matthew, Mark, and Luke) include a considerable amount of compiling of previously written sources. The leading source-critical theory, the two-source hypothesis, maintains that Matthew and Luke are predominantly composites of Mark and Q.[20] While source criticism of the Gospels cannot be absolutely substantiated, this is not the case with some books in the OT, where the

---

19. Ibid., 254.
20. It is a well-established fact among NT scholars that over 90 percent of Mark is included in Matthew and Luke. That material common to Matthew and Luke but absent from Mark was designated by German biblical scholars in the last century as "Source." This means that Matthew and Luke used Mark and one other written source in composing their Gospels. The German word for "Source" is *Quell*. Therefore, the abbreviation "Q" stands for "Source." C.F. Keil (C.F. Keil and F. Delitzsch, *Commentary on the Old Testament*, 10 vols. (rep. Grand Rapids: Eerdmans, 1983), 1:32, 46) states concerning at least the earlier chapters of Genesis that they "were unquestionably copied by Moses from ancient documents. . . . Nothing certain can be decided as to the period when it was committed to writing; probably some time before Moses, who inserted it as a written record."

discipline of source criticism was first thoroughly applied. Some OT authors name official state records and writings no longer available as source references for the compilation and/or verification of material in their books.[21] *If literary biblical critics are correct, the three Synoptists wrote their Gospels much like composite harmonists, employing the literary techniques of copying, combining, and editing their written sources.*

Besides his harmony of the Gospels, John Calvin wrote a harmony of *The Four Last Books of Moses,* viz., Exodus, Leviticus, Numbers, and Deuteronomy. In his preface, Calvin defends the legitimacy of commentators to rearrange chronologically the historical and doctrinal material of biblical books into one continuous reading. His following words apply equally to a composite harmony of the Gospels:

> Now, there cannot be a doubt that what was dictated to Moses was excellent in itself, and perfectly adapted for the instruction for the people; but what he delivered in Four Books, it has been my endeavour so to collect and arrange, that, at first sight, and before a full examination of the subject, it might seem I was trying to improve upon it, which would be an act of audacity akin to sacrilege. . . . For I have had no other intention than, by this arrangement, to assist unpractised readers, so that they might more easily, more commodiously, and more profitably acquaint themselves with THE WRITINGS OF MOSES; and whosoever would derive benefit from my labours should understand that I would by no means withdraw him from the study of each separate Book.[22]

Similar to the above assertion is the charge that a composite of the Gospels is tampering with the Scriptures. Actually, the composite harmony should be regarded as a commentary on the Gospels. No author of either a composite or parallel-column harmony claims

---

21. Some examples are as follows: Josh. 10:13; 2 Sam. 1:18; 1 Kings 11:41; 1 Chron. 29:29; 2 Chron. 9:29; 12:15; 20:34; 33:19; Es. 10:2. Furthermore, it is now well accepted among OT scholars that the author of Genesis used written sources.

22. John Calvin, *Commentaries on the Four Last Books of Moses, Arranged in the Form of a Harmony,* n.d., tr. Charles William Bingham (Edinburgh: Calvin Translation Society, 1852), pp. xiv-xv.

divine inspiration to rewrite the Gospels. *May the reader understand that this work is not intended to supplant or usurp authority over the Holy Scriptures. It is intended as a supplement to them,* including every detail from the four Gospels and providing an attempt at chronological arrangement of the events. This one coordinated whole makes for easy reading and can be a rewarding learning experience for both novices and regular Bible readers.

May God bless this effort to bring together the four Gospel accounts of the life of the Lord Jesus Christ, to the furtherance of his kingdom.

Principles of Composition.

1. The Gospels of Matthew, Mark, Luke, and John in the *New International Version* (NIV), 1984 edition, are interwoven into one continuous narrative, or composite, with the addition of Luke's Acts 1:2b-12a, 18-19, and 2:1-2, 4a, as well as Paul's 1 Corinthians 11:24-25 and 15:5b, 6a, 7. Note on page 29 the example of how details of the Gospels were interwoven.

2. Faithfulness to the NIV text was rigorously maintained in the interweaving process. No liberty was taken to change comparative material in order to obtain an artificial harmony. Great care was taken not to change NIV punctuation or sentence structure unnecessarily. Whenever adjustments were unavoidable due to the interweaving process, caution was exercised not to alter the meaning of the Gospel texts.

3. Duplication contained in the four Gospels is omitted, except when Jesus himself repeated a teaching on more than one occasion.

4. *The Gospels Interwoven* includes all of the Gospel material—every significant detail except Luke's personal greeting in Luke 1:1-4 and John's references to himself in John 19:35 and 21:24. Otherwise, every effort has been made to include every word of all four Gospels unless manifestly redundant or seemingly contradictory.

5. Apparent contradictions between Gospel accounts are discussed in Part Two, where 108 extensive endnotes are appended to the narrative. In the composite, locations where apparent discrepancies arise in the Gospels are noted by a number in superscript, which is keyed to an endnote expressed in question-and-answer form. These

notes are generally restricted to problems of harmonization and chronology. (See "Introduction to Harmonization Endnotes," page 273.)

6. The matter of choosing between different words or phrases from Gospel accounts of the same event is governed by the following principles, listed in order of priority:
   a. When evidence supports one variation of a quotation as the *ipsissma verba* (exact words), that wording is preferred for inclusion.
   b. The reading in the Gospel of Mark is sometimes granted additional weight, since it is regarded by contemporary scholarship to be the earliest written, as well as frequently to contain the *ipsissma verba*.
   c. Where two Evangelists record the same word(s), their reading was usually chosen over any differing Gospel writer.
   d. More descriptive words were chosen over those less descriptive.

7. In interweaving details from the four Gospels, the author occasionally adds a word not found in the NIV in order to achieve smooth readability. These few additional words are printed in *italics*. The NIV contains only a few words in *italics*, mostly Aramaic words spoken by Jesus. To prevent confusion between these and editorial additions, Aramaic words have been printed in standard type.

8. The NIV sectional headings are included and numbered. Occasionally a choice was required between differing NIV sectional headings of same sections in different Gospels. In rare instances it was necessary to add a heading, change one slightly, or combine two NIV headings.

9. NIV footnotes are included in *The Gospels Interwoven* with two minor exceptions:
   a. Footnotes citing manuscript variance—usually introduced by "Some manuscripts"—are omitted if that Gospel text occurs in another Gospel without such a footnote, thus being well attested by manuscript authority.
   b. Repeated NIV footnotes are usually omitted, being anticipated at the first occurrence with the author's appended words "and hereinafter."

Scripture references appended to certain NIV footnotes, as well as any words added by the author, are enclosed in brackets. For further explanation of the NIV footnotes, see "Excerpts from the Preface to the *New International Version*," page 13.

10. The chronology of events in *The Gospels Interwoven* was determined by appealing to the majority view of thirteen leading parallel-column harmonies of the four Gospels appearing in English over the past 325 years.[1] A unique and elaborate table produced by John M'Clintock and James Strong (of *Strong's Concordance*), called the "Comparative Table of Different Harmonies," was an invaluable aid.[2] It presents the sequence of events according to the nine leading parallel-column harmonies of the four Gospels published in English from 1655 to 1851. This author augmented the table by adding the arrangements of four leading parallel-column harmonies produced in this century. Thus the chronology of this narrative was not arbitrarily achieved. The author's expanded table is appended to this volume as "The Chronological Table," page 407.

---

1. The thirteen harmonies (the first nine names and titles shortened by M'Clintock and Strong) are as follows:
   a. Lightfoot, *Chronicle*, 1655.
   b. Doddridge, *Expositor*, 1739.
   c. Macknight, *Harmony*, 1756.
   d. Newcome, *Harmony*, 1778.
   e. Townsend, *Arrangement*, 1821.
   f. Greswell, *Harmonia*, 1830.
   g. Jarvis, *Introduction*, 1844.
   h. Robinson, *Harmony*, 1845.
   i. Tischendorf, *Synopsis*, 1851.
   j. William A. Stevens and Ernest De Witt Burton, *A Harmony of the Gospels for Historical Study*, 1900.
   k. A.T. Robertson, *A Harmony of the Gospels*, 1922.
   l. Albert Cassel Wieand, *A New Harmony of the Gospels*, 1950.
   m. Robert L. Thomas and Stanley N. Gundry, *A Harmony of the Gospels*, 1978. Kurt Aland's excellent *Synopsis of the Four Gospels* was not used since Aland does not appear to have sought a chronological arrangement.
2. M'Clintock and Strong, *Cyclopaedia*, 3-4:79-81.

17. JOHN THE BAPTIST PREPARES THE WAY
Matthew 3:1-12; Mark 1:1-8; Luke 3:1-18; John 1:6-9, 15

The beginning of the gospel about Jesus Christ, the Son of God. — Mark 1:1

In the fifteenth year of the reign of Tiberius Caesar—when Pontius Pilate was governor of Judea, Herod tetrarch of Galilee, his brother Phillip tetrarch of Iturea and Traconitis, and Lysanias tetrarch of Abilene—during the high priesthood of Annas and Caiaphas, there came a man who was sent from God; his name was John. — Luke 3:1-2a / John 1:6 / Luke 3:2b

The word of God came to John son of Zechariah in the desert. He came as a witness to testify concerning that light, so that through him all men might believe. He himself was not the light; he came only as a witness to the light. The true light that gives light to every man was coming into the world. — John 1:7-9

In those days John the Baptist went into all the country around — Matt. 3:1a / Luke 3:3a
the Jordan, baptizing in the Desert of Judea and preaching a baptism — Mark 1:4a
of repentance for the forgiveness of sins and saying, "Repent, for the — Matt. 3:1b
kingdom of heaven is near." This is he who was spoken of through — Mark 1:4b
the prophet Isaiah: — Matt. 3:2-3a

"I will send my messenger ahead of you,
who will prepare your way"— — Mark 1:2b
"a voice of one calling in the desert,
'Prepare the way for the Lord,
make straight paths for him. — Matt. 3:3b / Mark 1:3 / Luke 3:4b
Every valley shall be filled in,
every mountain and hill made low.
The crooked roads shall become straight,
the rough ways smooth.
And all mankind will see God's salvation.' ". — Luke 3:5-6

John's clothes were made of camel's hair, and he had a leather belt around his waist. His food was locusts and wild honey. People went out to him from Jerusalem and all Judea and the whole region of the Jordan. Confessing their sins, they were baptized by him in the Jordan River.

But when he saw many of the Pharisees and Sadducees coming to — Matt. 3:4-7a
where he was baptizing, he said to them: "You brood of vipers! — Matt. 3:7b; Luke 3:7b

29

Outline and Scripture Index.

PART

1

THE GOSPELS
INTERWOVEN

A Chronological Narrative of the Life of Jesus

ONE.
BIRTHS OF JOHN THE BAPTIST AND JESUS

1. THE BEGINNING
John 1:1-5, 10-14, 16-18

In the beginning was the Word, and the Word was with God, and the Word was God. He was with God in the beginning.

Through him all things were made; without him nothing was made that has been made. In him was life, and that life was the light of men. The light shines in the darkness, but the darkness has not understood[a] it.

He was in the world, and though the world was made through him, the world did not recognize him. He came to that which was his own, but his own did not receive him. Yet to all who received him, to those who believed in his name, he gave the right to become children of God—children born not of natural descent,[b] nor of human decision or a husband's will, but born of God.

The Word became flesh and made his dwelling among us. We have seen his glory, the glory of the One and Only,[c] who came from the Father, full of grace and truth. From the fullness of his grace we have all received one blessing after another. For the law was given through Moses; grace and truth came through Jesus Christ. No one has ever seen God, but God the One and Only,[c][d] who is at the Father's side, has made him known.

---

a. Or *darkness, and the darkness has not overcome*
b. Greek *of bloods*
c. Or *the Only Begotten*
d. Some manuscripts [of John 1:18] *but the only* (or *only begotten*) *Son*

2. THE BIRTH OF JOHN THE BAPTIST FORETOLD
Luke 1:5-25

In the time of Herod king of Judea there was a priest named Zechariah, who belonged to the priestly division of Abijah; his wife Elizabeth was also a descendant of Aaron. Both of them were upright in the sight of God, observing all the Lord's commandments and regulations blamelessly. But they had no children, because Elizabeth was barren; and they were both well along in years.

Once when Zechariah's division was on duty and he was serving as priest before God, he was chosen by lot, according to the custom of the priesthood, to go into the temple of the Lord and burn incense. And when the time for the burning of incense came, all the assembled worshipers were praying outside.

Then an angel of the Lord appeared to him, standing at the right side of the altar of incense. When Zechariah saw him, he was startled and was gripped with fear. But the angel said to him: "Do not be afraid, Zechariah; your prayer has been heard. Your wife Elizabeth will bear you a son, and you are to give him the name John. He will be a joy and delight to you, and many will rejoice because of his birth, for he will be great in the sight of the Lord. He is never to take wine or other fermented drink, and he will be filled with the Holy Spirit even from birth.[c] Many of the people of Israel will he bring back to the Lord their God. And he will go on before the Lord, in the spirit and power of Elijah, to turn the hearts of the fathers to their children and the disobedient to the wisdom of the righteous— to make ready a people prepared for the Lord."

Zechariah asked the angel, "How can I be sure of this? I am an old man and my wife is well along in years."

The angel answered, "I am Gabriel. I stand in the presence of God, and I have been sent to speak to you and to tell you this good news. And now you will be silent and not able to speak until the day this happens, because you did not believe my words, which will come true at their proper time."

Meanwhile, the people were waiting for Zechariah and wondering why he stayed so long in the temple. When he came out, he could not speak to them. They realized he had seen a vision in the temple, for he kept making signs to them but remained unable to speak.

When his time of service was completed, he returned home. After

---

c. Or *from his mother's womb*

The Birth of Jesus and Escape to Egypt and Back

SECTION

10 Joseph and Mary go from Nazareth to Bethlehem to be taxed

12 Joseph and Mary present Jesus to the Lord at Jerusalem

13 The Magi enter Jerusalem, then travel to Bethlehem to worship the Child Jesus

14 Joseph and Mary escape with Jesus to Egypt

15 The family returns to Nazareth

16 Attending the Passover, the Boy Jesus reveals his wisdom

Mary and Joseph

The Magi

Jesus as a boy

Miles 5 0 10 20

Kms 5 0 10 20 30

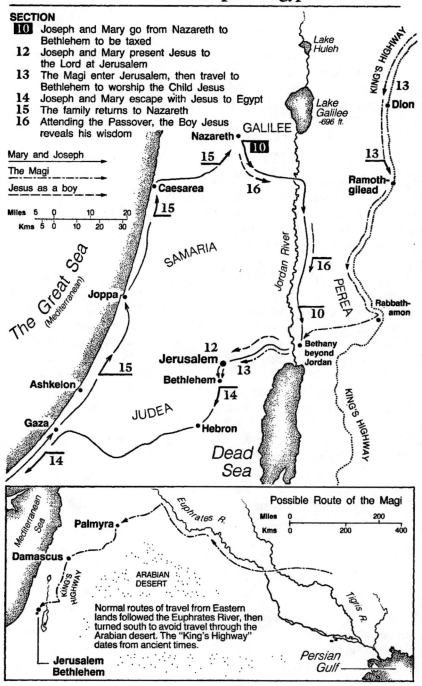

Lake Huleh

KING'S HIGHWAY

Lake Galilee -696 ft.

GALILEE

Nazareth **10**

Caesarea

15

15

16

13 Dion

13

Ramoth-gilead

The Great Sea (Mediterranean)

SAMARIA

Jordan River

PEREA

16

10

Rabbath-amon

Joppa

15

Jerusalem **12**

Bethlehem

Ashkelon

13

14

JUDEA

Gaza

Hebron

14

Bethany beyond Jordan

Dead Sea

KING'S HIGHWAY

Possible Route of the Magi

Mediterranean Sea

Palmyra

Euphrates R.

Miles 0 200

Kms 0 200 400

Damascus

KING'S HIGHWAY

ARABIAN DESERT

Tigris R.

Normal routes of travel from Eastern lands followed the Euphrates River, then turned south to avoid travel through the Arabian desert. The "King's Highway" dates from ancient times.

Jerusalem Bethlehem

Persian Gulf

this his wife Elizabeth became pregnant and for five months remained in seclusion. "The Lord has done this for me," she said. "In these days he has shown his favor and taken away my disgrace among the people."

3. THE BIRTH OF JESUS FORETOLD
Luke 1:26-38

In the sixth month, God sent the angel Gabriel to Nazareth, a town in Galilee, to a virgin pledged to be married to a man named Joseph, a descendant of David. The virgin's name was Mary. The angel went to her and said, "Greetings, you who are highly favored! The Lord is with you."

Mary was greatly troubled at his words and wondered what kind of greeting this might be. But the angel said to her, "Do not be afraid, Mary; you have found favor with God. You will be with child and give birth to a son, and you are to give him the name Jesus. He will be great and will be called the Son of the Most High. The Lord God will give him the throne of his father David, and he will reign over the house of Jacob forever; his kingdom will never end."

"How will this be," Mary asked the angel, "since I am a virgin?"

The angel answered, "The Holy Spirit will come upon you, and the power of the Most High will overshadow you. So the holy one to be born will be called[f] the Son of God. Even Elizabeth your relative is going to have a child in her old age, and she who was said to be barren is in her sixth month. For nothing is impossible with God."

"I am the Lord's servant," Mary answered. "May it be to me as you have said." Then the angel left her.

4. MARY VISITS ELIZABETH
Luke 1:39-45

At that time Mary got ready and hurried to a town in the hill country of Judea, where she entered Zechariah's home and greeted Elizabeth. When Elizabeth heard Mary's greeting, the baby leaped in her womb, and Elizabeth was filled with the Holy Spirit. In a loud

---

f. Or *So the child to be born will be called holy,*

voice she exclaimed: "Blessed are you among women, and blessed is the child you will bear! But why am I so favored, that the mother of my Lord should come to me? As soon as the sound of your greeting reached my ears, the baby in my womb leaped for joy. Blessed is she who has believed that what the Lord has said to her will be accomplished!"

5. MARY'S SONG
Luke 1:46-56

And Mary said:

> "My soul glorifies the Lord
> and my spirit rejoices in God my Savior,
> for he has been mindful
> of the humble state of his servant.
> From now on all generations will call me blessed,
> for the Mighty One has done great things for me—
> holy is his name.
> His mercy extends to those who fear him,
> from generation to generation.
> He has performed mighty deeds with his arm;
> he has scattered those who are proud
> in their inmost thoughts.
> He has brought down rulers from their thrones
> but has lifted up the humble.
> He has filled the hungry with good things
> but has sent the rich away empty.
> He has helped his servant Israel,
> remembering to be merciful
> to Abraham and his descendants forever,
> even as he said to our fathers."

Mary stayed with Elizabeth for about three months and then returned home.

6. THE BIRTH OF JOHN THE BAPTIST
Luke 1:57-66

When it was time for Elizabeth to have her baby, she gave birth to a son. Her neighbors and relatives heard that the Lord had shown her great mercy, and they shared her joy.

On the eighth day they came to circumcise the child, and they were going to name him after his father Zechariah, but his mother spoke up and said, "No! He is to be called John."

They said to her, "There is no one among your relatives who has that name."

Then they made signs to his father, to find out what he would like to name the child. He asked for a writing tablet, and to everyone's astonishment he wrote, "His name is John." Immediately his mouth was opened and his tongue was loosed, and he began to speak, praising God. The neighbors were all filled with awe, and throughout the hill country of Judea people were talking about all these things. Everyone who heard this wondered about it, asking, "What then is this child going to be?" For the Lord's hand was with him.

7. ZECHARIAH'S SONG
Luke 1:67-80

His father Zechariah was filled with the Holy Spirit and prophesied:

"Praise be to the Lord, the God of Israel,
because he has come and has redeemed his people.
He has raised up a horn[g] of salvation for us
in the house of his servant David
(as he said through his holy prophets of long ago),
salvation from our enemies
and from the hand of all who hate us—
to show mercy to our fathers
and to remember his holy covenant,
the oath he swore to our father Abraham:
to rescue us from the hand of our enemies,
and to enable us to serve him without fear
in holiness and righteousness before him all our days.

---

g. *Horn* here symbolizes strength.

48

And you, my child, will be called
a prophet of the Most High;
for you will go on before the Lord
to prepare the way for him,
to give his people the knowledge of salvation
through the forgiveness of their sins,
because of the tender mercy of our God,
by which the rising sun
will come to us from heaven
to shine on those living in darkness
and in the shadow of death,
to guide our feet into the path of peace."

And the child grew and became strong in spirit; and he lived in the desert until he appeared publicly to Israel.

8. JOSEPH'S DREAM
Matthew 1:18b-25a

Mary was pledged to be married to Joseph, but before they came together, she was found to be with child[1] through the Holy Spirit. Because Joseph her husband was a righteous man and did not want to expose her to public disgrace, he had in mind to divorce her quietly.

But after he had considered this, an angel of the Lord appeared to him in a dream[2] and said, "Joseph son of David, do not be afraid to take Mary home as your wife, because what is conceived in her is from the Holy Spirit. She will give birth to a son, and you are to give him the name Jesus,[h] because he will save his people from their sins."

All this took place to fulfill what the Lord had said through the prophet: "The virgin will be with child and will give birth to a son, and they will call him Immanuel"[i]—which means, "God with us."

When Joseph woke up, he did what the angel of the Lord had

1. See p. 285: Did Joseph know of Mary's pregnancy soon after her virginal conception (Luke 1:26) or only after her condition was discovered (Matthew 1:18)?
2. See p. 285: Did Joseph have his dream before the birth of John (Matthew 1:18-24) or afterward (Luke 1:56-57)?
h. _Jesus_ is the Greek form of _Joshua_, which means _the LORD saves_.
i. Isaiah 7:14

commanded him and took Mary home as his wife. But he had no union with her until she gave birth to a son.

9. THE GENEALOGIES OF JESUS
Matthew 1:1-17; Luke 3:23b-38

He[3] was the son, so it was thought, of Joseph,
the son of Heli, the son of Matthat,
the son of Levi, the son of Melki,
the son of Jannai, the son of Joseph,
the son of Mattathias, the son of Amos,
the son of Nahum, the son of Esli,
the son of Naggai, the son of Maath,
the son of Mattathias, the son of Semein,
the son of Josech, the son of Joda,
the son of Joanan, the son of Rhesa,
the son of Zerubbabel, the son of Shealtiel,
the son of Neri, the son of Melki,
the son of Addi, the son of Cosam,
the son of Elmadam, the son of Er,
the son of Joshua, the son of Eliezer,
the son of Jorim, the son of Matthat,
the son of Levi, the son of Simeon,
the son of Judah, the son of Joseph,
the son of Jonam, the son of Eliakim,
the son of Melea, the son of Menna,
the son of Mattatha, the son of Nathan,
the son of David, the son of Jesse,
the son of Obed, the son of Boaz,
the son of Salmon,[j] the son of Nahshon,
the son of Amminadab, the son of Ram,[k]
the son of Hezron, the son of Perez,
the son of Judah, the son of Jacob,
the son of Isaac, the son of Abraham,

---

3. See p. 286: What is the correct genealogy of Jesus (Matthew 1:1-17; Luke 3:23-38)?
j. Some early manuscripts [of Luke 3:32] *Sala*
k. Some manuscripts [of Luke 3:33] *Amminadab, the son of Admin, the son of Arni*; other manuscripts vary widely.

the son of Terah, the son of Nahor,
the son of Serug, the son of Reu,
the son of Peleg, the son of Eber,
the son of Shelah, the son of Cainan,
the son of Arphaxad, the son of Shem,
the son of Noah, the son of Lamech,
the son of Methuselah, the son of Enoch,
the son of Jared, the son of Mahalalel,
the son of Kenan, the son of Enosh,
the son of Seth, the son of Adam,
the son of God.

Another record of the genealogy of Jesus Christ the son of David,
the son of Abraham:

Abraham was the father of Isaac,
Isaac the father of Jacob,
Jacob the father of Judah and his brothers,
Judah the father of Perez and Zerah,
whose mother was Tamar,
Perez the father of Hezron,
Hezron the father of Ram,
Ram the father of Amminadab,
Amminadab the father of Nahshon,
Nahshon the father of Salmon,
Salmon the father of Boaz,
whose mother was Rahab,
Boaz the father of Obed,
whose mother was Ruth,
Obed the father of Jesse,
and Jesse the father of King David.

David was the father of Solomon,
whose mother had been Uriah's wife,
Solomon the father of Rehoboam,
Rehoboam the father of Abijah,
Abijah the father of Asa,
Asa the father of Jehoshaphat,
Jehoshaphat the father of Jehoram,

Jehoram the father of Uzziah,
Uzziah the father of Jotham,
Jotham the father of Ahaz,
Ahaz the father of Hezekiah,
Hezekiah the father of Manasseh,
Manasseh the father of Amon,
Amon the father of Josiah,
and Josiah the father of Jeconiah[l]
and his brothers at the time
of the exile to Babylon.

After the exile to Babylon:
Jeconiah was the father of Shealtiel,
Shealtiel the father of Zerubbabel,
Zerubbabel the father of Abiud,
Abiud the father of Eliakim,
Eliakim the father of Azor,
Azor the father of Zadok,
Zadok the father of Akim,
Akim the father of Eliud,
Eliud the father of Eleazar,
Eleazar the father of Matthan,
Matthan the father of Jacob,
and Jacob the father of Joseph,
the husband of Mary,
of whom was born Jesus,
who is called Christ.

Thus there were fourteen generations in all from Abraham to David, fourteen from David to the exile to Babylon, and fourteen from the exile to the Christ.[m]

10. THE BIRTH OF JESUS CHRIST
Matthew 1:18a; Luke 2:1-7

This is how the birth of Jesus Christ came about.
In those days Caesar Augustus issued a decree that a census should

---

l. That is, Jehoiachin [and hereinafter]
m. Or *Messiah* [and hereinafter]. "The Christ" (Greek) and "the Messiah" (Hebrew) both mean "the Anointed One."

be taken of the entire Roman world. (This was the first census that took place while Quirinius was governor of Syria.) And everyone went to his own town to register.

So Joseph also went up from the town of Nazareth in Galilee to Judea, to Bethlehem the town of David, because he belonged to the house and line of David. He went there to register with Mary, who was pledged to be married to him and was expecting a child. While they were there, the time came for the baby to be born, and she gave birth to her firstborn, a son. She wrapped him in cloths and placed him in a manger, because there was no room for them in the inn.

11. THE SHEPHERDS AND THE ANGELS
Luke 2:8-20

And there were shepherds living out in the fields nearby, keeping watch over their flocks at night. An angel of the Lord appeared to them, and the glory of the Lord shone around them, and they were terrified. But the angel said to them, "Do not be afraid. I bring you good news of great joy that will be for all the people. Today in the town of David a Savior has been born to you; he is Christ the Lord. This will be a sign to you: You will find a baby wrapped in cloths and lying in a manger."

Suddenly a great company of the heavenly host appeared with the angel, praising God and saying,

"Glory to God in the highest,
and on earth peace to men
on whom his favor rests."

When the angels had left them and gone into heaven, the shepherds said to one another, "Let's go to Bethlehem and see this thing that has happened, which the Lord has told us about."

So they hurried off and found Mary and Joseph, and the baby, who was lying in the manger. When they had seen him, they spread the word concerning what had been told them about this child, and all who heard it were amazed at what the shepherds said to them. But Mary treasured up all these things and pondered them in her heart. The shepherds returned, glorifying and praising God for all the things they had heard and seen, which were just as they had been told.

12. JESUS PRESENTED IN THE TEMPLE
Matthew 1:25b; Luke 2:21-39a

On the eighth day, when it was time to circumcise him, *Joseph* gave him the name Jesus, the name the angel had given him before he had been conceived.

When the time of their purification according to the Law of Moses had been completed, Joseph and Mary took him to Jerusalem to present him to the Lord (as it is written in the Law of the Lord, "Every firstborn male is to be consecrated to the Lord"[n]), and to offer a sacrifice in keeping with what is said in the Law of the Lord: "a pair of doves or two young pigeons."[o]

Now there was a man in Jerusalem called Simeon, who was righteous and devout. He was waiting for the consolation of Israel, and the Holy Spirit was upon him. It had been revealed to him by the Holy Spirit that he would not die before he had seen the Lord's Christ. Moved by the Spirit, he went into the temple courts. When the parents brought in the child Jesus to do for him what the custom of the Law required, Simeon took him in his arms and praised God, saying:

> "Sovereign Lord, as you have promised,
> you now dismiss[p] your servant in peace.
> For my eyes have seen your salvation,
> which you have prepared
> in the sight of all people,
> a light for revelation to the Gentiles
> and for glory to your people Israel."

The child's father and mother marveled at what was said about him. Then Simeon blessed them and said to Mary, his mother: "This child is destined to cause the falling and rising of many in Israel, and to be a sign that will be spoken against, so that the thoughts of many hearts will be revealed. And a sword will pierce your own soul too."

There was also a prophetess, Anna, the daughter of Phanuel, of the tribe of Asher. She was very old; she had lived with her husband seven years after her marriage, and then was a widow until she was

n. Exodus 13:2, 12
o. Leviticus 12:8
p. Or *promised, / now dismiss*

eighty-four.[q] She never left the temple but worshiped night and day, fasting and praying. Coming up to them at that very moment, she gave thanks to God and spoke about the child to all who were looking forward to the redemption of Jerusalem.

When Joseph and Mary had done everything required by the Law of the Lord, they returned.[4]

13. THE VISIT OF THE MAGI
Matthew 2:1-12

After Jesus was born in Bethlehem in Judea, during the time of King Herod, Magi[r] from the east came to Jerusalem and asked, "Where is the one who has been born king of the Jews? We saw his star in the east[s] and have come to worship him."

When King Herod heard this he was disturbed, and all Jerusalem with him. When he had called together all the people's chief priests and teachers of the law, he asked them where the Christ was to be born. "In Bethlehem in Judea," they replied, "for this is what the prophet has written:

" 'But you, Bethlehem, in the land of Judah,
are by no means least among the rulers of Judah;
for out of you will come a ruler
who will be the shepherd of my people Israel.'[t]"

Then Herod called the Magi secretly and found out from them the exact time the star had appeared. He sent them to Bethlehem and said, "Go and make a careful search for the child. As soon as you find him, report to me, so that I too may go and worship him."

After they had heard the king, they went on their way, and the star they had seen in the east[u] went ahead of them until it stopped over the place where the child was. When they saw the star, they were overjoyed. On coming to the house, they saw the child with his

q. Or *widow for eighty-four years*
4. See p. 289: What is the order of events immediately following the birth of Jesus (Matthew 2; Luke 2:1-39)?
r. Traditionally *Wise Men*
s. Or *star when it rose*
t. Micah 5:2
u. Or *seen when it rose*

mother Mary, and they bowed down and worshiped him. Then they opened their treasures and presented him with gifts of gold and of incense and of myrrh. And having been warned in a dream not to go back to Herod, they returned to their country by another route.

14. THE ESCAPE TO EGYPT
Matthew 2:13-18

When they had gone, an angel of the Lord appeared to Joseph in a dream. "Get up," he said, "take the child and his mother and escape to Egypt. Stay there until I tell you, for Herod is going to search for the child to kill him."

So he got up, took the child and his mother during the night and left for Egypt, where he stayed until the death of Herod. And so was fulfilled what the Lord had said through the prophet: "Out of Egypt I called my son."[v]

When Herod realized that he had been outwitted by the Magi, he was furious, and he gave orders to kill all the boys in Bethlehem and its vicinity who were two years old and under, in accordance with the time he had learned from the Magi. Then what was said through the prophet Jeremiah was fulfilled:

> "A voice is heard in Ramah,
> weeping and great mourning,
> Rachel weeping for her children
> and refusing to be comforted,
> because they are no more."[w]

15. THE RETURN TO NAZARETH
Matthew 2:19-23; Luke 2:39b-40

After Herod died, an angel of the Lord appeared in a dream to Joseph in Egypt and said, "Get up, take the child and his mother and go to the land of Israel, for those who were trying to take the child's life are dead."

So he got up, took the child and his mother and went to the land

---

v. Hosea 11:1
w. Jeremiah 31:15

of Israel. But when he heard that Archelaus was reigning in Judea in place of his father Herod, he was afraid to go there. Having been warned in a dream, he withdrew to the district of Galilee, and he went and lived in their own town of Nazareth. So was fulfilled what was said through the prophets: "He will be called a Nazarene."

And the child grew and became strong; he was filled with wisdom, and the grace of God was upon him.

16. THE BOY JESUS AT THE TEMPLE
Luke 2:41-52

Every year his parents went to Jerusalem for the Feast of the Passover. When he was twelve years old, they went up to the Feast, according to the custom. After the Feast was over, while his parents were returning home, the boy Jesus stayed behind in Jerusalem, but they were unaware of it. Thinking he was in their company, they traveled on for a day. Then they began looking for him among their relatives and friends. When they did not find him, they went back to Jerusalem to look for him. After three days they found him in the temple courts, sitting among the teachers, listening to them and asking them questions. Everyone who heard him was amazed at his understanding and his answers. When his parents saw him, they were astonished. His mother said to him, "Son, why have you treated us like this? Your father and I have been anxiously searching for you."

"Why were you searching for me?" he asked. "Didn't you know I had to be in my Father's house?" But they did not understand what he was saying to them.

Then he went down to Nazareth with them and was obedient to them. But his mother treasured all these things in her heart. And Jesus grew in wisdom and stature, and in favor with God and men.

TWO.
PREPARATION FOR MINISTRY

17. JOHN THE BAPTIST PREPARES THE WAY
Matthew 3:1-12; Mark 1:1-8; Luke 3:1-18; John 1:6-9, 15

The beginning[1] of the gospel about Jesus Christ, the Son of God.[a] In the fifteenth year of the reign of Tiberius Caesar—when Pontius Pilate was governor of Judea, Herod tetrarch of Galilee, his brother Phillip tetrarch of Iturea and Traconitis, and Lysanias tetrarch of Abilene—during the high priesthood of Annas and Caiaphas, there came a man who was sent from God; his name was John.

The word of God came to John son of Zechariah in the desert. He came as a witness to testify concerning that light, so that through him all men might believe. He himself was not the light; he came only as a witness to the light. The true light that gives light to every man was coming into the world.[b]

In those days John the Baptist went into all the country around the Jordan, baptizing in the Desert of Judea and preaching a baptism of repentance for the forgiveness of sins and saying, "Repent, for the kingdom of heaven is near." This is he who was spoken of through the prophet Isaiah:

> "I will send my messenger ahead of you,
> who will prepare your way"[c]—
> "a voice of one calling in the desert,
> 'Prepare the way for the Lord,
> make straight paths for him.

---

1. See p. 290: Does Mark's *beginning* (Mark 1:1) mean the same as John's *beginning* (John 1:1)?
a. Some manuscripts [of Mark 1:1] do not have *the Son of God*.
b. Or *This was the true light that gives light to every man who comes into the world*
c. Malachi 3:1

58

Every valley shall be filled in,
every mountain and hill made low.
The crooked roads shall become straight,
the rough ways smooth.
And all mankind will see God's salvation.' "[d]

John's clothes were made of camel's hair, and he had a leather belt around his waist. His food was locusts and wild honey. People went out to him from Jerusalem and all Judea and the whole region of the Jordan. Confessing their sins, they were baptized by him in the Jordan River.

But when he saw many of the Pharisees and Sadducees coming to where he was baptizing, he said to them: "You brood of vipers! Who warned you to flee from the coming wrath? Produce fruit in keeping with repentance. And do not think you can say to yourselves, 'We have Abraham as our father.' I tell you that out of these stones God can raise up children for Abraham. The ax is already at the root of the trees, and every tree that does not produce good fruit will be cut down and thrown into the fire."

"What should we do then?" the crowd asked.

John answered, "The man with two tunics should share with him who has none, and the one who has food should do the same."

Tax collectors also came to be baptized. "Teacher," they asked, "what should we do?"

"Don't collect any more than you are required to," he told them.

Then some soldiers asked him, "And what should we do?"

He replied, "Don't extort money and don't accuse people falsely— be content with your pay."

The people were waiting expectantly and were all wondering in their hearts if John might possibly be the Christ. John answered them all, "I baptize you with water for repentance. But after me one more powerful than I will come, the thongs of whose sandals I am not worthy to stoop down and untie. He who comes after me has surpassed me because he was before me. He will baptize you with the Holy Spirit and with fire. His winnowing fork is in his hand to clear his threshing floor and to gather his wheat into the barn, but he will burn up the chaff with unquenchable fire." And with many other words John exhorted the people and preached the good news to them.

---

d. Isaiah 40:3-5

18. THE BAPTISM OF JESUS
Matthew 3:13-17; Mark 1:9-11; Luke 3:21-23a

At that time Jesus came from Nazareth in Galilee to the Jordan to be baptized by John.

When all the people were being baptized, Jesus came to be baptized too. John tried to deter him, saying, "I need to be baptized by you, and do you come to me?" Jesus replied, "Let it be so now; it is proper for us to do this to fulfill all righteousness." Then John consented, and Jesus was baptized by John in the Jordan. As Jesus went up out of the water he was praying. At that moment he saw heaven being torn open and the Spirit of God descending in bodily form like a dove and lighting on him. And a voice came from heaven: "You are my Son, whom I love; with you I am well pleased."[2]

Now Jesus himself was about thirty years old when he began his ministry.

19. THE TEMPTATION OF JESUS
Matthew 4:1-11; Mark 1:12-13; Luke 4:1-13

At once Jesus, full of the Holy Spirit, returned from the Jordan and was led by the Spirit out into the desert to be tempted by the devil. For forty days he was being tempted by Satan. Fasting forty days and forty nights, he ate nothing, and at the end of those days he was hungry.

The tempter came to him and said, "If you are the Son of God, tell these stones to become bread."[3]

Jesus answered, "It is written: 'Man does not live on bread alone, but on every word that comes from the mouth of God.'"[c]

Then the devil took him to the holy city, Jerusalem, and had him stand on the highest point of the temple. "If you are the Son of God," he said, "throw yourself down from here. For it is written:

---

2. See p. 290: Are the exact words of the voice from heaven at Jesus' baptism recorded in Matthew 3:17 or in Mark 1:11 and Luke 3:22?
3. See p. 291: In what order did Jesus' second and third temptations occur (Matthew 4:5-10; Luke 4:5-12)?
c. Deuteronomy 8:3

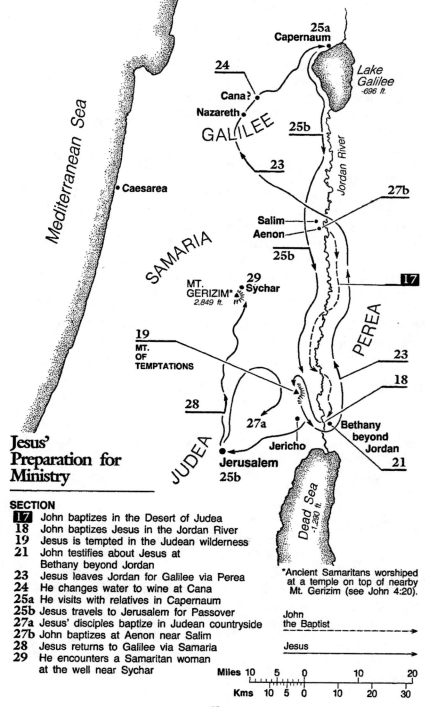

25a
Capernaum

Lake Galilee -696 ft.

24

Cana?
Nazareth

GALILEE

25b

Mediterranean Sea

23

Jordan River

27b

• **Caesarea**

Salim
Aenon

25b

SAMARIA

29
MT.
GERIZIM* **Sychar**
2,849 ft.

PEREA

17

19
MT.
OF
TEMPTATIONS

23

18

28

27a

Bethany
beyond
Jordan

21

JUDEA

Jericho

Jerusalem
25b

Jesus' Preparation for Ministry

Dead Sea -1,290 ft.

SECTION

17 John baptizes in the Desert of Judea
18 John baptizes Jesus in the Jordan River
19 Jesus is tempted in the Judean wilderness
21 John testifies about Jesus at
Bethany beyond Jordan
23 Jesus leaves Jordan for Galilee via Perea
24 He changes water to wine at Cana
25a He visits with relatives in Capernaum
25b Jesus travels to Jerusalem for Passover
27a Jesus' disciples baptize in Judean countryside
27b John baptizes at Aenon near Salim
28 Jesus returns to Galilee via Samaria
29 He encounters a Samaritan woman
at the well near Sychar

*Ancient Samaritans worshiped
at a temple on top of nearby
Mt. Gerizim (see John 4:20).

John
the Baptist ——————————→

Jesus ——————————→

Miles 10   5   0   10   20

Kms   10 5 0   10   20   30

61

" 'He will command his angels concerning you,
to guard you carefully;
they will lift you up in their hands,
so that you will not strike your foot
against a stone.'[f]"

Jesus answered him, "It is also written: 'Do not put the Lord your God to the test.'[g]"

Again, the devil took him to a very high mountain and showed him in an instant all the kingdoms of the world. And he said to him, "All this authority and splendor I will give you, for it has been given to me, and I can give it to anyone I want to. So if you will bow down and worship me, it will all be yours."

Jesus said to him, "Away from me, Satan! For it is written: 'Worship the Lord your God, and serve him only.'[h]"

When the devil had finished all this tempting, he left him until an opportune time. *Jesus* was with the wild animals, and angels came and attended him.

20. JOHN THE BAPTIST DENIES BEING THE CHRIST
John 1:19-28

Now this was John's testimony when the Jews of Jerusalem sent priests and Levites to ask him who he was. He did not fail to confess, but confessed freely, "I am not the Christ."

They asked him, "Then who are you? Are you Elijah?"

He said, "I am not."

"Are you the Prophet?"

He answered, "No."

Finally they said, "Who are you? Give us an answer to take back to those who sent us. What do you say about yourself?"

John replied in the words of Isaiah the prophet, "I am the voice of one calling in the desert, 'Make straight the way for the Lord.' "[i]

Now some Pharisees who had been sent questioned him, "Why then do you baptize if you are not the Christ, nor Elijah, nor the Prophet?"

---

f. Psalm 91:11-12
g. Deuteronomy 6:16
h. Deuteronomy 6:13
i. Isaiah 40:3

"I baptize with[j] water," John replied, "but among you stands one you do not know. He is the one who comes after me, the thongs of whose sandals I am not worthy to untie."

This all happened at Bethany on the other side of the Jordan, where John was baptizing.

21. JESUS THE LAMB OF GOD
John 1:29-34

The next day John saw Jesus coming toward him and said, "Look, the Lamb of God, who takes away the sin of the world! This is the one I meant when I said, 'A man who comes after me has surpassed me because he was before me.' I myself did not know him, but the reason I came baptizing with water was that he might be revealed to Israel."

Then John gave this testimony: "I saw the Spirit come down from heaven as a dove and remain on him. I would not have known him, except that the one who sent me to baptize with water told me, 'The man on whom you see the Spirit come down and remain is he who will baptize with the Holy Spirit.' I have seen and I testify that this is the Son of God."

22. JESUS' FIRST DISCIPLES
John 1:35-42

The next day John was there again with two of his disciples. When he saw Jesus passing by, he said, "Look, the Lamb of God!"

When the two disciples heard him say this, they followed Jesus. Turning around, Jesus saw them following and asked, "What do you want?"

They said, "Rabbi" (which means Teacher), "where are you staying?"

"Come," he replied, "and you will see."

So they went and saw where he was staying, and spent that day with him. It was about the tenth hour.

Andrew, Simon Peter's brother, was one of the two who heard what John had said and who had followed Jesus. The first thing

---

j. Or *in* [and hereinafter, following *baptize*]

Andrew did was to find his brother Simon and tell him, "We have found the Messiah" (that is, the Christ). And he brought him to Jesus.

Jesus looked at him and said, "You are Simon son of John. You will be called Cephas" (which, when translated, is Peter[k]).

23. JESUS CALLS PHILIP AND NATHANAEL
John 1:43-51

The next day Jesus decided to leave for Galilee. Finding Philip, he said to him, "Follow me."

Philip, like Andrew and Peter, was from the town of Bethsaida. Philip found Nathanael and told him, "We have found the one Moses wrote about in the Law, and about whom the prophets also wrote—Jesus of Nazareth, the son of Joseph."

"Nazareth! Can anything good come from there?" Nathanael asked.

"Come and see," said Philip.

When Jesus saw Nathanael approaching, he said of him, "Here is a true Israelite, in whom there is nothing false."

"How do you know me?" Nathanael asked.

Jesus answered, "I saw you while you were still under the fig tree before Philip called you."

Then Nathanael declared, "Rabbi, you are the Son of God; you are the King of Israel."

Jesus said, "You believe[l] because I told you I saw you under the fig tree. You shall see greater things than that." He then added, "I tell you[m] the truth, you[m] shall see heaven open, and the angels of God ascending and descending on the Son of Man."

24. JESUS CHANGES WATER TO WINE
John 2:1-11

On the third day a wedding took place at Cana in Galilee. Jesus' mother was there, and Jesus and his disciples had also been invited

---

k. Both *Cephas* (Aramaic) and *Peter* (Greek) mean *rock.*
l. Or *Do you believe . . . ?*
m. The Greek is plural.

to the wedding. When the wine was gone, Jesus' mother said to him, "They have no more wine."

"Dear woman, why do you involve me?" Jesus replied. "My time has not yet come."

His mother said to the servants, "Do whatever he tells you."

Nearby stood six stone water jars, the kind used by the Jews for ceremonial washing, each holding from twenty to thirty gallons.[n]

Jesus said to the servants, "Fill the jars with water"; so they filled them to the brim.

Then he told them, "Now draw some out and take it to the master of the banquet."

They did so, and the master of the banquet tasted the water that had been turned into wine. He did not realize where it had come from, though the servants who had drawn the water knew. Then he called the bridegroom aside and said, "Everyone brings out the choice wine first and then the cheaper wine after the guests have had too much to drink; but you have saved the best till now."

This, the first of his miraculous signs, Jesus performed in Cana of Galilee. He thus revealed his glory, and his disciples put their faith in him.

25. JESUS CLEARS THE TEMPLE
John 2:12-25

After this he went down to Capernaum with his mother and brothers and his disciples. There they stayed for a few days.

When it was almost time for the Jewish Passover, Jesus went up to Jerusalem. In the temple courts he found men selling cattle, sheep and doves, and others sitting at tables exchanging money. So he made a whip out of cords, and drove all from the temple area, both sheep and cattle; he scattered the coins of the money changers and overturned their tables. To those who sold doves he said, "Get these out of here! How dare you turn my Father's house into a market!"

His disciples remembered that it is written: "Zeal for your house will consume me."[o]

Then the Jews demanded of him, "What miraculous sign can you show us to prove your authority to do all this?"

---

n. Greek *two to three metretes* (probably about 75 to 115 liters)
o. Psalm 69:9

Jesus answered them, "Destroy this temple, and I will raise it again in three days."

The Jews replied, "It has taken forty-six years to build this temple, and you are going raise it in three days?" But the temple he had spoken of was his body. After he was raised from the dead, his disciples recalled what he had said. Then they believed the Scripture and the words that Jesus had spoken.

Now while he was in Jerusalem at the Passover Feast, many people saw the miraculous signs he was doing and believed in his name.[p] But Jesus would not entrust himself to them, for he knew all men. He did not need man's testimony about man, for he knew what was in a man.

26. JESUS TEACHES NICODEMUS
John 3:1-21

Now there was a man of the Pharisees named Nicodemus, a member of the Jewish ruling council. He came to Jesus at night and said, "Rabbi, we know you are a teacher who has come from God. For no one could perform the miraculous signs you are doing if God were not with him."

In reply Jesus declared, "I tell you the truth, no one can see the kingdom of God unless he is born again.[q]"

"How can a man be born when he is old?" Nicodemus asked. "Surely he cannot enter a second time into his mother's womb to be born!"

Jesus answered, "I tell you the truth, no one can enter the kingdom of God unless he is born of water and the Spirit. Flesh gives birth to flesh, but the Spirit[r] gives birth to spirit. You should not be surprised at my saying, 'You[s] must be born again.' The wind blows wherever it pleases. You hear its sound, but you cannot tell where it comes from or where it is going. So it is with everyone born of the Spirit."

"How can this be?" Nicodemus asked.

"You are Israel's teacher," said Jesus, "and do you not understand

---

p. Or *and believed in him*
q. Or *born from above* [and hereinafter]
r. Or *but spirit*
s. The Greek is plural.

these things? I tell you the truth, we speak of what we know, and we testify to what we have seen, but still you people do not accept our testimony. I have spoken to you of earthly things and you do not believe; how then will you believe if I speak of heavenly things? No one has ever gone into heaven except the one who came from heaven—the Son of Man.ᵗ Just as Moses lifted up the snake in the desert, so the Son of Man must be lifted up, that everyone who believes in him may have eternal life.ᵘ

"For God so loved the world that he gave his one and only Son,ᵛ that whoever believes in him shall not perish but have eternal life. For God did not send his Son into the world to condemn the world, but to save the world through him. Whoever believes in him is not condemned, but whoever does not believe stands condemned already because he has not believed in the name of God's one and only Son.ʷ This is the verdict: Light has come into the world, but men loved darkness instead of light because their deeds were evil. Everyone who does evil hates the light, and will not come into the light for fear that his deeds will be exposed. But whoever lives by the truth comes into the light, so that it may be seen plainly that what he has done has been done through God."ˣ

27. JOHN THE BAPTIST'S TESTIMONY ABOUT JESUS
John 3:22-36

After this, Jesus and his disciples went out into the Judean countryside, where he spent some time with them, and baptized. Now John also was baptizing at Aenon near Salim, because there was plenty of water, and people were constantly coming to be baptized. (This was before John was put in prison.) An argument developed between some of John's disciples and a certain Jewʸ over the matter of ceremonial washing. They came to John and said to him, "Rabbi, that man who was with you on the other side of the Jordan—the one you testified about—well, he is baptizing, and everyone is going to him."

---

t. Some manuscripts [of John 3:13] *Man, who is in heaven*
u. Or *believes may have eternal life in him*
v. Or *his only begotten Son*
w. Or *God's only begotten Son*
x. Some interpreters end the quotation after [the previous paragraph].
y. Some manuscripts [of John 3:25] *and certain Jews*

To this John replied, "A man can receive only what is given him from heaven. You yourselves can testify that I said, 'I am not the Christ but am sent ahead of him.' The bride belongs to the bridegroom. The friend who attends the bridegroom waits and listens for him, and is full of joy when he hears the bridegroom's voice. That joy is mine, and it is now complete. He must become greater; I must become less.

"The one who comes from above is above all; the one who is from the earth belongs to the earth, and speaks as one from the earth. The one who comes from heaven is above all. He testifies to what he has seen and heard, but no one accepts his testimony. The man who has accepted it has certified that God is truthful. For the one whom God has sent speaks the words of God, for God[z] gives the Spirit without limit. The Father loves the Son and has placed everything in his hands. Whoever believes in the Son has eternal life, but whoever rejects the Son will not see life, for God's wrath remains on him."[aa]

28. JOHN THE BAPTIST IMPRISONED
Matthew 4:12; 14:3-5; Mark 1:14a; 6:17-18; Luke 3:19-20; 4:14a; John 4:1-3

Herod the tetrarch had given orders to have John arrested. He did this because of Herodias, his brother Philip's wife, whom he had married. For John had been saying to Herod, "It is not lawful for you to have your brother's wife." John rebuked Herod because of all the other evil things he had done. Herod added this to them all: He had John bound and locked up in prison. Herod wanted to kill John, but he was afraid of the people, because they considered him a prophet.

The Pharisees heard that Jesus was gaining and baptizing more disciples than John, although in fact it was not Jesus who baptized, but his disciples. When the Lord learned of this *and* heard that John had been put in prison, he left Judea and returned once more to Galilee in the power of the Spirit.

---

z. Greek *he*
aa. Some interpreters end the quotation after [the previous paragraph].

29. JESUS TALKS WITH A SAMARITAN WOMAN
John 4:4-26

Now he had to go through Samaria. So he came to a town in Samaria called Sychar, near the plot of ground Jacob had given to his son Joseph. Jacob's well was there, and Jesus, tired as he was from the journey, sat down by the well. It was about the sixth hour.

When a Samaritan woman came to draw water, Jesus said to her, "Will you give me a drink?" (His disciples had gone into the town to buy food.)

The Samaritan woman said to him, "You are a Jew and I am a Samaritan woman. How can you ask me for a drink?" (For Jews do not associate with Samaritans.bb)

Jesus answered her, "If you knew the gift of God and who it is that asks you for a drink, you would have asked him and he would have given you living water."

"Sir," the woman said, "you have nothing to draw with and the well is deep. Where can you get this living water? Are you greater than our father Jacob, who gave us the well and drank from it himself, as did also his sons and his flocks and herds?"

Jesus answered, "Everyone who drinks this water will be thirsty again, but whoever drinks the water I give him will never thirst. Indeed, the water I give him will become in him a spring of water welling up to eternal life."

The woman said to him, "Sir, give me this water so that I won't get thirsty and have to keep coming here to draw water."

He told her, "Go, call your husband and come back."

"I have no husband," she replied.

Jesus said to her, "You are right when you say you have no husband. The fact is, you have had five husbands, and the man you now have is not your husband. What you have just said is quite true."

"Sir," the woman said, "I can see that you are a prophet. Our fathers worshiped on this mountain, but you Jews claim that the place where we must worship is in Jerusalem."

Jesus declared, "Believe me, woman, a time is coming when you will worship the Father neither on this mountain nor in Jerusalem. You Samaritans worship what you do not know; we worship what we do know, for salvation is from the Jews. Yet a time is coming and

bb. Or *do not use dishes Samaritans have used*

69

has now come when the true worshipers will worship the Father in spirit and truth, for they are the kind of worshipers the Father seeks. God is spirit, and his worshipers must worship in spirit and in truth."

The woman said, "I know that Messiah" (called Christ) "is coming. When he comes, he will explain everything to us."

Then Jesus declared, "I who speak to you am he."

30. THE DISCIPLES REJOIN JESUS
John 4:27-38

Just then his disciples returned and were surprised to find him talking with a woman. But no one asked, "What do you want?" or "Why are you talking with her?"

Then, leaving her water jar, the woman went back to the town and said to the people, "Come, see a man who told me everything I ever did. Could this be the Christ?" They came out of the town and made their way toward him.

Meanwhile his disciples urged him, "Rabbi, eat something."

But he said to them, "I have food to eat that you know nothing about."

Then his disciples said to each other, "Could someone have brought him food?"

"My food," said Jesus, "is to do the will of him who sent me and to finish his work. Do you not say, 'Four months more and then the harvest'? I tell you, open your eyes and look at the fields! They are ripe for harvest. Even now the reaper draws his wages, even now he harvests the crop for eternal life, so that the sower and the reaper may be glad together. Thus the saying 'One sows and another reaps' is true. I sent you to reap what you have not worked for. Others have done the hard work, and you have reaped the benefits of their labor."

31. MANY SAMARITANS BELIEVE
John 4:39-42

Many of the Samaritans from that town believed in him because of the woman's testimony, "He told me everything I ever did." So when the Samaritans came to him, they urged him to stay with them, and he stayed two days. And because of his words many more became believers.

They said to the woman, "We no longer believe just because of what you said; now we have heard for ourselves, and we know that this man really is the Savior of the world."

THREE.
GALILEAN MINISTRY

32. JESUS BEGINS TO PREACH
Matthew 4:17; Mark 1:14b-15; Luke 4:14b-15; John 4:43-45

After the two days Jesus left for Galilee. (Now Jesus himself had pointed out that a prophet has no honor in his own country.) When he arrived in Galilee, the Galileans welcomed him. They had seen all that he had done in Jerusalem at the Passover Feast, for they also had been there.

From that time on Jesus began to preach, proclaiming the good news of God. News about him spread through the whole countryside. He taught in their synagogues, and everyone praised him. "The time has come," he said. "The kingdom of God is near. Repent and believe the good news!"

33. JESUS HEALS THE OFFICIAL'S SON
John 4:46-54

Once more he visited Cana in Galilee, where he had turned the water into wine. And there was a certain royal official whose son lay sick at Capernaum. When this man heard that Jesus had arrived in Galilee from Judea, he went to him and begged him to come and heal his son, who was close to death.

"Unless you people see miraculous signs and wonders," Jesus told him, "you will never believe."

The royal official said, "Sir, come down before my child dies."

Jesus replied, "You may go. Your son will live."

The man took Jesus at his word and departed. While he was still on the way, his servants met him with the news that his boy was living. When he inquired as to the time when his son got better, they said to him, "The fever left him yesterday at the seventh hour."

72

Then the father realized that this was the exact time at which Jesus had said to him, "Your son will live." So he and all his household believed.

This was the second miraculous sign that Jesus performed, having come from Judea to Galilee.

34. JESUS REJECTED AT NAZARETH
Luke 4:16-30

He went to Nazareth, where he had been brought up, and on the Sabbath day he went into the synagogue, as was his custom. And he stood up to read. The scroll of the prophet Isaiah was handed to him. Unrolling it, he found the place where it is written:

"The Spirit of the Lord is on me,
because he has anointed me
to preach good news to the poor.
He has sent me to proclaim
freedom for the prisoners
and recovery of sight for the blind,
to release the oppressed,
to proclaim the year of the Lord's favor."[a]

Then he rolled up the scroll, gave it back to the attendant and sat down. The eyes of everyone in the synagogue were fastened on him, and he began by saying to them, "Today this scripture is fulfilled in your hearing."

All spoke well of him and were amazed at the gracious words that came from his lips. "Isn't this Joseph's son?" they asked.

Jesus said to them, "Surely you will quote this proverb to me: 'Physician, heal yourself! Do here in your hometown what we have heard that you did in Capernaum.'"

"I tell you the truth," he continued, "no prophet is accepted in his hometown. I assure you that there were many widows in Israel in Elijah's time, when the sky was shut for three and a half years and there was a severe famine throughout the land. Yet Elijah was not sent to any of them, but to a widow in Zarephath in the region of

---

a. Isaiah 61:1-2

Sidon. And there were many in Israel with leprosy[b] in the time of Elisha the prophet, yet not one of them was cleansed—only Naaman the Syrian."

All the people in the synagogue were furious when they heard this. They got up, drove him out of the town, and took him to the brow of the hill on which the town was built, in order to throw him down the cliff. But he walked right through the crowd and went on his way.

35. JESUS SETTLES AT CAPERNAUM
Matthew 4:13-16

Leaving Nazareth, he went and lived in Capernaum, a town in Galilee, which was by the lake in the area of Zebulun and Naphtali—to fulfill what was said through the prophet Isaiah:

"Land of Zebulun and land of Naphtali,
the way to the sea, along the Jordan,
Galilee of the Gentiles—
the people living in darkness
have seen a great light;
on those living in the land
of the shadow of death
a light has dawned."[c]

36. THE CALLING OF THE FIRST DISCIPLES
Matthew 4:18-22; Mark 1:16-20; Luke 5:1-11

One day as Jesus was walking beside the Sea of Galilee (the Lake of Gennesaret), he saw two brothers, Simon called Peter and his brother Andrew. They were casting a net into the lake, for they were fishermen. As Jesus was standing by the sea, with the people crowding around him and listening to the word of God, he saw at the water's edge two boats, left there by the fishermen, who were washing their nets. He got into one of the boats, the one belonging

b. The Greek word was used for various diseases affecting the skin—not necessarily leprosy [and hereinafter].
c. Isaiah 9:1-2

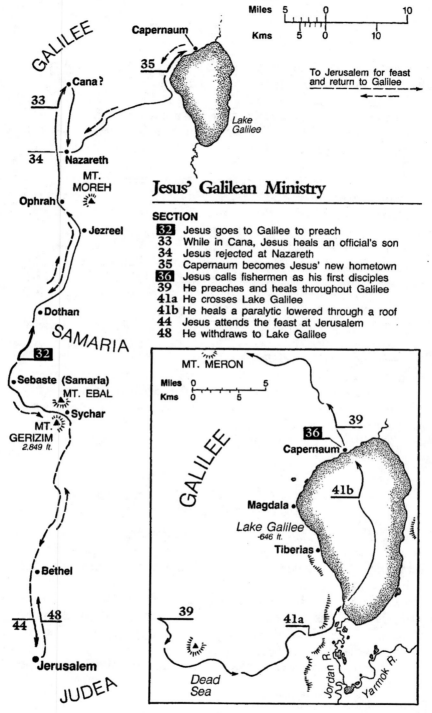

Jesus' Galilean Ministry

SECTION

32 Jesus goes to Galilee to preach
33 While in Cana, Jesus heals an official's son
34 Jesus rejected at Nazareth
35 Capernaum becomes Jesus' new hometown
36 Jesus calls fishermen as his first disciples
39 He preaches and heals throughout Galilee
41a He crosses Lake Galilee
41b He heals a paralytic lowered through a roof
44 Jesus attends the feast at Jerusalem
48 He withdraws to Lake Galilee

75

to Simon, and asked him to put out a little from shore. Then he sat down and taught the people from the boat.

When he had finished speaking, he said to Simon, "Put out into deep water, and let down the nets for a catch."

Simon answered, "Master, we've worked hard all night and haven't caught anything. But because you say so, I will let down the nets."

When they had done so, they caught such a large number of fish that their nets began to break. So they signaled their partners in the other boat to come and help them, and they came and filled both boats so full that they began to sink.

When Simon Peter saw this, he fell at Jesus' knees and said, "Go away from me, Lord; I am a sinful man!" For he and all his companions were astonished at the catch of fish they had taken.

Then Jesus said to Simon, "Don't be afraid; from now on you will catch men."

"Come, follow me," Jesus said, "and I will make you fishers of men." So they pulled their boats up on shore. At once they left their nets, left everything and followed him.

When he had gone a little farther, he saw two other brothers, James son of Zebedee and his brother John, Simon's partners. They were in a boat with their father Zebedee, preparing their nets. Without delay Jesus called them, and immediately they left their father Zebedee in the boat with the hired men and followed him.

37. JESUS DRIVES OUT AN EVIL SPIRIT
Mark 1:21-28; Luke 4:31-37

They went to Capernaum, and when the Sabbath came, Jesus went into the synagogue and began to teach. The people were amazed at his teaching, because he taught them as one who had authority, not as the teachers of the law.

In the synagogue there was a man possessed by a demon, an evil[d] spirit. He cried out at the top of his voice, "Ha! What do you want with us, Jesus of Nazareth? Have you come to destroy us? I know who you are—the Holy One of God!"

"Be quiet!" Jesus said sternly. "Come out of him!" Then the

---

d. Greek *unclean* [and hereinafter]

demon threw the man down before them all, shook the man violently and came out of him with a shriek, without injuring him.

The people were all so amazed that they asked each other, "What is this? A new teaching? With authority and power he gives orders to evil spirits and they obey him and come out!" News about him spread quickly throughout the surrounding area, over the whole region of Galilee.

38. JESUS HEALS MANY
Matthew 8:14-17; Mark 1:29-34; Luke 4:38-41

As soon as they left the synagogue, they went with James and John to the home of Simon and Andrew. Now Simon Peter's mother-in-law was lying in bed suffering from a high fever. They told Jesus about her and asked *him* to help her. When Jesus came into Peter's house, he went to her, rebuked the fever, and it left her. He bent over, took her hand and helped her up. She got up at once and began to wait on them.

That evening, when the sun was setting, the people brought to Jesus all who had various kinds of sickness and diseases and many who were demon-possessed. The whole town gathered at the door. Laying his hands on each one, he healed all the sick. This was to fulfill what was spoken through the prophet Isaiah:

> "He took up our infirmities
> and carried our diseases."[e]

Moreover, he drove out the spirits with a word; demons came out of many people, shouting, "You are the Son of God!" But he rebuked them and would not allow them to speak, because they knew who he was. They knew he was the Christ.

39. JESUS PRAYS, PREACHES, AND HEALS
Matthew 4:23; Mark 1:35-39; Luke 4:42-44

Very early in the morning, while it was still dark, Jesus got up. At daybreak Jesus left the house and went out to a solitary place, where

---

e. Isaiah 53:4

he prayed. Simon and his companions went to look for him, and when they found him, they exclaimed: "Everyone is looking for you!"

Jesus replied, "Let us go somewhere else—to the nearby villages—so I can preach there also. That is why I have come."

The people were looking for him and when they came to where he was, they tried to keep him from leaving them. But he said, "I must preach the good news of the kingdom of God to the other towns also, because that is why I was sent." So he traveled throughout Galilee,[f] and he kept on teaching in their synagogues, preaching[1] the good news of the kingdom, healing every disease and sickness among the people, and driving out demons.

40. THE MAN WITH LEPROSY
Matthew 8:2-4; Mark 1:40-45; Luke 5:12-16

While Jesus was in one of the towns, a man came along who was covered with leprosy. When he saw Jesus, he fell before him, and with his face to the ground, begged him on his knees, "Lord, if you are willing, you can make me clean."

Filled with compassion, Jesus reached out his hand and touched the man. "I am willing," he said. "Be clean!" Immediately the leprosy left him and he was cured.[g]

Then Jesus sent him away at once *and* ordered him with a strong warning: "See that you don't tell this to anyone. But go, show yourself to the priest and offer the sacrifices that Moses commanded for your cleansing, as a testimony to them." Instead he went out and began to talk freely, spreading the news. As a result, Jesus could no longer enter a town openly but stayed outside in lonely places. Yet the news about him spread all the more, so that crowds of people from everywhere came to hear him and to be healed of their sicknesses. But Jesus often withdrew to lonely places and prayed.

---

f. [*Judea* in Luke 4:44] Or *the land of the Jews*; some manuscripts *Galilee*
1. See p. 293: Did Jesus begin preaching in the synagogues of Galilee (Matthew 4:23; Mark 1:39) or Judea (Luke 4:44)?
g. Greek *made clean* [and hereinafter]

41. JESUS HEALS A PARALYTIC
Matthew 9:1-8; Mark 2:1-12; Luke 5:17-26

A few days later Jesus stepped into a boat, crossed over and again entered his own town, Capernaum. The people heard that he had come home.[2] So many gathered that there was no room left, not even outside the door, and he preached the word to them. As he was teaching, Pharisees and teachers of the law, who had come from every village of Galilee and from Judea and Jerusalem, were sitting there. And the power of the Lord was present for him to heal the sick. Some men came, bringing to him a paralytic lying on a mat carried by four of them. They tried to take him into the house to lay him before Jesus. When they could not find a way to do this because of the crowd, they went up on the roof. They made an opening in the roof above Jesus and, after digging through it,[3] lowered him on his mat through the tiles into the middle of the crowd, right in front of Jesus.

"Take heart, son," Jesus said to the paralytic when he saw their faith. "Friend, your sins are forgiven."

Now the Pharisees and some teachers of the law were sitting there, thinking to themselves, "Who is this fellow? Why does this fellow talk like that? He's blaspheming! Who can forgive sins but God alone?"

Immediately Jesus knew in his spirit that this was what they were thinking in their hearts, and he said to them, "Why are you thinking these things? Why do you entertain evil thoughts in your hearts? Which is easier: to say to the paralytic, 'Your sins are forgiven,' or to say, 'Get up, take your mat and walk'? But so that you may know that the Son of Man has authority on earth to forgive sins. . . ." Then he said to the paralyzed man, "I tell you, get up, take your mat and go home." Immediately the man stood up in full view of them all, took his mat he had been lying on, walked out and went home praising God. When the crowd saw this, everyone was amazed and gave praise to God, who had given such authority to men. They were filled with awe and said, "We have never seen anything like this! We have seen remarkable things today."

---

2. See p. 293: Was Jesus' hometown Nazareth (Luke 4:24) or Capernaum (Matthew 9:1)?

3. See p. 294: Did the men carrying the paralytic on a mat dig through the roof of the house (Mark 2:4) or only remove the tiles (Luke 5:19)?

42. THE CALLING OF LEVI (MATTHEW)
Matthew 9:9-13; Mark 2:13-17; Luke 5:27-32

After this, Jesus went on from there. He once again went out beside the lake. A large crowd came to him, and he began to teach them. As he walked along, he saw a tax collector by the name of Levi,[4] son of Alphaeus, sitting at his tax booth. "Follow me," Jesus told him, and Levi got up, left everything and followed him.

Then Levi held a great banquet for Jesus at his house. A large crowd of tax collectors and "sinners" were eating with him and his disciples, for there were many who followed him. But when the Pharisees and the teachers of the law who belonged to their sect saw him eating with the "sinners" and tax collectors, they complained to his disciples: "Why do you *and* your teacher eat and drink with tax collectors and 'sinners'?"

On hearing this, Jesus answered them, "It is not the healthy who need a doctor, but the sick. But go and learn what this means: 'I desire mercy, not sacrifice.'[h] I have not come to call the righteous, but sinners to repentance."

43. JESUS QUESTIONED ABOUT FASTING
Matthew 9:14-17; Mark 2:18-22; Luke 5:33-39

Now John's disciples and the Pharisees were fasting. Then John's disciples[5] came and asked Jesus, "How is it that we and the disciples of the Pharisees often fast and pray, but your disciples do not fast, but go on eating and drinking?"[6]

Jesus answered, "How can you make the guests of the bridegroom mourn *and* fast while he is with them? They cannot, so long as they have him with them. But the time will come when the bridegroom will be taken from them; in those days they will fast."

He told them this parable: "No one tears a patch from a new garment and sews *the* unshrunk cloth on an old garment. If he does,

---

4. See p. 294: Was one of Jesus' apostles named Matthew (Matthew 9:9) or Levi (Mark 2:14; Luke 5:27)?
h. Hosea 6:6
5. See p. 295: Was it John's disciples (Matthew 9:14) or those of the Pharisees (Luke 5:30) who questioned Jesus about fasting?
6. See p. 295: Did Matthew's banquet and the question on fasting immediately follow his call or was it later?

he will have torn the new garment, and the patch from the new will not match the old. The new piece will pull away from the old, making the tear worse. And no one pours new wine into old wineskins. If he does, the new wine will burst the skins, the wine will run out, and both the wine and the wineskins will be ruined. No, he pours new wine into new wineskins, and both are preserved. And no one after drinking old wine wants the new, for he says, 'The old is better.' "

44. THE HEALING AT THE POOL
John 5:1-15

Some time later, Jesus went up to Jerusalem for a feast of the Jews.[7] Now there is in Jerusalem near the Sheep Gate a pool, which in Aramaic is called Bethesda[i] and which is surrounded by five covered colonnades. Here a great number of disabled people used to lie—the blind, the lame, the paralyzed.[j] One who was there had been an invalid for thirty-eight years. When Jesus saw him lying there and learned that he had been in this condition for a long time, he asked him, "Do you want to get well?"

"Sir," the invalid replied, "I have no one to help me into the pool when the water is stirred. While I am trying to get in, someone else goes down ahead of me."

Then Jesus said to him, "Get up! Pick up your mat and walk." At once the man was cured; he picked up his mat and walked.

The day on which this took place was a Sabbath, and so the Jews said to the man who had been healed, "It is the Sabbath; the law forbids you to carry your mat."

But he replied, "The man who made me well said to me, 'Pick up your mat and walk.'"

So they asked him, "Who is this fellow who told you to pick it up and walk?"

The man who was healed had no idea who it was, for Jesus had slipped away into the crowd that was there.

---

7. See p. 295: How long was the Lord Jesus' public ministry?
i. Some manuscripts [of John 5:2] *Bethzatha*; other manuscripts *Bethsaida*
j. Some less important manuscripts [of John 5:3-4] *paralyzed—and they waited for the moving of the waters. From time to time an angel of the Lord would come down and stir up the waters. The first one into the pool after each such disturbance would be cured of whatever disease he had.*

Later Jesus found him at the temple and said to him, "See, you are well again. Stop sinning or something worse may happen to you." The man went away and told the Jews that it was Jesus who had made him well.

45. LIFE THROUGH THE SON
John 5:16-30

So, because Jesus was doing these things on the Sabbath, the Jews persecuted him. Jesus said to them, "My Father is always at his work to this very day, and I too am working." For this reason the Jews tried all the harder to kill him; not only was he breaking the Sabbath, but he was even calling God his own Father, making himself equal with God.

Jesus gave them this answer: "I tell you the truth, the Son can do nothing by himself; he can do only what he sees his Father doing, because whatever the Father does the Son also does. For the Father loves the Son and shows him all he does. Yes, to your amazement he will show him even greater things than these. For just as the Father raises the dead and gives them life, even so the Son gives life to whom he is pleased to give it. Moreover, the Father judges no one, but has entrusted all judgment to the Son, that all may honor the Son just as they honor the Father. He who does not honor the Son does not honor the Father, who sent him.

"I tell you the truth, whoever hears my word and believes him who sent me has eternal life and will not be condemned; he has crossed over from death to life. I tell you the truth, a time is coming and has now come when the dead will hear the voice of the Son of God and those who hear will live. For as the Father has life in himself, so he has granted the Son to have life in himself. And he has given him authority to judge because he is the Son of Man.

"Do not be amazed at this, for a time is coming when all who are in their graves will hear his voice and come out—those who have done good will rise to live, and those who have done evil will rise to be condemned. By myself I can do nothing; I judge only as I hear, and my judgment is just, for I seek not to please myself but him who sent me.

46. TESTIMONIES ABOUT JESUS
John 5:31-47

"If I testify about myself, my testimony is not valid. There is another who testifies in my favor, and I know that his testimony about me is valid.

"You have sent to John and he has testified to the truth. Not that I accept human testimony; but I mention it that you may be saved. John was a lamp that burned and gave light, and you chose for a time to enjoy his light.

"I have testimony weightier than that of John. For the very work that the Father has given me to finish, and which I am doing, testifies that the Father has sent me. And the Father who sent me has himself testified concerning me. You have never heard his voice nor seen his form, nor does his word dwell in you, for you do not believe the one he sent. You diligently study[k] the Scriptures because you think that by them you possess eternal life. These are the Scriptures that testify about me, yet you refuse to come to me to have life.

"I do not accept praise from men, but I know you. I know that you do not have the love of God in your hearts. I have come in my Father's name, and you do not accept me; but if someone else comes in his own name, you will accept him. How can you believe if you accept praise from one another, yet make no effort to obtain the praise that comes from the only God[l]?

"But do not think I will accuse you before the Father. Your accuser is Moses, on whom your hopes are set. If you believed Moses, you would believe me, for he wrote about me. But since you do not believe what he wrote, how are you going to believe what I say?"

47. LORD OF THE SABBATH
Matthew 12:1-14; Mark 2:23–3:6; Luke 6:1-11

One Sabbath Jesus was going through the grainfields, and his disciples walked along. They were hungry and began to pick some heads of grain, rub them in their hands and eat the kernels. When the Pharisees saw this, they said to him, "Look! Why are your disciples doing what is unlawful on the Sabbath?"

Jesus answered them, "Have you never read what David did when

---

k. Or *Study diligently* (the imperative)
l. Some early manuscripts [of John 5:44] *the Only One*

he and his companions were hungry and in need? In the days of Abiathar the high priest, he entered the house of God, and taking the consecrated bread, he ate what is lawful only for priests to eat. And he also gave some to his companions. Or haven't you read in the Law that on the Sabbath the priests in the temple desecrate the day and yet are innocent? I tell you that one[m] greater than the temple is here. If you had known what these words mean, 'I desire mercy, not sacrifice,'[n] you would not have condemned the innocent."

Then he said to them, "The Sabbath was made for man, not man for the Sabbath. So the Son of Man is Lord even of the Sabbath."

Going on from that place, on another Sabbath he went into their synagogue and was teaching, and a man was there whose right hand was shriveled. The Pharisees and the teachers of the law were looking for a reason to accuse Jesus, so they watched him closely to see if he would heal on the Sabbath. They asked him, "Is it lawful to heal on the Sabbath?"

Jesus knew what they were thinking and said to the man with the shriveled hand, "Get up and stand up in front of everyone." So he got up and stood there.

Then Jesus said to them, "I ask you, which is lawful on the Sabbath: to do good or to do evil, to save life or to destroy it?" But they remained silent.

He said to them, "If any of you has a sheep and it falls into a pit on the Sabbath, will you not take hold of it and lift it out? How much more valuable is a man than a sheep! Therefore it is lawful to do good on the Sabbath."

He looked around at them all in anger and, deeply distressed at their stubborn hearts, said to the man, "Stretch out your hand." He stretched it out, and his hand was completely restored, just as sound as the other. But they were furious. Then the Pharisees went out and began to plot with the Herodians what they might do, how they might kill Jesus.

48. CROWDS FOLLOW JESUS, GOD'S CHOSEN SERVANT
Matthew 4:24-25; 12:15-21; Mark 3:7-12

Aware of this, Jesus withdrew with his disciples from that place to the lake, and a large crowd from Galilee followed. News about him

---

m. Or *something*
n. Hosea 6:6

spread all over Syria, and people brought to him all who were ill with various diseases, those suffering severe pain, the demon-possessed, those having seizures, and the paralyzed, and he healed them. Large crowds came to him from Galilee, the Decapolis, Judea, Jerusalem, Idumea, and the regions across the Jordan and around Tyre and Sidon. Many followed him.

Because of the crowd he told his disciples to have a small boat ready for him, to keep the people from crowding him. For he had healed many, so that those with diseases were pushing forward to touch him. He healed all their sick, warning them not to tell who he was. Whenever the evil spirits saw him, they fell down before him and cried out, "You are the Son of God." But he gave them strict orders not to tell who he was. This was to fulfill what was spoken through the prophet Isaiah:

"Here is my servant whom I have chosen,
the one I love, in whom I delight;
I will put my Spirit on him,
and he will proclaim justice to the nations.
He will not quarrel or cry out;
no one will hear his voice in the streets.
A bruised reed he will not break,
and a smoldering wick he will not snuff out,
till he leads justice to victory.
In his name the nations will put their hope."o

o. Isaiah 42:1-4

FOUR.
CHOOSING THE TWELVE AND
SERMON ON THE MOUNT

49. THE APPOINTING OF THE TWELVE APOSTLES
Matthew 5:1a; 10:2-4; Mark 3:13-19; Luke 6:12-16

Now when he saw the crowds, Jesus went up on a mountainside to pray, and spent the night praying to God. When morning came, he called to him those disciples he wanted, and they came to him. He appointed twelve of them, whom he also designated apostles, that they might be with him and that he might send them out to preach and to have authority to drive out demons. These are the names of the twelve apostles: first, Simon (to whom he gave the name Peter) and his brother Andrew; James son of Zebedee and his brother John (to them he gave the name Boanerges, which means Sons of Thunder); Philip and Bartholomew; Thomas and Matthew the tax collector; James son of Alphaeus, and Thaddaeus (Judas son of James)[1]; Simon who was called the Zealot and Judas Iscariot, who became a traitor.

50. BLESSINGS AND WOES
Matthew 5:1b-12; Luke 6:17-26

He went down with them and stood on a level place.[2] A large crowd of his disciples came to him there, and a great number of people from all over Judea, from Jerusalem, and from the coast of Tyre and Sidon, who had come to hear him and to be healed of their diseases.

---

1. See p. 297: Was the apostle named Thaddaeus (Matthew 10:4; Mark 3:19) the same as Judas son of James (Luke 6:16; Acts 1:13)?
2. See p. 297: Are the Sermon on the Mount (Matthew 5-7) and the Sermon on the Plain (Luke 6) the same or two separate sermons?

Those troubled by evil spirits were cured, and the people all tried to touch him, because power was coming from him and healing them all.

Looking at his disciples, he sat down and began to teach them, saying:

"Blessed are the poor in spirit,
for theirs is the kingdom of heaven.
Blessed are those who mourn,
for they will be comforted.
Blessed are the meek,
for they will inherit the earth.
Blessed are those who hunger
and thirst for righteousness,
for they will be filled.
Blessed are the merciful,
for they will be shown mercy.
Blessed are the pure in heart,
for they will see God.
Blessed are the peacemakers,
for they will be called sons of God.
Blessed are those who are persecuted
because of righteousness,
for theirs is the kingdom of heaven.

"Blessed are you who are poor,[3]
for yours is the kingdom of God.
Blessed are you who hunger now,
for you will be satisfied.
Blessed are you who weep now,
for you will laugh.

"Blessed are you when people hate you,
when they exclude you and insult you,
persecute you and falsely say all kinds of evil against you
and reject your name as evil,
because of me, the Son of Man.

---

3. See p. 299: If Matthew and Luke record the same sermon, do Matthew 5:3-11 and Luke 6:20-22 reflect different beatitudes or are they the same, with Matthew as editor?

"Rejoice in that day and leap for joy. Be glad, because great is your reward in heaven. For in the same way their fathers persecuted the prophets who were before you.

"But woe to you who are rich,
for you have already received your comfort.
Woe to you who are well fed now,
for you will go hungry.
Woe to you who laugh now,
for you will mourn and weep.
Woe to you when all men speak well of you,
for that is how their fathers
treated the false prophets.

51. SALT AND LIGHT
Matthew 5:13-16

"You are the salt of the earth. But if the salt loses its saltiness, how can it be made salty again? It is no longer good for anything, except to be thrown out and trampled by men.

"You are the light of the world. A city on a hill cannot be hidden. Neither do people light a lamp and put it under a bowl. Instead they put it on its stand, and it gives light to everyone in the house. In the same way, let your light shine before men, that they may see your good deeds and praise your Father in heaven.

52. THE FULFILLMENT OF THE LAW
Matthew 5:17-20

"Do not think that I have come to abolish the Law or the Prophets; I have not come to abolish them but to fulfill them. I tell you the truth, until heaven and earth disappear, not the smallest letter, not the least stroke of a pen, will by any means disappear from the Law until everything is accomplished. Anyone who breaks one of the least of these commandments and teaches others to do the same will be called least in the kingdom of heaven, but whoever practices and teaches these commands will be called great in the kingdom of heaven. For I tell you that unless your righteousness surpasses that of the Pharisees and the teachers of the law, you will certainly not enter the kingdom of heaven.

53. MURDER
Matthew 5:21-22

"You have heard that it was said to the people long ago, 'Do not murder,[a] and anyone who murders will be subject to judgment.' But I tell you that anyone who is angry with his brother[b] will be subject to judgment. Again, anyone who says to his brother, 'Raca,'[c] is answerable to the Sanhedrin. But anyone who says, 'You fool!' will be in danger of the fire of hell.

Mountainside Experiences

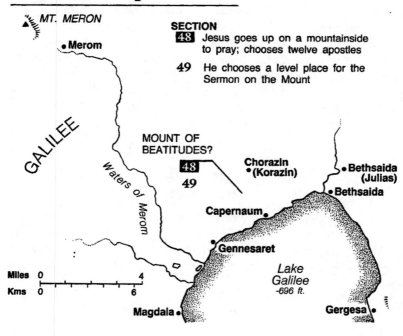

SECTION

48 Jesus goes up on a mountainside to pray; chooses twelve apostles

49 He chooses a level place for the Sermon on the Mount

a. Exodus 20:13
b. Some manuscripts *brother without cause*
c. An Aramaic term of contempt

89

54. RECONCILIATION
Matthew 5:23-26

"Therefore, if you are offering your gift at the altar and there remember that your brother has something against you, leave your gift there in front of the altar. First go and be reconciled to your brother; then come and offer your gift.

"Settle matters quickly with your adversary who is taking you to court. Do it while you are still with him on the way, or he may hand you over to the judge, and the judge may hand you over to the officer, and you may be thrown into prison. I tell you the truth, you will not get out until you have paid the last penny.[d]

55. ADULTERY
Matthew 5:27-30

"You have heard that it was said, 'Do not commit adultery.'[e] But I tell you that anyone who looks at a woman lustfully has already committed adultery with her in his heart. If your right eye causes you to sin, gouge it out and throw it away. It is better for you to lose one part of your body than for your whole body to be thrown into hell. And if your right hand causes you to sin, cut it off and throw it away. It is better for you to lose one part of your body than for your whole body to go into hell.

56. DIVORCE
Matthew 5:31-32

"It has been said, 'Anyone who divorces his wife must give her a certificate of divorce.'[f] But I tell you that anyone who divorces his wife, except for marital unfaithfulness, causes her to become an adulteress, and anyone who marries the divorced woman commits adultery.

---

d. Greek *kodrantes*
e. Exodus 20:14
f. Deuteronomy 24:1

57. OATHS
Matthew 5:33-37

"Again, you have heard that it was said to the people long ago, 'Do not break your oath, but keep the oaths you have made to the Lord.' But I tell you, Do not swear at all: either by heaven, for it is God's throne; or by the earth, for it is his footstool; or by Jerusalem, for it is the city of the Great King. And do not swear by your head, for you cannot make even one hair white or black. Simply let your 'Yes' be 'Yes,' and your 'No,' 'No'; anything beyond this comes from the evil one.

58. AN EYE FOR AN EYE
Matthew 5:38-42; Luke 6:29-31

"You have heard that it was said, 'Eye for eye, and tooth for tooth.'[g] But I tell you, Do not resist an evil person. If someone strikes you on the right cheek, turn to him the other also. And if someone wants to sue you and take your tunic, let him have your cloak as well. If someone takes your cloak, do not stop him from taking your tunic. If someone forces you to go one mile, go with him two miles. Give to everyone who asks you, and do not turn away from the one who wants to borrow from you. If anyone takes what belongs to you, do not demand it back. Do to others as you would have them do to you.

59. LOVE FOR ENEMIES
Matthew 5:43-48; Luke 6:27-28, 32-36

"You have heard that it was said, 'Love your neighbor[h] and hate your enemy.' But I tell you who hear me: Love your enemies, do good to those who hate you, bless those who curse you, pray for those who mistreat you *and* persecute you, that you may be sons of your Father in heaven. He causes his sun to rise on the evil and the good, and sends rain on the righteous and the unrighteous.

"If you love those who love you, what credit is that to you? What

---

g. Exodus 21:24; Leviticus 24:20; Deuteronomy 19:21
h. Leviticus 19:18

reward will you get? Are not even the tax collectors doing that? Even 'sinners' love those who love them. And if you do good to those who are good to you, what credit is that to you? Even 'sinners' do that. And if you greet only your brothers, what are you doing more than others? Do not even pagans do that? And if you lend to those from whom you expect repayment, what credit is that to you? Even 'sinners' lend to 'sinners,' expecting to be repaid in full. But love your enemies, do good to them, and lend to them without expecting to get anything back. Then your reward will be great, and you will be sons of the Most High, because he is kind to the ungrateful and wicked. Be merciful, just as your Father is merciful.

"Be perfect, therefore, as your heavenly Father is perfect.

60. GIVING TO THE NEEDY
Matthew 6:1-4

"Be careful not to do your 'acts of righteousness' before men, to be seen by them. If you do, you will have no reward from your Father in heaven.

"So when you give to the needy, do not announce it with trumpets, as the hypocrites do in the synagogues and on the streets, to be honored by men. I tell you the truth, they have received their reward in full. But when you give to the needy, do not let your left hand know what your right hand is doing, so that your giving may be in secret. Then your Father, who sees what is done in secret, will reward you.

61. PRAYER
Matthew 6:5-15

"And when you pray, do not be like the hypocrites, for they love to pray standing in the synagogues and on the street corners to be seen by men. I tell you the truth, they have received their reward in full. But when you pray, go into your room, close the door and pray to your Father, who is unseen. Then your Father, who sees what is done in secret, will reward you. And when you pray, do not keep on babbling like pagans, for they think they will be heard because of their many words. Do not be like them, for your Father knows what you need before you ask him.

"This, then, is how you should pray:

" 'Our Father in heaven,
hallowed be your name,
your kingdom come,
your will be done
on earth as it is in heaven.
Give us today our daily bread.
Forgive us our debts,
as we also have forgiven our debtors.
And lead us not into temptation,
but deliver us from the evil one.'ᵇ

For if you forgive men when they sin against you, your heavenly Father will also forgive you. But if you do not forgive men their sins, your Father will not forgive your sins.

62. FASTING
Matthew 6:16-18

"When you fast, do not look somber as the hypocrites do, for they disfigure their faces to show men they are fasting. I tell you the truth, they have received their reward in full. But when you fast, put oil on your head and wash your face, so that it will not be obvious to men that you are fasting, but only to your Father, who is unseen; and your Father, who sees what is done in secret, will reward you.

63. TREASURES IN HEAVEN
Matthew 6:19-24

"Do not store up for yourselves treasures on earth, where moth and rust destroy, and where thieves break in and steal. But store up for yourselves treasures in heaven, where moth and rust do not destroy, and where thieves do not break in and steal. For where your treasure is, there your heart will be also.

---

i. Or *from evil*; some late manuscripts [of Matthew 6:13] *one, / for yours is the kingdom and the power and the glory forever. Amen.*

"The eye is the lamp of the body. If your eyes are good, your whole body will be full of light. But if your eyes are bad, your whole body will be full of darkness. If then the light within you is darkness, how great is that darkness!

"No one can serve two masters. Either he will hate the one and love the other, or he will be devoted to the one and despise the other. You cannot serve both God and Money.

64. DO NOT WORRY
Matthew 6:25-34

"Therefore I tell you, do not worry about your life, what you will eat or drink; or about your body, what you will wear. Is not life more important than food, and the body more important than clothes? Look at the birds of the air; they do not sow or reap or store away in barns, and yet your heavenly Father feeds them. Are you not much more valuable than they? Who of you by worrying can add a single hour to his life?[j]

"And why do you worry about clothes? See how the lilies of the field grow. They do not labor or spin. Yet I tell you that not even Solomon in all his splendor was dressed like one of these. If that is how God clothes the grass of the field, which is here today and tomorrow is thrown into the fire, will he not much more clothe you, O you of little faith? So do not worry, saying, 'What shall we eat?' or 'What shall we wear?' For the pagans run after all these things, and your heavenly Father knows that you need them. But seek first his kingdom and his righteousness, and all these things will be given to you as well. Therefore do not worry about tomorrow, for tomorrow will worry about itself. Each day has enough trouble of its own.

65. JUDGING OTHERS
Matthew 7:1-6; Luke 6:37-42

"Do not judge, or you too will be judged. For in the same way you judge others, you will be judged. Do not condemn, and you will not be condemned. Forgive, and you will be forgiven. Give, and it will be given to you. A good measure, pressed down, shaken together and running over, will be poured into your lap. For with the measure you use, it will be measured to you."

---

j. Or *single cubit to his height*

He also told them this parable: "Can a blind man lead a blind man? Will they not both fall into a pit? A student is not above his teacher, but everyone who is fully trained will be like his teacher.

"Why do you look at the speck of sawdust in your brother's eye and pay no attention to the plank in your own eye? How can you say to your brother, 'Brother, let me take the speck out of your eye,' when all the time you yourself fail to see there is a plank in your own eye? You hypocrite, first take the plank out of your own eye, and then you will see clearly to remove the speck from your brother's eye.

"Do not give dogs what is sacred; do not throw your pearls to pigs. If you do, they may trample them under their feet, and then turn and tear you to pieces.

66. ASK, SEEK, KNOCK
Matthew 7:7-12

"Ask and it will be given to you; seek and you will find; knock and the door will be opened to you. For everyone who asks receives; he who seeks finds; and to him who knocks, the door will be opened.

"Which of you, if his son asks for bread, will give him a stone? Or if he asks for a fish, will give him a snake? If you, then, though you are evil, know how to give good gifts to your children, how much more will your Father in heaven give good gifts to those who ask him! So in everything, do to others what you would have them do to you, for this sums up the Law and the Prophets.

67. THE NARROW AND WIDE GATES
Matthew 7:13-14

"Enter through the narrow gate. For wide is the gate and broad is the road that leads to destruction, and many enter through it. But small is the gate and narrow the road that leads to life, and only a few find it.

68. A TREE AND ITS FRUIT
Matthew 7:15-23; Luke 6:43-46

"Watch out for false prophets. They come to you in sheep's clothing, but inwardly they are ferocious wolves. By their fruit you will recognize them. Do people pick grapes from thornbushes, or figs from thistles? People do not pick figs from thornbushes, or grapes from briers. Likewise every good tree bears good fruit, but a bad tree bears bad fruit. A good tree cannot bear bad fruit, and a bad tree cannot bear good fruit. Every tree that does not bear good fruit is cut down and thrown into the fire.

"Each tree is recognized by its own fruit. Thus, by their fruit you will recognize them. The good man brings good things out of the good stored up in his heart, and the evil man brings evil things out of the evil stored up in his heart. For out of the overflow of his heart his mouth speaks.

"Why do you call me, 'Lord, Lord,' and do not do what I say? Not everyone who says to me, 'Lord, Lord,' will enter the kingdom of heaven, but only he who does the will of my Father who is in heaven. Many will say to me on that day, 'Lord, Lord, did we not prophesy in your name, and in your name drive out demons and perform many miracles?' Then I will tell them plainly, 'I never knew you. Away from me, you evildoers!'

69. THE WISE AND FOOLISH BUILDERS
Matthew 7:24-29; Luke 6:47-49

"Therefore everyone who comes to me and hears these words of mine and puts them into practice is like a wise man building a house, who dug down deep and laid the foundation on rock. The rain came down, the streams rose, and the winds blew and beat against that house. When a flood came, the torrent struck that house but could not shake it, because it was well built. It did not fall, because it had its foundation on the rock. But everyone who hears these words of mine and does not put them into practice is like a foolish man who built his house on sand, on the ground without a foundation. The rain came down, the streams rose, and the winds blew and beat against that house. The moment the torrent struck, it collapsed and fell with a great crash, and its destruction was complete."

When Jesus had finished saying these things, the crowds were amazed at his teaching, because he taught as one who had authority, and not as their teachers of the law.

FIVE.
MORE GALILEAN MINISTRY
AND PARABLES

70. THE FAITH OF THE CENTURION
Matthew 8:1, 5-13; Luke 7:1-10

When Jesus came down from the mountainside, large crowds followed him. He entered Capernaum. There a centurion's servant, whom his master valued highly, was sick and about to die. The centurion heard of Jesus and sent some elders of the Jews to him, asking him to come and heal his servant: "Lord, my servant lies at home paralyzed and in terrible suffering."[1] When they came to Jesus, they pleaded earnestly with him, "This man deserves to have you do this, because he loves our nation and has built our synagogue."

Jesus said, "I will go and heal him." So Jesus went with them.

He was not far from the house when the centurion sent friends to say to him: "Lord, don't trouble yourself, for I do not deserve to have you come under my roof. That is why I did not even consider myself worthy to come to you. But just say the word, and my servant will be healed. For I myself am a man under authority, with soldiers under me. I tell this one, 'Go,' and he goes; and that one, 'Come,' and he comes. I say to my servant, 'Do this,' and he does it."

When Jesus heard this, he was amazed at him, and turning to the crowd following him, he said, "I tell you the truth, I have not found anyone with such great faith even in Israel. I say to you that many will come from the east and the west, and will take their places at the

---

1. See p. 301: Did the centurion himself approach Jesus to request his servant's healing (Matthew 8:5-13) or did others make the request (Luke 7:1-10)? Was the healing of the centurion's servant the same as that of the royal official's son (John 4:46-54?

feast with Abraham, Isaac and Jacob in the kingdom of heaven. But the subjects of the kingdom will be thrown outside, into the darkness, where there will be weeping and gnashing of teeth."

Then Jesus said to the centurion, "Go! It will be done just as you believed it would." And his servant was healed at that very hour. Then the men who had been sent returned to the house and found the servant well.

71. JESUS RAISES A WIDOW'S SON
Luke 7:11-17

Soon afterward, Jesus went to a town called Nain, and his disciples and a large crowd went along with him. As he approached the town gate, a dead person was being carried out—the only son of his mother, and she was a widow. And a large crowd from the town was with her. When the Lord saw her, his heart went out to her and he said, "Don't cry."

Then he went up and touched the coffin, and those carrying it stood still. He said, "Young man, I say to you, get up!" The dead man sat up and began to talk, and Jesus gave him back to his mother.

They were all filled with awe and praised God. "A great prophet has appeared among us," they said. "God has come to help his people." This news about Jesus spread throughout Judea[a] and the surrounding country.

72. JESUS AND JOHN THE BAPTIST
Matthew 11:2-19; Luke 7:18-35

John's disciples told John in prison about all these things Christ was doing. Calling two of them, he sent them to the Lord to ask him, "Are you the one who was to come, or should we expect someone else?"

When the men came to Jesus, they said, "John the Baptist sent us to you to ask, 'Are you the one who was to come, or should we expect someone else?' "

At that very time Jesus cured many who had diseases, sicknesses and evil spirits, and gave sight to many who were blind. So he

a. Or *the land of the Jews*

98

replied to the messengers, "Go back and report to John what you have seen and heard: The blind receive sight, the lame walk, those who have leprosy are cured, the deaf hear, the dead are raised, and the good news is preached to the poor. Blessed is the man who does not fall away on account of me."

As John's disciples were leaving, Jesus began to speak to the crowd about John: "What did you go out into the desert to see? A reed swayed by the wind? If not, what did you go out to see? A man dressed in fine clothes? No, those who wear fine, expensive clothes and indulge in luxury are in kings' palaces. Then what did you go out to see? A prophet? Yes, I tell you, and more than a prophet. This

More Galilean Ministry and Parables

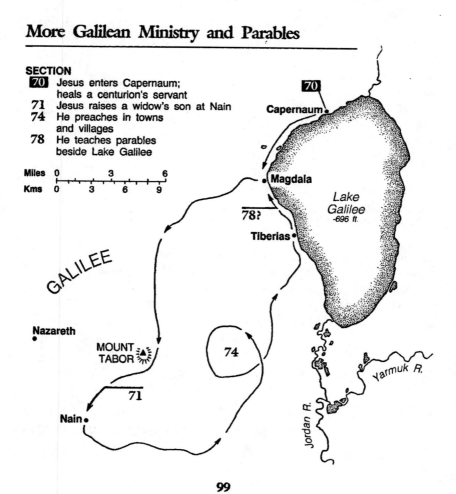

SECTION
70 Jesus enters Capernaum; heals a centurion's servant
71 Jesus raises a widow's son at Nain
74 He preaches in towns and villages
78 He teaches parables beside Lake Galilee

| Miles | 0 | | 3 | | 6 |
| Kms | 0 | 3 | 6 | 9 | |

70 Capernaum

Magdala

Lake Galilee -696 ft.

78?

Tiberias

GALILEE

Nazareth

MOUNT TABOR

74

71

Nain

Jordan R.

Yarmuk R.

99

is the one about whom it is written:

> " 'I will send my messenger ahead of you,
> who will prepare your way before you.'[b]

I tell you the truth: Among those born of women there has not risen anyone greater than John the Baptist; yet the one who is least in the kingdom of God is greater than he. From the days of John the Baptist until now, the kingdom of heaven has been forcefully advancing, and forceful men lay hold of it. For all the Prophets and the Law prophesied until John. And if you are willing to accept it, he is the Elijah who was to come. He who has ears, let him hear.

(All the people, even the tax collectors, when they heard Jesus' words, acknowledged that God's way was right, because they had been baptized by John. But the Pharisees and experts in the law rejected God's purpose for themselves, because they had not been baptized by John.)

"To what, then, can I compare the people of this generation? What are they like? They are like children sitting in the marketplaces and calling out to each other:

> " 'We played the flute for you,
> and you did not dance;
> we sang a dirge,
> and you did not cry.'

For John the Baptist came neither eating bread nor drinking wine, and you say, 'He has a demon.' The Son of Man came eating and drinking, and you say, 'Here is a glutton and a drunkard, a friend of tax collectors and "sinners." ' But wisdom is proved right by all her children, by her actions."

73. JESUS ANOINTED BY A SINFUL WOMAN
Luke 7:36-50

Now one of the Pharisees invited Jesus to have dinner with him, so he went to the Pharisee's house and reclined at the table. When a

---

b. Malachi 3:1

woman who had lived a sinful life in that town learned that Jesus was eating at the Pharisee's house, she brought an alabaster jar of perfume, and as she stood behind him at his feet weeping, she began to wet his feet with her tears. Then she wiped them with her hair, kissed them and poured perfume on them.

When the Pharisee who had invited him saw this, he said to himself, "If this man were a prophet, he would know who is touching him and what kind of woman she is—that she is a sinner."

Jesus answered him, "Simon, I have something to tell you."

"Tell me, teacher," he said.

"Two men owed money to a certain moneylender. One owed him five hundred denarii,[c] and the other fifty. Neither of them had the money to pay him back, so he canceled the debts of both. Now which of them will love him more?"

Simon replied, "I suppose the one who had the bigger debt canceled."

"You have judged correctly," Jesus said.

Then he turned toward the woman and said to Simon, "Do you see this woman? I came into your house. You did not give me any water for my feet, but she wet my feet with her tears and wiped them with her hair. You did not give me a kiss, but this woman, from the time I entered, has not stopped kissing my feet. You did not put oil on my head, but she has poured perfume on my feet. Therefore, I tell you, her many sins have been forgiven—for she loved much. But he who has been forgiven little loves little."

Then Jesus said to her, "Your sins are forgiven. Your faith has saved you; go in peace."

The other guests began to say among themselves, "Who is this who even forgives sins?"

74. WOMEN HELPERS
Luke 8:1-3

After this, Jesus traveled about from one town and village to another, proclaiming the good news of the kingdom of God. The Twelve were with him, and also some women who had been cured of evil spirits and diseases: Mary (called Magdalene) from whom seven

---

c. A denarius was a coin worth about a day's wages.

demons had come out; Joanna the wife of Cuza, the manager of Herod's household; Susanna; and many others. These women were helping to support them out of their own means.

75. JESUS AND BEELZEBUB
Matthew 12:22-37; Mark 3:20-30

Then Jesus entered a house, and again a crowd gathered, so that he and his disciples were not even able to eat. When his family heard about this, they went to take charge of him, for they said, "He is out of his mind."

Then *the crowd* brought him a demon-possessed man who was blind and mute, and Jesus healed him, so that he could both talk and see. All the people were astonished and said, "Could this be the Son of David?"

But when the Pharisees and the teachers of the law who came down from Jerusalem heard this, they said, "He is possessed by Beelzebub!ᵈ It is only by Beelzebub, the prince of demons, that this fellow is driving out demons."

Jesus knew their thoughts, called them and spoke to them in parables: "How can Satan drive out Satan? Every kingdom divided against itself cannot stand *and* will be ruined, and every city or household divided against itself will not stand. And if Satan opposes himself, he is divided against himself. How then can his kingdom stand? His end has come. And if I drive out demons by Beelzebub, by whom do your people drive them out? So then, they will be your judges. But if I drive out demons by the Spirit of God, then the kingdom of God has come upon you.

"In fact, no one can enter a strong man's house and carry off his possessions unless he first ties up the strong man. Then he can rob his house.

"He who is not with me is against me, and he who does not gather with me scatters. And so I tell you the truth, every sin and blasphemy will be forgiven men, but the blasphemy against the Spirit will not be forgiven. Anyone who speaks a word against the Son of Man will be forgiven, but anyone who blasphemes against the Holy Spirit will never be forgiven, either in this age or in the age to come; he is guilty of an eternal sin."

---

d. Greek *Beezeboul* or *Beelzeboul* [and hereinafter]

He said this because they were saying, "He has an evil spirit."

"Make a tree good and its fruit will be good, or make a tree bad and its fruit will be bad, for a tree is recognized by its fruit. You brood of vipers, how can you who are evil say anything good? For out of the overflow of the heart the mouth speaks. The good man brings good things out of the good stored up in him, and the evil man brings evil things out of the evil stored up in him. But I tell you that men will have to give account on the day of judgment for every careless word they have spoken. For by your words you will be acquitted, and by your words you will be condemned."

76. THE SIGN OF JONAH
Matthew 12:38-45

Then some of the Pharisees and teachers of the law said to him, "Teacher, we want to see a miraculous sign from you."

He answered, "A wicked and adulterous generation asks for a miraculous sign! But none will be given it except the sign of the prophet Jonah. For as Jonah was three days and three nights in the belly of a huge fish, so the Son of Man will be three days and three nights in the heart of the earth. The men of Nineveh will stand up at the judgment with this generation and condemn it; for they repented at the preaching of Jonah, and now one^c greater than Jonah is here. The Queen of the South will rise at the judgment with this generation and condemn it; for she came from the ends of the earth to listen to Solomon's wisdom, and now one^c greater than Solomon is here.

"When an evil spirit comes out of a man, it goes through arid places seeking rest and does not find it. Then it says, 'I will return to the house I left.' When it arrives, it finds the house unoccupied, swept clean and put in order. Then it goes and takes with it seven other spirits more wicked than itself, and they go in and live there. And the final condition of that man is worse than the first. That is how it will be with this wicked generation."

---

c. Or *something*

77. JESUS' MOTHER AND BROTHERS
Matthew 12:46-50; Mark 3:31-35; Luke 8:19-21

Now Jesus' mother and brothers arrived to see him, but they were not able to get near him because of the crowd. While Jesus was still talking to the crowd, his mother and brothers stood outside, wanting to speak to him. They sent someone in to call him. A crowd was sitting around him, and they told him, "Your mother and brothers are standing outside looking for you, wanting to speak to you."[f]

"Who is my mother, and who are my brothers?" he asked.

Then he looked at those seated in a circle around him. Pointing to his disciples, he said, "Here are my mother and my brothers—those who hear God's word and put it into practice. For whoever does the will of my Father in heaven[2] is my brother and sister and mother."

78. THE PARABLE OF THE SOWER
Matthew 13:1-23; Mark 4:1-20; Luke 8:4-15

On another occasion that same day, Jesus went out of the house, sat by the lake and began to teach. People were coming from town after town. Such large crowds gathered around him that he got into a boat and sat in it out on the lake, while all the people stood along the shore at the water's edge. Then he taught them many things by parables. In his teaching he told this parable: "Listen! A farmer went out to sow his seed. As he was scattering the seed, some fell along the path; it was trampled on, and the birds of the air came and ate it up. Some fell on rocky places, where it did not have much soil. It sprang up quickly, because the soil was shallow. But when the sun came up, the plants were scorched; they withered because they had no moisture, no root. Other seed fell among thorns, which grew up with it and choked the plants, so that they did not bear grain. Still other seed fell on good soil. It came up, grew and produced a crop, multiplying thirty, sixty or even a hundred times more than what was sown."

When he said this, he called out, "He who has ears to hear, let him hear."

When he was alone, the Twelve and the others around him came

---

f. Some manuscripts do not have [this sentence in Matthew 12:47].
2. See p. 302: When Jesus' relatives came to get him, did he refer to *the will of my Father in heaven* (Matthew 12:50) or *God's will* (Mark 3:35)?

and asked him about the parables, *and* what this parable meant. The disciples asked, "Why do you speak to the people in parables?"

He replied, "The knowledge of the secrets of the kingdom of heaven has been given to you, but not to them. Whoever has will be given more, and he will have an abundance. Whoever does not have, even what he has will be taken from him. This is why to those others on the outside I speak everything in parables, so that,

> " 'Though seeing, they do not see;
> though hearing, they do not
> hear or understand.'[g]

In them is fulfilled the prophecy of Isaiah:

> " 'You will be ever hearing
> but never understanding;
> you will be ever seeing but never perceiving.
> For this people's heart has become calloused;
> they hardly hear with their ears,
> and they have closed their eyes.
> Otherwise they might see with their eyes,
> hear with their ears,
> understand with their hearts
> and turn, and I would heal them
> and they might be forgiven.'[h]

But blessed are your eyes because they see, and your ears because they hear. For I tell you the truth, many prophets and righteous men longed to see what you see but did not see it, and to hear what you hear but did not hear it."

Then Jesus said to them, "Don't you understand this parable? How then will you understand any parable? Listen then to what the parable of the sower means: The seed is the word of God. The farmer sows the word. Some people are like seed along the path, where the word is sown. As soon as they hear the message about the kingdom and *do* not understand it, Satan comes and snatches away the word that was sown in their hearts, so that they may not believe

---

g. Isaiah 6:9
h. Isaiah 6:9-10

105

and be saved. Others, like seed sown on rocky places, are the ones who hear the word and at once receive it with joy. But since they have no root, they last only a short time. They believe for a while, but in the time of testing, when trouble or persecution comes because of the word, they quickly fall away. Still others, like seed sown among thorns, hear the word, but as they go on their way they are choked by the worries of this life, the deceitfulness of wealth, and the desires for pleasures and other things, and they do not mature, making *them* unfruitful. But the seed sown on good soil stands for others who, with a noble and good heart, hear the word, understand, accept and retain it, and by persevering produce a crop—thirty, sixty or even a hundred times what was sown."

79. A LAMP ON A STAND
Mark 4:21-25; Luke 8:16-18

He said to them, "Do you bring in a lamp to put it under a bowl or a bed? No one lights a lamp and hides it in a jar or puts it under a bed. Instead, don't you put it on its stand, so that those who come in can see the light? For there is nothing hidden that will not be disclosed, and nothing concealed that will not be known or brought out into the open. If anyone has ears to hear, let him hear. Therefore consider carefully how you listen. With the measure you use, it will be measured to you—and even more. Whoever has will be given more; whoever does not have, even what he thinks he has will be taken from him."

80. THE PARABLE OF THE GROWING SEED
Mark 4:26-29

He also said, "This is what the kingdom of God is like. A man scatters seed on the ground. Night and day, whether he sleeps or gets up, the seed sprouts and grows, though he does not know how. All by itself the soil produces grain—first the stalk, then the head, then the full kernel in the head. As soon as the grain is ripe, he puts the sickle to it, because the harvest has come."

81. THE PARABLE OF THE WEEDS
Matthew 13:24-30

Jesus told them another parable: "The kingdom of heaven is like a man who sowed good seed in his field. But while everyone was sleeping, his enemy came and sowed weeds among the wheat, and went away. When the wheat sprouted and formed heads, then the weeds also appeared.

"The owner's servants came to him and said, 'Sir, didn't you sow good seed in your field? Where then did the weeds come from?'

" 'An enemy did this,' he replied.

"The servants asked him, 'Do you want us to go and pull them up?'

" 'No,' he answered, 'because while you are pulling the weeds, you may root up the wheat with them. Let both grow together until the harvest. At that time I will tell the harvesters: First collect the weeds and tie them in bundles to be burned; then gather the wheat and bring it into my barn.' "

82. THE PARABLES OF THE MUSTARD SEED AND THE YEAST
Matthew 13:31-35; Mark 4:30-34

Again he told them another parable: "What shall we say the kingdom of God is like, or what parable shall we use to describe it? The kingdom of heaven is like a mustard seed, which a man took and planted in his field. Though it is the smallest of all your seeds you plant in the ground, yet when planted, it grows and becomes the largest of all garden plants, a tree with such big branches that the birds of the air can come and perch in shade in its branches."

He told them still another parable: "The kingdom of heaven is like yeast that a woman took and mixed into a large amount[i] of flour until it worked all through the dough."

With many similar parables Jesus spoke the word to them, as much as they could understand. Jesus spoke all these things to the crowd in parables. He did not say anything to them without using a parable. So was fulfilled what was spoken through the prophet:

---

i. Greek *three satas* (probably about 1/2 bushel or 22 liters)

"I will open my mouth in parables,
I will utter things hidden
since the creation of the world."[j]

But when he was alone with his own disciples, he explained everything.

83. THE PARABLE OF THE WEEDS EXPLAINED
Matthew 13:36-43

Then he left the crowd and went into the house. His disciples came to him and said, "Explain to us the parable of the weeds in the field."

He answered, "The one who sowed the good seed is the Son of Man. The field is the world, and the good seed stands for the sons of the kingdom. The weeds are the sons of the evil one, and the enemy who sows them is the devil. The harvest is the end of the age, and the harvesters are angels.

"As the weeds are pulled up and burned in the fire, so it will be at the end of the age. The Son of Man will send out his angels, and they will weed out of his kingdom everything that causes sin and all who do evil. They will throw them into the fiery furnace, where there will be weeping and gnashing of teeth. Then the righteous will shine like the sun in the kingdom of their Father. He who has ears, let him hear.

84. THE PARABLES OF THE HIDDEN TREASURE
AND THE PEARL
Matthew 13:44-46

"The kingdom of heaven is like treasure hidden in a field. When a man found it, he hid it again, and then in his joy went and sold all he had and bought that field.

"Again, the kingdom of heaven is like a merchant looking for fine pearls. When he found one of great value, he went away and sold everything he had and bought it.

---

j. Psalm 78:2

85. THE PARABLE OF THE NET
Matthew 13:47-53

"Once again, the kingdom of heaven is like a net that was let down into the lake and caught all kinds of fish. When it was full, the fishermen pulled it up on the shore. Then they sat down and collected the good fish in baskets, but threw the bad away. This is how it will be at the end of the age. The angels will come and separate the wicked from the righteous and throw them into the fiery furnace, where there will be weeping and gnashing of teeth."

"Have you understood all these things?" Jesus asked.

"Yes," they replied.

He said to them, "Therefore every teacher of the law who has been instructed about the kingdom of heaven is like the owner of a house who brings out of his storeroom new treasures as well as old."

When Jesus had finished these parables, he moved on from there.

SIX.
MINISTRY OF MIRACLES

86. JESUS CALMS THE STORM
Matthew 8:18, 23-27; Mark 4:35-41; Luke 8:22-25

That day when evening came *and* Jesus saw the crowd around him, he gave orders to his disciples: "Let us cross over to the other side of the lake." Then he got into the boat and his disciples followed him. Leaving the crowd behind, they took him along, just as he was, in the boat.[1] There were also other boats with him. They set out. As they sailed, he fell asleep. Without warning, a furious squall came up on the lake, so that the waves swept over the boat. The boat was being swamped, and they were in great danger.

Jesus was in the stern, sleeping on a cushion. The disciples went and woke him, saying, "Master, Master, save us! We're going to drown!" "Teacher, don't you care if we drown?"

He replied, "You of little faith, why are you so afraid?" Then he got up, rebuked the wind and said to the raging waters, "Quiet! Be still!" Then the storm subsided, the wind died down, and all was completely calm.

"Where is your faith?" he asked his disciples. "Do you still have no faith?"

They were terrified. In fear and amazement they asked one another, "Who is this? What kind of man is this? He commands even the winds and the waves, and they obey him."

---

1. See p. 304: When Jesus finished teaching the many parables, did he remain in the boat and leave the shore (Mark 4:36) or get out and later get back in to leave (Matthew 8:23)?

87. THE HEALING OF TWO DEMON-POSSESSED MEN
Matthew 8:28-34; Mark 5:1-20; Luke 8:26-39

They sailed to the region of the Gerasenes (Gadarenes),[a] which is across the lake from Galilee. When he arrived at the other side, Jesus got out of the boat. When Jesus stepped ashore, he was met by two demon-possessed men[2] coming from the tombs. They were so violent that no one could pass that way. *One,* a demon-possessed man from the town, for a long time had not worn clothes or lived in a house, but had lived in the tombs. No one could bind him any more, not even with a chain. Many times an evil spirit had seized him, and though he was chained hand and foot and kept under guard, he tore the chains apart and broke the irons on his feet. No one was strong enough to subdue him. He had been driven by the demon into solitary places. Night and day among the tombs and in the hills he would cry out and cut himself with stones.

When he saw Jesus from a distance, he ran and fell on his knees at his feet. He cried out, shouting at the top of his voice, "What do you want with me, Jesus, Son of the Most High God? Have you come here to torture us before the appointed time? I beg you, don't torture me! Swear to God that you won't torture me!" For Jesus had commanded him, "Come out of this man, you evil spirit!"

Then Jesus asked him, "What is your name?"

"My name is Legion," he replied, "for we are many," because many demons had gone into him. And he begged Jesus again and again not to send them out of the area, not to order them to go into the Abyss.

Some distance from them a large herd of pigs was feeding on the nearby hillside. The demons begged Jesus, "If you drive us out, send us into the herd of pigs; allow us to go into them." He gave them permission. He said to them, "Go!" When the demons came out, they went into the pigs. The whole herd, about two thousand in number, rushed down the steep bank into the lake and were drowned.

---

a. Some manuscripts *Gadarenes*; other manuscripts *Gergesenes* [and hereinafter]
2. See p. 304: How many times did Jesus permit demons to enter a herd of pigs? Did Jesus heal one demoniac (Mark 5:2; Luke 8:27) or two (Matthew 8:28)? Did the swine incident occur in the region of the Gadarenes (Matthew 8:28) or Gerasenes (Mark 5:1; Luke 8:26)? Was one of the demoniacs from Gerasa (Luke 8:26-27, 39) or the Decapolis (Mark 5:20)?

When those tending the pigs saw what had happened, they ran off and reported all this, including what had happened to the demon-possessed men, in the town and countryside. Then the whole town went out to see what had happened. When they came to Jesus, they saw the man who had been possessed by the legion of demons, sitting there at Jesus' feet, dressed and in his right mind; and they were afraid. Those who had seen it told the people how the demon-possessed man had been cured—and told about the pigs as well. Then all the people of the region of the Gerasenes began to plead with Jesus to leave their region, because they were overcome with fear. So he got into the boat and left.

As Jesus was getting into the boat, the man from whom the demons had gone out begged to go with him. Jesus did not let him, but sent him away, saying, "Return home to your family and tell them how much God has done for you, and how the Lord has had mercy on you." So the man went away and told all over town, and began to tell in the Decapolis[b] how much Jesus had done for him. And all the people were amazed.

88. A DEAD GIRL AND A SICK WOMAN
Matthew 9:18-26; Mark 5:21-43; Luke 8:40-56

Now when Jesus had again crossed over by boat to the other side of the lake, a large crowd gathered around while he was by the lake *and* welcomed him, for they were all expecting him. Just then one of the synagogue rulers, a man named Jairus, came there[3] because his only daughter, a girl of about twelve, was dying. Seeing Jesus, he knelt at his feet and pleaded earnestly with him to come to his house, and said, "My little daughter is dying.[4] Please come and put your hands on her so that she will be healed and live." So Jesus got up and went with him, and so did his disciples.

As Jesus was on his way, a large crowd followed and pressed

---

b. That is, the Ten Cities [and hereinafter]
3. See p. 307: Did Jesus encounter Jairus immediately after healing the two demoniacs and crossing the lake (Mark 5:21-22; Luke 8:40-41), or later at Matthew's house (Matthew 9:10-18)?
4. See p. 308: Was Jairus' daughter dying (Mark 5:23; Luke 8:42) or already dead (Matthew 9:18) when he first approached Jesus with his request?

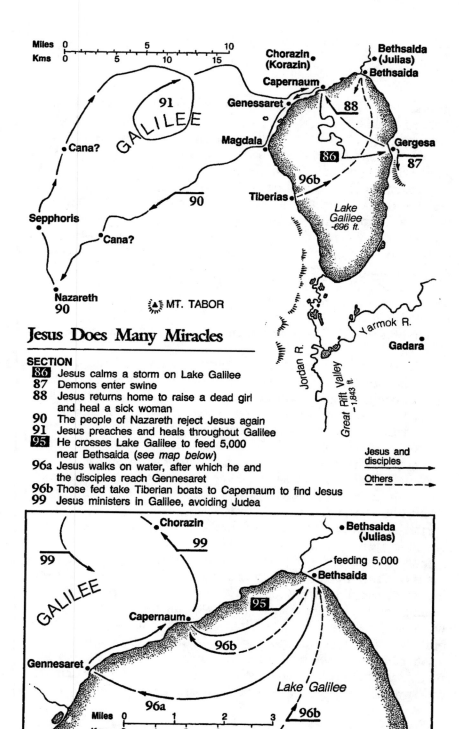

Miles 0 ... 5 ... 10
Kms 0 ... 5 ... 10 ... 15

Chorazin (Korazin)
Bethsaida (Julias)
Bethsaida
Capernaum
Genessaret
91
88
GALILEE
Cana?
Magdala
Gergesa
86
87
Sepphoris
96b
90
Tiberias
Lake Galilee -696 ft.
Cana?
Nazareth
90
MT. TABOR
Yarmok R.
Gadara
Jordan R.
Great Rift Valley -1,843 ft.

Jesus Does Many Miracles

SECTION

86 Jesus calms a storm on Lake Galilee
87 Demons enter swine
88 Jesus returns home to raise a dead girl and heal a sick woman
90 The people of Nazareth reject Jesus again
91 Jesus preaches and heals throughout Galilee
95 He crosses Lake Galilee to feed 5,000 near Bethsaida (see map below)
96a Jesus walks on water, after which he and the disciples reach Gennesaret
96b Those fed take Tiberian boats to Capernaum to find Jesus
99 Jesus ministers in Galilee, avoiding Judea

Jesus and disciples ⟶

Others ⇢

Chorazin
99
Bethsaida (Julias)
99
feeding 5,000
Bethsaida
GALILEE
95
Capernaum
96b
Gennesaret
Lake Galilee
96a
96b
Miles 0 ... 1 ... 2 ... 3
Kms 0 ... 1 ... 2 ... 3 ... 4

113

around him. The crowds almost crushed him. And a woman was there who had been subject to bleeding for twelve years,[c] but no one could heal her. She had suffered a great deal under the care of many doctors and had spent all she had, yet instead of getting better she grew worse. When she heard about Jesus, she said to herself, "If I only touch his cloak, I will be healed." She came up behind him in the crowd and touched the edge of his cloak. Immediately her bleeding stopped, and the woman was healed from that moment. She felt in her body that she was freed from her suffering.

At once Jesus realized that power had gone out from him. He turned around in the crowd and asked, "Who touched my clothes?"

When they all denied it, Peter said, "Master, you see the people are crowding and pressing against you, and yet you can ask, 'Who touched me?' "

But Jesus said, "Someone touched me; I know that power has gone out from me."

Looking around to see who had done it, Jesus turned and saw her. Then the woman, knowing what had happened to her *and* seeing that she could not go unnoticed, came trembling with fear and fell at his feet. In the presence of all the people, she told him the whole truth: why she had touched him and how she had been instantly healed. Then he said to her, "Take heart, daughter, your faith has healed you. Go in peace and be freed from your suffering."

While Jesus was still speaking, some men came from the house of Jairus, the synagogue ruler. "Your daughter is dead," they said. "Why bother the teacher any more?"

Hearing this *but* ignoring what they said, Jesus told Jairus, "Don't be afraid; just believe, and she will be healed."

Jesus did not let anyone follow him except Peter, James and John the brother of James. They entered the ruler's house and saw the flute players and the noisy commotion with all the people crying and wailing loudly, mourning for her. "Why all this commotion and wailing?" Jesus said. "Stop wailing. Go away. The girl is not dead but asleep." But they laughed at him, knowing that she was dead.

After he put all the crowd outside, he took the child's father and mother and the disciples who were with him, and went in where the child was. He took her by the hand and said to her, "Talitha koum!"

---

c. Many manuscripts [of Luke 8:43] *years, and she had spent all she had on doctors*

(which means, "Little girl, I say to you, get up!"). Immediately her spirit returned, and the girl stood up and walked around. Then he told them to give her something to eat. Her parents were completely astonished, but he gave them strict orders not to tell anyone about what had happened.

News of this spread through all that region.

89. JESUS HEALS THE BLIND AND MUTE
Matthew 9:27-34

As Jesus went on from there, two blind men followed him, calling out, "Have mercy on us, Son of David!"

When he had gone indoors, the blind men came to him, and he asked them, "Do you believe that I am able to do this?"

"Yes, Lord," they replied.

Then he touched their eyes and said, "According to your faith will it be done to you"; and their sight was restored. Jesus warned them sternly, "See that no one knows about this." But they went out and spread the news about him all over that region.

While they were going out, a man who was demon-possessed and could not talk was brought to Jesus. And when the demon was driven out, the man who had been mute spoke. The crowd was amazed and said, "Nothing like this has ever been seen in Israel."

But the Pharisees said, "It is by the prince of demons that he drives out demons."

90. A PROPHET WITHOUT HONOR
Matthew 13:54-58; Mark 6:1-6a

Jesus left there and went to his hometown, accompanied by his disciples. When the Sabbath came, he began to teach the people in the synagogue, and many who heard him were amazed.

"Where did this man get this wisdom and these miraculous powers?" they asked. "Isn't this the carpenter? Isn't this the carpenter's son? Isn't his mother's name Mary, and aren't his brothers James, Joseph,[d] Simon and Judas? Aren't all his sisters here with us? Where

---

d. Greek *Joses*, a variant of *Joseph*

then did this man get all these things?" And they took offense at him.

But Jesus said to them, "Only in his hometown,[5] among his relatives and in his own house is a prophet without honor." Because of their lack of faith, he could not[6] do any miracles there, except lay his hands on a few sick people and heal them. And he was amazed at their lack of faith.

91. THE WORKERS ARE FEW
Matthew 9:35-38; Mark 6:6b

Then Jesus went through all the towns and villages, teaching in their synagogues, preaching the good news of the kingdom and healing every disease and sickness. When he saw the crowds, he had compassion on them, because they were harassed and helpless, like sheep without a shepherd. Then he said to his disciples, "The harvest is plentiful but the workers are few. Ask the Lord of the harvest, therefore, to send out workers into his harvest field."

92. JESUS SENDS OUT THE TWELVE
Matthew 10:1, 5–11:1; Mark 6:7-13; Luke 9:1-6

When Jesus had called the Twelve together to him, he gave them power and authority to drive out all demons and to heal every disease and sickness. He sent them out two by two to preach the kingdom of God and to heal the sick.

These were his instructions: "Do not go among the Gentiles or enter any town of the Samaritans. Go rather to the lost sheep of Israel. As you go, preach this message: 'The kingdom of heaven is near.' Heal the sick, raise the dead, cleanse those who have leprosy, drive out demons. Freely you have received, freely give. Take nothing for the journey except a staff. Wear sandals. Do not take along any gold or silver or copper money in your belts; take no bag for the

---

5. See p. 308: Was Jesus rejected at Nazareth once (Matthew 13:54-58; Mark 6:1-6) or twice (Luke 4:16-30)?
6. See p. 309: Was Jesus unable to do many miracles at Nazareth (Mark 6:5), or did he choose not to do many (Matthew 13:58)?

journey, no bread, no extra tunic or sandals or staff'; for the worker is worth his keep.

"Whatever town or village you enter, search for some worthy person there and stay at his house until you leave that town. As you enter the home, give it your greeting. If the home is deserving, let your peace rest on it; if it is not, let your peace return to you. If anyone will not welcome you or listen to your words, shake the dust off your feet when you leave that home or town, as a testimony against them. I tell you the truth, it will be more bearable for Sodom and Gomorrah on the day of judgment than for that town. I am sending you out like sheep among wolves. Therefore be as shrewd as snakes and as innocent as doves.

"Be on your guard against men; they will hand you over to the local councils and flog you in their synagogues. On my account you will be brought before governors and kings as witnesses to them and to the Gentiles. But when they arrest you, do not worry about what to say or how to say it. At that time you will be given what to say, for it will not be you speaking, but the Spirit of your Father speaking through you.

"Brother will betray brother to death, and a father his child; children will rebel against their parents and have them put to death. All men will hate you because of me, but he who stands firm to the end will be saved. When you are persecuted in one place, flee to another. I tell you the truth, you will not finish going through the cities of Israel before the Son of Man comes.

"A student is not above his teacher, nor a servant above his master. It is enough for the student to be like his teacher, and the servant like his master. If the head of the house has been called Beelzebub, how much more the members of his household!

"So do not be afraid of them. There is nothing concealed that will not be disclosed, or hidden that will not be made known. What I tell you in the dark, speak in the daylight; what is whispered in your ear, proclaim from the roofs. Do not be afraid of those who kill the body but cannot kill the soul. Rather, be afraid of the One who can destroy both soul and body in hell. Are not two sparrows sold for a penny[e]? Yet not one of them will fall to the ground apart from the

---

7. See p. 310: Did Jesus instruct his twelve apostles to take a staff and a pair of sandals on their first missionary journey (Mark 6:8-9) or not (Matthew 10:10; Luke 9:3)?
e. Greek *an assarion*

will of your Father. And even the very hairs of your head are all numbered. So don't be afraid; you are worth more than many sparrows.

"Whoever acknowledges me before men, I will also acknowledge him before my Father in heaven. But whoever disowns me before men, I will disown him before my Father in heaven.

"Do not suppose that I have come to bring peace to the earth. I did not come to bring peace, but a sword. For I have come to turn

> " 'a man against his father,
> a daughter against her mother,
> a daughter-in-law against her mother-in-law—
> a man's enemies will be
> the members of his own household.'[f]

"Anyone who loves his father or mother more than me is not worthy of me; anyone who loves his son or daughter more than me is not worthy of me; and anyone who does not take his cross and follow me is not worthy of me. Whoever finds his life will lose it, and whoever loses his life for my sake will find it.

"He who receives you receives me, and he who receives me receives the one who sent me. Anyone who receives a prophet because he is a prophet will receive a prophet's reward, and anyone who receives a righteous man because he is a righteous man will receive a righteous man's reward. And if anyone gives even a cup of cold water to one of these little ones because he is my disciple, I tell you the truth, he will certainly not lose his reward."

So they set out and went from village to village, preaching the gospel, and that people should repent. Everywhere they went they drove out many demons and anointed many sick people with oil and healed them.

After Jesus had finished instructing his twelve disciples, he went on from there to teach and preach in the towns of Galilee.[g]

93. JOHN THE BAPTIST BEHEADED

Matthew 14:6-12; Mark 6:19-29

Herodias, *Herod's wife,* nursed a grudge against John *the Baptist* and

f. Micah 7:6
g. Greek *in their towns*

wanted to kill him. But she was not able to, because Herod feared John and protected him,[8] knowing him to be a righteous and holy man. When Herod heard John, he was greatly puzzled[h]; yet he liked to listen to him.

Finally the opportune time came. On his birthday Herod gave a banquet for his high officials and military commanders and the leading men of Galilee. When the daughter of Herodias came in and danced for them, she pleased Herod and his dinner guests.

The king said to the girl, "Ask me for anything you want, and I'll give it to you." And he promised her with an oath, "Whatever you ask I will give you, up to half my kingdom."

She went out and said to her mother, "What shall I ask for?"

"The head of John the Baptist," she answered.

At once the girl hurried in to the king with the request prompted by her mother. She said, "I want you to give me here right now the head of John the Baptist on a platter."

The king was greatly distressed, but because of his oaths and his dinner guests, he did not want to refuse that her request be granted. So he immediately sent an executioner with orders to bring John's head. The man went, beheaded John in the prison, and brought back his head on a platter. He presented it to the girl, and she carried it to her mother. On hearing of this, John's disciples came and took his body and laid it in a tomb. Then they went and told Jesus.

94. JESUS KNOWN TO HEROD
Matthew 14:1-2; Mark 6:14-16; Luke 9:7-9

Later King Herod the tetrarch heard the reports about Jesus *and* all that was going on, for Jesus' name had become well known. And he was perplexed, because some were saying,[i] "John the Baptist has been raised from the dead, and that is why miraculous powers are at work in him."

But Herod said, "I beheaded John. Who, then, is this I hear such things about?"

Others said, "He is Elijah."

---

8. See p. 310: When Herod imprisoned John the Baptist, did he want to kill John (Matthew 14:5), or did he fear and protect him (Luke 6:20)?
h. Some early manuscripts [of Mark 6:20] *he did many things*
i. Some early manuscripts [of Mark 6:14] *he was saying*

And still others claimed, "He is a prophet, like one of the prophets of long ago, come back to life."

When Herod heard this, he said to his attendants, "This is John the Baptist; he has risen from the dead! That is why miraculous powers are at work in him." And he tried to see him.

95. JESUS FEEDS THE FIVE THOUSAND
Matthew 14:13-21; Mark 6:30-44; Luke 9:10-17; John 6:1-14

When the apostles returned, they gathered around Jesus and reported to him all they had done and taught. When Jesus heard what had happened *to John, and* because so many people were coming and going that they did not even have a chance to eat, he said to them, "Come with me by yourselves to a quiet place and get some rest."

So he took them with him. They withdrew by themselves in a boat *and* crossed to the far shore of the Sea of Galilee (that is, the Sea of Tiberias) to a town called Bethsaida. But many who saw them leaving recognized them and ran on foot from all the towns and got there ahead of them. A great crowd of people learned about it and followed him on foot from the towns because they saw the miraculous signs he had performed on the sick.

When Jesus landed, he went up on a mountainside to a solitary place and sat down with his disciples. When Jesus looked up and saw a great crowd coming toward him, he had compassion on them, because they were like sheep without a shepherd. He welcomed them and began teaching them many things about the kingdom of God, and he healed those who needed healing. The Jewish Passover Feast was near.

By this time it was late in the afternoon, so the Twelve came to him and said, "This is a remote place, and it's already getting very late. Send the people away so they can go to the surrounding countryside and villages and buy themselves something to eat and find lodging."

Jesus replied, "They do not need to go away. You give them something to eat." He said to Philip, "Where shall we buy bread for these people to eat?" He asked this only to test him, for he already had in mind what he was going to do.

Philip answered him, "Eight months' wages[j] would not buy

j. Greek *two hundred denarii*

enough bread for each one to have a bite!" They said to him, "Are we to go and spend that much on bread and give it to them to eat?"

"How many loaves do you have?" he asked. "Go and see."

When they found out, Andrew, Simon Peter's brother, spoke up, "Here is a boy with five small barley loaves and two small fish, but how far will they go among so many?"

"Bring them here to me," he said. Then Jesus directed them to have all the people sit down on the green grass in groups of about fifty each. The disciples did so. There was plenty of grass in that place, and everybody sat down in groups of hundreds and fifties. Taking the five loaves and the two fish and looking up to heaven, Jesus gave thanks and broke the loaves. Then he gave them to the disciples, and the disciples distributed to those who were seated as much as they wanted. He also divided the two fish among them all. They all ate and were satisfied.

When they had all had enough to eat, he said to his disciples, "Gather the pieces that are left over. Let nothing be wasted." So they gathered them up and filled twelve baskets of broken pieces of the five barley loaves of bread and fish that were left over. The number of those who ate was about five thousand men, besides women and children.

After the people saw the miraculous sign that Jesus did, they began to say, "Surely this is the Prophet who is to come into the world."

96. JESUS WALKS ON THE WATER
Matthew 14:22-36; Mark 6:45-56; John 6:15-24

Knowing that they intended to come and make him king by force, immediately Jesus made his disciples get into the boat and go on ahead of him to Bethsaida, while he dismissed the crowd. After he had dismissed them, he withdrew again. He went up on a mountainside by himself to pray. When evening came, he was there alone.

His disciples went down to the lake, where they got into a boat and set off across the lake for Capernaum.[9]

9. See p. 311: Following the feeding of the 5,000, did the disciples leave in a boat to go to Bethsaida (Mark 6:45) or to Capernaum (John 6:17)? Was it before Jesus went up to pray (Matthew 14:22-23) or afterward (John 6:15-17)? Did Jesus walk on the water to approach the disciples (Matthew 14:25) or to pass by them (Mark 6:48)? Did they land at Capernaum (John 6:17) or Gennesaret (Matthew 14:34; Mark 6:53)?

By now it was dark, and Jesus had not yet joined them. A strong wind was blowing and the waters grew rough. The boat was already a considerable distance[k] from land, in the middle of the lake, buffeted by the waves because the wind was against it. Alone on land, he saw the disciples straining at the oars.

About the fourth watch of the night, when they had rowed three or three and a half miles,[l] Jesus went out to them, walking on the lake. He was about to pass by them when they saw Jesus approaching the boat, walking on the water. They all saw him and were terrified. "It's a ghost," they said, and cried out in fear.

But Jesus immediately spoke to them and said, "Take courage! It is I. Don't be afraid."

"Lord, if it's you," Peter replied, "tell me to come to you on the water."

"Come," he said.

Then Peter got down out of the boat, walked on the water and came toward Jesus. But when he saw the wind, he was afraid and, beginning to sink, cried out, "Lord, save me!"

Immediately Jesus reached out his hand and caught him. "You of little faith," he said, "why did you doubt?"

Then they were willing to take him into the boat. And when they climbed into the boat with them, the wind died down. Then those who were in the boat worshiped him, saying, "Truly you are the Son of God." They were completely amazed, for they had not understood about the loaves; their hearts were hardened.

Immediately the boat reached the shore where they were heading. They landed at Gennesaret and anchored there. As soon as they got out of the boat, the people of that place recognized Jesus. They sent word to all the surrounding country. They ran throughout that whole region and carried the sick on mats to wherever they heard he was. And wherever he went—into villages, towns or countryside—they placed the sick in the marketplaces. They begged him to let the sick just touch even the edge of his cloak, and all who touched him were healed.

The next day the crowd that had stayed on the opposite shore of the lake realized that only one boat had been there, and that Jesus had not entered it with his disciples, but that they had gone away

---

k. Greek *many stadia*
l. Greek *rowed twenty-five or thirty stadia* (about 5 or 6 kilometers)

alone. Then some boats from Tiberias landed near the place where the people had eaten the bread after the Lord had given thanks. Once the crowd realized that neither Jesus nor his disciples were there, they got into the boats and went to Capernaum in search of Jesus.

97. JESUS THE BREAD OF LIFE
John 6:25-59

When they found him on the other side of the lake, they asked him, "Rabbi, when did you get here?"

Jesus answered, "I tell you the truth, you are looking for me, not because you saw miraculous signs but because you ate the loaves and had your fill. Do not work for food that spoils, but for food that endures to eternal life, which the Son of Man will give you. On him God the Father has placed his seal of approval."

Then they asked him, "What must we do to do the works God requires?"

Jesus answered, "The work of God is this: to believe in the one he has sent."

So they asked him, "What miraculous sign then will you give that we may see it and believe you? What will you do? Our forefathers ate the manna in the desert; as it is written: 'He gave them bread from heaven to eat.'m"

Jesus said to them, "I tell you the truth, it is not Moses who has given you the bread from heaven, but it is my Father who gives you the true bread from heaven. For the bread of God is he who comes down from heaven and gives life to the world."

"Sir," they said, "from now on give us this bread."

Then Jesus declared, "I am the bread of life. He who comes to me will never go hungry, and he who believes in me will never be thirsty. But as I told you, you have seen me and still you do not believe. All that the Father gives me will come to me, and whoever comes to me I will never drive away. For I have come down from heaven not to do my will but to do the will of him who sent me. And this is the will of him who sent me, that I shall lose none of all that he has given me, but raise them up at the last day. For my

---

m. Exodus 16:4; Nehemiah 9:15; Psalm 78:24-25

Father's will is that everyone who looks to the Son and believes in him shall have eternal life, and I will raise him up at the last day."

At this the Jews began to grumble about him because he said, "I am the bread that came down from heaven." They said, "Is this not Jesus, the son of Joseph, whose father and mother we know? How can he now say, 'I came down from heaven'?"

"Stop grumbling among yourselves," Jesus answered. "No one can come to me unless the Father who sent me draws him, and I will raise him up at the last day. It is written in the Prophets: 'They will all be taught by God.'ⁿ Everyone who listens to the Father and learns from him comes to me. No one has seen the Father except the one who is from God; only he has seen the Father. I tell you the truth, he who believes has everlasting life. I am the bread of life. Your forefathers ate the manna in the desert, yet they died. But here is the bread that comes down from heaven, which a man may eat and not die. I am the living bread that came down from heaven. If anyone eats of this bread, he will live forever. This bread is my flesh, which I will give for the life of the world."

Then the Jews began to argue sharply among themselves, "How can this man give us his flesh to eat?"

Jesus said to them, "I tell you the truth, unless you eat the flesh of the Son of Man and drink his blood, you have no life in you. Whoever eats my flesh and drinks my blood has eternal life, and I will raise him up at the last day. For my flesh is real food and my blood is real drink. Whoever eats my flesh and drinks my blood remains in me, and I in him. Just as the living Father sent me and I live because of the Father, so the one who feeds on me will live because of me. This is the bread that came down from heaven. Your forefathers ate manna and died, but he who feeds on this bread will live forever." He said this while teaching in the synagogue in Capernaum.

98. MANY DISCIPLES DESERT JESUS
John 6:60-71

On hearing it, many of his disciples said, "This is a hard teaching. Who can accept it?"

---

n. Isaiah 54:13

Aware that his disciples were grumbling about this, Jesus said to them, "Does this offend you? What if you see the Son of Man ascend to where he was before! The Spirit gives life; the flesh counts for nothing. The words I have spoken to you are spirit° and they are life. Yet there are some of you who do not believe." For Jesus had known from the beginning which of them did not believe and who would betray him. He went on to say, "This is why I told you that no one can come to me unless the Father has enabled him."

From this time many of his disciples turned back and no longer followed him.

"You do not want to leave too, do you?" Jesus asked the Twelve.

Simon Peter answered him, "Lord, to whom shall we go? You have the words of eternal life. We believe and know that you are the Holy One of God."

Then Jesus replied, "Have I not chosen you, the Twelve? Yet one of you is a devil!" (He meant Judas, the son of Simon Iscariot, who, though one of the Twelve, was later to betray him.)

99. CLEAN AND UNCLEAN
Matthew 15:1-20; Mark 7:1-23; John 7:1

After this, Jesus went around in Galilee, purposely staying away from Judea because the Jews there were waiting to take his life.

Then some Pharisees and teachers of the law who had come from Jerusalem gathered around Jesus and saw some of his disciples eating food with hands that were "unclean," that is, unwashed. (The Pharisees and all the Jews do not eat unless they give their hands a ceremonial washing, holding to the tradition of the elders. When they come from the marketplace they do not eat unless they wash. And they observe many other traditions, such as the washing of cups, pitchers and kettles.ᴾ)

So the Pharisees and teachers of the law asked Jesus, "Why do your disciples break the tradition of the elders, eating their food with 'unclean' hands? They don't wash their hands before they eat."

He replied, "Isaiah was right when he prophesied about you hypocrites; as it is written:

---

o. Or *Spirit*
p. Some early manuscripts [of Mark 7:4] *pitchers, kettles and dining couches*

> " 'These people honor me with their lips,
> but their hearts are far from me.
> They worship me in vain;
> their teachings are but rules taught by men.'q

You have let go of the commands of God and are holding on to the traditions of men."

And he said to them: "And why do you break the command of God? You have a fine way of setting aside the commands of God in order to observe[r] your own traditions! For God *through* Moses said, 'Honor your father and mother,'[s] and, 'Anyone who curses his father or mother must be put to death.'[t] But you say that if a man says to his father or mother: 'Whatever help you might otherwise have received from me is Corban' (that is, a gift devoted to God), then he is not to 'honor his father'[u] with it. You no longer let him do anything for his father or mother. Thus you nullify the word of God for the sake of your tradition that you have handed down. And you do many things like that."

Again Jesus called the crowd to him and said, "Listen to me, everyone, and understand this. Nothing outside a man can make him 'unclean' by going into him. What goes into a man's mouth does not make him 'unclean.' Rather, it is what comes out of a man, out of his mouth, that makes him 'unclean.'"[v]

After he had left the crowd and entered the house, his disciples came to him and asked, "Do you know that the Pharisees were offended when they heard this?"

He replied, "Every plant that my heavenly Father has not planted will be pulled up by the roots. Leave them; they are blind guides.[w] If a blind man leads a blind man, both will fall into a pit."

Peter said, "Explain the parable to us."

"Are you still so dull?" Jesus asked them. "Don't you see that nothing that enters a man from the outside can make him 'unclean'?

---

q. Isaiah 29:13
r. Some manuscripts [of Mark 7:9] *set up*
s. Exodus 20:12; Deuteronomy 5:16
t. Exodus 21:17; Leviticus 20:9
u. Some manuscripts [of Matthew 15:6] *father or his mother*
v. Some early manuscripts [of Mark 7:15] *'unclean.' If anyone has ears to hear, let him hear.*
w. Some manuscripts [of Matthew 15:14] *guides of the blind*

For it doesn't go into his heart. Whatever enters his mouth goes into his stomach and then out of his body." (In saying this, Jesus declared all foods "clean.")

He went on: "What comes out of a man is what makes him 'unclean.' The things that come out of the mouth come from the heart, and these make a man 'unclean.' For from within, out of men's hearts, come evil thoughts, murder, adultery, sexual immorality, theft, false testimony, greed, malice, deceit, lewdness, envy, slander, arrogance and folly. All these evils come from inside and are what make a man 'unclean'; but eating with unwashed hands does not make him 'unclean.' "

SEVEN.
MINISTRY BEYOND GALILEE

100. THE FAITH OF A SYROPHOENICIAN WOMAN
Matthew 15:21-28; Mark 7:24-30

Leaving that place, Jesus withdrew to the region of Tyre and Sidon. He entered a house and did not want anyone to know it; yet he could not keep his presence secret. In fact, as soon as she heard about him, a Canaanite Greek woman from that vicinity, born in Syrian Phoenicia,[1] came to him, crying out, "Lord, Son of David, have mercy on me! My daughter is suffering terribly from demon-possession." She begged Jesus to drive the demon out of her daughter.

Jesus did not answer a word. So his disciples came to him and urged him, "Send her away, for she keeps crying out after us."

He answered, "I was sent only to the lost sheep of Israel."

The woman came and knelt before him. "Lord, help me!" she said.

"First let the children eat all they want," he told her, "for it is not right to take the children's bread and toss it to their dogs."

"Yes, Lord," she replied, "but even the dogs under the table eat the children's crumbs that fall from their masters' table."

Then Jesus told her, "Woman, you have great faith! For such a reply, you may go. Your request is granted; the demon has left your daughter." And her daughter was healed from that very hour. She went home and found her child lying on the bed, and the demon gone.

---

1. See p. 313: Was the woman with the demon-possessed daughter a Canaanite (Matthew 15:22) or a Syrian-Phoenician (Mark 7:26)?

101. THE HEALING OF A DEAF AND MUTE MAN
Matthew 15:29-31; Mark 7:31-37

Then Jesus left the vicinity of Tyre and went through Sidon, down to and along the Sea of Galilee and into the region of the Decapolis. Then he went up on a mountainside and sat down. Great crowds came to him, bringing the lame, the blind, the crippled, the mute and many others, and laid them at his feet; and he healed them. The people were amazed when they saw the mute speaking, the crippled made well, the lame walking and the blind seeing. And they praised the God of Israel.

There some people brought to him a man who was deaf and could hardly talk, and they begged him to place his hand on the man.

After he took him aside, away from the crowd, Jesus put his fingers into the man's ears. Then he spit and touched the man's tongue. He looked up to heaven and with a deep sigh said to him, "Ephphatha!" (which means, "Be opened!"). At this, the man's ears were opened, his tongue was loosened and he began to speak plainly.

Jesus commanded them not to tell anyone. But the more he did so, the more they kept talking about it. People were overwhelmed with amazement. "He has done everything well," they said. "He even makes the deaf hear and the mute speak."

102. JESUS FEEDS THE FOUR THOUSAND
Matthew 15:32-39; Mark 8:1-10

During those days another large crowd gathered. Since they had nothing to eat, Jesus called his disciples to him and said, "I have compassion for these people; they have already been with me three days and have nothing to eat. If I send them home hungry, they will collapse on the way, because some of them have come a long distance."

His disciples answered, "But where in this remote place can anyone get enough bread to feed such a crowd?"

"How many loaves do you have?" Jesus asked.

"Seven," they replied, "and a few small fish."

He told the crowd to sit down on the ground. Then he took the seven loaves, and when he had given thanks, he broke them and gave them to his disciples to set before the people, and they did so. He gave thanks for the fish also and told his disciples to distribute them. All the people ate and were satisfied. Afterward the disciples picked up seven basketfuls of broken pieces that were left over. The number of those present who ate was about four thousand men, besides women and children. After Jesus had sent the crowd away, he got into the boat with his disciples and went to the region of Magadan (Dalmanutha).[2]

103. THE DEMAND FOR A SIGN
Matthew 16:1-4; Mark 8:11-13

The Pharisees and Sadducees came and began to question Jesus. To test him, they asked him to show them a sign from heaven. He sighed deeply and said, "Why does this generation ask for a miraculous sign? When evening comes, you say, 'It will be fair weather, for the sky is red,' and in the morning, 'Today it will be stormy, for the sky is red and overcast.' You know how to interpret the appearance of the sky, but you cannot interpret the signs of the times.[a] A wicked and adulterous generation looks for a miraculous sign. I tell you the truth, no sign will be given to it except the sign of Jonah." Jesus then left them, got back into the boat and crossed to the other side.

104. THE YEAST OF THE PHARISEES, SADDUCEES, AND HEROD
Matthew 16:5-12; Mark 8:14-21

When they went across the lake, the disciples forgot to bring bread, except for one loaf they had with them in the boat. "Be careful; be on your guard," Jesus warned them. "Watch out for the yeast of the Pharisees and Sadducees, and that of Herod."

They discussed this among themselves and said, "It is because we didn't bring any bread."

Aware of their discussion, Jesus asked them: "You of little faith, why are you talking among yourselves about having no bread? Do you still not see or understand? Are your hearts hardened? Do you

---

2. See p. 313: After Jesus fed the 4,000, did he go to Magadan (Matthew 15:39) or Dalmanutha (Mark 8:10)?
a. Some early manuscripts do not have the [two previous sentences of Matthew 16:2-3].

Jesus Ministers Beyond Galilee

SECTION
100 A Syrophenician woman near Tyre shows her faith in Jesus
101 Jesus travels through Sidon, along Lake Galilee, and into Decapolis
102 After feeding 4,000, Jesus and the disciples cross Lake Galilee to Magdala
103 Jesus crosses Lake Galilee to Bethsaida
106 Near Caesarea Philippi, Peter confesses Jesus is Christ
108 Jesus is transfigured on a high mountain*
110 Arriving home at Capernaum, Peter pays the temple tax

Note: This entire route is quite uncertain

*The traditional site for the
Transfiguration is Mt. Tabor,
but Mt. Hermon is the more
likely location.*

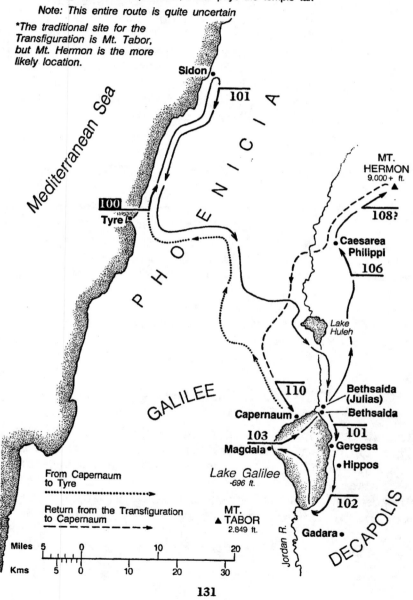

131

have eyes but fail to see, and ears but fail to hear? And don't you remember? When I broke the five loaves for the five thousand, how many basketfuls of pieces did you pick up?"

"Twelve," they replied.

"And when I broke the seven loaves for the four thousand, how many basketfuls of pieces did you pick up?"

They answered, "Seven."

He said to them, "How is it you still don't understand that I was not talking to you about bread? But be on your guard against the yeast of the Pharisees and Sadducees." Then they understood that he was not telling them to guard against the yeast used in bread, but against the teaching of the Pharisees and Sadducees.

105. THE HEALING OF A BLIND MAN AT BETHSAIDA
Mark 8:22-26

They came to Bethsaida, and some people brought a blind man and begged Jesus to touch him. He took the blind man by the hand and led him outside the village. When he had spit on the man's eyes and put his hands on him, Jesus asked, "Do you see anything?"

He looked up and said, "I see people; they look like trees walking around."

Once more Jesus put his hands on the man's eyes. Then his eyes were opened, his sight was restored, and he saw everything clearly. Jesus sent him home, saying, "Don't go into the village.[b]"

106. PETER'S CONFESSION OF CHRIST
Matthew 16:13-20; Mark 8:27-30; Luke 9:18-21

Jesus and his disciples went on to the villages around Caesarea Philippi. On the way, when Jesus was praying in private and his disciples were with him, he asked them, "Who do people say I, the Son of Man, am?"

They replied, "Some say John the Baptist; others say Elijah; and still others, that Jeremiah or one of the prophets of long ago has come back to life."

"But what about you?" he asked. "Who do you say I am?"

---

b. Some manuscripts [of Mark 8:26] *Don't go and tell anyone in the village*

Simon Peter answered, "You are the Christ, the Son of the living God."

Jesus replied, "Blessed are you, Simon son of Jonah, for this was not revealed to you by man, but by my Father in heaven. And I tell you that you are Peter,^c and on this rock I will build my church, and the gates of Hades^d will not overcome it.^e I will give you the keys of the kingdom of heaven; whatever you bind on earth will be^f bound in heaven, and whatever you loose on earth will be^f loosed in heaven." Then Jesus strictly warned his disciples not to tell anyone that he was the Christ.

107. JESUS PREDICTS HIS DEATH
Matthew 16:21-28; Mark 8:31–9:1; Luke 9:22-27

From that time on Jesus began to explain to his disciples that he must go to Jerusalem. And he said, "The Son of Man must be rejected and suffer many things at the hands of the elders, chief priests and teachers of the law, and he must be killed and on the third day be raised to life."[3] He spoke plainly about this.

Peter took him aside and began to rebuke him. "Never, Lord!" he said. "This shall never happen to you!"

But when Jesus turned and looked at his disciples, he rebuked Peter. "Get behind me, Satan!" he said to Peter. "You are a stumbling block to me; you do not have in mind the things of God, but the things of men."

Then he called the crowd to him along with his disciples and said to them all: "If anyone would come after me, he must deny himself and take up his cross daily and follow me. For whoever wants to save his life[g] will lose it, but whoever loses his life for me and for the gospel will save it. What good is it for a man to gain the whole world, and yet lose or forfeit his soul, his very self? Or what can a man give in exchange for his soul? If anyone is ashamed of me and my words in this adulterous and sinful generation, the Son of Man

c. *Peter* means *rock.*
d. Or *hell*
e. Or *not prove stronger than it*
f. Or *have been*
3. See p. 314: Did Jesus rise from the dead on the third day (Matthew 16:21; Luke 9:22), after three days (Mark 8:31), or after three days and three nights (Matthew 12:40)? On what day of the week was Jesus crucified?
g. The Greek word means either *life* or *soul* [and hereinafter].

will be ashamed of him when he comes in his glory and in the glory of the Father and of the holy angels. And then he will reward each person according to what he has done."

And he said to them, "I tell you the truth, some who are standing here will not taste death before they see the Son of Man coming in his kingdom, the kingdom of God, with power."

108. THE TRANSFIGURATION
Matthew 17:1-13; Mark 9:2-13; Luke 9:28-36

After six days[4] Jesus took with him Peter, James and John the brother of James, and led them up onto a high mountain by themselves, where they were all alone to pray. As he was praying there, he was transfigured before them. The appearance of his face changed and shone like the sun. His clothes became dazzling white, whiter than anyone in the world could bleach them, as white as the light, bright as a flash of lightning. Just then there appeared before them two men in glorious splendor, Moses and Elijah, who were talking with Jesus. They spoke about his departure, which he was about to bring to fulfillment at Jerusalem. Peter and his companions were very sleepy, but when they became fully awake, they saw his glory and the two men standing with him. As the men were leaving Jesus, Peter said to him, "Rabbi,[5] it is good for us to be here. Let us put up three shelters—one for you, one for Moses and one for Elijah." (He did not know what he was saying, they were so frightened.)

While he was still speaking, a bright cloud appeared and enveloped them, and they were afraid as they entered the cloud. A voice came from the cloud, saying, "This is my Son, whom I love, whom I have chosen; with him I am well pleased. Listen to him!"

When the disciples heard this, they fell facedown to the ground, terrified. But Jesus came and touched them. "Get up," he said. "Don't be afraid." Suddenly, when they looked up, they no longer saw anyone with them except Jesus.

---

4. See p. 316: After Jesus first predicted his death, did six days (Matthew 17:1; Mark 9:2) or eight days (Luke 9:28) pass before he and the three apostles ascended the Mount of Transfiguration?

5. See p. 317: On the Mount of Transfiguration, did Peter address Jesus as *Lord* (Matthew 17:4), *Rabbi* (Mark 9:5), or *Master* (Luke 9:33)?

As they were coming down the mountain, Jesus instructed them, "Don't tell anyone what you have seen, until the Son of Man has been raised from the dead." They kept the matter to themselves, discussing what "rising from the dead" meant.

The disciples asked him, "Why then do the teachers of the law say that Elijah must come first?"

Jesus replied, "To be sure, Elijah does come first, and restores all things. Why then is it written that the Son of Man must suffer much and be rejected? But I tell you, Elijah has already come, and they did not recognize him, but have done to him everything they wished, just as it is written about him. In the same way the Son of Man is going to suffer at their hands." Then the disciples understood that he was talking to them about John the Baptist.[6]

The disciples told no one at that time what they had seen.

109. THE HEALING OF A BOY WITH AN EVIL SPIRIT
Matthew 17:14-23; Mark 9:14-32; Luke 9:37-45

The next day, when they came down from the mountain to the other disciples, they saw a large crowd around them and the teachers of the law arguing with them. As soon as all the people saw Jesus, they were overwhelmed with wonder and ran to greet him.

"What are you arguing with them about?" he asked.

A man in the crowd called out, "Teacher, I beg you to look at my son, for he is my only child." He approached Jesus and knelt before him. "Lord, have mercy on my son, who is possessed by a spirit that has robbed him of speech," he said. "He has seizures and is suffering greatly. Whenever *the* spirit seizes him, he suddenly screams; it throws him to the ground into convulsions. He foams at the mouth, gnashes his teeth and becomes rigid. It scarcely ever leaves him and is destroying him. I brought him *and* begged your disciples to drive out the spirit, but they could not."

"O unbelieving and perverse generation," Jesus replied, "how long shall I stay with you? How long shall I put up with you? Bring the boy here to me."

So they brought him. Even while the boy was coming, the spirit saw Jesus. The demon immediately threw the boy into a convulsion.

---

6. See p. 318: Was John the Baptist Elijah (Matthew 17:12; Mark 9:13) or not (John 1:21)?

He fell to the ground and rolled around, foaming at the mouth.

Jesus asked the boy's father, "How long has he been like this?"

"From childhood," he answered. "It has often thrown him into fire or water to kill him. But if you can do anything, take pity on us and help us."

"'If you can'?" said Jesus. "Everything is possible for him who believes."

Immediately the boy's father exclaimed, "I do believe; help me overcome my unbelief!"

When Jesus saw that a crowd was running to the scene, he rebuked the evil spirit. "You deaf and mute spirit," he said, "I command you, come out of him and never enter him again."

The spirit shrieked, convulsed him violently and came out. The boy looked so much like a corpse that many said, "He's dead." But Jesus took him by the hand and lifted him to his feet, and he stood up. He was healed from that moment. Jesus gave him back to his father. And they were all amazed at the greatness of God.

After Jesus had gone indoors, his disciples asked him privately, "Why couldn't we drive it out?"

He replied, "Because you have so little faith. I tell you the truth, if you have faith as small as a mustard seed, you can say to this mountain, 'Move from here to there' and it will move. Nothing will be impossible for you. *But* this kind can come out only by prayer."[h]

While everyone was marveling at all that Jesus did, they left that place and passed through Galilee. Jesus did not want anyone to know where they were, because he was teaching his disciples. He said to them, "Listen carefully to what I am about to tell you: The Son of Man is going to be betrayed into the hands of men. They will kill him, and on the third day he will be raised to life." And the disciples were filled with grief. But they did not understand what he meant. It was hidden from them, so that they did not grasp it, and they were afraid to ask him about it.

110. THE TEMPLE TAX
Matthew 17:24-27; Mark 9:33a

After Jesus and his disciples arrived in Capernaum, the collectors of

---

h. Some manuscripts [of Mark 9:29] *prayer and fasting*; some manuscripts [of Matthew 17:21] *you. But this kind does not go out except by prayer and fasting.*

the two-drachma tax came to Peter and asked, "Doesn't your teacher pay the temple tax[i]?"

"Yes, he does," he replied.

When Peter came into the house, Jesus was the first to speak. "What do you think, Simon?" he asked. "From whom do the kings of the earth collect duty and taxes—from their own sons or from others?"

"From others," Peter answered.

"Then the sons are exempt," Jesus said to him. "But so that we may not offend them, go to the lake and throw out your line. Take the first fish you catch; open its mouth and you will find a four-drachma coin. Take it and give it to them for my tax and yours."

111. THE GREATEST IN THE KINGDOM OF HEAVEN
Matthew 18:1-5; Mark 9:33b-37; Luke 9:46-48

On the way, an argument started among the disciples as to which of them would be the greatest. When he was in the house, the disciples came to Jesus and asked, "Who is the greatest in the kingdom of heaven?"

Jesus, knowing their thoughts, asked them, "What were you arguing about on the road?" But they kept quiet.

Sitting down, Jesus called the Twelve and said, "If anyone wants to be first, he must be the very last, and the servant of all."

He called a little child and had him stand beside him. Taking him in his arms, he said to them, "I tell you the truth, unless you change and become like little children, you will never enter the kingdom of heaven. Therefore, whoever humbles himself like this child is the greatest in the kingdom of heaven. And whoever welcomes a little child like this in my name welcomes me; and whoever welcomes me does not welcome me but the one who sent me. For he who is least among you all—he is the greatest."

112. WHOEVER IS NOT AGAINST US IS FOR US
Mark 9:38-41; Luke 9:49-50

"Master," said John, "we saw a man driving out demons in your

---

i. Greek *the two drachmas*

name and we told him to stop, because he was not one of us."

"Do not stop him," Jesus said. "No one who does a miracle in my name can in the next moment say anything bad about me, for whoever is not against us is for us. I tell you the truth, anyone who gives you a cup of water in my name, because you belong to Christ, will certainly not lose his reward.

113. CAUSING TO SIN
Matthew 18:6-9; Mark 9:42-50

"But if anyone causes one of these little ones who believe in me to sin, it would be better for him to have a large millstone hung around his neck and to be thrown into the sea to be drowned in the depths.

"Woe to the world because of the things that cause people to sin! Such things must come, but woe to the man through whom they come! If your hand causes you to sin, cut it off and throw it away. It is better for you to enter life maimed than with two hands to go into eternal hell, where the fire never goes out.[j] And if your foot causes you to sin, cut it off. It is better for you to enter life crippled than to have two feet and be thrown into hell.[k] And if your eye causes you to sin, gouge it out and throw it away. It is better for you to enter the kingdom of God with one eye than to have two eyes and be thrown into the fire of hell, where

> " 'their worm does not die,
> and the fire is not quenched.'[l]

Everyone will be salted with fire.

"Salt is good, but if it loses its saltiness, how can you make it salty again? Have salt in yourselves, and be at peace with each other."

114. THE PARABLE OF THE LOST SHEEP
Matthew 18:10-14

"See that you do not look down on one of these little ones. For I tell

---

j. Some manuscripts [of Mark 9:44] *out, where / " 'their worm does not die, / and the fire is not quenched.'*
k. Some manuscripts [of Mark 9:46] *hell, where / " 'their worm does not die, / and the fire is not quenched.'*
l. Isaiah 66:24

you that their angels in heaven always see the face of my Father in heaven.[m]

"What do you think? If a man owns a hundred sheep, and one of them wanders away, will he not leave the ninety-nine on the hills and go to look for the one that wandered off? And if he finds it, I tell you the truth, he is happier about that one sheep than about the ninety-nine that did not wander off. In the same way your Father in heaven is not willing that any of these little ones should be lost.

115. A BROTHER WHO SINS AGAINST YOU
Matthew 18:15-20

"If your brother sins against you,[n] go and show him his fault, just between the two of you. If he listens to you, you have won your brother over. But if he will not listen, take one or two others along, so that 'every matter may be established by the testimony of two or three witnesses.'[o] If he refuses to listen to them, tell it to the church; and if he refuses to listen even to the church, treat him as you would a pagan or a tax collector.

"I tell you the truth, whatever you bind on earth will be[p] bound in heaven, and whatever you loose on earth will be[p] loosed in heaven.

"Again, I tell you that if two of you on earth agree about anything you ask for, it will be done for you by my Father in heaven. For where two or three come together in my name, there am I with them."

116. THE PARABLE OF THE UNMERCIFUL SERVANT
Matthew 18:21-35

Then Peter came to Jesus and asked, "Lord, how many times shall I forgive my brother when he sins against me? Up to seven times?"

Jesus answered, "I tell you, not seven times, but seventy-seven times.[q]

---

m. Some manuscripts [of Matthew 18:11] *heaven. The Son of Man came to save what was lost.*
n. Some manuscripts [of Matthew 18:15] do not have *against you.*
o. Deuteronomy 19:15
p. Or *have been*
q. Or *seventy times seven*

"Therefore, the kingdom of heaven is like a king who wanted to settle accounts with his servants. As he began the settlement, a man who owed him ten thousand talents[r] was brought to him. Since he was not able to pay, the master ordered that he and his wife and his children and all that he had be sold to repay the debt.

"The servant fell on his knees before him. 'Be patient with me,' he begged, 'and I will pay back everything.' The servant's master took pity on him, canceled the debt and let him go.

"But when that servant went out, he found one of his fellow servants who owed him a hundred denarii.[s] He grabbed him and began to choke him. 'Pay back what you owe me!' he demanded.

"His fellow servant fell to his knees and begged him, 'Be patient with me, and I will pay you back.'

"But he refused. Instead, he went off and had the man thrown into prison until he could pay the debt. When the other servants saw what had happened, they were greatly distressed and went and told their master everything that had happened.

"Then the master called the servant in. 'You wicked servant,' he said, 'I canceled all that debt of yours because you begged me to. Shouldn't you have had mercy on your fellow servant just as I had on you?' In anger his master turned him over to the jailers to be tortured, until he should pay back all he owed.

"This is how my heavenly Father will treat each of you unless you forgive your brother from your heart."

---

r. That is, millions of dollars
s. That is, a few dollars

EIGHT.
LAST FEAST
OF TABERNACLES

117. THE ADVICE OF JESUS' UNBELIEVING BROTHERS
John 7:2-9

When the Jewish Feast of Tabernacles was near, Jesus' brothers said to him, "You ought to leave here and go to Judea, so that your disciples may see the miracles you do. No one who wants to become a public figure acts in secret. Since you are doing these things, show yourself to the world." For even his own brothers did not believe in him.

Therefore Jesus told them, "The right time for me has not yet come; for you any time is right. The world cannot hate you, but it hates me because I testify that what it does is evil. You go to the Feast. I am not yet[a] going up to this Feast, because for me the right time has not yet come." Having said this, he stayed in Galilee.

118. SAMARITAN OPPOSITION
Luke 9:51-56

As the time approached for him to be taken up to heaven, Jesus resolutely set out for Jerusalem.[1] And he sent messengers on ahead, who went into a Samaritan village to get things ready for him; but the people there did not welcome him, because he was heading for Jerusalem. When the disciples James and John saw this, they asked, "Lord, do you want us to call fire down from heaven to destroy

---

a. Some early manuscripts [of John 7:8] do not have *yet*.
1. See p. 319: Is Luke 9:51–18:14 chronological? Does it include any incidents recorded in the other Gospels?

them[b]?" But Jesus turned and rebuked them, and[c] they went to another village.

119. THE COST OF FOLLOWING JESUS
Matthew 8:19-22; Luke 9:57-62

Then,[2] as they were walking along the road, a teacher of the law came to him and said, "Teacher, I will follow you wherever you go."[3]

Jesus replied, "Foxes have holes and birds of the air have nests, but the Son of Man has no place to lay his head."

He said to another disciple, "Follow me."

But the man replied, "Lord, first let me go and bury my father."

But Jesus said to him, "Let the dead bury their own dead, but you go and proclaim the kingdom of God."

Still another said, "I will follow you, Lord; but first let me go back and say good-by to my family."

Jesus replied, "No one who puts his hand to the plow and looks back is fit for service in the kingdom of God."

120. JESUS TEACHES AT THE FEAST OF TABERNACLES
John 7:10-24

After his brothers had left for the Feast, *Jesus* went also, not publicly, but in secret. Now at the Feast the Jews were watching for him and asking, "Where is that man?"

Among the crowds there was widespread whispering about him. Some said, "He is a good man."

Others replied, "No, he deceives the people." But no one would say anything publicly about him for fear of the Jews.

Not until halfway through the Feast did Jesus go up to the temple courts and begin to teach. The Jews were amazed and asked, "How

---

b. Some manuscripts [of Luke 9:54] *them, even as Elijah did*

c. Some manuscripts [of Luke 9:56] *them. And he said, "You do not know what kind of spirit you are of, for the Son of Man did not come to destroy men's lives, but to save them." And*

2. See p. 321: How can Matthew dislocate an incident in time yet begin it with the word *Then* (Matthew 8:23)?

3. See p. 322: When and where did Jesus encounter those disciples who had not counted the cost (Matthew 8:18-22; Luke 9:52, 56-62)?

did this man get such learning without having studied?"

Jesus answered, "My teaching is not my own. It comes from him who sent me. If anyone chooses to do God's will, he will find out whether my teaching comes from God or whether I speak on my own. He who speaks on his own does so to gain honor for himself, but he who works for the honor of the one who sent him is a man of truth; there is nothing false about him. Has not Moses given you the law? Yet not one of you keeps the law. Why are you trying to kill me?"

"You are demon-possessed," the crowd answered. "Who is trying to kill you?"

Jesus said to them, "I did one miracle, and you are all astonished. Yet, because Moses gave you circumcision (though actually it did not come from Moses, but from the patriarchs), you circumcise a child on the Sabbath. Now if a child can be circumcised on the Sabbath so that the law of Moses may not be broken, why are you angry with me for healing the whole man on the Sabbath? Stop judging by mere appearances, and make a right judgment."

121. IS JESUS THE CHRIST?
John 7:25-44

At that point some of the people of Jerusalem began to ask, "Isn't this the man they are trying to kill? Here he is, speaking publicly, and they are not saying a word to him. Have the authorities really concluded that he is the Christ? But we know where this man is from; when the Christ comes, no one will know where he is from."

Then Jesus, still teaching in the temple courts, cried out, "Yes, you know me, and you know where I am from. I am not here on my own, but he who sent me is true. You do not know him, but I know him because I am from him and he sent me."

At this they tried to seize him, but no one laid a hand on him, because his time had not yet come. Still, many in the crowd put their faith in him. They said, "When the Christ comes, will he do more miraculous signs than this man?"

The Pharisees heard the crowd whispering such things about him. Then the chief priests and the Pharisees sent temple guards to arrest him.

Jesus said, "I am with you for only a short time, and then I go to the one who sent me. You will look for me, but you will not find me; and where I am, you cannot come."

The Jews said to one another, "Where does this man intend to go that we cannot find him? Will he go where our people live scattered among the Greeks, and teach the Greeks? What did he mean when he said, 'You will look for me, but you will not find me,' and 'Where I am, you cannot come'?"

On the last and greatest day of the Feast, Jesus stood and said in a loud voice, "If anyone is thirsty, let him come to me and drink. Whoever believes in me, as[d] the Scripture has said, streams of living water will flow from within him." By this he meant the Spirit, whom those who believed in him were later to receive. Up to that time the Spirit had not been given, since Jesus had not yet been glorified.

On hearing his words, some of the people said, "Surely this man is the Prophet."

Others said, "He is the Christ."

Still others asked, "How can the Christ come from Galilee? Does not the Scripture say that the Christ will come from David's family[e] and from Bethlehem, the town where David lived?" Thus the people were divided because of Jesus. Some wanted to seize him, but no one laid a hand on him.

122. UNBELIEF OF THE JEWISH LEADERS
John 7:45-53

Finally the temple guards went back to the chief priests and Pharisees, who asked them, "Why didn't you bring him in?"

"No one ever spoke the way this man does," the guards declared.

"You mean he has deceived you also?" the Pharisees retorted. "Has any of the rulers or of the Pharisees believed in him? No! But this mob that knows nothing of the law—there is a curse on them."

Nicodemus, who had gone to Jesus earlier and who was one of their own number, asked, "Does our law condemn anyone without first hearing him to find out what he is doing?"

They replied, "Are you from Galilee, too? Look into it, and you will find that a prophet[f] does not come out of Galilee."

d. Or / *If anyone is thirsty, let him come to me. / And let him drink, who believes in me. / As*

e. Greek *seed*

f. Two early manuscripts [of John 7:52] *the Prophet*

[Then each went to his own home.g

123. THE WOMAN CAUGHT IN ADULTERY
John 8:1-11g

But Jesus went to the Mount of Olives. At dawn he appeared again in the temple courts, where all the people gathered around him, and he sat down to teach them. The teachers of the law and the Pharisees brought in a woman caught in adultery. They made her stand before the group and said to Jesus, "Teacher, this woman was caught in the act of adultery. In the Law Moses commanded us to stone such women. Now what do you say?" They were using this question as a trap, in order to have a basis for accusing him.

But Jesus bent down and started to write on the ground with his finger. When they kept on questioning him, he straightened up and said to them, "If any one of you is without sin, let him be the first to throw a stone at her." Again he stooped down and wrote on the ground.

At this, those who heard began to go away one at a time, the older ones first, until only Jesus was left, with the woman still standing there. Jesus straightened up and asked her, "Woman, where are they? Has no one condemned you?"

"No one, sir," she said.

"Then neither do I condemn you," Jesus declared. "Go now and leave your life of sin."]

124. THE VALIDITY OF JESUS' TESTIMONY
John 8:12-30

When Jesus spoke again to the people, he said, "I am the light of the world. Whoever follows me will never walk in darkness, but will have the light of life."

The Pharisees challenged him, "Here you are, appearing as your own witness; your testimony is not valid."

Jesus answered, "Even if I testify on my own behalf, my testimony is valid, for I know where I came from and where I am going. But

g. The earliest and most reliable manuscripts and other ancient witnesses do not have John 7:53–8:11 [the contents of which are placed in brackets].

you have no idea where I come from or where I am going. You judge by human standards; I pass judgment on no one. But if I do judge, my decisions are right, because I am not alone. I stand with the Father, who sent me. In your own Law it is written that the testimony of two men is valid. I am one who testifies for myself; my other witness is the Father, who sent me."

Then they asked him, "Where is your father?"

"You do not know me or my Father," Jesus replied. "If you knew me, you would know my Father also." He spoke these words while teaching in the temple area near the place where the offerings were put. Yet no one seized him, because his time had not yet come.

Once more Jesus said to them, "I am going away, and you will look for me, and you will die in your sin. Where I go, you cannot come."

This made the Jews ask, "Will he kill himself? Is that why he says, 'Where I go, you cannot come'?"

But he continued, "You are from below; I am from above. You are of this world; I am not of this world. I told you that you would die in your sins; if you do not believe that I am [the one I claim to be],[h] you will indeed die in your sins."

"Who are you?" they asked.

"Just what I have been claiming all along," Jesus replied. "I have much to say in judgment of you. But he who sent me is reliable, and what I have heard from him I tell the world."

They did not understand that he was telling them about his Father. So Jesus said, "When you have lifted up the Son of Man, then you will know who I am [the one I claim to be][h] and that I do nothing on my own but speak just what the Father has taught me. The one who sent me is with me; he has not left me alone, for I always do what pleases him." Even as he spoke, many put their faith in him.

125. THE CHILDREN OF ABRAHAM
John 8:31-41

To the Jews who had believed him, Jesus said, "If you hold to my teaching, you are really my disciples. Then you will know the truth, and the truth will set you free."

h. Or *I am he*

They answered him, "We are Abraham's descendants[i] and have never been slaves of anyone. How can you say that we shall be set free?"

Jesus replied, "I tell you the truth, everyone who sins is a slave to sin. Now a slave has no permanent place in the family, but a son belongs to it forever. So if the Son sets you free, you will be free indeed. I know you are Abraham's descendants.[i] Yet you are ready to kill me, because you have no room for my word. I am telling you what I have seen in the Father's presence, and you do what you have heard from your father.[j]"

"Abraham is our father," they answered.

"If you were Abraham's children," said Jesus, "then you would[k] do the things Abraham did. As it is, you are determined to kill me, a man who has told you the truth that I heard from God. Abraham did not do such things. You are doing the things your own father does."

"We are not illegitimate children," they protested. "The only Father we have is God himself."

126. THE CHILDREN OF THE DEVIL
John 8:42-47

Jesus said to them, "If God were your Father, you would love me, for I came from God and now am here. I have not come on my own; but he sent me. Why is my language not clear to you? Because you are unable to hear what I say. You belong to your father, the devil, and you want to carry out your father's desire. He was a murderer from the beginning, not holding to the truth, for there is no truth in him. When he lies, he speaks his native language, for he is a liar and the father of lies. Yet because I tell the truth, you do not believe me! Can any of you prove me guilty of sin? If I am telling the truth, why don't you believe me? He who belongs to God hears what God says. The reason you do not hear is that you do not belong to God."

---

i. Greek *seed*
j. Or *presence. Therefore do what you have heard from the Father.*
k. Some early manuscripts [of John 8:39] *"If you are Abraham's children," said Jesus, "then*

127. THE CLAIMS OF JESUS ABOUT HIMSELF
John 8:48-59

The Jews answered him, "Aren't we right in saying that you are a Samaritan and demon-possessed?"

"I am not possessed by a demon," said Jesus, "but I honor my Father and you dishonor me. I am not seeking glory for myself; but there is one who seeks it, and he is the judge. I tell you the truth, if anyone keeps my word, he will never see death."

At this the Jews exclaimed, "Now we know that you are demon-possessed! Abraham died and so did the prophets, yet you say that if anyone keeps your word, he will never taste death. Are you greater than our father Abraham? He died, and so did the prophets. Who do you think you are?"

Jesus replied, "If I glorify myself, my glory means nothing. My Father, whom you claim as your God, is the one who glorifies me. Though you do not know him, I know him. If I said I did not, I would be a liar like you, but I do know him and keep his word. Your father Abraham rejoiced at the thought of seeing my day; he saw it and was glad."

"You are not yet fifty years old," the Jews said to him, "and you have seen Abraham!"

"I tell you the truth," Jesus answered, "before Abraham was born, I am!" At this, they picked up stones to stone him, but Jesus hid himself, slipping away from the temple grounds.

128. JESUS HEALS A MAN BORN BLIND
John 9:1-12

As he went along, he saw a man blind from birth. His disciples asked him, "Rabbi, who sinned, this man or his parents, that he was born blind?"

"Neither this man nor his parents sinned," said Jesus, "but this happened so that the work of God might be displayed in his life. As long as it is day, we must do the work of him who sent me. Night is coming, when no one can work. While I am in the world, I am the light of the world."

Having said this, he spit on the ground, made some mud with the saliva, and put it on the man's eyes. "Go," he told him, "wash in the Pool of Siloam" (this word means Sent). So the man went and washed, and came home seeing.

His neighbors and those who had formerly seen him begging asked, "Isn't this the same man who used to sit and beg?" Some claimed that he was.

Others said, "No, he only looks like him."

But he himself insisted, "I am the man."

"How then were your eyes opened?" they demanded.

He replied, "The man they call Jesus made some mud and put it on my eyes. He told me to go to Siloam and wash. So I went and washed, and then I could see."

"Where is this man?" they asked him.

"I don't know," he said.

129. THE PHARISEES INVESTIGATE THE HEALING
John 9:13-34

They brought to the Pharisees the man who had been blind. Now the day on which Jesus had made the mud and opened the man's eyes was a Sabbath. Therefore the Pharisees also asked him how he had received his sight. "He put mud on my eyes," the man replied, "and I washed, and now I see."

Some of the Pharisees said, "This man is not from God, for he does not keep the Sabbath."

But others asked, "How can a sinner do such miraculous signs?" So they were divided.

Finally they turned again to the blind man, "What have you to say about him? It was your eyes he opened."

The man replied, "He is a prophet."

The Jews still did not believe that he had been blind and had received his sight until they sent for the man's parents. "Is this your son?" they asked. "Is this the one you say was born blind? How is it that now he can see?"

"We know he is our son," the parents answered, "and we know he was born blind. But how he can see now, or who opened his eyes, we don't know. Ask him. He is of age; he will speak for himself." His parents said this because they were afraid of the Jews, for already the Jews had decided that anyone who acknowledged that Jesus was the Christ would be put out of the synagogue. That was why his parents said, "He is of age; ask him."

A second time they summoned the man who had been blind. "Give glory to God,[1]" they said. "We know this man is a sinner."

He replied, "Whether he is a sinner or not, I don't know. One thing I do know. I was blind but now I see!"

Then they asked him, "What did he do to you? How did he open your eyes?"

He answered, "I have told you already and you did not listen. Why do you want to hear it again? Do you want to become his disciples, too?"

Then they hurled insults at him and said, "You are this fellow's disciple! We are disciples of Moses! We know that God spoke to Moses, but as for this fellow, we don't even know where he comes from."

The man answered, "Now that is remarkable! You don't know where he comes from, yet he opened my eyes. We know that God does not listen to sinners. He listens to the godly man who does his will. Nobody has ever heard of opening the eyes of a man born blind. If this man were not from God, he could do nothing."

To this they replied, "You were steeped in sin at birth; how dare you lecture us!" And they threw him out.

130. SPIRITUAL BLINDNESS
John 9:35-41

Jesus heard that they had thrown him out, and when he found him, he said, "Do you believe in the Son of Man?"

"Who is he, sir?" the man asked. "Tell me so that I may believe in him."

Jesus said, "You have now seen him; in fact, he is the one speaking with you."

Then the man said, "Lord, I believe," and he worshiped him.

Jesus said, "For judgment I have come into this world, so that the blind will see and those who see will become blind."

Some Pharisees who were with him heard him say this and asked, "What? Are we blind too?"

Jesus said, "If you were blind, you would not be guilty of sin; but now that you claim you can see, your guilt remains.

---

1. A solemn charge to tell the truth (see Joshua 7:19)

131. THE SHEPHERD AND HIS FLOCK
John 10:1-21

"I tell you the truth, the man who does not enter the sheep pen by the gate, but climbs in by some other way, is a thief and a robber. The man who enters by the gate is the shepherd of his sheep. The watchman opens the gate for him, and the sheep listen to his voice. He calls his own sheep by name and leads them out. When he has brought out all his own, he goes on ahead of them, and his sheep follow him because they know his voice. But they will never follow a stranger; in fact, they will run away from him because they do not recognize a stranger's voice." Jesus used this figure of speech, but they did not understand what he was telling them.

Therefore Jesus said again, "I tell you the truth, I am the gate for the sheep. All who ever came before me were thieves and robbers, but the sheep did not listen to them. I am the gate; whoever enters through me will be saved.ᵐ He will come in and go out, and find pasture. The thief comes only to steal and kill and destroy; I have come that they may have life, and have it to the full.

"I am the good shepherd. The good shepherd lays down his life for the sheep. The hired hand is not the shepherd who owns the sheep. So when he sees the wolf coming, he abandons the sheep and runs away. Then the wolf attacks the flock and scatters it. The man runs away because he is a hired hand and cares nothing for the sheep.

"I am the good shepherd; I know my sheep and my sheep know me—just as the Father knows me and I know the Father—and I lay down my life for the sheep. I have other sheep that are not of this sheep pen. I must bring them also. They too will listen to my voice, and there shall be one flock and one shepherd. The reason my Father loves me is that I lay down my life—only to take it up again. No one takes it from me, but I lay it down of my own accord. I have authority to lay it down and authority to take it up again. This command I received from my Father."

At these words the Jews were again divided. Many of them said, "He is demon-possessed and raving mad. Why listen to him?"

But others said, "These are not the sayings of a man possessed by a demon. Can a demon open the eyes of the blind?"

---

m. Or *kept safe*

NINE.
MORE (JUDEAN?) MINISTRY

132. JESUS SENDS OUT THE SEVENTY-TWO
Luke 10:1-12

After this the Lord appointed seventy-two[a] others and sent them two by two ahead of him to every town and place where he was about to go. He told them, "The harvest is plentiful, but the workers are few. Ask the Lord of the harvest, therefore, to send out workers into his harvest field. Go! I am sending you out like lambs among wolves. Do not take a purse or bag or sandals; and do not greet anyone on the road.

"When you enter a house, first say, 'Peace to this house.' If a man of peace is there, your peace will rest on him; if not, it will return to you. Stay in that house, eating and drinking whatever they give you, for the worker deserves his wages. Do not move around from house to house.

"When you enter a town and are welcomed, eat what is set before you. Heal the sick who are there and tell them, 'The kingdom of God is near you.' But when you enter a town and are not welcomed, go into its streets and say, 'Even the dust of your town that sticks to our feet we wipe off against you. Yet be sure of this: The kingdom of God is near.' I tell you, it will be more bearable on that day for Sodom than for that town."

:

133. WOE ON UNREPENTANT CITIES
Matthew 11:20-24; Luke 10:13-16

Then Jesus began to denounce the cities in which most of his miracles had been performed, because they did not repent. "Woe to

---

a. Some manuscripts [of Luke 10:1] *seventy*

you, Korazin! Woe to you, Bethsaida! For if the miracles that were performed in you had been performed in Tyre and Sidon, they would have repented long ago, sitting in sackcloth and ashes. But I tell you, it will be more bearable for Tyre and Sidon on the day of judgment than for you. And you, Capernaum, will you be lifted up to the skies? No, you will go down to the depths.[b] If the miracles that were performed in you had been performed in Sodom, it would have remained to this day. But I tell you that it will be more bearable for Sodom on the day of judgment than for you.

"He who listens to you listens to me; he who rejects you rejects me; but he who rejects me rejects him who sent me."

134. THE SEVENTY-TWO RETURN
Matthew 11:25-30; Luke 10:17-24

The seventy-two[c] returned with joy and said, "Lord, even the demons submit to us in your name."

He replied, "I saw Satan fall like lightning from heaven. I have given you authority to trample on snakes and scorpions and to overcome all the power of the enemy; nothing will harm you. However, do not rejoice that the spirits submit to you, but rejoice that your names are written in heaven."

At that time Jesus, full of joy through the Holy Spirit, said, "I praise you, Father, Lord of heaven and earth, because you have hidden these things from the wise and learned, and revealed them to little children. Yes, Father, for this was your good pleasure.

"All things have been committed to me by my Father. No one knows who the Son is except the Father, and no one knows who the Father is except the Son and those to whom the Son chooses to reveal him.

"Come to me, all you who are weary and burdened, and I will give you rest. Take my yoke upon you and learn from me, for I am gentle and humble in heart, and you will find rest for your souls. For my yoke is easy and my burden is light."

Then he turned to his disciples and said privately, "Blessed are the eyes that see what you see. For I tell you that many prophets and

---

b. Greek *Hades* [and hereinafter]
c. Some manuscripts [of Luke 10:17] *seventy*

kings wanted to see what you see but did not see it, and to hear what you hear but did not hear it."

135. THE PARABLE OF THE GOOD SAMARITAN
Luke 10:25-37

On one occasion an expert in the law stood up to test Jesus. "Teacher," he asked, "what must I do to inherit eternal life?"

"What is written in the Law?" he replied. "How do you read it?"

He answered: "'Love the Lord your God with all your heart and with all your soul and with all your strength and with all your mind'd; and, 'Love your neighbor as yourself.'e"

"You have answered correctly," Jesus replied. "Do this and you will live."

But he wanted to justify himself, so he asked Jesus, "And who is my neighbor?"

In reply Jesus said: "A man was going down from Jerusalem to Jericho, when he fell into the hands of robbers. They stripped him of his clothes, beat him and went away, leaving him half dead. A priest happened to be going down the same road, and when he saw the man, he passed by on the other side. So too, a Levite, when he came to the place and saw him, passed by on the other side. But a Samaritan, as he traveled, came where the man was; and when he saw him, he took pity on him. He went to him and bandaged his wounds, pouring on oil and wine. Then he put the man on his own donkey, took him to an inn and took care of him. The next day he took out two silver coinsf and gave them to the innkeeper. 'Look after him,' he said, 'and when I return, I will reimburse you for any extra expense you may have.'

"Which of these three do you think was a neighbor to the man who fell into the hands of robbers?"

The expert in the law replied, "The one who had mercy on him." Jesus told him, "Go and do likewise."

---

d. Deuteronomy 6:5
e. Leviticus 19:18
f. Greek *two denarii*

136. AT THE HOME OF MARTHA AND MARY
Luke 10:38-42

As Jesus and his disciples were on their way, he came to a village where a woman named Martha opened her home to him. She had a sister called Mary, who sat at the Lord's feet listening to what he said. But Martha was distracted by all the preparations that had to be made. She came to him and asked, "Lord, don't you care that my sister has left me to do the work by myself? Tell her to help me!"

"Martha, Martha," the Lord answered, "you are worried and upset about many things, but only one thing is needed.ᵍ Mary has chosen what is better, and it will not be taken away from her."

137. JESUS' TEACHING ON PRAYER
Luke 11:1-13

One day Jesus was praying in a certain place. When he finished, one of his disciples said to him, "Lord, teach us to pray, just as John taught his disciples."

He said to them, "When you pray, say:[1]

" 'Father,ʰ
hallowed be your name,
your kingdom come.ⁱ
Give us each day our daily bread.
Forgive us our sins,
for we also forgive everyone
who sins against us.ʲ
And lead us not into temptation.' "ᵏ

Then he said to them, "Suppose one of you has a friend, and he goes to him at midnight and says, 'Friend, lend me three loaves of bread, because a friend of mine on a journey has come to me, and I

g. Some manuscripts [of Luke 10:42] *but few things are needed—or only one*
1. See p. 323: Do the Gospels record that Jesus delivered two "Lord's Prayers" or one (Matthew 6:9-13; Luke 11:2-4)?
h. Some manuscripts [of Luke 11:2] *Our Father in heaven*
i. Some manuscripts [of Luke 11:2] *come. May your will be done on earth as it is in heaven.*
j. Greek *everyone who is indebted to us*
k. Some manuscripts [of Luke 11:4] *temptation but deliver us from the evil one*

have nothing to set before him.'

"Then the one inside answers, 'Don't bother me. The door is already locked, and my children are with me in bed. I can't get up and give you anything.' I tell you, though he will not get up and give him the bread because he is his friend, yet because of the man's boldness[l] he will get up and give him as much as he needs.

"So I say to you: Ask and it will be given to you; seek and you will find; knock and the door will be opened to you. For everyone who asks receives; he who seeks finds; and to him who knocks, the door will be opened.

"Which of you fathers, if your son asks for[m] a fish, will give him a snake instead? Or if he asks for an egg, will give him a scorpion? If you then, though you are evil, know how to give good gifts to your children, how much more will your Father in heaven give the Holy Spirit to those who ask him!"

138. JESUS AND BEELZEBUB AGAIN
Luke 11:14-28

Jesus was driving out a demon that was mute. When the demon left, the man who had been mute spoke, and the crowd was amazed. But some of them said, "By Beelzebub, the prince of demons, he is driving out demons." Others tested him by asking for a sign from heaven.

Jesus knew their thoughts and said to them: "Any kingdom divided against itself will be ruined, and a house divided against itself will fall. If Satan is divided against himself, how can his kingdom stand? I say this because you claim that I drive out demons by Beelzebub. Now if I drive out demons by Beelzebub, by whom do your followers drive them out? So then, they will be your judges. But if I drive out demons by the finger of God, then the kingdom of God has come to you.

"When a strong man, fully armed, guards his own house, his possessions are safe. But when someone stronger attacks and overpowers him, he takes away the armor in which the man trusted and divides up the spoils.

---

l. Or *persistence*
m. Some manuscripts [of Luke 11:11] *for bread, will give him a stone; or if he asks for*

"He who is not with me is against me, and he who does not gather with me, scatters.

"When an evil spirit comes out of a man, it goes through arid places seeking rest and does not find it. Then it says, 'I will return to the house I left.' When it arrives, it finds the house swept clean and put in order. Then it goes and takes seven other spirits more wicked than itself, and they go in and live there. And the final condition of that man is worse than the first."

As Jesus was saying these things, a woman in the crowd called out, "Blessed is the mother who gave you birth and nursed you."

He replied, "Blessed rather are those who hear the word of God and obey it."

139. THE SIGN OF JONAH AGAIN
Luke 11:29-32

As the crowds increased, Jesus said, "This is a wicked generation. It asks for a miraculous sign, but none will be given it except the sign of Jonah.[2] For as Jonah was a sign to the Ninevites, so also will the Son of Man be to this generation. The Queen of the South will rise at the judgment with the men of this generation and condemn them; for she came from the ends of the earth to listen to Solomon's wisdom, and now one[n] greater than Solomon is here. The men of Nineveh will stand up at the judgment with this generation and condemn it; for they repented at the preaching of Jonah, and now one[n] greater than Jonah is here.

140. THE LAMP OF THE BODY
Luke 11:33-36

"No one lights a lamp and puts it in a place where it will be hidden, or under a bowl. Instead he puts it on its stand, so that those who come in may see the light. Your eye is the lamp of your body. When your eyes are good, your whole body also is full of light. But when

---

2. See p. 324: How many times do the Gospels record that Jesus spoke of the sign of Jonah (Matthew 12:38-45; 16:1-4; Luke 11:29-32)?
n. Or *something*

157

they are bad, your body also is full of darkness. See to it, then, that the light within you is not darkness. Therefore, if your whole body is full of light, and no part of it dark, it will be completely lighted, as when the light of a lamp shines on you."

141. SIX WOES
Luke 11:37-54

When Jesus had finished speaking, a Pharisee invited him to eat with him; so he went in and reclined at the table. But the Pharisee, noticing that Jesus did not first wash before the meal, was surprised.

Then the Lord said to him, "Now then, you Pharisees clean the outside of the cup and dish, but inside you are full of greed and wickedness. You foolish people! Did not the one who made the outside make the inside also? But give what is inside [the dish]° to the poor, and everything will be clean for you.

"Woe to you Pharisees, because you give God a tenth of your mint, rue and all other kinds of garden herbs, but you neglect justice and the love of God. You should have practiced the latter without leaving the former undone.

"Woe to you Pharisees, because you love the most important seats in the synagogues and greetings in the marketplaces.

"Woe to you, because you are like unmarked graves, which men walk over without knowing it."

One of the experts in the law answered him, "Teacher, when you say these things, you insult us also."

Jesus replied, "And you experts in the law, woe to you, because you load people down with burdens they can hardly carry, and you yourselves will not lift one finger to help them.

"Woe to you, because you build tombs for the prophets, and it was your forefathers who killed them. So you testify that you approve of what your forefathers did; they killed the prophets, and you build their tombs. Because of this, God in his wisdom said, 'I will send them prophets and apostles, some of whom they will kill and others they will persecute.' Therefore this generation will be held responsible for the blood of all the prophets that has been shed since the beginning of the world, from the blood of Abel to the blood of Zechariah, who was killed between the altar and the

---

o. Or *what you have*

sanctuary. Yes, I tell you, this generation will be held responsible for it all.

"Woe to you experts in the law, because you have taken away the key to knowledge. You yourselves have not entered, and you have hindered those who were entering."

When Jesus left there, the Pharisees and the teachers of the law began to oppose him fiercely and to besiege him with questions, waiting to catch him in something he might say.

142. WARNINGS AND ENCOURAGEMENTS
Luke 12:1-12

Meanwhile, when a crowd of many thousands had gathered, so that they were trampling on one another, Jesus began to speak first to his disciples, saying: "Be on your guard against the yeast of the Pharisees, which is hypocrisy. There is nothing concealed that will not be disclosed, or hidden that will not be made known. What you have said in the dark will be heard in the daylight, and what you have whispered in the ear in the inner rooms will be proclaimed from the roofs.

"I tell you, my friends, do not be afraid of those who kill the body and after that can do no more. But I will show you whom you should fear: Fear him who, after the killing of the body, has power to throw you into hell. Yes, I tell you, fear him. Are not five sparrows sold for two pennies?[p] Yet not one of them is forgotten by God. Indeed, the very hairs of your head are all numbered. Don't be afraid; you are worth more than many sparrows.

"I tell you, whoever acknowledges me before men, the Son of Man will also acknowledge him before the angels of God. But he who disowns me before men will be disowned before the angels of God. And everyone who speaks a word against the Son of Man will be forgiven, but anyone who blasphemes against the Holy Spirit will not be forgiven.

"When you are brought before synagogues, rulers and authorities, do not worry about how you will defend yourselves or what you will say, for the Holy Spirit will teach you at that time what you should say."

---

p. Greek *two assaria*

143. THE PARABLE OF THE RICH FOOL

Luke 12:13-21

Someone in the crowd said to him, "Teacher, tell my brother to divide the inheritance with me."

Jesus replied, "Man, who appointed me a judge or an arbiter between you?" Then he said to them, "Watch out! Be on your guard against all kinds of greed; a man's life does not consist in the abundance of his possessions."

And he told them this parable: "The ground of a certain rich man produced a good crop. He thought to himself, 'What shall I do? I have no place to store my crops.'

"Then he said, 'This is what I'll do. I will tear down my barns and build bigger ones, and there I will store all my grain and my goods. And I'll say to myself, "You have plenty of good things laid up for many years. Take life easy; eat, drink and be merry." '

"But God said to him, 'You fool! This very night your life will be demanded from you. Then who will get what you have prepared for yourself?'

"This is how it will be with anyone who stores up things for himself but is not rich toward God."

144. DO NOT WORRY

Luke 12:22-34

Then Jesus said to his disciples: "Therefore I tell you, do not worry about your life, what you will eat; or about your body, what you will wear. Life is more than food, and the body more than clothes. Consider the ravens: They do not sow or reap, they have no storeroom or barn; yet God feeds them. And how much more valuable you are than birds! Who of you by worrying can add a single hour to his life?[q] Since you cannot do this very little thing, why do you worry about the rest?

"Consider how the lilies grow. They do not labor or spin. Yet I tell you, not even Solomon in all his splendor was dressed like one of these. If that is how God clothes the grass of the field, which is here today, and tomorrow is thrown into the fire, how much more will he clothe you, O you of little faith! And do not set your heart on

---

q. Or *single cubit to his height*

what you will eat or drink; do not worry about it. For the pagan world runs after all such things, and your Father knows that you need them. But seek his kingdom, and these things will be given to you as well.

"Do not be afraid, little flock, for your Father has been pleased to give you the kingdom. Sell your possessions and give to the poor. Provide purses for yourselves that will not wear out, a treasure in heaven that will not be exhausted, where no thief comes near and no moth destroys. For where your treasure is, there your heart will be also.

145. WATCHFULNESS
Luke 12:35-48

"Be dressed ready for service and keep your lamps burning, like men waiting for their master to return from a wedding banquet, so that when he comes and knocks they can immediately open the door for him. It will be good for those servants whose master finds them watching when he comes. I tell you the truth, he will dress himself to serve, will have them recline at the table and will come and wait on them. It will be good for those servants whose master finds them ready, even if he comes in the second or third watch of the night. But understand this: If the owner of the house had known at what hour the thief was coming, he would not have let his house be broken into. You also must be ready, because the Son of Man will come at an hour when you do not expect him."

Peter asked, "Lord, are you telling this parable to us, or to everyone?"

The Lord answered, "Who then is the faithful and wise manager, whom the master puts in charge of his servants to give them their food allowance at the proper time? It will be good for that servant whom the master finds doing so when he returns. I tell you the truth, he will put him in charge of all his possessions. But suppose the servant says to himself, 'My master is taking a long time in coming,' and he then begins to beat the menservants and maidservants and to eat and drink and get drunk. The master of that servant will come on a day when he does not expect him and at an hour he is not aware of. He will cut him to pieces and assign him a place with the unbelievers.

"That servant who knows his master's will and does not get ready or does not do what his master wants will be beaten with many blows. But the one who does not know and does things deserving punishment will be beaten with few blows. From everyone who has been given much, much will be demanded; and from the one who has been entrusted with much, much more will be asked.

146. NOT PEACE BUT DIVISION
Luke 12:49-53

"I have come to bring fire on the earth, and how I wish it were already kindled! But I have a baptism to undergo, and how distressed I am until it is completed! Do you think I came to bring peace on earth? No, I tell you, but division. From now on there will be five in one family divided against each other, three against two and two against three. They will be divided, father against son and son against father, mother against daughter and daughter against mother, mother-in-law against daughter-in-law and daughter-in-law against mother-in-law."

147. INTERPRETING THE TIMES
Luke 12:54-59

He said to the crowd: "When you see a cloud rising in the west, immediately you say, 'It's going to rain,' and it does. And when the south wind blows, you say, 'It's going to be hot,' and it is. Hypocrites! You know how to interpret the appearance of the earth and the sky. How is it that you don't know how to interpret this present time?

"Why don't you judge for yourselves what is right? As you are going with your adversary to the magistrate, try hard to be reconciled to him on the way, or he may drag you off to the judge, and the judge turn you over to the officer, and the officer throw you into prison. I tell you, you will not get out until you have paid the last penny."

---

r. Greek *lepton*

148. REPENT OR PERISH
Luke 13:1-9

Now there were some present at that time who told Jesus about the Galileans whose blood Pilate had mixed with their sacrifices. Jesus answered, "Do you think that these Galileans were worse sinners than all the other Galileans because they suffered this way? I tell you, no! But unless you repent, you too will all perish. Or those eighteen who died when the tower in Siloam fell on them—do you think they were more guilty than all the others living in Jerusalem? I tell you, no! But unless you repent, you too will all perish."

Then he told this parable: "A man had a fig tree, planted in his vineyard, and he went to look for fruit on it, but did not find any. So he said to the man who took care of the vineyard, 'For three years now I've been coming to look for fruit on this fig tree and haven't found any. Cut it down! Why should it use up the soil?'

" 'Sir,' the man replied, 'leave it alone for one more year, and I'll dig around it and fertilize it. If it bears fruit next year, fine! If not, then cut it down.' "

TEN.
PEREAN MINISTRY AND RAISING OF LAZARUS

149. THE UNBELIEF OF THE JEWS
John 10:22-42

Then came the Feast of Dedication[a] at Jerusalem. It was winter, and Jesus was in the temple area walking in Solomon's Colonnade. The Jews gathered around him, saying, "How long will you keep us in suspense? If you are the Christ, tell us plainly."

Jesus answered, "I did tell you, but you do not believe. The miracles I do in my Father's name speak for me, but you do not believe because you are not my sheep. My sheep listen to my voice; I know them, and they follow me. I give them eternal life, and they shall never perish; no one can snatch them out of my hand. My Father, who has given them to me, is greater than all[b]; no one can snatch them out of my Father's hand. I and the Father are one."

Again the Jews picked up stones to stone him, but Jesus said to them, "I have shown you many great miracles from the Father. For which of these do you stone me?"

"We are not stoning you for any of these," replied the Jews, "but for blasphemy, because you, a mere man, claim to be God."

Jesus answered them, "Is it not written in your Law, 'I have said you are gods'[c]? If he called them 'gods,' to whom the word of God came—and the Scripture cannot be broken—what about the one whom the Father set apart as his very own and sent into the world? Why then do you accuse me of blasphemy because I said, 'I am God's Son'? Do not believe me unless I do what my Father does. But

a. That is, Hanukkah
b. Many early manuscripts [of John 10:29] *What my Father has given me is greater than all*
c. Psalm 82:6

164

if I do it, even though you do not believe me, believe the miracles, that you may know and understand that the Father is in me, and I in the Father." Again they tried to seize him, but he escaped their grasp.

Then Jesus went back across the Jordan to the place where John had been baptizing in the early days. Here he stayed and many people came to him. They said, "Though John never performed a miraculous sign, all that John said about this man was true." And in that place many believed in Jesus.

150. A CRIPPLED WOMAN HEALED ON THE SABBATH
Luke 13:10-17

On a Sabbath Jesus was teaching in one of the synagogues, and a woman was there who had been crippled by a spirit for eighteen years. She was bent over and could not straighten up at all. When Jesus saw her, he called her forward and said to her, "Woman, you are set free from your infirmity." Then he put his hands on her, and immediately she straightened up and praised God.

Indignant because Jesus had healed on the Sabbath, the synagogue ruler said to the people, "There are six days for work. So come and be healed on those days, not on the Sabbath."

The Lord answered him, "You hypocrites! Doesn't each of you on the Sabbath untie his ox or donkey from the stall and lead it out to give it water? Then should not this woman, a daughter of Abraham, whom Satan has kept bound for eighteen long years, be set free on the Sabbath day from what bound her?"

When he said this, all his opponents were humiliated, but the people were delighted with all the wonderful things he was doing.

151. THE PARABLES OF THE MUSTARD SEED AND THE YEAST AGAIN
Luke 13:18-21

Then Jesus asked, "What is the kingdom of God like? What shall I compare it to? It is like a mustard seed, which a man took and planted in his garden. It grew and became a tree, and the birds of the air perched in its branches."

Again he asked, "What shall I compare the kingdom of God to? It is like yeast that a woman took and mixed into a large amount[d] of flour until it worked all through the dough."

152. THE NARROW DOOR
Luke 13:22-30

Then Jesus went through the towns and villages, teaching as he made his way to Jerusalem. Someone asked him, "Lord, are only a few people going to be saved?"

He said to them, "Make every effort to enter through the narrow door, because many, I tell you, will try to enter and will not be able to. Once the owner of the house gets up and closes the door, you will stand outside knocking and pleading, 'Sir, open the door for us.'

"But he will answer, 'I don't know you or where you come from.'

"Then you will say, 'We ate and drank with you, and you taught in our streets.'

"But he will reply, 'I don't know you or where you come from. Away from me, all you evildoers!'

"There will be weeping there, and gnashing of teeth, when you see Abraham, Isaac and Jacob and all the prophets in the kingdom of God, but you yourselves thrown out. People will come from east and west and north and south, and will take their places at the feast in the kingdom of God. Indeed there are those who are last who will be first, and first who will be last."

153. JESUS' SORROW FOR JERUSALEM
Luke 13:31-35

At that time some Pharisees came to Jesus and said to him, "Leave this place and go somewhere else. Herod wants to kill you."

He replied, "Go tell that fox, 'I will drive out demons and heal people today and tomorrow, and on the third day I will reach my goal.' In any case, I must keep going today and tomorrow and the next day—for surely no prophet can die outside Jerusalem!

"O Jerusalem, Jerusalem, you who kill the prophets and stone

---

d. Greek *three satas* (probably about 1/2 bushel or 22 liters)

those sent to you, how often I have longed to gather your children together, as a hen gathers her chicks under her wings, but you were not willing! Look, your house is left to you desolate. I tell you, you will not see me again until you say, 'Blessed is he who comes in the name of the Lord.'[e][1]

Perean Ministry and Raising of Lazarus

SECTION

149a Jesus attends the Feast of Dedication at Jerusalem
149b He goes to Bethany beyond Jordan
164 Jesus returns to Bethany of Judea to raise Lazarus
166 Jesus withdraws from the Jews to stay at Ephraim

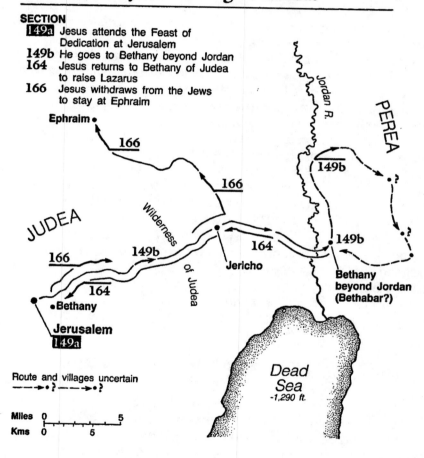

e. Psalm 118:26
1. See p. 325: Did Jesus lament over Jerusalem once (Luke 13:34-35) or twice (Matthew 23:37-39)?

167

154. JESUS AT A PHARISEE'S HOUSE
Luke 14:1-14

One Sabbath, when Jesus went to eat in the house of a prominent Pharisee, he was being carefully watched. There in front of him was a man suffering from dropsy. Jesus asked the Pharisees and experts in the law, "Is it lawful to heal on the Sabbath or not?" But they remained silent. So taking hold of the man, he healed him and sent him away.

Then he asked them, "If one of you has a son[f] or an ox that falls into a well on the Sabbath day, will you not immediately pull him out?" And they had nothing to say.

When he noticed how the guests picked the places of honor at the table, he told them this parable: "When someone invites you to a wedding feast, do not take the place of honor, for a person more distinguished than you may have been invited. If so, the host who invited both of you will come and say to you, 'Give this man your seat.' Then, humiliated, you will have to take the least important place. But when you are invited, take the lowest place, so that when your host comes, he will say to you, 'Friend, move up to a better place.' Then you will be honored in the presence of all your fellow guests. For everyone who exalts himself will be humbled, and he who humbles himself will be exalted."

Then Jesus said to his host, "When you give a luncheon or dinner, do not invite your friends, your brothers or relatives, or your rich neighbors; if you do, they may invite you back and so you will be repaid. But when you give a banquet, invite the poor, the crippled, the lame, the blind, and you will be blessed. Although they cannot repay you, you will be repaid at the resurrection of the righteous."

155. THE PARABLE OF THE GREAT BANQUET
Luke 14:15-24

When one of those at the table with him heard this, he said to Jesus, "Blessed is the man who will eat at the feast in the kingdom of God."

Jesus replied: "A certain man was preparing a great banquet and invited many guests. At the time of the banquet he sent his servant to tell those who had been invited, 'Come, for everything is now ready.'

f. Some manuscripts [of Luke 14:5] *donkey*

"But they all alike began to make excuses. The first said, 'I have just bought a field, and I must go and see it. Please excuse me.'

"Another said, 'I have just bought five yoke of oxen, and I'm on my way to try them out. Please excuse me.'

"Still another said, 'I just got married, so I can't come.'

"The servant came back and reported this to his master. Then the owner of the house became angry and ordered his servant, 'Go out quickly into the streets and alleys of the town and bring in the poor, the crippled, the blind and the lame.'

" 'Sir,' the servant said, 'what you ordered has been done, but there is still room.'

"Then the master told his servant, 'Go out to the roads and country lanes and make them come in, so that my house will be full. I tell you, not one of those men who were invited will get a taste of my banquet.' "

156. THE COST OF BEING A DISCIPLE
Luke 14:25-35

Large crowds were traveling with Jesus, and turning to them he said: "If anyone comes to me and does not hate his father and mother, his wife and children, his brothers and sisters—yes, even his own life—he cannot be my disciple. And anyone who does not carry his cross and follow me cannot be my disciple.

"Suppose one of you wants to build a tower. Will he not first sit down and estimate the cost to see if he has enough money to complete it? For if he lays the foundation and is not able to finish it, everyone who sees it will ridicule him, saying, 'This fellow began to build and was not able to finish.'

"Or suppose a king is about to go to war against another king. Will he not first sit down and consider whether he is able with ten thousand men to oppose the one coming against him with twenty thousand? If he is not able, he will send a delegation while the other is still a long way off and will ask for terms of peace. In the same way, any of you who does not give up everything he has cannot be my disciple.

"Salt is good, but if it loses its saltiness, how can it be made salty again? It is fit neither for the soil nor for the manure pile; it is thrown out.

"He who has ears to hear, let him hear."

157. ANOTHER PARABLE OF THE LOST SHEEP
Luke 15:1-7

Now the tax collectors and "sinners" were all gathering around to hear him. But the Pharisees and the teachers of the law muttered, "This man welcomes sinners and eats with them."

Then Jesus told them this parable:[2] "Suppose one of you has a hundred sheep and loses one of them. Does he not leave the ninety-nine in the open country and go after the lost sheep until he finds it? And when he finds it, he joyfully puts it on his shoulders and goes home. Then he calls his friends and neighbors together and says, 'Rejoice with me; I have found my lost sheep.' I tell you that in the same way there will be more rejoicing in heaven over one sinner who repents than over ninety-nine righteous persons who do not need to repent.

158. THE PARABLE OF THE LOST COIN
Luke 15:8-10

"Or suppose a woman has ten silver coins[g] and loses one. Does she not light a lamp, sweep the house and search carefully until she finds it? And when she finds it, she calls her friends and neighbors together and says, 'Rejoice with me; I have found my lost coin.' In the same way, I tell you, there is rejoicing in the presence of the angels of God over one sinner who repents."

159. THE PARABLE OF THE LOST SON
Luke 15:11-32

Jesus continued: "There was a man who had two sons. The younger one said to his father, 'Father, give me my share of the estate.' So he divided his property between them.

---

2. See p. 326: Do the Gospels record that Jesus taught the Parable of the Lost Sheep on one or two occasions (Matthew 18:12-14; Luke 15:3-7)?
g. Greek *ten drachmas*, each worth about a day's wages

"Not long after that, the younger son got together all he had, set off for a distant country and there squandered his wealth in wild living. After he had spent everything, there was a severe famine in that whole country, and he began to be in need. So he went and hired himself out to a citizen of that country, who sent him to his fields to feed pigs. He longed to fill his stomach with the pods that the pigs were eating, but no one gave him anything.

"When he came to his senses, he said, 'How many of my father's hired men have food to spare, and here I am starving to death! I will set out and go back to my father and say to him: Father, I have sinned against heaven and against you. I am no longer worthy to be called your son; make me like one of your hired men.' So he got up and went to his father.

"But while he was still a long way off, his father saw him and was filled with compassion for him; he ran to his son, threw his arms around him and kissed him.

"The son said to him, 'Father, I have sinned against heaven and against you. I am no longer worthy to be called your son.'*h*

"But the father said to his servants, 'Quick! Bring the best robe and put it on him. Put a ring on his finger and sandals on his feet. Bring the fattened calf and kill it. Let's have a feast and celebrate. For this son of mine was dead and is alive again; he was lost and is found.' So they began to celebrate.

"Meanwhile, the older son was in the field. When he came near the house, he heard music and dancing. So he called one of the servants and asked him what was going on. 'Your brother has come,' he replied, 'and your father has killed the fattened calf because he has him back safe and sound.'

"The older brother became angry and refused to go in. So his father went out and pleaded with him. But he answered his father, 'Look! All these years I've been slaving for you and never disobeyed your orders. Yet you never gave me even a young goat so I could celebrate with my friends. But when this son of yours who has squandered your property with prostitutes comes home, you kill the fattened calf for him!'

" 'My son,' the father said, 'you are always with me, and everything I have is yours. But we had to celebrate and be glad, because this brother of yours was dead and is alive again; he was lost and is found.' "

---

h. Some early manuscripts [of Luke 15:21] *son. Make me like one of your hired men.*

160. THE PARABLE OF THE SHREWD MANAGER
Luke 16:1-18

Jesus told his disciples: "There was a rich man whose manager was accused of wasting his possessions. So he called him in and asked him, 'What is this I hear about you? Give an account of your management, because you cannot be manager any longer.'

"The manager said to himself, 'What shall I do now? My master is taking away my job. I'm not strong enough to dig, and I'm ashamed to beg—I know what I'll do so that, when I lose my job here, people will welcome me into their houses.'

"So he called in each one of his master's debtors. He asked the first, 'How much do you owe my master?'

" 'Eight hundred gallons[i] of olive oil,' he replied.

"The manager told him, 'Take your bill, sit down quickly, and make it four hundred.'

"Then he asked the second, 'And how much do you owe?'

" 'A thousand bushels[j] of wheat,' he replied.

"He told him, 'Take your bill and make it eight hundred.'

"The master commended the dishonest manager because he had acted shrewdly. For the people of this world are more shrewd in dealing with their own kind than are the people of the light. I tell you, use worldly wealth to gain friends for yourselves, so that when it is gone, you will be welcomed into eternal dwellings.

"Whoever can be trusted with very little can also be trusted with much, and whoever is dishonest with very little will also be dishonest with much. So if you have not been trustworthy in handling worldly wealth, who will trust you with true riches? And if you have not been trustworthy with someone else's property, who will give you property of your own?

"No servant can serve two masters. Either he will hate the one and love the other, or he will be devoted to the one and despise the other. You cannot serve both God and Money."

The Pharisees, who loved money, heard all this and were sneering at Jesus. He said to them, "You are the ones who justify yourselves in the eyes of men, but God knows your hearts. What is highly valued among men is detestable in God's sight.

---

i. Greek *one hundred batous* (probably about 3 kiloliters)
j. Greek *one hundred korous* (probably about 35 kiloliters)

"The Law and the Prophets were proclaimed until John. Since that time, the good news of the kingdom of God is being preached, and everyone is forcing his way into it. It is easier for heaven and earth to disappear than for the least stroke of a pen to drop out of the Law.

"Anyone who divorces his wife and marries another woman commits adultery, and the man who marries a divorced woman commits adultery.

161. THE RICH MAN AND LAZARUS
Luke 16:19-31

"There was a rich man who was dressed in purple and fine linen and lived in luxury every day. At his gate was laid a beggar named Lazarus, covered with sores and longing to eat what fell from the rich man's table. Even the dogs came and licked his sores.

"The time came when the beggar died and the angels carried him to Abraham's side. The rich man also died and was buried. In hell, where he was in torment, he looked up and saw Abraham far away, with Lazarus by his side. So he called to him, 'Father Abraham, have pity on me and send Lazarus to dip the tip of his finger in water and cool my tongue, because I am in agony in this fire.'

"But Abraham replied, 'Son, remember that in your lifetime you received your good things, while Lazarus received bad things, but now he is comforted here and you are in agony. And besides all this, between us and you a great chasm has been fixed, so that those who want to go from here to you cannot, nor can anyone cross over from there to us.'

"He answered, 'Then I beg you, father, send Lazarus to my father's house, for I have five brothers. Let him warn them, so that they will not also come to this place of torment.'

"Abraham replied, 'They have Moses and the Prophets; let them listen to them.'

"'No, father Abraham,' he said, 'but if someone from the dead goes to them, they will repent.'

"He said to him, 'If they do not listen to Moses and the Prophets, they will not be convinced even if someone rises from the dead.' "

162. SIN, FAITH, DUTY
Luke 17:1-10

Jesus said to his disciples: "Things that cause people to sin are bound to come, but woe to that person through whom they come. It would be better for him to be thrown into the sea with a millstone tied around his neck than for him to cause one of these little ones to sin. So watch yourselves.

"If your brother sins, rebuke him, and if he repents, forgive him. If he sins against you seven times in a day, and seven times comes back to you and says, 'I repent,' forgive him."

The apostles said to the Lord, "Increase our faith!"

He replied, "If you have faith as small as a mustard seed, you can say to this mulberry tree, 'Be uprooted and planted in the sea,' and it will obey you.

"Suppose one of you had a servant plowing or looking after the sheep. Would he say to the servant when he comes in from the field, 'Come along now and sit down to eat'? Would he not rather say, 'Prepare my supper, get yourself ready and wait on me while I eat and drink; after that you may eat and drink'? Would he thank the servant because he did what he was told to do? So you also, when you have done everything you were told to do, should say, 'We are unworthy servants; we have only done our duty.' "

163. THE DEATH OF LAZARUS
John 11:1-16

Now a man named Lazarus was sick. He was from Bethany, the village of Mary and her sister Martha. This Mary, whose brother Lazarus now lay sick, was the same one who poured perfume on the Lord and wiped his feet with her hair. So the sisters sent word to Jesus, "Lord, the one you love is sick."

When he heard this, Jesus said, "This sickness will not end in death. No, it is for God's glory so that God's Son may be glorified through it." Jesus loved Martha and her sister and Lazarus. Yet when he heard that Lazarus was sick, he stayed where he was two more days.

Then he said to his disciples, "Let us go back to Judea."

"But, Rabbi," they said, "a short while ago the Jews tried to stone you, and yet you are going back there?"

Jesus answered, "Are there not twelve hours of daylight? A man who walks by day will not stumble, for he sees by this world's light. It is when he walks by night that he stumbles, for he has no light."

After he had said this, he went on to tell them, "Our friend Lazarus has fallen asleep; but I am going there to wake him up."

His disciples replied, "Lord, if he sleeps, he will get better." Jesus had been speaking of his death, but his disciples thought he meant natural sleep.

So then he told them plainly, "Lazarus is dead, and for your sake I am glad I was not there, so that you may believe. But let us go to him."

Then Thomas (called Didymus) said to the rest of the disciples, "Let us also go, that we may die with him."

164. JESUS COMFORTS THE SISTERS
John 11:17-37

On his arrival, Jesus found that Lazarus had already been in the tomb for four days. Bethany was less than two miles[k] from Jerusalem, and many Jews had come to Martha and Mary to comfort them in the loss of their brother. When Martha heard that Jesus was coming, she went out to meet him, but Mary stayed at home.

"Lord," Martha said to Jesus, "if you had been here, my brother would not have died. But I know that even now God will give you whatever you ask."

Jesus said to her, "Your brother will rise again."

Martha answered, "I know he will rise again in the resurrection at the last day."

Jesus said to her, "I am the resurrection and the life. He who believes in me will live, even though he dies; and whoever lives and believes in me will never die. Do you believe this?"

"Yes, Lord," she told him, "I believe that you are the Christ, the Son of God, who was to come into the world."

And after she had said this, she went back and called her sister Mary aside. "The Teacher is here," she said, "and is asking for you." When Mary heard this, she got up quickly and went to him. Now Jesus had not yet entered the village, but was still at the place where

---

k. Greek *fifteen stadia* (about 3 kilometers)

Martha had met him. When the Jews who had been with Mary in the house, comforting her, noticed how quickly she got up and went out, they followed her, supposing she was going to the tomb to mourn there.

When Mary reached the place where Jesus was and saw him, she fell at his feet and said, "Lord, if you had been here, my brother would not have died."

When Jesus saw her weeping, and the Jews who had come along with her also weeping, he was deeply moved in spirit and troubled. "Where have you laid him?" he asked.

"Come and see, Lord," they replied.

Jesus wept.

Then the Jews said, "See how he loved him!"

But some of them said, "Could not he who opened the eyes of the blind man have kept this man from dying?"

165. JESUS RAISES LAZARUS FROM THE DEAD
John 11:38-44

Jesus, once more deeply moved, came to the tomb. It was a cave with a stone laid across the entrance. "Take away the stone," he said.

"But, Lord," said Martha, the sister of the dead man, "by this time there is a bad odor, for he has been there four days."

Then Jesus said, "Did I not tell you that if you believed, you would see the glory of God?"

So they took away the stone. Then Jesus looked up and said, "Father, I thank you that you have heard me. I knew that you always hear me, but I said this for the benefit of the people standing here, that they may believe that you sent me."

When he had said this, Jesus called in a loud voice, "Lazarus, come out!" The dead man came out, his hands and feet wrapped with strips of linen, and a cloth around his face.

Jesus said to them, "Take off the grave clothes and let him go."

166. THE PLOT TO KILL JESUS
John 11:45-54

Therefore many of the Jews who had come to visit Mary, and had seen what Jesus did, put their faith in him. But some of them went

176

to the Pharisees and told them what Jesus had done. Then the chief priests and the Pharisees called a meeting of the Sanhedrin.

"What are we accomplishing?" they asked. "Here is this man performing many miraculous signs. If we let him go on like this, everyone will believe in him, and then the Romans will come and take away both our place[1] and our nation."

Then one of them, named Caiaphas, who was high priest that year, spoke up, "You know nothing at all! You do not realize that it is better for you that one man die for the people than that the whole nation perish."

He did not say this on his own, but as high priest that year he prophesied that Jesus would die for the Jewish nation, and not only for that nation but also for the scattered children of God, to bring them together and make them one. So from that day on they plotted to take his life.

Therefore Jesus no longer moved about publicly among the Jews. Instead he withdrew to a region near the desert, to a village called Ephraim, where he stayed with his disciples.

:

---

1. Or *temple*

ELEVEN.
LAST TRIP TO JERUSALEM

167. TEN HEALED OF LEPROSY
Luke 17:11-19

Now on his way to Jerusalem, Jesus traveled along the border between Samaria and Galilee. As he was going into a village, ten men who had leprosy met him. They stood at a distance and called out in a loud voice, "Jesus, Master, have pity on us!"

When he saw them, he said, "Go, show yourselves to the priests." And as they went, they were cleansed.

One of them, when he saw he was healed, came back, praising God in a loud voice. He threw himself at Jesus' feet and thanked him—and he was a Samaritan.

Jesus asked, "Were not all ten cleansed? Where are the other nine? Was no one found to return and give praise to God except this foreigner?" Then he said to him, "Rise and go; your faith has made you well."

168. THE COMING OF THE KINGDOM OF GOD
Luke 17:20-37

Once, having been asked by the Pharisees when the kingdom of God would come, Jesus replied, "The kingdom of God does not come with your careful observation, nor will people say, 'Here it is,' or 'There it is,' because the kingdom of God is within[a] you."

Then he said to his disciples, "The time is coming when you will long to see one of the days of the Son of Man, but you will not see it. Men will tell you, 'There he is!' or 'Here he is!' Do not go

---

a. Or *among*

178

running off after them. For the Son of Man in his day[b] will be like the lightning, which flashes and lights up the sky from one end to the other. But first he must suffer many things and be rejected by this generation.

"Just as it was in the days of Noah, so also will it be in the days of the Son of Man. People were eating, drinking, marrying and being given in marriage up to the day Noah entered the ark. Then the flood came and destroyed them all.

"It was the same in the days of Lot. People were eating and drinking, buying and selling, planting and building. But the day Lot left Sodom, fire and sulfur rained down from heaven and destroyed them all.

"It will be just like this on the day the Son of Man is revealed. On that day no one who is on the roof of his house, with his goods inside, should go down to get them. Likewise, no one in the field should go back for anything. Remember Lot's wife! Whoever tries to keep his life will lose it, and whoever loses his life will preserve it. I tell you, on that night two people will be in one bed; one will be taken and the other left. Two women will be grinding grain together; one will be taken and the other left.[c]"

"Where, Lord?" they asked.

He replied, "Where there is a dead body, there the vultures will gather."

169. THE PARABLE OF THE PERSISTENT WIDOW
Luke 18:1-8

Then Jesus told his disciples a parable to show them that they should always pray and not give up. He said: "In a certain town there was a judge who neither feared God nor cared about men. And there was a widow in that town who kept coming to him with the plea, 'Grant me justice against my adversary.'

"For some time he refused. But finally he said to himself, 'Even though I don't fear God or care about men, yet because this widow keeps bothering me, I will see that she gets justice, so that she won't eventually wear me out with her coming!'"

b. Some manuscripts [of Luke 17:24] do not have *in his day.*
c. Some manuscripts [of Luke 17:35] *left. Two men will be in the field; one will be taken and the other left.*

179

And the Lord said, "Listen to what the unjust judge says. And will not God bring about justice for his chosen ones, who cry out to him day and night? Will he keep putting them off? I tell you, he will see that they get justice, and quickly. However, when the Son of Man comes, will he find faith on the earth?"

170. THE PARABLE OF THE PHARISEE AND THE TAX COLLECTOR
Luke 18:9-14

To some who were confident of their own righteousness and looked down on everybody else, Jesus told this parable: "Two men went up to the temple to pray, one a Pharisee and the other a tax collector. The Pharisee stood up and prayed about[d] himself: 'God, I thank you that I am not like other men—robbers, evildoers, adulterers—or even like this tax collector. I fast twice a week and give a tenth of all I get.'

"But the tax collector stood at a distance. He would not even look up to heaven, but beat his breast and said, 'God, have mercy on me, a sinner.'

"I tell you that this man, rather than the other, went home justified before God. For everyone who exalts himself will be humbled, and he who humbles himself will be exalted."

171. CERTIFICATE OF DIVORCE
Matthew 19:1-12; Mark 10:1-12

When Jesus had finished saying these things, he left Galilee and went into the region of Judea to the other side of the Jordan. Again large crowds of people came and followed him. He healed them there, and as was his custom, he taught them.

Some Pharisees came to him to test him. They asked, "Is it lawful for a man to divorce his wife for any and every reason?"

"What did Moses command you?" he replied.

They said, "Moses permitted a man to write a certificate of divorce and send her away."

---

d. Or *to*

"Haven't you read," he replied, "that at the beginning of creation God 'made them male and female,'[e] and said, 'For this reason a man will leave his father and mother and be united to his wife, and the two will become one flesh'[f]? So they are no longer two, but one. Therefore what God has joined together, let man not separate."

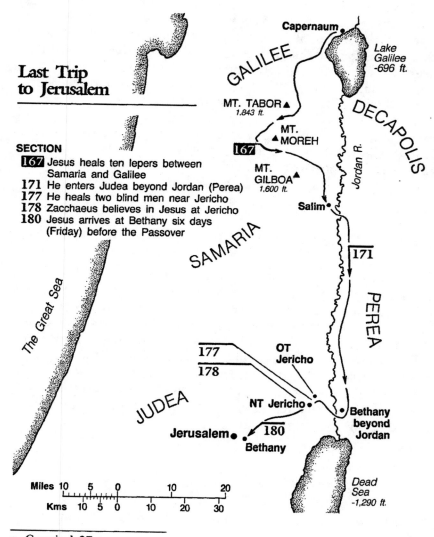

Last Trip to Jerusalem

SECTION

167 Jesus heals ten lepers between Samaria and Galilee
171 He enters Judea beyond Jordan (Perea)
177 He heals two blind men near Jericho
178 Zacchaeus believes in Jesus at Jericho
180 Jesus arrives at Bethany six days (Friday) before the Passover

Capernaum
Lake Galilee -696 ft.
GALILEE
MT. TABOR ▲ 1,843 ft.
DECAPOLIS
MT. ▲ MOREH
167
MT. GILBOA ▲ 1,600 ft.
Jordan R.
Salim
The Great Sea
SAMARIA
171
PEREA
177
178
OT Jericho
JUDEA
NT Jericho
Bethany beyond Jordan
Jerusalem
180
Bethany
Dead Sea -1,290 ft.

Miles 10 5 0 10 20
Kms 10 5 0 10 20 30

e. Genesis 1:27
f. Genesis 2:24

"Why then," they asked, "did Moses command that a man give his wife a certificate of divorce and send her away?"

Jesus replied, "It was because your hearts were hard that Moses wrote you this law *and* permitted you to divorce your wives. But it was not this way from the beginning."

When they were in the house again, the disciples asked Jesus about this. He answered, "I tell you that anyone who divorces his wife, except for marital unfaithfulness, and marries another woman commits adultery against her. And if she divorces her husband and marries another man, she commits adultery."

The disciples said to him, "If this is the situation between a husband and wife, it is better not to marry."

Jesus replied, "Not everyone can accept this word, but only those to whom it has been given. For some are eunuchs because they were born that way; others were made that way by men; and others have renounced marriage[g] because of the kingdom of heaven. The one who can accept this should accept it."

172. THE LITTLE CHILDREN AND JESUS
Matthew 19:13-15; Mark 10:13-16; Luke 18:15-17

Then people were bringing little children to Jesus for him to place his hands on them and pray for them. People were also bringing babies to Jesus to have him touch them. But when the disciples saw this, they rebuked those who brought them. When Jesus saw this, he was indignant. He called the children to him and said, "Let the little children come to me, and do not hinder them, for the kingdom of heaven belongs to such as these. I tell you the truth, anyone who will not receive the kingdom of God like a little child will never enter it." And he took the children in his arms, put his hands on them and blessed them. He went on from there.

173. THE RICH YOUNG RULER
Matthew 19:16-30; Mark 10:17-31; Luke 18:18-30

As Jesus started on his way, a certain ruler ran up to him and fell on

---

g. Or *have made themselves eunuchs*

his knees before him. "Good teacher," he asked, "what good thing must I do to inherit eternal life?"

"Why do you call me good?" Jesus answered. "There is only One who is good—God alone. Why do you ask me about what is good?[1] If you want to enter life, obey the commandments."

"Which ones?" the man inquired.

Jesus replied, "You know the commandments: 'Do not murder, do not commit adultery, do not steal, do not give false testimony, do not defraud, honor your father and mother,[h] and 'love your neighbor as yourself.'[i]"

"Teacher," the young man declared, "all these I have kept since I was a boy. What do I still lack?"

When Jesus heard this, he looked at him and loved him. "You still lack one thing," he said. "If you want to be perfect, go, sell your possessions, everything you have, and give to the poor, and you will have treasure in heaven. Then come, follow me."

When he heard this, the young man's face fell. He went away very sad, because he was a man of great wealth.

Jesus looked at him, looked around and said to his disciples, "I tell you the truth, how hard it is for the rich to enter the kingdom of heaven!"

The disciples were amazed at his words. But Jesus said again, "Children, how hard it is[j] to enter the kingdom of God! Indeed, it is easier for a camel to go through the eye of a needle than for a rich man to enter the kingdom of God."

When the disciples heard this, they were greatly astonished and asked each other, "Who then can be saved?"

Jesus looked at them and replied, "With man this is impossible, but not with God; all things are possible with God."

Peter answered him, "We have left everything we had to follow you! What then will there be for us?"

"I tell you the truth," Jesus replied to them, "at the renewal of all things, when the Son of Man sits on his glorious throne, you who have followed me will also sit on twelve thrones, judging the twelve tribes of Israel. And everyone who has left home or wife or brothers

---

1. See p. 327: Do Mark 10:18 and Luke 18:19 relate the exact dialogue between Jesus and the rich young ruler, or does Matthew 19:17?
h. Exodus 20:12-16; Deuteronomy 5:16-20
i. Leviticus 19:18
j. Some manuscripts [of Mark 10:24] *is for those who trust in riches*

or sisters or father or mother or children or fields for me and the gospel, for the sake of the kingdom of God, will receive a hundred times as much in this present age (homes, brothers, sisters, mothers, children and fields—and with them, persecutions) and in the age to come, eternal life. But many who are first will be last, and many who are last will be first.

174. THE PARABLE OF THE WORKERS IN THE VINEYARD
Matthew 20:1-16

"For the kingdom of heaven is like a landowner who went out early in the morning to hire men to work in his vineyard. He agreed to pay them a denarius for the day and sent them into his vineyard.

"About the third hour he went out and saw others standing in the marketplace doing nothing. He told them, 'You also go and work in my vineyard, and I will pay you whatever is right.' So they went.

"He went out again about the sixth hour and the ninth hour and did the same thing. About the eleventh hour he went out and found still others standing around. He asked them, 'Why have you been standing here all day long doing nothing?'

" 'Because no one has hired us,' they answered.

"He said to them, 'You also go and work in my vineyard.'

"When evening came, the owner of the vineyard said to his foreman, 'Call the workers and pay them their wages, beginning with the last ones hired and going on to the first.'

"The workers who were hired about the eleventh hour came and each received a denarius. So when those came who were hired first, they expected to receive more. But each one of them also received a denarius. When they received it, they began to grumble against the landowner. 'These men who were hired last worked only one hour,' they said, 'and you have made them equal to us who have borne the burden of the work and the heat of the day.'

"But he answered one of them, 'Friend, I am not being unfair to you. Didn't you agree to work for a denarius? Take your pay and go. I want to give the man who was hired last the same as I gave you. Don't I have the right to do what I want with my own money? Or are you envious because I am generous?'

"So the last will be first, and the first will be last."

175. JESUS AGAIN PREDICTS HIS DEATH
Matthew 20:17-19; Mark 10:32-34; Luke 18:31-34

They were on their way up to Jerusalem, with Jesus leading the way, and the disciples were astonished, while those who followed were afraid. Again he took the twelve disciples aside and told them what was going to happen to him. "We are going up to Jerusalem," he said, "and everything that is written by the prophets about the Son of Man will be fulfilled. He will be betrayed to the chief priests and the teachers of the law. They will condemn him to death and will hand him over to the Gentiles. They will mock him, insult him, spit on him, flog him and kill him. On the third day he will rise to life again."

The disciples did not understand any of this. Its meaning was hidden from them, and they did not know what he was talking about.

176. THE REQUEST OF JAMES, JOHN, AND THEIR MOTHER
Matthew 20:20-28; Mark 10:35-45

Then James and John, the sons of Zebedee, came to Jesus *with their mother*. "Teacher," they said, "we want you to do for us whatever we ask."[2]

"What is it you want me to do for you?" he asked.

Then the mother, kneeling down, asked a favor of him.

She said, "Grant that one of these two sons of mine may sit at your right and the other at your left in your kingdom glory." They replied *similarly*.

"You don't know what you are asking," Jesus said to them. "Can you drink the cup I am going to drink or be baptized with the baptism I am baptized with?"

"We can," they answered.

Jesus said to them, "You will indeed drink the cup I drink and be baptized with the baptism I am baptized with, but to sit at my right or left is not for me to grant. These places belong to those for whom they have been prepared by my Father."

---

2. See p. 328: Did James and John (Mark 10:35), or did their mother (Matthew 20:20), make the request to Jesus that the two brothers sit on Jesus' immediate right and left hand in his kingdom?

When the ten heard about this, they became indignant with James and John. Jesus called them together and said, "You know that those who are regarded as rulers of the Gentiles lord it over them, and their high officials exercise authority over them. Not so with you. Instead, whoever wants to become great among you must be your servant, and whoever wants to be first must be slave of all. For even the Son of Man did not come to be served, but to serve, and to give his life as a ransom for many."

177. TWO BLIND MEN RECEIVE THEIR SIGHT
Matthew 20:29-34; Mark 10:46-52; Luke 18:35-43

Then they came to Jericho. As Jesus and his disciples were leaving the city,[3] a large crowd followed him. Two blind men[4] were sitting by the roadside begging. *One was* Bartimaeus (that is, the Son of Timaeus). When he heard the crowd going by, he asked what was happening. When they heard, "Jesus of Nazareth is passing by," they shouted, "Jesus, Son of David, have mercy on us!"

Those who led the way rebuked them and told them to be quiet, but they shouted all the louder, "Lord, Son of David, have mercy on us!"

Jesus stopped and called them, and ordered *them* to be brought to him.

So they called to the blind *men*, "Cheer up! On your feet! He's calling you." Throwing his cloak aside, *Bartimaeus* jumped to his feet and came to Jesus.

When he came near, Jesus asked him, "What do you want me to do for you?"

"Lord," he replied, "we want our sight."

Jesus had compassion on them and touched their eyes. "Go," said Jesus, "your faith has healed you." Immediately they received their sight and followed Jesus along the road, praising God. When all the people saw it, they also praised God.

---

3. See p. 328: Did Jesus heal the two blind men on his entry into Jericho (Luke 18:35) or on his departure (Matthew 20:29; Mark 10:46)?
4. See p. 330: On his last approach to Jerusalem, did Jesus heal one blind man near Jericho (Mark 10:46; Luke 18:35) or two (Matthew 20:30)?

178. ZACCHAEUS THE TAX COLLECTOR
Luke 19:1-10

Jesus entered Jericho and was passing through. A man was there by the name of Zacchaeus; he was a chief tax collector and was wealthy. He wanted to see who Jesus was, but being a short man he could not, because of the crowd. So he ran ahead and climbed a sycamore-fig tree to see him, since Jesus was coming that way.

When Jesus reached the spot, he looked up and said to him, "Zacchaeus, come down immediately. I must stay at your house today." So he came down at once and welcomed him gladly.

All the people saw this and began to mutter, "He has gone to be the guest of a 'sinner.'"

But Zacchaeus stood up and said to the Lord, "Look, Lord! Here and now I give half of my possessions to the poor, and if I have cheated anybody out of anything, I will pay back four times the amount."

Jesus said to him, "Today salvation has come to this house, because this man, too, is a son of Abraham. For the Son of Man came to seek and to save what was lost."

179. THE PARABLE OF THE TEN MINAS
Luke 19:11-28

While they were listening to this, he went on to tell them a parable, because he was near Jerusalem and the people thought that the kingdom of God was going to appear at once. He said: "A man of noble birth went to a distant country to have himself appointed king and then to return. So he called ten of his servants and gave them ten minas.[k] 'Put this money to work,' he said, 'until I come back.'

"But his subjects hated him and sent a delegation after him to say, 'We don't want this man to be our king.'

"He was made king, however, and returned home. Then he sent for the servants to whom he had given the money, in order to find out what they had gained with it.

"The first one came and said, 'Sir, your mina has earned ten more.'

"'Well done, my good servant!' his master replied. 'Because you

---

k. A mina was about three months' wages.

have been trustworthy in a very small matter, take charge of ten cities.'

"The second came and said, 'Sir, your mina has earned five more.'

"His master answered, 'You take charge of five cities.'

"Then another servant came and said, 'Sir, here is your mina; I have kept it laid away in a piece of cloth. I was afraid of you, because you are a hard man. You take out what you did not put in and reap what you did not sow.'

"His master replied, 'I will judge you by your own words, you wicked servant! You knew, did you, that I am a hard man, taking out what I did not put in, and reaping what I did not sow? Why then didn't you put my money on deposit, so that when I came back, I could have collected it with interest?'

"Then he said to those standing by, 'Take his mina away from him and give it to the one who has ten minas.'

" 'Sir,' they replied, 'he already has ten!'

"He replied, 'I tell you that to everyone who has, more will be given, but as for the one who has nothing, even what he has will be taken away. But those enemies of mine who did not want me to be king over them—bring them here and kill them in front of me.' "

After Jesus had said this, he went on ahead, going up to Jerusalem.

180. THE PASSOVER CROWD AWAITS JESUS
John 11:55–12:1, 9-11

When it was almost time for the Jewish Passover, many went up from the country to Jerusalem for their ceremonial cleansing before the Passover. They kept looking for Jesus, and as they stood in the temple area they asked one another, "What do you think? Isn't he coming to the Feast at all?" But the chief priests and Pharisees had given orders that if anyone found out where Jesus was, he should report it so that they might arrest him.

Six days before the Passover, Jesus arrived at Bethany, where Lazarus lived, whom Jesus had raised from the dead. A large crowd of Jews found out that Jesus was there and came, not only because of him but also to see Lazarus, whom he had raised from the dead. So the chief priests made plans to kill Lazarus as well, for on account of him many of the Jews were going over to Jesus and putting their faith in him.

TWELVE.
LAST JERUSALEM MINISTRY

181. THE TRIUMPHAL ENTRY
Matthew 21:1-11; Mark 11:1-11; Luke 19:29-44; John 12:12-19

The next day, as they approached Jerusalem and came to Bethphage and Bethany at the hill called the Mount of Olives, Jesus sent two of his disciples, saying to them, "Go to the village ahead of you, and just as you enter it, you will find a donkey tied there, with her colt by her, which no one has ever ridden. Untie them and bring them here to me. If anyone asks you, 'Why are you doing this?' tell him, 'The Lord needs them, and he will send them back here right away.' "

The disciples went and did as Jesus had instructed them. They found a colt just as he had told them, outside in the street, tied at a doorway. As they were untying the colt, its owners asked them, "What are you doing? Why are you untying that colt?"

They answered as Jesus had told them, "The Lord needs it," and the people let them go. They brought the donkey and the colt to Jesus, threw their cloaks on the colt and put Jesus on it.[1]

This took place to fulfill what was spoken through the prophet:

"Say to the Daughter of Zion,
'Do not be afraid.
See, your king comes to you,
gentle and riding on a donkey,
on a colt, the foal of a donkey.' "[a]

At first his disciples did not understand all this. Only after Jesus

---

1. See p. 331: At his Triumphal Entry into Jerusalem, did Jesus have one donkey (Mark 11:7; Luke 19:35; John 12:14) or two (Matthew 21:7)? Did he sit simultaneously on both the donkey and her colt?
a. Zechariah 9:9

189

was glorified did they realize that these things had been written about him and that they had done these things to him.

The great crowd that had come for the Feast heard that Jesus was on his way to Jerusalem. Now the crowd that was with him when he called Lazarus from the tomb and raised him from the dead continued to spread the word. Many people, because they had heard that he had given this miraculous sign, went out to meet him.

As he went along, people spread their cloaks on the road, while others cut palm branches from the trees in the fields and spread them on the road.

When he came near the place where the road goes down the Mount of Olives, the whole crowd of disciples that went ahead of him, and those that followed, began joyfully to praise God in loud voices for all the miracles they had seen, shouting:

"Hosanna![b]"
"Hosanna to the Son of David!"
"Blessed is he who comes
in the name of the Lord![c]"
"Blessed is the King of Israel!"
"Blessed is the coming kingdom
of our father David!"
"Peace in heaven and glory in the highest!"
"Hosanna in the highest!"

Some of the Pharisees in the crowd said to Jesus, "Teacher, rebuke your disciples!"

"I tell you," he replied, "if they keep quiet, the stones will cry out."

So the Pharisees said to one another, "See, this is getting us nowhere. Look how the whole world has gone after him!"

As he approached Jerusalem and saw the city, he wept over it and said, "If you, even you, had only known on this day what would bring you peace—but now it is hidden from your eyes. The days will come upon you when your enemies will build an embankment against you and encircle you and hem you in on every side. They will

---

b. A Hebrew expression meaning "Save!" which became an exclamation of praise [and hereinafter]
c. Psalm 118:25-26

Passion Week Begins

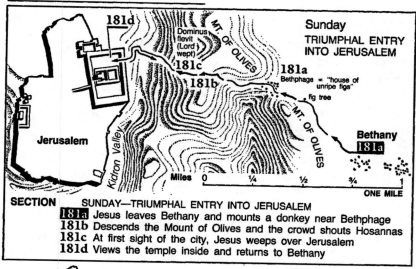

Sunday
TRIUMPHAL ENTRY INTO JERUSALEM

181d

Dominus flevit (Lord wept)

MT. OF OLIVES

181c

181b

181a

Bethphage = "house of unripe figs"

fig tree

MT. OF OLIVES

Jerusalem

Kidron Valley

Bethany
181a

Miles 0 ¼ ½ ¾ 1
ONE MILE

SECTION SUNDAY—TRIUMPHAL ENTRY INTO JERUSALEM
181a Jesus leaves Bethany and mounts a donkey near Bethphage
181b Descends the Mount of Olives and the crowd shouts Hosannas
181c At first sight of the city, Jesus weeps over Jerusalem
181d Views the temple inside and returns to Bethany

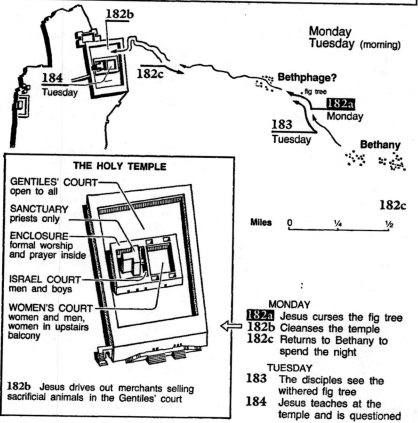

182b

Monday
Tuesday (morning)

184
Tuesday

182c

Bethphage?

fig tree

182a
Monday

183
Tuesday

Bethany

THE HOLY TEMPLE

GENTILES' COURT—
open to all

SANCTUARY
priests only

ENCLOSURE—
formal worship
and prayer inside

ISRAEL COURT—
men and boys

WOMEN'S COURT—
women and men,
women in upstairs
balcony

182c

Miles 0 ¼ ½

182b Jesus drives out merchants selling
sacrificial animals in the Gentiles' court

MONDAY
182a Jesus curses the fig tree
182b Cleanses the temple
182c Returns to Bethany to
spend the night

TUESDAY
183 The disciples see the
withered fig tree
184 Jesus teaches at the
temple and is questioned

191

dash you to the ground, you and the children within your walls. They will not leave one stone on another, because you did not recognize the time of God's coming to you."

When Jesus entered Jerusalem, the whole city was stirred and asked, "Who is this?"

The crowds answered, "This is Jesus, the prophet from Nazareth in Galilee."

Jesus went to the temple. He looked around at everything, but since it was already late, he went out to Bethany with the Twelve.

182. JESUS CURSES THE FIG TREE AND CLEARS THE TEMPLE
Matthew 21:12-19; Mark 11:12-19; Luke 19:45-48

Early in the morning the next day, they were leaving Bethany. On his way back to the city, Jesus was hungry. Seeing in the distance a fig tree in leaf by the road, he went up to it to find out if it had any fruit. When he reached it, he found nothing on it except leaves, because it was not the season for figs. Then he said to the tree, "May you never bear fruit again. May no one ever eat fruit from you again." And his disciples heard him say it. Immediately the tree withered.

On reaching Jerusalem, Jesus entered the temple area and began driving out all those who were buying and selling there. He overturned the tables of the money changers and the benches of those selling doves, and would not allow anyone to carry merchandise through the temple courts.[2] And as he taught them, he said, "Is it not written:

" 'My house will be called
a house of prayer for all nations'[d]?

But you have made it 'a den of robbers.'[e][3]

Every day he was teaching at the temple. The blind and the lame

2. See p. 331: Did Jesus cleanse the temple on Sunday (Matthew 21:1-17; Luke 19:29-46) or Monday (Mark 11:1-17) of Passion Week?
d. Isaiah 56:7
e. Jeremiah 7:11
3. See p. 332: Did Jesus cleanse the temple by expelling the moneychangers once (Matthew 21:12; Mark 11:15; Luke 19:45) or twice (John 2:13-16)?

came to him, and he healed them. But when the chief priests and the teachers of the law saw the wonderful things he did and the children shouting in the temple area, "Hosanna to the Son of David," they were indignant.

"Do you hear what these children are saying?" they asked him. "Yes," replied Jesus, "have you never read,

" 'From the lips of children and infants
you have ordained praise'[f]?"

The chief priests, the teachers of the law, and the leaders among the people heard this and began looking for a way to kill him, for they feared him. Yet they could not find any way to do it, because all the people, amazed at his teaching, hung on his words.

When evening came, he left them and went out of the city to Bethany, where he spent the night.

183. THE WITHERED FIG TREE
Matthew 21:20-22; Mark 11:20-26

In the morning, as they went along, they saw the fig tree withered from the roots.[4] Peter remembered and said to Jesus, "Rabbi, look! The fig tree you cursed has withered!" The disciples were amazed. "How did the fig tree wither so quickly?" they asked.

"Have[g] faith in God," Jesus answered. "I tell you the truth, not only can you do what was done to the fig tree, but if anyone says to this mountain, 'Go, throw yourself into the sea,' and does not doubt in his heart but believes that what he says will happen, it will be done for him. Therefore I tell you, whatever you ask for in prayer, believe that you have received it, and it will be yours. And when you stand praying, if you hold anything against anyone, forgive him, so that your Father in heaven may forgive you your sins.[h]"

---

f. Psalm 8:2
4. See p. 333: Did the disciples see the fig tree withered on Monday, the same day Jesus cursed it (Matthew 21:20), or on Tuesday, the day following the curse (Mark 11:20)?
g. Some early manuscripts [of Mark 11:22] *If you have*
h. Some manuscripts [of Mark 11:26] *sins. But if you do not forgive, neither will your Father who is in heaven forgive your sins.*

184. THE AUTHORITY OF JESUS QUESTIONED
Matthew 21:23-27; Mark 11:27-33; Luke 20:1-8

They arrived again in Jerusalem and Jesus entered the temple courts, teaching the people and preaching the gospel. While Jesus was walking in the temple courts, the chief priests and the teachers of the law, together with the elders of the people, came up to him. "Tell us by what authority you are doing these things," they said. "And who gave you authority to do this?"

Jesus replied, "I will also ask you one question. If you answer me, I will tell you by what authority I am doing these things. Tell me, John's baptism—where did it come from? Was it from heaven, or from men?"

They discussed it among themselves and said, "If we say, 'From heaven,' he will ask, 'Then why didn't you believe him?' But if we say, 'From men'—we are afraid of the people. All the people will stone us, because they are persuaded that John really was a prophet."

So they answered Jesus, "We don't know where it was from."

Then Jesus said, "Neither will I tell you by what authority I am doing these things."

185. THE PARABLE OF THE TWO SONS
Matthew 21:28-32; Mark 12:1a

He then began to speak to them in parables. "What do you think? There was a man who had two sons. He went to the first and said, 'Son, go and work today in the vineyard.'

" 'I will not,' he answered, but later he changed his mind and went.

"Then the father went to the other son and said the same thing. He answered, 'I will, sir,' but he did not go.

"Which of the two did what his father wanted?"

"The first," they answered.

Jesus said to them, "I tell you the truth, the tax collectors and the prostitutes are entering the kingdom of God ahead of you. For John came to you to show you the way of righteousness, and you did not believe him, but the tax collectors and the prostitutes did. And even after you saw this, you did not repent and believe him.

186. THE PARABLE OF THE TENANTS
Matthew 21:33-46; Mark 12:1b-12; Luke 20:9-19

"Listen to another parable: There was a landowner who planted a vineyard. He put a wall around it, dug a pit for the winepress in it and built a watchtower. Then he rented the vineyard to some farmers and went away on a journey for a long time. When the harvest time approached, he sent a servant to the tenants to collect from them some of the fruit of the vineyard. But the tenants seized him, beat him and sent him away empty-handed. Then he sent another servant to them; but that one also they struck on the head, treated shamefully and sent away empty-handed. He sent still a third; they stoned and wounded him and threw him out. He sent still another, and that one they killed. Then he sent many other servants to them, more than the first time, and the tenants treated them the same way; some of them they beat, others they killed.

"Then the owner of the vineyard said, 'What shall I do?' He had one left to send, a son, whom he loved. He sent him last of all, saying, 'I will send my son, whom I love; perhaps they will respect him.'

"But when the tenants saw the son, they talked the matter over. They said to each other, 'This is the heir. Come, let's kill him, and his inheritance will be ours.' So they took him and threw him out of the vineyard and killed him.

"Therefore, when the owner of the vineyard comes, what then will he do to those tenants?"

"He will bring those wretches to a wretched end," they replied, "and he will rent the vineyard to other tenants, who will give him his share of the crop at harvest time."

Jesus said to them, "He will come and kill those tenants and give the vineyard to others."

When the people heard this, they said, "May this never be!"

Jesus looked directly at them and asked, "Then what is the meaning of that which is written? Have you never read this scripture:

"'The stone the builders rejected
has become the capstone[i];
the Lord has done this,
and it is marvelous in our eyes'[j]?

i. Or *cornerstone*
j. Psalm 118:22-23

195

"Therefore I tell you that the kingdom of God will be taken away from you and given to a people who will produce its fruit. Everyone who falls on that stone will be broken to pieces, but he on whom it falls will be crushed."[k]

When the chief priests and the Pharisees heard Jesus' parables, they knew he was talking about them. Then they looked for a way to arrest him immediately. But they were afraid of the crowd because the people held that he was a prophet. So they left him and went away.

187. THE PARABLE OF THE WEDDING BANQUET
Matthew 22:1-14

Jesus spoke to them again in parables, saying: "The kingdom of heaven is like a king who prepared a wedding banquet for his son. He sent his servants to those who had been invited to the banquet to tell them to come, but they refused to come.

"Then he sent some more servants and said, 'Tell those who have been invited that I have prepared my dinner: My oxen and fattened cattle have been butchered, and everything is ready. Come to the wedding banquet.'

"But they paid no attention and went off—one to his field, another to his business. The rest seized his servants, mistreated them and killed them. The king was enraged. He sent his army and destroyed those murderers and burned their city.

"Then he said to his servants, 'The wedding banquet is ready, but those I invited did not deserve to come. Go to the street corners and invite to the banquet anyone you find.' So the servants went out into the streets and gathered all the people they could find, both good and bad, and the wedding hall was filled with guests.

"But when the king came in to see the guests, he noticed a man there who was not wearing wedding clothes. 'Friend,' he asked, 'how did you get in here without wedding clothes?' The man was speechless.

"Then the king told the attendants, 'Tie him hand and foot, and throw him outside, into the darkness, where there will be weeping and gnashing of teeth.'

"For many are invited, but few are chosen."

---

k. Some manuscripts do not have [this sentence in Matthew 21:44].

188. PAYING TAXES TO CAESAR
Matthew 22:15-22; Mark 12:13-17; Luke 20:20-26

Then the Pharisees went out and laid plans to trap him in his words. They hoped to catch Jesus in something he said so that they might hand him over to the power and authority of the governor. Keeping a close watch on him, they sent their disciples to him, along with the Herodians. So the spies, who pretended to be honest, questioned him: "Teacher, we know you are a man of integrity and that you teach the way of God in accordance with the truth. We know that you speak and teach what is right. You aren't swayed by men, because you pay no attention to who they are. You do not show partiality. Tell us then, what is your opinion? Is it right for us to pay taxes to Caesar or not? Should we pay or shouldn't we?"

But Jesus, knowing their evil intent, saw through their duplicity and said to them, "You hypocrites, why are you trying to trap me? Show me the coin used for paying the tax. Bring me a denarius and let me look at it." They brought him a denarius, and he asked them, "Whose portrait is this on it? And whose inscription?"

"Caesar's," they replied.

Then Jesus said to them, "Give to Caesar what is Caesar's and to God what is God's."

When they heard this, they were amazed at him. And astonished by his answer, they became silent. They were unable to trap him in what he had said there in public. So they left him and went away.

189. NO MARRIAGE AT THE RESURRECTION
Matthew 22:23-33; Mark 12:18-27; Luke 20:27-39

That same day some of the Sadducees, who say there is no resurrection, came to Jesus with a question. "Teacher," they said, "Moses wrote for us that if a man's brother dies and leaves a wife but no children, the man must marry the widow and have children for his brother. Now there were seven brothers among us. The first one married a woman and died childless. The second one married the widow, but he also died, leaving no child. It was the same with the third. In fact, none of the seven left any children. Last of all, the woman died too. Now then, at the resurrection,[1] whose wife will she be, since all seven of them were married to her?"

---

1. Some manuscripts [of Mark 12:23] *resurrection, when men rise from the dead,*

Jesus replied, "You are in error because you do not know the Scriptures or the power of God. The people of this age marry and are given in marriage. But those who are considered worthy of taking part in that age and in the resurrection from the dead will neither marry nor be given in marriage, and they can no longer die; for they will be like the angels in heaven. They are God's children, since they are children of the resurrection. But about the resurrection of the dead—have you not read in the book of Moses, in the account of the bush, how God said to him, 'I am the God of Abraham, the God of Isaac, and the God of Jacob'[m]? He is not the God of the dead, but of the living, for to him all are alive. You are badly mistaken!"

When the crowds heard this, they were astonished at his teaching. Some of the teachers of the law responded, "Well said, teacher!"

190. THE GREATEST COMMANDMENT
Matthew 22:34-40; Mark 12:28-34a

One of the teachers of the law came and heard them debating. *He noticed* that Jesus had given them a good answer. Hearing that Jesus had silenced the Sadducees, the Pharisees got together. One of them, *the* expert in the law, tested him with this question: "Teacher, of all the commandments, which is the most important?"

"The most important one," answered Jesus, "is this: 'Hear, O Israel, the Lord our God, the Lord is one.[n] Love the Lord your God with all your heart and with all your soul and with all your mind and with all your strength.'[o] This is the first and greatest commandment. And the second is like it: 'Love your neighbor as yourself.'[p] There is no commandment greater than these. All the Law and the Prophets hang on these two commandments."

"Well said, teacher," the man replied. "You are right in saying that God is one and there is no other but him. To love him with all your heart, with all your understanding and with all your strength, and to love your neighbor as yourself is more important than all burnt offerings and sacrifices."

---

m. Exodus 3:6
n. Or *the Lord our God is one Lord*
o. Deuteronomy 6:4-5
p. Leviticus 19:18

When Jesus saw that he had answered wisely, he said to him, "You are not far from the kingdom of God."

191. WHOSE SON IS THE CHRIST?
Matthew 22:41-46; Mark 12:34b-37; Luke 20:40-44

While the Pharisees were gathered together, Jesus asked them, "What do you think about the Christ? Whose son is he?"

"The son of David," they replied.

Then Jesus said to them, "How is it that the teachers of the law say that the Christ is the son of David? David, speaking by the Holy Spirit, calls him 'Lord' in the Book of Psalms. For David himself declares:

" 'The Lord said to my Lord:
"Sit at my right hand
until I make your enemies
a footstool for your feet." 'q

If David himself calls him 'Lord,' how then can he be his son?"

The large crowd listened to him with delight. No one could say a word in reply, and from that day on no one dared to ask him any more questions.

192. WARNING ABOUT TEACHERS OF THE LAW
Matthew 23:1-12; Mark 12:38-40; Luke 20:45-47

While all the people were listening, Jesus said to the crowds and to his disciples, "The teachers of the law and the Pharisees sit in Moses' seat. So you must obey them and do everything they tell you. But do not do what they do, for they do not practice what they preach. They tie up heavy loads and put them on men's shoulders, but they themselves are not willing to lift a finger to move them.

"Beware of the teachers of the law. Everything they do is done for men to see: They make their phylacteries[r] wide and the tassels on their garments long. They like to walk around in flowing robes and

---

q. Psalm 110:1
r. That is, boxes containing Scripture verses, worn on forehead and arm

love to be greeted in the marketplaces and to have men call them 'Rabbi.' They love the place of honor at banquets and the most important seats in the synagogues. They devour widows' houses and for a show make lengthy prayers. Such men will be punished most severely.

"But you are not to be called 'Rabbi,' for you have only one Master and you are all brothers. And do not call anyone on earth 'father,' for you have one Father, and he is in heaven. Nor are you to be called 'teacher,' for you have one Teacher, the Christ. The greatest among you will be your servant. For whoever exalts himself will be humbled, and whoever humbles himself will be exalted.

193. SEVEN WOES
Matthew 23:13-36

"Woe to you, teachers of the law and Pharisees, you hypocrites! You shut the kingdom of heaven in men's faces. You yourselves do not enter, nor will you let those enter who are trying to.[s]

"Woe to you, teachers of the law and Pharisees, you hypocrites! You travel over land and sea to win a single convert, and when he becomes one, you make him twice as much a son of hell as you are.

"Woe to you, blind guides! You say, 'If anyone swears by the temple, it means nothing; but if anyone swears by the gold of the temple, he is bound by his oath.' You blind fools! Which is greater: the gold, or the temple that makes the gold sacred? You also say, 'If anyone swears by the altar, it means nothing; but if anyone swears by the gift on it, he is bound by his oath.' You blind men! Which is greater: the gift, or the altar that makes the gift sacred? Therefore, he who swears by the altar swears by it and by everything on it. And he who swears by the temple swears by it and by the one who dwells in it. And he who swears by heaven swears by God's throne and by the one who sits on it.

"Woe to you, teachers of the law and Pharisees, you hypocrites! You give a tenth of your spices—mint, dill and cummin. But you have neglected the more important matters of the law—justice, mercy and faithfulness. You should have practiced the latter, without

---

s. Some manuscripts [of Matthew 23:14] *to. Woe to you, teachers of the law and Pharisees, you hypocrites! You devour widows' houses and for a show make lengthy prayers. Therefore you will be punished more severely.*

neglecting the former. You blind guides! You strain out a gnat but swallow a camel.

"Woe to you, teachers of the law and Pharisees, you hypocrites! You clean the outside of the cup and dish, but inside they are full of greed and self-indulgence. Blind Pharisee! First clean the inside of the cup and dish, and then the outside also will be clean.

"Woe to you, teachers of the law and Pharisees, you hypocrites! You are like whitewashed tombs, which look beautiful on the outside but on the inside are full of dead men's bones and everything unclean. In the same way, on the outside you appear to people as righteous but on the inside you are full of hypocrisy and wickedness.

"Woe to you, teachers of the law and Pharisees, you hypocrites! You build tombs for the prophets and decorate the graves of the righteous. And you say, 'If we had lived in the days of our forefathers, we would not have taken part with them in shedding the blood of the prophets.' So you testify against yourselves that you are the descendants of those who murdered the prophets. Fill up, then, the measure of the sin of your forefathers!

"You snakes! You brood of vipers! How will you escape being condemned to hell? Therefore I am sending you prophets and wise men and teachers. Some of them you will kill and crucify; others you will flog in your synagogues and pursue from town to town. And so upon you will come all the righteous blood that has been shed on earth, from the blood of righteous Abel to the blood of Zechariah son of Berekiah, whom you murdered between the temple and the altar. I tell you the truth, all this will come upon this generation.

194. LAMENT OVER JERUSALEM
Matthew 23:37-39

"O Jerusalem, Jerusalem, you who kill the prophets and stone those sent to you, how often I have longed to gather your children together, as a hen gathers her chicks under her wings, but you were not willing. Look, your house is left to you desolate. For I tell you, you will not see me again until you say, 'Blessed is he who comes in the name of the Lord.'"

---

t. Psalm 118:26

195. THE WIDOW'S OFFERING
Mark 12:41-44; Luke 21:1-4

Jesus sat down opposite the place where the offerings were put. He looked up and watched the crowd putting their money into the temple treasury. Many rich people threw in large amounts. But a poor widow came and put in two very small copper coins,[u] worth only a fraction of a penny.[v]

Calling his disciples to him, Jesus said, "I tell you the truth, this poor widow has put more into the treasury than all the others. All these people gave their gifts out of their wealth; but she out of her poverty put in everything—all she had to live on."

196. THE GREEKS SEEK JESUS
John 12:20-36

Now there were some Greeks among those who went up to worship at the Feast. They came to Philip, who was from Bethsaida in Galilee, with a request. "Sir," they said, "we would like to see Jesus." Philip went to tell Andrew; Andrew and Philip in turn told Jesus.

Jesus replied, "The hour has come for the Son of Man to be glorified. I tell you the truth, unless a kernel of wheat falls to the ground and dies, it remains only a single seed. But if it dies, it produces many seeds. The man who loves his life will lose it, while the man who hates his life in this world will keep it for eternal life. Whoever serves me must follow me; and where I am, my servant also will be. My Father will honor the one who serves me.

"Now my heart is troubled, and what shall I say? 'Father, save me from this hour'? No, it was for this very reason I came to this hour. Father, glorify your name!"

Then a voice came from heaven, "I have glorified it, and will glorify it again." The crowd that was there and heard it said it had thundered; others said an angel had spoken to him.

Jesus said, "This voice was for your benefit, not mine. Now is the time for judgment on this world; now the prince of this world will be driven out. But I, when I am lifted up from the earth, will draw all men to myself." He said this to show the kind of death he was going to die.

---

u. Greek *two lepta*
v. Greek *kodrantes*

The crowd spoke up, "We have heard from the Law that the Christ will remain forever, so how can you say, 'The Son of Man must be lifted up'? Who is this 'Son of Man'?"

Then Jesus told them, "You are going to have the light just a little while longer. Walk while you have the light, before darkness overtakes you. The man who walks in the dark does not know where he is going. Put your trust in the light while you have it, so that you may become sons of light." When he had finished speaking, Jesus left and hid himself from them.

197. THE JEWS CONTINUE IN THEIR UNBELIEF
John 12:37-50

Even after Jesus had done all these miraculous signs in their presence, they still would not believe in him. This was to fulfill the word of Isaiah the prophet:

"Lord, who has believed our message
and to whom has the arm of the Lord been revealed?"w

For this reason they could not believe, because, as Isaiah says elsewhere:

"He has blinded their eyes
and deadened their hearts,
so they can neither see with their eyes,
nor understand with their hearts,
nor turn—and I would heal them."x

Isaiah said this because he saw Jesus' glory and spoke about him.

Yet at the same time many even among the leaders believed in him. But because of the Pharisees they would not confess their faith for fear they would be put out of the synagogue; for they loved praise from men more than praise from God.

Then Jesus cried out, "When a man believes in me, he does not believe in me only, but in the one who sent me. When he looks at

---

w. Isaiah 53:1
x. Isaiah 6:10

me, he sees the one who sent me. I have come into the world as a light, so that no one who believes in me should stay in darkness.

"As for the person who hears my words but does not keep them, I do not judge him. For I did not come to judge the world, but to save it. There is a judge for the one who rejects me and does not accept my words; that very word which I spoke will condemn him at the last day. For I did not speak of my own accord, but the Father who sent me commanded me what to say and how to say it. I know that his command leads to eternal life. So whatever I say is just what the Father has told me to say."

THIRTEEN.
PREDICTING THE FUTURE

198. SIGNS OF THE END OF THE AGE
Matthew 24:1-35; Mark 13:1-31; Luke 21:5-33

Jesus was leaving the temple and walking away when his disciples came up to him to call his attention to its buildings. Some of his disciples were remarking about how the temple was adorned with beautiful stones and with gifts dedicated to God. One of his disciples said to him, "Look, Teacher! What massive stones! What magnificent buildings!"

"Do you see all these great buildings?" replied Jesus. "I tell you the truth, as for what you see here, the time will come when not one stone here will be left on another; every one of them will be thrown down."

As Jesus was sitting on the Mount of Olives opposite the temple, Peter, James, John and Andrew asked him privately, "Teacher, tell us, when will these things happen? And what will be the sign that they are all about to take place, and what will be the sign of your coming and of the end of the age?"

Jesus answered: "Watch out that no one deceives you. For many will come in my name, claiming, 'I am he, I am the Christ. The time is near,' and will deceive many. Do not follow them. You will hear of wars and revolutions and rumors of wars, but see to it that you are not alarmed. Do not be frightened. These things must happen first, but the end will not come right away. The end is still to come."

Then he said to them: "Nation will rise against nation, and kingdom against kingdom. There will be great earthquakes, famines and pestilences in various places, and fearful events and great signs from heaven. All these are the beginning of birth pains.

"You must be on your guard. Before all this, they will lay hands on you and persecute you. You will be handed over to the local councils and flogged in the synagogues. They will deliver you to prisons. On account of my name you will be brought before governors and kings. This will result in your being witnesses to them. Whenever you are arrested and brought to trial, make up your mind not to worry beforehand how you will defend yourselves. For I will give you words and wisdom that none of your adversaries will be able to resist or contradict. Just say whatever is given you at the time, for it is not you speaking, but the Holy Spirit.

"At that time many will turn away from the faith and will betray and hate each other, and many false prophets will appear and deceive many people. You will be betrayed even by parents, brothers, relatives and friends, and they will put some of you to death. Brother will betray brother to death, and a father his child. Children will rebel against their parents and have them put to death. All men will hate you because of me. Because of the increase of wickedness, the love of most will grow cold, but he who stands firm to the end will be saved; not a hair of your head will perish. By standing firm you will gain life. And this gospel of the kingdom will first be preached in the whole world as a testimony to all nations, and then the end will come.

"When you see Jerusalem being surrounded by armies, when you see 'the abomination that causes desolation,'[a] spoken of through the prophet Daniel, standing in the holy place where it[b] does not belong—let the reader understand—you will know that its desolation is near. Then let those who are in Judea flee to the mountains, let those in the city get out, and let those in the country not enter the city. Let no one on the roof of his house go down to take anything out of the house. Let no one in the field go back to get his cloak. For this is the time of punishment in fulfillment of all that has been written. How dreadful it will be in those days for pregnant women and nursing mothers! Pray that your flight will not take place in winter or on the Sabbath.

"For then there will be days of great distress in the land and wrath against this people, unequaled from the beginning, when God created the world, until now—and never to be equaled again. They will fall by the sword and will be taken as prisoners to all the nations. Jerusalem will be trampled on by the Gentiles until the times of the

---

a. Daniel 9:27; 11:31; 12:11
b. Or *he*

206

Gentiles are fulfilled. If the Lord had not cut short those days, no one would survive. But for the sake of the elect, whom he has chosen, those days will be shortened.

"At that time if anyone says to you, 'Look, here is the Christ!' or, 'Look, there he is!' do not believe it. For false Christs and false prophets will appear and perform great signs and miracles to deceive even the elect—if that were possible. So be on your guard. See, I have told you everything ahead of time.

"So if anyone tells you, 'There he is, out in the desert,' do not go out; or, 'Here he is, in the inner rooms,' do not believe it. For as lightning that comes from the east is visible even in the west, so will be the coming of the Son of Man. Wherever there is a carcass, there the vultures will gather.

"Immediately after the distress of those days, there will be signs in the sun, moon and stars:

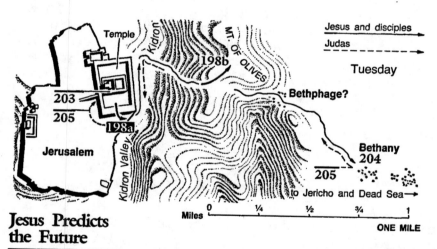

Jesus Predicts the Future

SECTION

TUESDAY

198a Leaving the temple, Jesus predicts its destruction
198b Sitting on the Mount of Olives, He teaches about the future
203 Religious authorities plot Jesus' death

TUESDAY OR POSSIBLY WEDNESDAY

204 Mary anoints Jesus at dinner in Bethany
205 Judas goes to the authorities to plot his betrayal

The upper western slope of Mt. Olivet provided a spectacular view of Jerusalem. The Kidron Valley's springtime green was dotted with ancient gray tombstones. Above rose the pride of Jerusalem—the temple—which occupied one-sixth of the city. Its buildings of massive white marble stones glistened in the sunlight.

'the sun will be darkened,
and the moon will not give its light;
the stars will fall from the sky,
and the heavenly bodies will be shaken.'[x]

On the earth, nations will be in anguish and perplexity at the roaring and tossing of the sea. Men will faint from terror, apprehensive of what is coming on the world.

"At that time the sign of the Son of Man will appear in the sky, and all the nations of the earth will mourn. They will see the Son of Man coming in the clouds of the sky, with power and great glory. When these things begin to take place, stand up and lift up your heads, because your redemption is drawing near. And he will send his angels with a loud trumpet call, and they will gather his elect from the four winds, from the ends of the earth, from one end of the heavens to the other."

He told them this parable: "Now learn this lesson from the fig tree and all the trees: As soon as its twigs get tender and its leaves sprout, you can see for yourselves and know that summer is near. Even so, when you see all these things happening, you know that it[d] is near; the kingdom of God is near, right at the door. I tell you the truth, this generation[e] will certainly not pass away until all these things have happened. Heaven and earth will pass away, but my words will never pass away.

199. THE DAY AND HOUR UNKNOWN
Matthew 24:36-51; Mark 13:32-37; Luke 21:34-36

"No one knows about that day or hour, not even the angels in heaven, nor the Son, but only the Father. As it was in the days of Noah, so it will be at the coming of the Son of Man. For in the days before the flood, people were eating and drinking, marrying and giving in marriage, up to the day Noah entered the ark; and they knew nothing about what would happen until the flood came and took them all away. That is how it will be at the coming of the Son

---

c. Isaiah 13:10; 34:4
d. Or *he*
e. Or *race*

of Man. Two men will be in the field; one will be taken and the other left. Two women will be grinding with a hand mill; one will be taken and the other left.

"Therefore keep watch, because you do not know on what day your Lord will come. But understand this: If the owner of the house had known at what time of night the thief was coming, he would have kept watch and would not have let his house be broken into. So you also must be ready, because the Son of Man will come at an hour when you do not expect him.

"Be on guard! Be alert[f]! You do not know when that time will come. It's like a man going away: He leaves his house and puts his servants in charge, each with his assigned task, and tells the one at the door to keep watch. Therefore keep watch because you do not know when the owner of the house will come back—whether in the evening, or at midnight, or when the rooster crows, or at dawn. If he comes suddenly, do not let him find you sleeping. What I say to you, I say to everyone: 'Watch!'

"Be careful, or your hearts will be weighed down with dissipation, drunkenness and the anxieties of life, and that day will close on you unexpectedly like a trap. For it will come upon all those who live on the face of the whole earth. Be always on the watch, and pray that you may be able to escape all that is about to happen, and that you may be able to stand before the Son of Man.

"Who then is the faithful and wise servant, whom the master has put in charge of the servants in his household to give them their food at the proper time? It will be good for that servant whose master finds him doing so when he returns. I tell you the truth, he will put him in charge of all his possessions. But suppose that servant is wicked and says to himself, 'My master is staying away a long time,' and he then begins to beat his fellow servants and to eat and drink with drunkards. The master of that servant will come on a day when he does not expect him and at an hour he is not aware of. He will cut him to pieces and assign him a place with the hypocrites, where there will be weeping and gnashing of teeth.

200. THE PARABLE OF THE TEN VIRGINS
Matthew 25:1-13

"At that time the kingdom of heaven will be like ten virgins who

---

f. Some manuscripts [of Mark 13:33] *alert and pray*

took their lamps and went out to meet the bridegroom. Five of them were foolish and five were wise. The foolish ones took their lamps but did not take any oil with them. The wise, however, took oil in jars along with their lamps. The bridegroom was a long time in coming, and they all became drowsy and fell asleep.

"At midnight the cry rang out: 'Here's the bridegroom! Come out to meet him!'

"Then all the virgins woke up and trimmed their lamps. The foolish ones said to the wise, 'Give us some of your oil; our lamps are going out.'

" 'No,' they replied, 'there may not be enough for both us and you. Instead, go to those who sell oil and buy some for yourselves.'

"But while they were on their way to buy the oil, the bridegroom arrived. The virgins who were ready went in with him to the wedding banquet. And the door was shut.

"Later the others also came. 'Sir! Sir!' they said. 'Open the door for us!'

"But he replied, 'I tell you the truth, I don't know you.'

"Therefore keep watch, because you do not know the day or the hour.

201. THE PARABLE OF THE TALENTS
Matthew 25:14-30

"Again, it will be like a man going on a journey, who called his servants and entrusted his property to them. To one he gave five talents[g] of money, to another two talents, and to another one talent, each according to his ability. Then he went on his journey. The man who had received the five talents went at once and put his money to work and gained five more. So also, the one with the two talents gained two more. But the man who had received the one talent went off, dug a hole in the ground and hid his master's money.

"After a long time the master of those servants returned and settled accounts with them. The man who had received the five talents brought the other five. 'Master,' he said, 'you entrusted me with five talents. See, I have gained five more.'

"His master replied, 'Well done, good and faithful servant! You

---

g. A talent was worth more than a thousand dollars.

have been faithful with a few things; I will put you in charge of many things. Come and share your master's happiness!'

"The man with the two talents also came. 'Master,' he said, 'you entrusted me with two talents; see, I have gained two more.'

"His master replied, 'Well done, good and faithful servant! You have been faithful with a few things; I will put you in charge of many things. Come and share your master's happiness!'

"Then the man who had received the one talent came. 'Master,' he said, 'I knew that you are a hard man, harvesting where you have not sown and gathering where you have not scattered seed. So I was afraid and went out and hid your talent in the ground. See, here is what belongs to you.'

"His master replied, 'You wicked, lazy servant! So you knew that I harvest where I have not sown and gather where I have not scattered seed? Well then, you should have put my money on deposit with the bankers, so that when I returned I would have received it back with interest.

" 'Take the talent from him and give it to the one who has the ten talents. For everyone who has will be given more, and he will have an abundance. Whoever does not have, even what he has will be taken from him. And throw that worthless servant outside, into the darkness, where there will be weeping and gnashing of teeth.'

202. THE SHEEP AND THE GOATS
Matthew 25:31-46; Luke 21:37-38

"When the Son of Man comes in his glory, and all the angels with him, he will sit on his throne in heavenly glory. All the nations will be gathered before him, and he will separate the people one from another as a shepherd separates the sheep from the goats. He will put the sheep on his right and the goats on his left.

"Then the King will say to those on his right, 'Come, you who are blessed by my Father; take your inheritance, the kingdom prepared for you since the creation of the world. For I was hungry and you gave me something to eat, I was thirsty and you gave me something to drink, I was a stranger and you invited me in, I needed clothes and you clothed me, I was sick and you looked after me, I was in prison and you came to visit me.'

"Then the righteous will answer him, 'Lord, when did we see you hungry and feed you, or thirsty and give you something to drink? When did we see you a stranger and invite you in, or needing clothes and clothe you? When did we see you sick or in prison and go to visit you?'

"The King will reply, 'I tell you the truth, whatever you did for one of the least of these brothers of mine, you did for me.'

"Then he will say to those on his left, 'Depart from me, you who are cursed, into the eternal fire prepared for the devil and his angels. For I was hungry and you gave me nothing to eat, I was thirsty and you gave me nothing to drink, I was a stranger and you did not invite me in, I needed clothes and you did not clothe me, I was sick and in prison and you did not look after me.'

"They also will answer, 'Lord, when did we see you hungry or thirsty or a stranger or needing clothes or sick or in prison, and did not help you?'

"He will reply, 'I tell you the truth, whatever you did not do for one of the least of these, you did not do for me.'

"Then they will go away to eternal punishment, but the righteous to eternal life."

Each day Jesus was teaching at the temple, and each evening he went out to spend the night on the hill called the Mount of Olives, and all the people came early in the morning to hear him at the temple.

203. THE PLOT AGAINST JESUS
Matthew 26:1-5; Mark 14:1-2; Luke 22:1-2

When Jesus had finished saying all these things, he said to his disciples, "As you know, the Passover is two days away—and the Son of Man will be handed over to be crucified."

Now the Feast of Unleavened Bread, called the Passover, was approaching, and the chief priests, the teachers of the law and the elders of the people assembled in the palace of the high priest, whose name was Caiaphas. Looking for some way to get rid of Jesus, they plotted to arrest *him* in some sly way and kill him. "But not during the Feast," they said, "or the people may riot," for they were afraid of the people.

204. JESUS ANOINTED AT BETHANY
Matthew 26:6-13; Mark 14:3-9; John 12:2-8

While he was in Bethany in the home of a man known as Simon the Leper, a dinner was given in Jesus' honor. Martha served, while Lazarus was among those reclining at the table with him. Then Mary took an alabaster jar of very expensive perfume, about a pint[h] of pure nard. She broke the jar and poured the perfume on *Jesus'* head as he was reclining at the table.[1] She poured it on Jesus' feet and wiped his feet with her hair. And the house was filled with the fragrance of the perfume.

When some of those disciples present saw this, they were indignant. "Why this waste?" they asked one another. And they rebuked her harshly. One of his disciples, Judas Iscariot, who was later to betray him, objected, "Why wasn't this perfume sold and the money given to the poor? It could have been sold for more than a year's wages.[i]" He did not say this because he cared about the poor but because he was a thief; as keeper of the money bag, he used to help himself to what was put into it.

Aware of this, Jesus said to them, "Why are you bothering this woman? Leave her alone. She has done a beautiful thing to me. It was intended that she should save this perfume for the day of my burial. You will always have the poor among you, and you can help them any time you want. But you will not always have me. She did what she could. When she poured this perfume on my body, she did it to prepare me for burial. I tell you the truth, wherever this gospel is preached throughout the world, what she has done will also be told, in memory of her."

205. JUDAS AGREES TO BETRAY JESUS
Matthew 26:14-16; Mark 14:10-11; Luke 22:3-6

Then Satan entered Judas, called Iscariot, one of the Twelve. And Judas went to the chief priests and the officers of the temple guard

---

h. Greek *a litra* (probably about 0.5 liter)
1. See p. 335: Do the Gospels account for one, two, or three anointings of Jesus while he was alive (Matthew 26:7; Mark 14:3; Luke 7:38; John 12:3)? If there were two anointings, was the one at Bethany two days before Passover (Matthew 26:2; Mark 14:1) or six days before (John 12:1)?
i. Greek *three hundred denarii*

and discussed with them how he might betray Jesus to them. They were delighted to hear this. Judas asked, "What are you willing to give me if I hand him over to you?" So they agreed to give him money and counted out for him thirty silver coins. He consented. So from then on Judas watched for an opportunity to hand Jesus over to them when no crowd was present.

FOURTEEN.
LAST SUPPER AND GETHSEMANE

206. THE PASSOVER MEAL IS PREPARED
Matthew 26:17-19; Mark 14:12-16; Luke 22:7-13

Then came the first day of the Feast of Unleavened Bread, when it was customary to sacrifice the Passover Lamb. Jesus' disciples came to him and asked, "Where do you want us to go and make preparations for you to eat the Passover?"

Jesus sent Peter and John, telling them, "Go into the city, and a man carrying a jar of water will meet you. Follow him to the house that he enters, and say to the owner of the house, 'The Teacher says: My appointed time is near. I am going to celebrate the Passover with my disciples at your house. Where is my guest room, where I may eat the Passover with my disciples?' He will show you a large upper room, all furnished and ready. Make preparations for us there."

So the disciples did as Jesus had directed them. They left, went into the city and found things just as Jesus had told them. So they prepared the Passover.

207. JESUS WASHES HIS DISCIPLES' FEET
Mark 14:17; John 13:1-20

When evening came, Jesus arrived with the Twelve. It was just before the Passover Feast. Jesus knew that the time had come for him to leave this world and go to the Father. Having loved his own who were in the world, he now showed them the full extent of his love.[a]

---

a. Or *he loved them to the last*

215

The evening meal was being served, and the devil had already prompted Judas Iscariot, son of Simon, to betray Jesus. Jesus knew that the Father had put all things under his power, and that he had come from God and was returning to God; so he got up from the meal, took off his outer clothing, and wrapped a towel around his waist. After that, he poured water into a basin and began to wash his disciples' feet, drying them with the towel that was wrapped around him.

He came to Simon Peter, who said to him, "Lord, are you going to wash my feet?"

Jesus replied, "You do not realize now what I am doing, but later you will understand."

"No," said Peter, "you shall never wash my feet."

Jesus answered, "Unless I wash you, you have no part with me."

"Then, Lord," Simon Peter replied, "not just my feet but my hands and my head as well!"

Jesus answered, "A person who has had a bath needs only to wash his feet; his whole body is clean. And you are clean, though not every one of you." For he knew who was going to betray him, and that was why he said not every one was clean.

When he had finished washing their feet, he put on his clothes and returned to his place. "Do you understand what I have done for you?" he asked them. "You call me 'Teacher' and 'Lord,' and rightly so, for that is what I am. Now that I, your Lord and Teacher, have washed your feet, you also should wash one another's feet. I have set you an example that you should do as I have done for you. I tell you the truth, no servant is greater than his master, nor is a messenger greater than the one who sent him. Now that you know these things, you will be blessed if you do them.

"I am not referring to all of you; I know those I have chosen. But this is to fulfill the scripture: 'He who shares my bread has lifted up his heel against me.'[b]

"I am telling you now before it happens, so that when it does happen you will believe that I am He. I tell you the truth, whoever accepts anyone I send accepts me; and whoever accepts me accepts the one who sent me."

---

b. Psalm 41:9

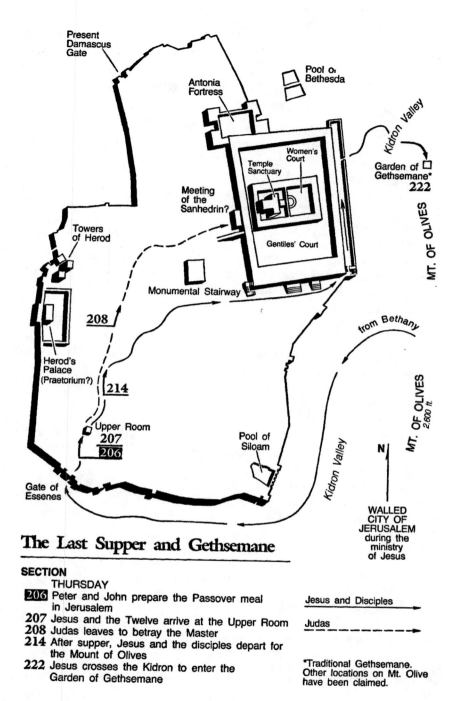

The Last Supper and Gethsemane

SECTION

    THURSDAY

206 Peter and John prepare the Passover meal in Jerusalem

207 Jesus and the Twelve arrive at the Upper Room

208 Judas leaves to betray the Master

214 After supper, Jesus and the disciples depart for the Mount of Olives

222 Jesus crosses the Kidron to enter the Garden of Gethsemane

Jesus and Disciples ⟶

Judas - - - - ⟶

*Traditional Gethsemane. Other locations on Mt. Olive have been claimed.

Miles 0   ⅓   ⅔

217

208. JESUS PREDICTS HIS BETRAYAL
Matthew 26:20-25; Mark 14:18-21; Luke 22:14-16, 21-23; John 13:21-30

When the hour came, Jesus and his apostles reclined at the table. And he said to them, "I have eagerly desired to eat this Passover with you before I suffer.[1] For I tell you, I will not eat it again until it finds fulfillment in the kingdom of God."

After he had said this, while they were eating,[2] Jesus was troubled in spirit and testified, "I tell you the truth, one of you is going to betray me—one who is eating with me, whose hand is with mine on the table."

His disciples stared at one another, at a loss to know which of them he meant. They were very sad. They began to question among themselves which of them it might be who would do this. And one by one they said to him, "Surely not I, Lord?"

"It is one of the Twelve," Jesus replied, "one who dips bread into the bowl with me. The Son of Man will go just as it is written about him. But woe to that man who betrays the Son of Man! It would be better for him if he had not been born."

Then Judas, the one who would betray him, said, "Surely not I, Rabbi?"

Jesus answered, "Yes, it is you."[c]

One of them, the disciple whom Jesus loved, was reclining next to him. Simon Peter motioned to this disciple and said, "Ask him which one he means."

Leaning back against Jesus, he asked him, "Lord, who is it?"

Jesus answered, "It is the one to whom I will give this piece of bread when I have dipped it in the dish." Then, dipping the piece of bread, he gave it to Judas Iscariot, son of Simon. As soon as Judas took the bread, Satan entered into him.

"What you are about to do, do quickly," Jesus told him, but no one at the meal understood why Jesus said this to him.[3] Since Judas had charge of the money, some thought Jesus was telling him to buy

---

1. See p. 339: Did Jesus and his apostles eat the Passover meal (Matthew 26:17-26; Mark 14:12-18; Luke 22:8-19) or not (Luke 22:15-16)?
2. See p. 340: Did Jesus and his apostles eat the Passover meal on the Day of Passover (Matthew 26:17; Mark 14:12; Luke 22:7) or the day before (John 18:28; 19:14)?
c. Or *"You yourself have said it"*
3. See p. 343: When Judas left the Upper Room, did the disciples understand that he would betray Jesus (Matthew 26:20, 25) or not (John 13:27-28)?

what was needed for the Feast, or to give something to the poor. As soon as Judas had taken the bread, he went out.[4] And it was night.

209. THE LAST SUPPER
Matthew 26:26-29; Mark 14:22-25; Luke 22:17-20; 1 Corinthians 11:24-25

After taking the cup, he gave thanks and said, "Take this and divide it among you. For I tell you I will not drink again of the fruit of the vine until the kingdom of God comes."

While they were eating, Jesus took bread, gave thanks and broke it, and gave it to his disciples, saying, "Take and eat; this is my body, which is given for you; do this in remembrance of me." ·

In the same way, after the supper he took the cup, gave thanks and offered it to them, saying, "Drink from it, all of you. This cup is the new covenant in my blood,[5] which is poured out for you, *and* for many, for the forgiveness of sins. Do this, whenever you drink it, in remembrance of me." And they all drank from it. "I tell you the truth, I will not drink again of the fruit of the vine from now on until that day when I drink it anew with you in my Father's kingdom."

210. THE DISCIPLES DISPUTE WHO IS GREATEST
Luke 22:24-30

A dispute arose among them as to which of them was considered to be greatest.[6] Jesus said to them, "The kings of the Gentiles lord it over them; and those who exercise authority over them call themselves Benefactors. But you are not to be like that. Instead, the greatest among you should be like the youngest, and the one who rules like the one who serves. For who is greater, the one who is at the table or the one who serves? Is it not the one who is at the table? But I am among you as one who serves. You are those who have

---

4. See p. 348: Was Judas present during the institution of the Communion service (Luke 22:17-22; John 13:26-30)?
5. See p. 349: When Jesus instituted the Communion service, are his exact words recorded in Matthew 26:26-28 and Mark 14:22-24 or in Luke 22:19-20 and 1 Corinthians 11:24-25?
6. See p. 349: Did the disciples' dispute over which of them was the greatest emerge before they ate the Passover or afterward (Luke 22:24)?

stood by me in my trials. And I confer on you a kingdom, just as my Father conferred one on me, so that you may eat and drink at my table in my kingdom and sit on thrones, judging the twelve tribes of Israel."

211. JESUS PREDICTS PETER'S DENIAL
Matthew 26:31-35; Mark 14:27-31; Luke 22:31-38; John 13:31-38

When *Judas* was gone, Jesus said, "Now is the Son of Man glorified and God is glorified in him. If God is glorified in him,[d] God will glorify the Son in himself, and will glorify him at once.

"My children, I will be with you only a little longer. You will look for me, and just as I told the Jews, so I tell you now: Where I am going, you cannot come.

"A new command I give you: Love one another. As I have loved you, so you must love one another. By this all men will know that you are my disciples, if you love one another."

Simon Peter asked him, "Lord, where are you going?"

Jesus replied, "Where I am going, you cannot follow now, but you will follow later."

Peter asked, "Lord, why can't I follow you now? I will lay down my life for you."

Then Jesus told them, "This very night you will all fall away on account of me, for it is written:

" 'I will strike the shepherd,
and the sheep of the flock will be scattered.'[e]

But after I have risen, I will go ahead of you into Galilee."

Peter declared, "Even if all fall away on account of you, I never will."

"Simon, Simon, Satan has asked to sift you[f] as wheat. But I have prayed for you, Simon, that your faith may not fail. And when you have turned back, strengthen your brothers."

But he replied, "Lord, I am ready to go with you to prison and to death."

---

d. Many early manuscripts [of John 13:32] do not have *If God is glorified in him.*
e. Zechariah 13:7
f. The Greek is plural.

Then Jesus answered, "Will you really lay down your life for me? I tell you the truth, Peter, today—yes, this very night—before the rooster crows twice[g] you yourself will disown me three times."[7]

But Peter insisted emphatically, "Even if I have to die with you, I will never disown you." And all the other disciples said the same.

Then Jesus asked them, "When I sent you without purse, bag or sandals, did you lack anything?"

"Nothing," they answered.

He said to them, "But now if you have a purse, take it, and also a bag; and if you don't have a sword, sell your cloak and buy one. It is written: 'And he was numbered with the transgressors'[h]; and I tell you that this must be fulfilled in me. Yes, what is written about me is reaching its fulfillment."

The disciples said, "See, Lord, here are two swords."

"That is enough," he replied.

212. JESUS COMFORTS HIS DISCIPLES
John 14:1-4

"Do not let your hearts be troubled. Trust in God[i]; trust also in me. In my Father's house are many rooms; if it were not so, I would have told you. I am going there to prepare a place for you. And if I go and prepare a place for you, I will come back and take you to be with me that you also may be where I am. You know the way to the place where I am going."

213. JESUS THE WAY TO THE FATHER
John 14:5-14

Thomas said to him, "Lord, we don't know where you are going, so how can we know the way?"

Jesus answered, "I am the way and the truth and the life. No one comes to the Father except through me. If you really knew me, you

---

g. Some early manuscripts [of Mark 14:30] do not have *twice*.
7. See p. 350: Did Jesus predict Peter's denials before they all left the Upper Room (Luke 22:34-39; John 13:38; 14:31) or afterward (Matthew 26:30-35; Mark 14:26-31)?
h. Isaiah 53:12
i. Or *You trust in God*

would know[j] my Father as well. From now on, you do know him and have seen him."

Philip said, "Lord, show us the Father and that will be enough for us."

Jesus answered: "Don't you know me, Philip, even after I have been among you such a long time? Anyone who has seen me has seen the Father. How can you say, 'Show us the Father'? Don't you believe that I am in the Father, and that the Father is in me? The words I say to you are not just my own. Rather, it is the Father, living in me, who is doing his work. Believe me when I say that I am in the Father and the Father is in me; or at least believe on the evidence of the miracles themselves. I tell you the truth, anyone who has faith in me will do what I have been doing. He will do even greater things than these, because I am going to the Father. And I will do whatever you ask in my name, so that the Son may bring glory to the Father. You may ask me for anything in my name, and I will do it.

214. JESUS PROMISES THE HOLY SPIRIT
Matthew 26:30; Mark 14:26; John 14:15-31

"If you love me, you will obey what I command. And I will ask the Father, and he will give you another Counselor to be with you forever—the Spirit of truth. The world cannot accept him, because it neither sees him nor knows him. But you know him, for he lives with you and will be[k] in you. I will not leave you as orphans; I will come to you. Before long, the world will not see me anymore, but you will see me. Because I live, you also will live. On that day you will realize that I am in my Father, and you are in me, and I am in you. Whoever has my commands and obeys them, he is the one who loves me. He who loves me will be loved by my Father, and I too will love him and show myself to him."

Then Judas (not Judas Iscariot) said, "But, Lord, why do you intend to show yourself to us and not to the world?"

Jesus replied, "If anyone loves me, he will obey my teaching. My Father will love him, and we will come to him and make our home with him. He who does not love me will not obey my teaching.

---

j. Some early manuscripts [of John 14:7] *If you really have known me, you will know*
k. Some early manuscripts [of John 14:17] *and is*

These words you hear are not my own; they belong to the Father who sent me.

"All this I have spoken while still with you. But the Counselor, the Holy Spirit, whom the Father will send in my name, will teach you all things and will remind you of everything I have said to you. Peace I leave with you; my peace I give you. I do not give to you as the world gives. Do not let your hearts be troubled and do not be afraid.

"You heard me say, 'I am going away and I am coming back to you.' If you loved me, you would be glad that I am going to the Father, for the Father is greater than I. I have told you now before it happens, so that when it does happen you will believe. I will not speak with you much longer, for the prince of this world is coming. He has no hold on me, but the world must learn that I love the Father and that I do exactly what my Father has commanded me.

"Come now; let us leave."

When they had sung a hymn, they went out to the Mount of Olives.[8]

215. THE VINE AND THE BRANCHES
John 15:1-17

"I am the true vine, and my Father is the gardener. He cuts off every branch in me that bears no fruit, while every branch that does bear fruit he prunes[1] so that it will be even more fruitful. You are already clean because of the word I have spoken to you. Remain in me, and I will remain in you. No branch can bear fruit by itself; it must remain in the vine. Neither can you bear fruit unless you remain in me.

"I am the vine; you are the branches. If a man remains in me and I in him, he will bear much fruit; apart from me you can do nothing. If anyone does not remain in me, he is like a branch that is thrown away and withers; such branches are picked up, thrown into the fire and burned. If you remain in me and my words remain in you, ask whatever you wish, and it will be given you. This is to my Father's glory, that you bear much fruit, showing yourselves to be my disciples.

---

8. See p. 351: Did Jesus and his apostles leave the Upper Room before his words in John 14–17 or afterward (Matthew 26:30; Mark 14:26; Luke 22:39)? What was the order of events surrounding their departure?
1. The Greek for *prunes* also means *cleans.*

"As the Father has loved me, so have I loved you. Now remain in my love. If you obey my commands, you will remain in my love, just as I have obeyed my Father's commands and remain in his love. I have told you this so that my joy may be in you and that your joy may be complete. My command is this: Love each other as I have loved you. Greater love has no one than this, that he lay down his life for his friends. You are my friends if you do what I command. I no longer call you servants, because a servant does not know his master's business. Instead, I have called you friends, for everything that I learned from my Father I have made known to you. You did not choose me, but I chose you and appointed you to go and bear fruit—fruit that will last. Then the Father will give you whatever you ask in my name. This is my command: Love each other.

216. THE WORLD HATES THE DISCIPLES
John 15:18–16:4

"If the world hates you, keep in mind that it hated me first. If you belonged to the world, it would love you as its own. As it is, you do not belong to the world, but I have chosen you out of the world. That is why the world hates you. Remember the words I spoke to you: 'No servant is greater than his master.'[m] If they persecuted me, they will persecute you also. If they obeyed my teaching, they will obey yours also. They will treat you this way because of my name, for they do not know the One who sent me. If I had not come and spoken to them, they would not be guilty of sin. Now, however, they have no excuse for their sin. He who hates me hates my Father as well. If I had not done among them what no one else did, they would not be guilty of sin. But now they have seen these miracles, and yet they have hated both me and my Father. But this is to fulfill what is written in their Law: 'They hated me without reason.'[n]

"When the Counselor comes, whom I will send to you from the Father, the Spirit of truth who goes out from the Father, he will testify about me. And you also must testify, for you have been with me from the beginning.

"All this I have told you so that you will not go astray. They will put you out of the synagogue; in fact, a time is coming when anyone

m. John 13:16
n. Psalms 35:19; 69:4

who kills you will think he is offering a service to God. They will do such things because they have not known the Father or me. I have told you this, so that when the time comes you will remember that I warned you. I did not tell you this at first because I was with you.

217. THE WORK OF THE HOLY SPIRIT
John 16:5-16

"Now I am going to him who sent me, yet none of you asks me, 'Where are you going?' Because I have said these things, you are filled with grief. But I tell you the truth: It is for your good that I am going away. Unless I go away, the Counselor will not come to you; but if I go, I will send him to you. When he comes, he will convict the world of guilt° in regard to sin and righteousness and judgment: in regard to sin, because men do not believe in me; in regard to righteousness, because I am going to the Father, where you can see me no longer; and in regard to judgment, because the prince of this world now stands condemned.

"I have much more to say to you, more than you can now bear. But when he, the Spirit of truth, comes, he will guide you into all truth. He will not speak on his own; he will speak only what he hears, and he will tell you what is yet to come. He will bring glory to me by taking from what is mine and making it known to you. All that belongs to the Father is mine. That is why I said the Spirit will take from what is mine and make it known to you.

"In a little while you will see me no more, and then after a little while you will see me."

218. THE DISCIPLES' GRIEF WILL TURN TO JOY
John 16:17-33

Some of his disciples said to one another, "What does he mean by saying, 'In a little while you will see me no more, and then after a little while you will see me,' and 'Because I am going to the Father'?" They kept asking, "What does he mean by 'a little while'? We don't understand what he is saying."

---

o. Or *will expose the guilt of the world*

Jesus saw that they wanted to ask him about this, so he said to them, "Are you asking one another what I meant when I said, 'In a little while you will see me no more, and then after a little while you will see me'? I tell you the truth, you will weep and mourn while the world rejoices. You will grieve, but your grief will turn to joy. A woman giving birth to a child has pain because her time has come; but when her baby is born she forgets the anguish because of her joy that a child is born into the world. So with you: Now is your time of grief, but I will see you again and you will rejoice, and no one will take away your joy. In that day you will no longer ask me anything. I tell you the truth, my Father will give you whatever you ask in my name. Until now you have not asked for anything in my name. Ask and you will receive, and your joy will be complete.

"Though I have been speaking figuratively, a time is coming when I will no longer use this kind of language but will tell you plainly about my Father. In that day you will ask in my name. I am not saying that I will ask the Father on your behalf. No, the Father himself loves you because you have loved me and have believed that I came from God. I came from the Father and entered the world; now I am leaving the world and going back to the Father."

Then Jesus' disciples said, "Now you are speaking clearly and without figures of speech. Now we can see that you know all things and that you do not even need to have anyone ask you questions. This makes us believe that you came from God."

"You believe at last!"p Jesus answered. "But a time is coming, and has come, when you will be scattered, each to his own home. You will leave me all alone. Yet I am not alone, for my Father is with me.

"I have told you these things, so that in me you may have peace. In this world you will have trouble. But take heart! I have overcome the world."

219. JESUS PRAYS FOR HIMSELF
John 17:1-5

After Jesus said this, he looked toward heaven and prayed:

"Father, the time has come. Glorify your Son, that your Son may glorify you. For you granted him authority over all people that he

---

p. Or *"Do you now believe?"*

might give eternal life to all those you have given him. Now this is eternal life: that they may know you, the only true God, and Jesus Christ, whom you have sent. I have brought you glory on earth by completing the work you gave me to do. And now, Father, glorify me in your presence with the glory I had with you before the world began.

220. JESUS PRAYS FOR HIS DISCIPLES
John 17:6-19

"I have revealed you[q] to those whom you gave me out of the world. They were yours; you gave them to me and they have obeyed your word. Now they know that everything you have given me comes from you. For I gave them the words you gave me and they accepted them. They knew with certainty that I came from you, and they believed that you sent me. I pray for them. I am not praying for the world, but for those you have given me, for they are yours. All I have is yours, and all you have is mine. And glory has come to me through them. I will remain in the world no longer, but they are still in the world, and I am coming to you. Holy Father, protect them by the power of your name—the name you gave me—so that they may be one as we are one. While I was with them, I protected them and kept them safe by that name you gave me. None has been lost except the one doomed to destruction so that Scripture would be fulfilled.

"I am coming to you now, but I say these things while I am still in the world, so that they may have the full measure of my joy within them. I have given them your word and the world has hated them, for they are not of the world any more than I am of the world. My prayer is not that you take them out of the world but that you protect them from the evil one. They are not of the world, even as I am not of it. Sanctify[r] them by the truth; your word is truth. As you sent me into the world, I have sent them into the world. For them I sanctify[r] myself, that they too may be truly sanctified.

---

q. Greek *your name*
r. Greek *hagiazo* (*set apart for sacred use* or *make holy*)

221. JESUS PRAYS FOR ALL BELIEVERS
John 17:20-26

"My prayer is not for them alone. I pray also for those who will believe in me through their message, that all of them may be one, Father, just as you are in me and I am in you. May they also be in us so that the world may believe that you have sent me. I have given them the glory that you gave me, that they may be one as we are one: I in them and you in me. May they be brought to complete unity to let the world know that you sent me and have loved them even as you have loved me.

"Father, I want those you have given me to be with me where I am, and to see my glory, the glory you have given me because you loved me before the creation of the world.

"Righteous Father, though the world does not know you, I know you, and they know that you have sent me. I have made you[s] known to them, and will continue to make you known in order that the love you have for me may be in them and that I myself may be in them."

222. GETHSEMANE
Matthew 26:36-46; Mark 14:32-42; Luke 22:39-46; John 18:1

When he had finished praying, Jesus went out as usual to the Mount of Olives, and his disciples followed him. They crossed the Kidron Valley. On the other side there was an olive grove called Gethsemane, and he and his disciples went into it.

On reaching the place, he said to his disciples, "Sit here while I go over there and pray. Pray that you will not fall into temptation." He took Peter, James and John along with him, and he began to be deeply distressed and troubled. Then he said to them, "My soul is overwhelmed with sorrow to the point of death. Stay here and keep watch with me."

Going a little farther, he withdrew about a stone's throw beyond them, knelt down, fell with his face to the ground and prayed that if possible the hour might pass from him. "Abba[t], My Father," he said, "everything is possible for you. If you are willing, take this cup from me. Yet not what I will, but what you will."[9]

---

s. Greek *your name*
t. Aramaic for *Father*
9. See p. 352: What were the exact words that Jesus prayed in Gethsemane (Matthew 26:39-44; Mark 14:36-39; Luke 22:42)?

Then he returned to his disciples and found them sleeping. "Simon," he said to Peter, "are you asleep? Could you men not keep watch with me for one hour? Watch and pray so that you will not fall into temptation. The spirit is willing, but the body is weak."

He went away a second time and prayed, "My Father, if it is not possible for this cup to be taken away unless I drink it, may your will be done." An angel from heaven appeared to him and strengthened him. And being in anguish, he prayed more earnestly, and his sweat was like drops of blood falling to the ground.[u]

When he rose from prayer and went back to the disciples, he again found them sleeping. Exhausted from sorrow, their eyes were heavy. "Why are you sleeping?" he asked them. They did not know what to say to him. "Get up and pray so that you will not fall into temptation." So he left them and went away once more and prayed the third time, saying the same thing.

Returning the third time, he said to them, "Are you still sleeping and resting? Enough! The hour has come. Look, the Son of Man is betrayed into the hands of sinners. Rise! Let us go! Here comes my betrayer!"

---

u. Some early manuscripts do not have [the previous two sentences in Luke 22:43-44].

FIFTEEN.
TRIALS, DEATH, AND BURIAL

223. JESUS ARRESTED
Matthew 26:47-56; Mark 14:43-52; Luke 22:47-54a; John 18:2-11

While *Jesus* was still speaking, a crowd came up. The man who was called Judas, one of the Twelve, was leading them. Now Judas, who betrayed him, knew the place, because Jesus had often met there with his disciples. So Judas came to the grove, guiding a detachment of soldiers, and some officials, sent from the chief priests, Pharisees, teachers of the law, and elders of the people. Carrying torches and lanterns, a large crowd armed with swords and clubs was with him.

Jesus, knowing all that was going to happen to him, went out and asked them, "Who is it you want?"

"Jesus of Nazareth," they replied.

"I am he," Jesus said. (And Judas the traitor was standing there with them.) When Jesus said, "I am he," they drew back and fell to the ground.

Again he asked them, "Who is it you want?"

And they said, "Jesus of Nazareth."

"I told you that I am he," Jesus answered. "If you are looking for me, then let these men go." This happened so that the words he had spoken would be fulfilled: "I have not lost one of those you gave me."[a]

Now the betrayer had arranged a signal with them: "The one I kiss is the man; arrest him and lead him away under guard." He approached Jesus at once to kiss him, but Jesus asked him, "Judas, are you betraying the Son of Man with a kiss?" Judas said, "Greetings, Rabbi!" and kissed him.

---

a. John 6:39

Jesus replied, "Friend, do what you came for."[b]

Then the men stepped forward, seized Jesus and arrested him. When Jesus' followers saw what was going to happen, they said, "Lord, should we strike with our swords?" Then Simon Peter, standing near, reached for his sword, drew it out and struck the servant of the high priest, cutting off his right ear. (The servant's name was Malchus.)

But Jesus commanded Peter, "No more of this! Put your sword back in its place, for all who draw the sword will die by the sword. Do you think I cannot call on my Father, and he will at once put at my disposal more than twelve legions of angels? But how then would the Scriptures be fulfilled that say it must happen in this way? Shall I not drink the cup the Father has given me?" And he touched the man's ear and healed him.

At that time Jesus said to the chief priests, the officers of the temple guard, and the elders, who had come for him, "Am I leading a rebellion, that you have come out with swords and clubs to capture me? Every day I was with you; I sat in the temple courts teaching, and you did not lay a hand on me *to* arrest me. But this has all taken place that the writings of the prophets might be fulfilled. This is your hour—when darkness reigns." Then all the disciples deserted him and fled.

A young man,[1] wearing nothing but a linen garment, was following Jesus. When they seized him, he fled naked, leaving his garment behind.

224. JESUS TAKEN TO ANNAS, THEN TO CAIAPHAS
Matthew 26:57; Mark 14:53; Luke 22:54b; John 18:12-14

Then the detachment of soldiers with its commander and the Jewish officials bound him and led him away. They brought him first to Annas, who was the father-in-law of Caiaphas, the high priest that year. Caiaphas was the one who had advised the Jews that it would be good if one man died for the people.

Then those who had arrested Jesus took him into the house of the

b. Or "Friend, why have you come?"
1. See p. 354: Who was the young man who fled Gethsemane naked, leaving his linen garment behind (Mark 14:51-52)?

high priest, Caiaphas, where all the chief priests, elders and teachers of the law had assembled.

225. PETER'S FIRST DENIAL
Matthew 26:58, 69-71a; Mark 14:54, 66-68;
Luke 22:54c-57; John 18:15-18

Simon Peter and another disciple[2] were following Jesus at a distance, right up to the courtyard of the high priest.[3] Because this disciple was known to the high priest, he went with Jesus into the high priest's courtyard, but Peter had to wait outside at the door. The other disciple, who was known to the high priest, came back, spoke to the girl on duty there and brought Peter into the courtyard.

It was cold, and the servants and officials stood around a fire they had kindled in the middle of the courtyard to keep warm. Peter entered and was standing with them, warming himself. When they sat down together, Peter sat down with the guards to see the outcome.

While Peter was sitting out in the courtyard, one of the servant girls of the high priest, the girl at the door, came by. When she saw Peter seated there in the firelight warming himself, she asked, "You are not one of this man's disciples, are you?"

He replied, "I am not."

She looked closely at him and said, "This man was with him. You also were with that Nazarene, Jesus of Galilee."

But he denied it before them all. "Woman, I don't know him. I don't know or understand what you are talking about," he said, and went out into the entryway.[c]

226. THE HIGH PRIEST QUESTIONS JESUS
John 18:19-24

Meanwhile, the high priest questioned Jesus about his disciples and his teaching.

---

2. See p. 354: Who was the other disciple who accompanied Peter at Jesus' trials (John 18:15-16)?
3. See p. 354: Did Peter make his first denial of Jesus in the courtyard of Annas (John 18:12-15, 24) or of Caiaphas (Matthew 26:57-58)?
c. Some early manuscripts [of Mark 14:68] *entryway and the rooster crowed.*

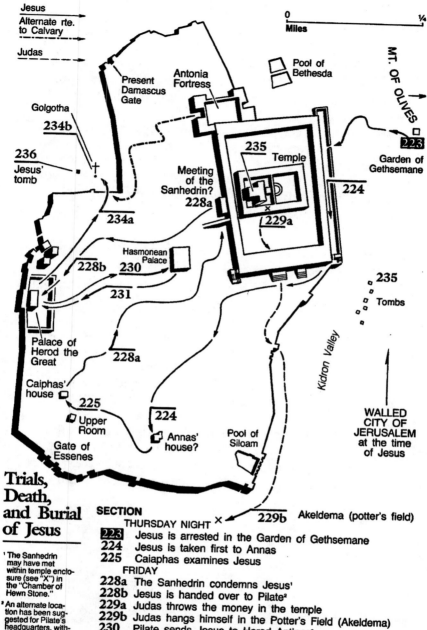

Jesus
Alternate rte.
to Calvary
Judas

0   ¼
Miles

MT. OF OLIVES →

Pool of
Bethesda

Present
Damascus
Gate

Antonia
Fortress

223
Garden of
Gethsemane

Golgotha
234b

235
Temple

236
Jesus'
tomb
†

Meeting
of the
Sanhedrin?
228a

224

234a

229a

Hasmonean
Palace
228b **230**

231

235
◦ ◦ ◦ ◦
Tombs

Kidron Valley

Palace of
Herod the
Great

228a

WALLED
CITY OF
JERUSALEM
at the time
of Jesus

Caiphas'
house
225
Upper
Room

Gate of
Essenes

224
Annas'
house?

Pool of
Siloam

Trials, Death, and Burial of Jesus

SECTION
THURSDAY NIGHT ×
229b Akeldema (potter's field)

223 Jesus is arrested in the Garden of Gethsemane
224 Jesus is taken first to Annas
225 Caiaphas examines Jesus
FRIDAY
228a The Sanhedrin condemns Jesus'
228b Jesus is handed over to Pilate²
229a Judas throws the money in the temple
229b Judas hangs himself in the Potter's Field (Akeldema)
230 Pilate sends Jesus to Herod Antipas³
231 Herod sends Jesus back to Pilate, who condemns Jesus
234a Soldiers lead Jesus to Golgotha;
Simon of Cyrene is forced to carry the cross
234b Jesus is crucified at Golgotha
235 Earthquake breaks open tombs and temple curtain torn
236 The body of Jesus is laid in a nearby tomb

¹ The Sanhedrin may have met within temple enclosure (see "X") in the "Chamber of Hewn Stone."

² An alternate location has been suggested for Pilate's headquarters, within the Antonia Fortress.

³ King Herod Antipas reigned in Galilee, was son of Herod the Great and may have stayed in the Hasmonean Palace.

233

"I have spoken openly to the world," Jesus replied. "I always taught in synagogues or at the temple, where all the Jews come together. I said nothing in secret. Why question me? Ask those who heard me. Surely they know what I said."

When Jesus said this, one of the officials nearby struck him in the face. "Is this the way you answer the high priest[4]?" he demanded.

"If I said something wrong," Jesus replied, "testify as to what is wrong. But if I spoke the truth, why did you strike me?" (Now Annas had sent him, still bound, to Caiaphas the high priest.)[d]

227. PETER'S SECOND AND THIRD DENIALS
Matthew 26:71b-75; Mark 14:69-72; Luke 22:58-62; John 18:25-27

A little later, Simon Peter stood warming himself.[5] When the servant girl saw him, she said again to those people standing around, "This fellow is one of them."

Another servant girl[6] saw him and said to the people there, "This fellow was with Jesus of Nazareth."

Someone else said, "You also are one of them."

He was asked, "You are not one of his disciples, are you?"

Peter denied it again, with an oath: "Man, I am not! I don't know the man!"

About an hour later, another asserted, "Certainly this fellow was with him, for he is a Galilean." Those standing there[7] went up to Peter and said, "Surely you are one of them, for your accent gives you away." One of the high priest's servants, a relative of the man

---

4. See p. 356: Who was the high priest: Caiaphas (Matthew 26:3, 57; John 11:49; 18:13-14) or Annas (Luke 3:2; Acts 4:6)? Which one examined Jesus while Peter made his first denial (John 18:19-24)?

d. Or *Then Annas sent him, still bound, to Caiaphas the high priest.* [The alternate reading in the NIV for John 18:24 is used herein. See EN 15:3, 4.]

5. See p. 359: Was Peter sitting in the courtyard or standing in the gateway when he made his first and second denials of Jesus (Matthew 26:69-72; Mark 14:66-70; Luke 22:54-58; John 18:17, 25)?

6. See p. 360: Who accused Peter at his second denial: the same servant girl as before (Mark 14:66, 69), another girl (Matthew 26:69, 71), or a man (Luke 22:58)?

7. See p. 361: Did one person question Peter the third time he denied Jesus (Luke 22:59; John 18:26), or did several people question him (Matthew 26:73; Mark 14:70)?

whose ear Peter had cut off, challenged him, "Didn't I see you with him in the olive grove?"

Again Peter denied it. He began to call down curses on himself, and he swore to them, "Man, I don't know what you're talking about! I don't know this man!"[8]

At that moment, just as he was speaking, the rooster began to crow the second time.[e] The Lord turned and looked straight at Peter. Then Peter remembered the word the Lord Jesus had spoken to him: "Before the rooster crows twice[f] today, you will disown me three times." And he went outside, broke down and wept bitterly.

228. BEFORE THE SANHEDRIN
Matthew 26:59-68; 27:1-2; Mark 14:55-65; 15:1;
Luke 22:63–23:1; John 18:28a

The chief priests and the whole Sanhedrin[10] were looking for false evidence against Jesus so that they could put him to death, but they did not find any. Though many false witnesses came forward *and* testified falsely against him, their statements did not agree.

Finally two stood up, and declared this false testimony against him: "This fellow said, 'I am able to destroy the temple of God and rebuild it in three days.' " "We heard him say, 'I will destroy this man-made temple and in three days will build another, not made by man.' " Yet even then their testimony did not agree.

Then the high priest stood up before them and asked Jesus, "Are you not going to answer? What is this testimony that these men are bringing against you?" But Jesus remained silent and gave no answer.

"If you are the Christ," they said, "tell us."

Jesus answered, "If I tell you, you will not believe me, and if I asked you, you would not answer. But from now on, the Son of

---

8. See p. 362: How many times did Peter deny Christ?

e. Some early manuscripts [of Mark 14:72] do not have *the second time*.

9. See p. 363: When Peter made his third denial, did the cock crow for the first time (Matthew 26:74; Luke 22:60; John 18:27) or the second time (Mark 14:30, 68, 72)?

f. Some early manuscripts [of Mark 14:72] do not have *twice*.

10. See p. 364: Did the Sanhedrin assemble at night, before Peter's denials (Matthew 26:59, 69; Mark 14:55, 68), or at daybreak, after them (Luke 22:57, 66)?

Man will be seated at the right hand of the mighty God."

They all asked, "Are you then the Son of God?"

Again the high priest said to him, "I charge you under oath by the living God: Tell us if you are the Christ, the Son of the Blessed One."

"You are right in saying I am," replied Jesus. "But I say to all of you: In the future you will see the Son of Man sitting at the right hand of the Mighty One and coming on the clouds of heaven."[11]

Then the high priest tore his clothes. "He has spoken blasphemy! Why do we need any more witnesses?" he asked. "Look, now you have heard the blasphemy. What do you think?"

"We have heard it from his own lips," they answered. "He is worthy of death." They all condemned him.

Then some began to spit in his face. They blindfolded him and struck him with their fists. Others slapped him and said, "Prophesy to us, Christ. Who hit you?" And the guards took him and began mocking and beating him. They demanded, "Prophesy! Who hit you?" And they said many other insulting things to him.

Very early in the morning, at daybreak, all the chief priests, with the elders of the people, the teachers of the law and the whole Sanhedrin, reached a decision to put Jesus to death. Then the whole assembly rose. They bound Jesus and led him away from Caiaphas to the palace of the Roman governor and handed him over to Pilate.

229. JUDAS HANGS HIMSELF
Matthew 27:3-10; Acts 1:18-19

When Judas, who had betrayed him, saw that Jesus was condemned, he was seized with remorse and returned the thirty silver coins to the chief priests and the elders. "I have sinned," he said, "for I have betrayed innocent blood."

"What is that to us?" they replied. "That's your responsibility."

So Judas threw the money into the temple and left.

The chief priests picked up the coins and said, "It is against the law to put this into the treasury, since it is blood money." So they

---

11. See p. 365: At Jesus' trial before the Sanhedrin, did the high priest ask the question that led to the charge of blasphemy (Matthew 26:63-65; Mark 14:61-64) or did others (Luke 22:66-70)? What was the form of the question and Jesus' answer to it?

decided to use the money to buy the potter's field as a burial place for foreigners. That is why it has been called the Field of Blood to this day. Then what was spoken by Jeremiah the prophet was fulfilled: "They took the thirty silver coins, the price set on him by the people of Israel, and they used them to buy the potter's field, as the Lord commanded me."[g]

Thus, with the reward he got for his wickedness, Judas bought a field.[12] Then he went away and hanged himself. There he fell head-long, his body burst open and all his intestines spilled out.[13] Everyone in Jerusalem heard about this, so they called that field in their language Akeldama, that is, Field of Blood.[14]

230. JESUS BEFORE PILATE
Matthew 27:11-14; Mark 15:2-5; Luke 23:2-7; John 18:28b-38

Meanwhile, by now it was early morning, and to avoid ceremonial uncleanness the Jews did not enter the palace; they wanted to be able to eat the Passover. So Pilate came out to them and asked, "What charges are you bringing against this man?"

"If he were not a criminal," they replied, "we would not have handed him over to you."

Pilate said, "Take him yourselves and judge him by your own law."

"But we have no right to execute anyone," the Jews objected. This happened so that the words Jesus had spoken indicating the kind of death he was going to die would be fulfilled.

And they began to accuse him, saying, "We have found this man subverting our nation. He opposes payment of taxes to Caesar and claims to be Christ, a king."

Pilate then went back inside the palace and summoned Jesus. Jesus stood before the governor, and the governor asked him, "Are you the king of the Jews?"

---

g. See Zechariah 11:12-13; Jeremiah 19:1-13; 32:6-9.
12. See p. 366: Did Judas buy the potter's field (Acts 1:18), or did the chief priests buy it (Matthew 27:7)?
13. See p. 367: Did Judas hang himself (Matthew 27:5), or did he fall to his death (Acts 1:18)?
14. See p. 367: Was the potter's field later called the *Field of Blood* because of the *blood money* (Matthew 27:6-8) or Judas' bloody fall (Acts 1:18-19)?

"Is that your own idea," Jesus asked, "or did others talk to you about me?"

"Am I a Jew?" Pilate replied. "It was your people and your chief priests who handed you over to me. What is it you have done?"

Jesus said, "My kingdom is not of this world. If it were, my servants would fight to prevent my arrest by the Jews. But now my kingdom is from another place."

"You are a king, then!" said Pilate.

Jesus answered, "You are right in saying I am a king. In fact, for this reason I was born, and for this I came into the world, to testify to the truth. Everyone on the side of truth listens to me."

"What is truth?" Pilate asked. With this he went out again to the Jews and said to the chief priests and the crowd, "I find no basis for a charge against this man."

When the chief priests and the elders accused him of many things, he gave no answer. Then Pilate asked him, "Aren't you going to answer? See how many things they are accusing you of. Don't you hear the testimony they are bringing against you?" But Jesus still made no reply, not even to a single charge—to the great amazement of the governor.

But they insisted, "He stirs up the people all over Judea[h] by his teaching. He started in Galilee and has come all the way here."

On hearing this, Pilate asked if the man was a Galilean. When he learned that Jesus was under Herod's jurisdiction, he sent him to Herod, who was also in Jerusalem at that time.

231. JESUS BEFORE HEROD
Luke 23:8-12

When Herod saw Jesus, he was greatly pleased, because for a long time he had been wanting to see him. From what he had heard about him, he hoped to see him perform some miracle. He plied him with many questions, but Jesus gave him no answer. The chief priests and the teachers of the law were standing there, vehemently accusing him. Then Herod and his soldiers ridiculed and mocked him. Dressing him in an elegant robe, they sent him back to Pilate. That day Herod and Pilate became friends—before this they had been enemies.

h. Or *over the land of the Jews*

232. JESUS AGAIN BEFORE PILATE
Matthew 27:15-23; Mark 15:6-14; Luke 23:13-22; John 18:39-40

Pilate called together the chief priests, the rulers and the people, and said to them, "You brought me this man as one who was inciting the people to rebellion. I have examined him in your presence and have found no basis for your charges against him. Neither has Herod, for he sent him back to us; as you can see, he has done nothing to deserve death. Therefore, I will punish him and then release him."

Now it was the governor's custom at the Feast of the Passover to release a prisoner chosen by the crowd. So the crowd came up and asked Pilate to do for them what he usually did.

"Do you want me to release to you the king of the Jews?" asked Pilate, for he knew it was out of envy that the chief priests had handed Jesus over to him.

At that time they had a notorious prisoner, called Barabbas, thrown into prison for an insurrection in the city, and for murder. The chief priests and the elders stirred up the crowd to have Pilate release Barabbas instead and to have Jesus executed. With one voice they shouted back, "No, not him! Away with this man! Give us Barabbas! Release Barabbas to us!"

While Pilate was sitting on the judge's seat, his wife sent him this message: "Don't have anything to do with that innocent man, for I have suffered a great deal today in a dream because of him."

Wanting to release Jesus, Pilate appealed to them again. "Which of the two do you want me to release to you: Barabbas, or Jesus who is called Christ?" asked the governor.

"Barabbas," they answered.

"What shall I do, then, with Jesus who is called Christ, the one you call the king of the Jews?" Pilate asked them.

They all answered, "Crucify him!" They kept shouting, "Crucify him!"

For the third time he spoke to them: "Why? What crime has this man committed? I have found in him no grounds for the death penalty. Therefore I will have him punished and then release him."

But they shouted all the louder, "Crucify him!"

233. JESUS SENTENCED TO BE CRUCIFIED
Matthew 27:24-31; Mark 15:15-20; Luke 23:23-25; John 19:1-16

Wanting to satisfy the crowd, Pilate released Barabbas to them. Then Pilate took Jesus and had him flogged. The soldiers led Jesus away into the palace (that is, the Praetorium) and called together the whole company of soldiers around him. They stripped him and put a purple robe on him, and then twisted together a crown of thorns and set it on his head.[15] They put a staff in his right hand. "Hail, O king of the Jews!" they began to call out to him. Falling on their knees in front of him, they worshiped him and mocked him. They spit on him, and took the staff and struck him on the head *and* face again and again.

Once more Pilate came out and said to the Jews, "Look, I am bringing him out to you to let you know that I find no basis for a charge against him." When Jesus came out wearing the crown of thorns and the purple robe, Pilate said to them, "Here is the man!"

As soon as the chief priests and their officials saw him, they shouted, "Crucify! Crucify!"

But Pilate answered, "You take him and crucify him. As for me, I find no basis for a charge against him."

The Jews insisted, "We have a law, and according to that law he must die, because he claimed to be the Son of God."

When Pilate heard this, he was even more afraid, and he went back inside the palace. "Where do you come from?" he asked Jesus, but Jesus gave him no answer. "Do you refuse to speak to me?" Pilate said. "Don't you realize I have power either to free you or to crucify you?"

Jesus answered, "You would have no power over me if it were not given to you from above. Therefore the one who handed me over to you is guilty of a greater sin."

From then on, Pilate tried to set Jesus free, but the Jews kept shouting, "If you let this man go, you are no friend of Caesar. Anyone who claims to be a king opposes Caesar."

When Pilate heard this, he brought Jesus out and sat down on the

---

15. See p. 368: How many times was Jesus mocked? Did the soldiers put a robe and a crown of thorns on Jesus once (Luke 23:11; John 19:1-2) or twice (Matthew 27:27-31; Mark 15:16-20)? What was the order of events surrounding the examinations of Jesus by the Roman authorities? Was the robe scarlet (Matthew 27:28) or purple (Mark 15:17; John 19:2)?

judge's seat at a place known as the Stone Pavement (which in Aramaic is Gabbatha). It was the day of Preparation of Passover Week, about the sixth hour.

"Here is your king," Pilate said to the Jews.

But they shouted, "Take him away! Take him away! Crucify him!"

"Shall I crucify your king?" Pilate asked.

"We have no king but Caesar," the chief priests answered.

With loud shouts they insistently demanded that he be crucified, and their shouts prevailed. When Pilate saw that he was getting nowhere, but that instead an uproar was starting, *he* decided to grant their demand. He took water and washed his hands in front of the crowd. "I am innocent of this man's blood," he said. "It is your responsibility!"

All the people answered, "Let his blood be on us and on our children!"

Finally Pilate surrendered Jesus to their will and handed him over to them to be crucified.[16]

So the soldiers took charge of Jesus. They took off the purple robe and put his own clothes on him. Then they led him away to crucify him.

234. THE CRUCIFIXION
Matthew 27:32-44; Mark 15:21-32; Luke 23:26-43; John 19:17-27

They led him away, carrying his own cross. As they were going out, they met a man from Cyrene, named Simon, the father of Alexander and Rufus. *He* was passing by on his way in from the country. They seized Simon, put the cross on him and forced him to carry it behind Jesus.[17] A large number of people followed him, including women who mourned and wailed for him. Jesus turned and said to them, "Daughters of Jerusalem, do not weep for me; weep for yourselves and for your children. For the time will come when you will say, 'Blessed are the barren women, the wombs that never bore and the breasts that never nursed!' Then

"'they will say to the mountains, "Fall on us!"
and to the hills, "Cover us!"'[i]

---

16. See p. 369: How many trials did Jesus endure?
17. See p. 370: Did Jesus carry his own cross (Matthew 27:32; Mark 15:21; Luke 23:26) or did Simon of Cyrene carry it (John 19:17)?
i. Hosea 10:8

241

For if men do these things when the tree is green, what will happen when it is dry?"

Two other men, both robbers, were also led out with him to be executed.

They came to a place called Golgotha in Aramaic (which means The Place of the Skull). Then they offered Jesus wine to drink, mixed with gall (myrrh); but after tasting it, he refused to drink it.[18] There they crucified him, along with the criminals—one on his right, the other on his left[j] and Jesus in the middle. It was the third hour when they crucified him.[19]

Jesus said, "Father, forgive them, for they do not know what they are doing."[k]

When the soldiers had crucified Jesus, they took his clothes, dividing them into four shares, one for each of them, with the undergarment remaining. This garment was seamless, woven in one piece from top to bottom.

"Let's not tear it," they said to one another. "Let's decide by lot who will get it." They cast lots.

This happened that the scripture might be fulfilled which said,

"They divided my garments among them
and cast lots for my clothing."[l]

So this is what the soldiers did. And sitting down, they kept watch over him there.

Pilate had a written notice of the charge against him prepared and fastened to the cross above his head. Many of the Jews read this sign, for the place where Jesus was crucified was near the city, and the sign was written in Aramaic, Latin and Greek.[20] It read:

---

18. See p. 371: Was the drink that Jesus refused at Golgotha wine mixed with gall (Matthew 27:34) or wine mixed with myrrh (Mark 15:23)?
j. Some manuscripts [of Mark 15:28] *left, and the scripture was fulfilled which says, "He was counted with the lawless ones"* (Isaiah 53:12)
19. See p. 371: Was Jesus crucified at the third hour (Mark 15:25) or after the sixth hour (John 19:14)?
k. Some early manuscripts [of Luke 23:34] do not have this sentence.
l. Psalm 22:18
20. See p. 377: Which of the four different inscriptions provided by the Evangelists was written on the sign attached to Jesus' cross (Matthew 27:37; Mark 15:26; Luke 23:38; John 19:19)?

JESUS OF NAZARETH, THE KING OF THE JEWS
THIS IS JESUS, THE KING OF THE JEWS
THIS IS THE KING OF THE JEWS

The chief priests of the Jews protested to Pilate, "Do not write 'The King of the Jews,' but that this man claimed to be king of the Jews."

Pilate answered, "What I have written, I have written."

Those who passed by hurled insults at him, shaking their heads and saying, "So! You who are going to destroy the temple and build it in three days, come down from the cross and save yourself, if you are the Son of God!"

The people stood watching, and the rulers even sneered at him. In the same way the chief priests, the teachers of the law and the elders mocked him among themselves. "He saved others," they said, "but he can't save himself!" "Let him save himself if he is the Christ of God, the Chosen One." "He's the King of Israel! Let this Christ, this King of Israel, come down now from the cross, that we may see and believe in him." "He trusts in God. Let God rescue him now if he wants him, for he said, 'I am the Son of God.' "

The soldiers also came up and mocked him. They offered him wine vinegar and said, "If you are the king of the Jews, save yourself."

In the same way the robbers who were crucified with him also heaped insults on him. One of the criminals who hung there hurled insults at him: "Aren't you the Christ? Save yourself and us!"

But the other criminal rebuked him. "Don't you fear God," he said, "since you are under the same sentence? We are punished justly, for we are getting what our deeds deserve. But this man has done nothing wrong."[21]

Then he said, "Jesus, remember me when you come into your kingdom."[m]

Jesus answered him, "I tell you the truth, today you will be with me in paradise."

Near the cross of Jesus stood his mother, his mother's sister, Mary the wife of Clopas, and Mary Magdalene. When Jesus saw his mother there, and the disciple whom he loved standing nearby, he said to his mother, "Dear woman, here is your son," and to the

---

21. See p. 378: Did both of the criminals crucified with Jesus insult him (Matthew 27:44; Mark 15:32), or did only one mock him (Luke 23:39)?
m. Some manuscripts [of Luke 23:42] *come with your kingly power*

disciple, "Here is your mother." From that time on, this disciple took her into his home.

235. THE DEATH OF JESUS
Matthew 27:45-56; Mark 15:33-41; Luke 23:44-49; John 19:28-34, 36-37

From the sixth hour until the ninth hour darkness came over all the land, for the sun stopped shining. And at the ninth hour Jesus cried out in a loud voice, "Eloi, Eloi,[n] lama sabachthani?"—which means, "My God, my God, why have you forsaken me?"[o]

When some of those standing there heard this, they said, "Listen, he's calling Elijah."

Later, knowing that all was now completed, and so that the Scripture would be fulfilled, Jesus said, "I am thirsty." A jar of wine vinegar was there. Immediately one man ran and got a sponge. He soaked it with wine vinegar, put the sponge on a stalk of the hyssop plant, and lifted it to Jesus' lips. The rest said, "Leave him alone now. Let's see if Elijah comes to save him, to take him down." When he had received the drink,[22] Jesus said, "It is finished."

Jesus cried out again with a loud voice, "Father, into your hands I commit my spirit." When he had said this, he breathed his last; he bowed his head and gave up his spirit.[23]

At that moment the curtain of the temple was torn in two from top to bottom. The earth shook and the rocks split. The tombs broke open and the bodies of many holy people who had died were raised to life. They came out of the tombs, and after Jesus' resurrection they went into the holy city and appeared to many people.

When the centurion and those with him who were guarding Jesus saw the earthquake and all that had happened, they were terrified. The centurion stood there in front of Jesus, heard his cry and[p] saw how he died. He praised God and exclaimed, "Surely this was a righteous man. Surely he was the Son[q] of God!"

---

n. Some manuscripts [of Matthew 27:46] *Eli, Eli*
o. Psalm 22:1
22. See p. 378: How many times was Jesus offered a drink at Golgotha (Matthew 27:34, 48; Mark 15:23, 36; Luke 23:36; John 19:29-30)?
23. See p. 379: What year was Jesus crucified? How old was Jesus when he died?
p. Some manuscripts [of Mark 15:39] do not have *heard his cry and*.
q. Or *a son*

When all the people who had gathered to witness this sight saw what took place, they beat their breasts and went away. But all those who knew him, including many women, stood at a distance, watching these things. Among them were Mary Magdalene, Mary the mother of James the younger and of Joses, and Salome, the mother of Zebedee's sons.[24] In Galilee these women had followed Jesus and cared for his needs. Many other women who had come up with him from Galilee to Jerusalem were also there.

Now it was the day of Preparation, and the next day was to be a special Sabbath. Because the Jews did not want the bodies left on the crosses during the Sabbath, they asked Pilate to have the legs broken and the bodies taken down. The soldiers therefore came and broke the legs of the first man who had been crucified with Jesus, and then those of the other. But when they came to Jesus and found that he was already dead, they did not break his legs. Instead, one of the soldiers pierced Jesus' side with a spear, bringing a sudden flow of blood and water. These things happened so that the scripture would be fulfilled: "Not one of his bones will be broken,"[r] and, as another scripture says, "They will look on the one they have pierced."[s]

236. THE BURIAL OF JESUS
Matthew 27:57-61; Mark 15:42-47; Luke 23:50-56; John 19:38-42

Now there was a rich man from the Judean town of Arimathea, named Joseph, a good and upright man who was himself waiting for the kingdom of God. Joseph had become a disciple of Jesus, but secretly because he feared the Jews. A prominent member of the Council, *he* had not consented to their decision and action.

It was Preparation Day (that is, the day before the Sabbath). So as evening approached, Joseph of Arimathea went boldly to Pilate and asked for Jesus' body. Pilate was surprised to hear that he was already dead. Summoning the centurion, he asked him if Jesus had already died. When he learned from the centurion that it was so, Pilate ordered that the body be given to Joseph. So Joseph bought some linen cloth.

---

24. See p. 380: Did Mary, the mother of Jesus, and Mary Magdalene stand near the cross (Matthew 27:55; Mark 15:40; Luke 23:49) or watch from a distance (John 19:25)?
r. Exodus 12:46; Numbers 9:12; Psalm 34:20
s. Zechariah 12:10

With Pilate's permission, Joseph came, took down the body *and* wrapped it in the linen cloth. He was accompanied by Nicodemus, the man who earlier had visited Jesus at night. Nicodemus brought a mixture of myrrh and aloes, about seventy-five pounds.[t] Taking Jesus' body, the two of them wrapped it, with the spices, in strips of clean linen cloth.[25] This was in accordance with Jewish burial customs.

At the place where Jesus was crucified, there was a garden, and in the garden a new tomb, *Joseph's* own new tomb that he had cut out of the rock. The Sabbath was about to begin, and since the tomb was nearby, they took Jesus' body and laid it there, *where* no one had ever been laid. Then *they* rolled a big stone against the entrance of the tomb and went away.

The women who had come with Jesus from Galilee followed Joseph and saw the tomb and how his body was laid in it. Mary Magdalene and the other Mary, the mother of Joses, were sitting there opposite the tomb. Then they went home and prepared spices and perfumes. But they rested on the Sabbath in obedience to the commandment.

237. THE GUARD AT THE TOMB
Matthew 27:62-66

The next day, the one after Preparation Day, the chief priests and the Pharisees went to Pilate. "Sir," they said, "we remember that while he was still alive that deceiver said, 'After three days I will rise again.' So give the order for the tomb to be made secure until the third day. Otherwise, his disciples may come and steal the body and tell the people that he has been raised from the dead. This last deception will be worse than the first."

"Take a guard," Pilate answered. "Go, make the tomb as secure as you know how." So they went and made the tomb secure by putting a seal on the stone and posting the guard.

---

t. Greek *a hundred litrai* (about 34 kilograms)
25. See p. 380: Was Jesus' body wrapped with a single linen cloth (Matthew 27:59; Mark 15:46; Luke 23:53) or with strips of linen (John 19:40)?

SIXTEEN.
RESURRECTION, APPEARANCES, AND ASCENSION

238. THE RESURRECTION[1]
Matthew 28:1-8; Mark 16:1-8; Luke 24:1-12; John 20:1-9

When the Sabbath was over, Mary Magdalene,[2] Mary the mother of James, and Salome bought spices[3] so that they might go to anoint Jesus' body.[4] Very early in the morning on the first day of the week, while it was still dark, the women took the spices they had prepared and went to the tomb.

There was a violent earthquake, for an angel of the Lord came down from heaven and, going to the tomb, rolled back the stone and sat on it. His appearance was like lightning, and his clothes were white as snow. The guards were so afraid of him that they shook and became like dead men.

Just after sunrise,[5] *the women* were on their way to the tomb and they asked each other, "Who will roll the stone away from the entrance of the tomb?" But when they looked up, they saw that the

---

1. See p. 381: Can the New Testament accounts of the resurrection of Jesus be harmonized?
2. See p. 383: When Mary Magdalene first visited the tomb on Easter morning, was she alone (John 20:1) or with the other women (Matthew 28:1; Mark 16:1; Luke 24:1)? If with others, why did John mention only that Mary Magdalene went to the tomb?
3. See p. 383: In order to anoint Jesus' body, did the women buy and prepare spices before the Sabbath (Luke 23:55-56) or afterward (Mark 16:1)?
4. See p. 384: If Jesus' body had already been anointed (John 19:39-40), the tomb sealed, and a Roman guard posted there (Matthew 27:66), why did the women visit the tomb to anoint the body (Mark 16:1; Luke 24:1)?
5. See p. 385: Did the women leave for the tomb during darkness (John 20:1) or after sunrise (Mark 16:2)?

stone, which was very large, had been rolled away from the tomb entrance. When they entered the tomb,[6] they did not find the body of the Lord Jesus. While they were wondering about this, suddenly two men[7] in clothes that gleamed like lightning stood beside them, *one*, a young man dressed in a white robe sitting[8] on the right side. They were alarmed. In their fright the women bowed down with their faces to the ground.

But the men said to the women, "Do not be afraid, for I know that you are looking for Jesus the Nazarene, who was crucified. Why do you look for the living among the dead? He is not here; he has risen, just as he said. Come and see the place where they laid him. Remember how he told you, while he was still with you in Galilee: 'The Son of Man must be delivered into the hands of sinful men, be crucified and on the third day be raised again.' " Then they remembered his words. "But go quickly, tell his disciples and Peter: 'He has risen from the dead and is going ahead of you into Galilee. There you will see him, just as he told you.' Now I have told you."[9]

Trembling and bewildered, the women went out and fled from the tomb. They said nothing to anyone, because they were afraid, yet filled with joy,[10] and ran to tell his disciples.

Mary Magdalene came running[11] to Simon Peter and the other disciple,[12] the one Jesus loved, and said, "They have taken the Lord out of the tomb, and we don't know where they have put him!"

When *the women* came back from the tomb, they told all these things to the Eleven and to all the others. It was Mary Magdalene, Joanna, Mary the mother of James, and the others with them who

6. See p. 386: Did the women first see the angel(s) outside the tomb (Matthew 28:2, 5) or inside it (Mark 16:4-5; Luke 24:2-4)?
7. See p. 387: Was there one man (Mark 16:5) or one angel at the tomb (Matthew 28:2), or were there two men (Luke 24:4) or two angels (Luke 24:23; John 20:12)?
8. See p. 388: Were the angels in the tomb sitting (Mark 16:5) or standing (Luke 24:4) when the women first saw them?
9. See p. 389: Did the angel conclude his announcement to the women by saying he had told them (Matthew 28:7), or that Jesus had told them (Mark 16:7)?
10. See p. 390: Were the women afraid (Mark 16:8) or joyful (Matthew 28:8) when they hurried off to tell the disciples of the empty tomb?
11. See p. 391: Did Mary Magdalene enter the tomb and hear the angel's announcement (Mark 16:1-8) on her first visit there Easter morning or not (John 20:1-2)? What is the order of events surrounding Mary Magdalene's two visits to the tomb?
12. See p. 393: Who was *the other disciple* (John 20:2, 4, 8) whom Mary Magdalene told about the empty tomb and who outran Peter there?

Ten Appearances of the Resurrected Jesus

Road to Emmaus, 7 miles

241

239a
Jesus' tomb

Miles 0 — ¼ — ½

Roads ....

Temple

Garden of Gethsemane

MT. OF OLIVES

Bethphage?

Jerusalem
240?

242

243
(1 week later)

• Upper Room

239b?

Road to Bethany

SECTION
239a Jesus first appears to Mary Magdalene
239b Then appears to other women
240 He appears to Simon Peter
241 He appears to two disciples on the road to Emmaus
242 Jesus appears to the gathered disciples in Jerusalem
243 He appears a second time to the disciples, with Thomas present

MERON MOUNTAINS

LATER

246?

244? He appears to seven disciples at Lake Galilee
246? He appears to more than 500 disciples on a mountain in Galilee

Capernaum   • **Bethsaida**

Tabgha •

244?

Cana •

Magdala •

Lake Galilee
-696 ft.

• **Gergesa**

Tiberias •

Sepphoris •

Miles 0 — 3 — 6
Kms 0 — 3 — 6 — 9

Nazareth •

FORTY DAYS LATER

247? He appears to James, presumably in Jerusalem
248 Jesus' last appearance and ascension from the Mount of Olives

Mt. of Ascension
248

MT. OF OLIVES -2,600 ft.

247?

Jerusalem

Miles 0 — ¼ — ½

told this to the apostles.[13] But they did not believe the women, because their words seemed to them like nonsense.

Peter and the other disciple, however, got up and started for the tomb. Both were running, but the other disciple outran Peter and reached the tomb first. He bent over and looked in at the strips of linen lying there but did not go in. Then Simon Peter, who was behind him, arrived and went into the tomb. Bending over, he saw the strips of linen lying there by themselves, as well as the burial cloth that had been around Jesus' head. The cloth was folded up by itself, separate from the linen. He went away, wondering to himself what had happened. Finally the other disciple, who had reached the tomb first, also went inside. He saw and believed. (They still did not understand from Scripture that Jesus had to rise from the dead.)

239. JESUS APPEARS TO MARY MAGDALENE AND THE OTHER WOMEN
Matthew 28:9-10; Mark 16:9-11; John 20:10-18

Then the disciples went back to their homes, but Mary stood outside the tomb crying. As she wept, she bent over to look into the tomb and saw two angels in white, seated where Jesus' body had been, one at the head and the other at the foot.

They asked her, "Woman, why are you crying?"

"They have taken my Lord away," she said, "and I don't know where they have put him." At this, she turned around and saw Jesus standing there, but she did not realize that it was Jesus.

"Woman," he said, "why are you crying? Who is it you are looking for?"

Thinking he was the gardener, she said, "Sir, if you have carried him away, tell me where you have put him, and I will get him."

Jesus said to her, "Mary."

She turned toward him and cried out in Aramaic, "Rabboni!" (which means Teacher).

Jesus said, "Do not hold on to me, for I have not yet returned to the Father. Go instead to my brothers and tell them, 'I am returning

---

13. See p. 393: How many women visited Jesus' tomb on Easter morning (Matthew 28:1; Mark 16:1; Luke 24:1, 10; John 20:1)? Why does each Evangelist report a different number of women who visited the tomb?

to my Father and your Father, to my God and your God.'"

a[*Thus* when Jesus rose early on the first day of the week, he appeared first to Mary Magdalene, out of whom he had driven seven demons.] She went to [those who had been with him and who were mourning and weeping] with the news: "I have seen the Lord!" And she told them that he had said these things to her. [When they heard that Jesus was alive, and that she had seen him, they did not believe it.]

Suddenly Jesus met *the other women*.[14] "Greetings," he said. They came to him, clasped his feet and worshiped him. Then Jesus said to them, "Do not be afraid. Go and tell my brothers to go to Galilee; there they will see me."[15]

240. THE GUARDS' REPORT
Matthew 28:11-15

While the women were on their way, some of the guards went into the city and reported to the chief priests everything that had happened. When the chief priests had met with the elders and devised a plan, they gave the soldiers a large sum of money, telling them, "You are to say, 'His disciples came during the night and stole him away while we were asleep.' If this report gets to the governor, we will satisfy him and keep you out of trouble." So the soldiers took the money and did as they were instructed. And this story has been widely circulated among the Jews to this very day.

241. ON THE ROAD TO EMMAUS
Mark 16:12-13; Luke 24:13-35; John 20:19a

Afterward that same day two of *Jesus' disciples* were [walking in the country], going to a village called Emmaus, about seven miles[b] from

---

a. The most reliable early manuscripts and other ancient witnesses do not have Mark 16:9-20 [the contents of which are placed in brackets hereinafter].
14. See p. 394: Did the risen Jesus appear to the other women on their way to tell the apostles of the empty tomb (Matthew 28:9) or afterward (Luke 24:9, 22-23)? What was the order of events on that Easter Sunday?
15. See p. 395: Why did Jesus give instructions for his disciples to go to Galilee to meet him (Matthew 28:7, 10), since he met them that evening in Jerusalem (Mark 16:14; Luke 24:36; John 20:19)?
b. Greek *sixty stadia* (about 11 kilometers)

Jerusalem. They were talking with each other about everything that had happened. As they talked and discussed these things with each other, Jesus himself came up and walked along with them; but they were kept from recognizing him. [Jesus appeared in a different form to them.]

He asked them, "What are you discussing together as you walk along?"

They stood still, their faces downcast. One of them, named Cleopas, asked him, "Are you only a visitor to Jerusalem and do not know the things that have happened there in these days?"

"What things?" he asked.

"About Jesus of Nazareth," they replied. "He was a prophet, powerful in word and deed before God and all the people. The chief priests and our rulers handed him over to be sentenced to death, and they crucified him; but we had hoped that he was the one who was going to redeem Israel. And what is more, it is the third day since all this took place. In addition, some of our women amazed us. They went to the tomb early this morning but didn't find his body. They came and told us that they had seen a vision of angels, who said he was alive. Then some of our companions went to the tomb and found it just as the women had said, but him they did not see."

He said to them, "How foolish you are, and how slow of heart to believe all that the prophets have spoken! Did not the Christ have to suffer these things and then enter his glory?" And beginning with Moses and all the Prophets, he explained to them what was said in all the Scriptures concerning himself.

As they approached the village to which they were going, Jesus acted as if he were going farther. But they urged him strongly, "Stay with us, for it is nearly evening; the day is almost over." So he went in to stay with them.

When he was at the table with them, he took bread, gave thanks, broke it and began to give it to them. Then their eyes were opened and they recognized him, and he disappeared from their sight. They asked each other, "Were not our hearts burning within us while he talked with us on the road and opened the Scriptures to us?"

They got up and returned at once to Jerusalem. On the evening of that first day of the week, there they found the Eleven disciples and those with them, assembled together with the doors locked for fear of the Jews, and saying, "It is true! The Lord has risen and has appeared to Simon." Then the two reported what had happened on the way, and how Jesus was recognized by them when he broke the bread. [But *the disciples* did not believe them either.][16]

242. JESUS APPEARS TO THE DISCIPLES
Mark 16:14; Luke 24:36-43; John 20:19b-23

While they were [eating] *and* still talking about this, Jesus himself came[17] and stood among [the Eleven][18] and said to them, "Peace be with you!"

They were startled and frightened, thinking they saw a ghost. He said to them, "Why are you troubled, and why do doubts rise in your minds?" [He rebuked them for their lack of faith and their stubborn refusal to believe those who had seen him after he had risen.] "Look at my hands and my feet. It is I myself! Touch me and see; a ghost does not have flesh and bones, as you see I have."

When he had said this, he showed them his hands and feet and side. And while they still did not believe it because of joy and amazement,[19] he asked them, "Do you have anything here to eat?" They gave him a piece of broiled fish, and he took it and ate it in their presence. So the disciples were overjoyed when they saw the Lord.

Again Jesus said, "Peace be with you! As the Father has sent me, I am sending you." And with that he breathed on them and said, "Receive the Holy Spirit. If you forgive anyone his sins, they are forgiven; if you do not forgive them, they are not forgiven."

243. JESUS APPEARS TO THOMAS
John 20:24-29

Now Thomas (called Didymus), one of the Twelve, was not with the disciples when Jesus came. So the other disciples told him, "We

16. See p. 397: As the disciples gathered in Jerusalem that first Easter evening, did they believe that Jesus had risen from the dead (Luke 24:34) or not (Luke 24:38; Mark 16:13-14)?
17. See p. 399: Did Jesus meet his disciples in and near Jerusalem (Luke 24:13-51) or in Galilee (Matthew 28:16)?
18. See p. 400: When Jesus appeared to his gathered disciples that first Easter evening, were there ten (John 20:24) or eleven (Luke 24:33) apostles present?
19. See p. 401: When Jesus appeared to the gathered disciples that first Easter evening, were they overjoyed (John 20:20) or doubtful (Luke 24:38)?

have seen the Lord!"

But he said to them, "Unless I see the nail marks in his hands and put my finger where the nails were, and put my hand into his side, I will not believe it."

A week later his disciples were in the house again, and Thomas was with them. Though the doors were locked, Jesus came and stood among them and said, "Peace be with you!" Then he said to Thomas, "Put your finger here; see my hands. Reach out your hand and put it into my side. Stop doubting and believe."

Thomas said to him, "My Lord and my God!"

Then Jesus told him, "Because you have seen me, you have believed; blessed are those who have not seen and yet have believed."

244. JESUS AND THE MIRACULOUS CATCH OF FISH
John 21:1-14

Afterward Jesus appeared again to his disciples, by the Sea of Tiberias.[c] It happened this way: Simon Peter, Thomas (called Didymus), Nathanael from Cana in Galilee, the sons of Zebedee, and two other disciples were together. "I'm going out to fish," Simon Peter told them, and they said, "We'll go with you." So they went out and got into the boat, but that night they caught nothing.

Early in the morning, Jesus stood on the shore, but the disciples did not realize that it was Jesus.

He called out to them, "Friends, haven't you any fish?"

"No," they answered.

He said, "Throw your net on the right side of the boat and you will find some." When they did, they were unable to haul the net in because of the large number of fish.

Then the disciple whom Jesus loved said to Peter, "It is the Lord!" As soon as Simon Peter heard him say, "It is the Lord," he wrapped his outer garment around him (for he had taken it off) and jumped into the water. The other disciples followed in the boat, towing the net full of fish, for they were not far from shore, about a hundred yards.[d] When they landed, they saw a fire of burning coals there with

c. That is, Sea of Galilee
d. Greek *about two hundred cubits* (about 90 meters)

fish on it, and some bread.

Jesus said to them, "Bring some of the fish you have just caught."

Simon Peter climbed aboard and dragged the net ashore. It was full of large fish, 153, but even with so many the net was not torn. Jesus said to them, "Come and have breakfast." None of the disciples dared ask him, "Who are you?" They knew it was the Lord. Jesus came, took the bread and gave it to them, and did the same with the fish. This was now the third time Jesus appeared to his disciples after he was raised from the dead.

245. JESUS REINSTATES PETER
John 21:15-23

When they had finished eating, Jesus said to Simon Peter, "Simon son of John, do you truly love me more than these?"

"Yes, Lord," he said, "you know that I love you."

Jesus said, "Feed my lambs."

Again Jesus said, "Simon son of John, do you truly love me?"

He answered, "Yes, Lord, you know that I love you."

Jesus said, "Take care of my sheep."

The third time he said to him, "Simon son of John, do you love me?"

Peter was hurt because Jesus asked him the third time, "Do you love me?" He said, "Lord, you know all things; you know that I love you."

Jesus said, "Feed my sheep. I tell you the truth, when you were younger you dressed yourself and went where you wanted; but when you are old you will stretch out your hands, and someone else will dress you and lead you where you do not want to go." Jesus said this to indicate the kind of death by which Peter would glorify God. Then he said to him, "Follow me!"

Peter turned and saw that the disciple whom Jesus loved was following them. (This was the one who had leaned back against Jesus at the supper and had said, "Lord, who is going to betray you?") When Peter saw him, he asked, "Lord, what about him?"

Jesus answered, "If I want him to remain alive until I return, what is that to you? You must follow me." Because of this, the rumor spread among the brothers that this disciple would not die. But Jesus did not say that he would not die; he only said, "If I want him to remain alive until I return, what is that to you?"

246. THE GREAT COMMISSION
Matthew 28:16-20; Mark 16:15-18; 1 Corinthians 15:6a

Then the eleven disciples went to Galilee, to the mountain where Jesus had told them to go. He appeared[20] to more than five hundred of the brothers at the same time.[21] When they saw him, they worshiped him; but some doubted. Then Jesus came to them and said, "All authority in heaven and on earth has been given to me. Therefore go [into all the world and preach the good news to all creation.] Make disciples of all nations, baptizing them in[e] the name of the Father and of the Son and of the Holy Spirit, and teaching them to obey everything I have commanded you. [Whoever believes and is baptized will be saved, but whoever does not believe will be condemned. And these signs will accompany those who believe: In my name they will drive out demons; they will speak in new tongues; they will pick up snakes with their hands; and when they drink deadly poison, it will not hurt them at all; they will place their hands on sick people, and they will get well.] And surely I am with you always, to the very end of the age."[22]

247. THE PROMISE OF THE HOLY SPIRIT
Luke 24:44-49; Acts 1:2b-5; 1 Corinthians 15:5b, 7

Then he appeared to James, then to all the apostles *besides* the Twelve. He showed himself to the apostles he had chosen and gave many convincing proofs that he was alive. He appeared to them over a period of forty days and spoke about the kingdom of God. On one occasion, while he was eating with them, he said, "This is what I told you while I was still with you: Everything must be fulfilled that is written about me in the Law of Moses, the Prophets and the Psalms."

Then he opened their minds so they could understand the Scriptures. He told them, "This is what is written: The Christ will suffer

---

20. See p. 401: When and where did Jesus appear to the disciples in Galilee (Matthew 28:16)?
21. See p. 402: Did Jesus appear to over 500 brethren (1 Corinthians 15:6) in Galilee (Matthew 28:16) or on the Mount of Olives (Luke 24:50; Acts 1:12)?
e. Or *into*; see Acts 8:16; 19:5; Romans 6:3; 1 Corinthians 1:13; 10:2; and Galatians 3:27.
22. See p. 403: Do the Gospels record that Jesus gave The Great Commission to his disciples once (Matthew 28:19-20) or twice (Mark 16:15)?

and rise from the dead on the third day, and repentance and forgiveness of sins will be preached in his name to all nations, beginning at Jerusalem. You are witnesses of these things. I am going to send you what my Father has promised; but stay in the city[23] until you have been clothed with power from on high. Do not leave Jerusalem, but wait for the gift my Father promised, which you have heard me speak about. For John baptized with water, but in a few days you will be baptized with the Holy Spirit."

248. JESUS TAKEN UP INTO HEAVEN
Mark 16:19; Luke 24:50-53; Acts 1:6-12a

So when they *last* met together, he led them out to the vicinity of Bethany. They asked him, "Lord, are you at this time going to restore the kingdom to Israel?"

He said to them: "It is not for you to know the times or dates the Father has set by his own authority. But you will receive power when the Holy Spirit comes on you; and you will be my witnesses in Jerusalem, and in all Judea and Samaria, and to the ends of the earth."

After [the Lord Jesus had] said this [to them,] he lifted up his hands and blessed them. While he was blessing them, he left them and was taken up into heaven before their very eyes, and a cloud hid him from their sight. [He sat at the right hand of God.]

They were looking intently up into the sky as he was going, when suddenly two men dressed in white stood beside them. "Men of Galilee," they said, "why do you stand here looking into the sky? This same Jesus, who has been taken from you into heaven, will come back in the same way you have seen him go into heaven."

Then they worshiped him and returned from the hill called the Mount of Olives[24] to Jerusalem with great joy. And they stayed continually at the temple, praising God.

---

23. See p. 403: Did Jesus give instructions for the disciples to go to Galilee (Matthew 28:7, 10; Mark 16:7) or to remain at Jerusalem (Luke 24:49)?
24. See p. 404: Did Jesus ascend to heaven from the Mount of Olives (Acts 1:9, 12) or from the vicinity of Bethany (Luke 24:50)?

249. THE SPIRIT COMES
Acts 2:1-2, 4a

When the day of Pentecost came, they were all together in one place. Suddenly a sound like the blowing of a violent wind came from heaven and filled the whole house where they were sitting. All of them were filled with the Holy Spirit.

250. THE GOSPEL IS PREACHED
Mark 16:20; John 20:30-31; 21:25

[Then the disciples went out and preached everywhere, and the Lord worked with them and confirmed his word by the signs that accompanied it.]

Jesus did many other miraculous signs in the presence of his disciples, which are not recorded in this book. If every one of them were written down, even the whole world would not have room for the books that would be written. But these are written that you may[f] believe that Jesus is the Christ, the Son of God, and that by believing you may have life in his name.

:

---

f. Some manuscripts [of John 20:31] *may continue to*

PART

2

HARMONIZATION
ENDNOTES

Help in Understanding Gospel Differences

Questions Discussed in Harmonization Endnotes.

CHAPTER ONE: BIRTHS OF JOHN THE BAPTIST AND JESUS

EN 1, p. 285: Did Joseph know of Mary's pregnancy soon after her virginal conception (Luke 1:26) or only after her condition was discovered (Matt. 1:18)?

EN 2, p. 285: Did Joseph have his dream before the birth of John (Matt. 1:18-24) or afterward (Luke 1:56-57)?

EN 3, p. 286: What is the correct genealogy of Jesus (Matt. 1:1-17; Luke 3:23-38)?

EN 4, p. 289: What is the order of events immediately following the birth of Jesus (Matt. 2; Luke 2:1-39)?

CHAPTER TWO: PREPARATION FOR MINISTRY

EN 1, p. 290: Does Mark's *beginning* (Mark 1:1) mean the same as John's *beginning* (John 1:1)?

EN 2, p. 290: Are the exact words of the voice from heaven at Jesus' baptism recorded in Matthew 3:17 or in Mark 1:11 and Luke 3:22?

EN 3, p. 291: In what order did Jesus' second and third temptations occur (Matt. 4:5-10; Luke 4:5-12)?

CHAPTER THREE: GALILEAN MINISTRY

EN 1, p. 293: Did Jesus begin preaching in the synagogues of Galilee (Matt. 4:23; Mark 1:39) or Judea (Luke 4:44)?

EN 2, p. 293: Was Jesus' hometown Nazareth (Luke 4:24) or Capernaum (Matt. 9:1)?

EN 3, p. 294: Did the men carrying the paralytic on a mat dig through the roof of the house (Mark 2:4) or only remove the tiles (Luke 5:19)?

EN 4, p. 294: Was one of Jesus' apostles named Matthew (Matt. 9:9) or Levi (Mark 2:14; Luke 5:27)?

EN 5, p. 295: Was it John's disciples (Matt. 9:14) or those of the Pharisees (Luke 5:30) who questioned Jesus about fasting?

EN 6, p. 295: Did Matthew's banquet and the question on fasting immediately follow his call or was it later?

EN 7, p. 295: How long was the Lord Jesus' public ministry?

CHAPTER FOUR: CHOOSING THE TWELVE AND SERMON ON THE MOUNT

EN 1, p. 297: Was the apostle named Thaddaeus (Matt. 10:4; Mark 3:19) the same as Judas son of James (Luke 6:16; Acts 1:13)?

EN 2, p. 297: Are the Sermon on the Mount (Matt. 5–7) and the Sermon on the Plain (Luke 6) the same or two separate sermons?

EN 3, p. 299: If Matthew and Luke record the same sermon, do Matthew 5:3-11 and Luke 6:20-22 reflect different beatitudes or are they the same, with Matthew as editor?

CHAPTER FIVE: MORE GALILEAN MINISTRY AND PARABLES

EN 1, p. 301: Did the centurion himself approach Jesus to request his servant's healing (Matt. 8:5-13) or did others make the request (Luke 7:1-10)? Was the healing of the centurion's servant the same as that of the royal official's son (John 4:46-54)?

EN 2, p. 302: When Jesus' relatives came to get him, did he refer to *the will of my Father in heaven* (Matt. 12:50) or *God's will* (Mark 3:35)?

CHAPTER SIX: MINISTRY OF MIRACLES

EN 1, p. 304: When Jesus finished teaching the many parables, did he remain in the boat and leave the shore (Mark 4:36) or get out and later get back in to leave (Matt. 8:23)?

EN 2, p. 304: How many times did Jesus permit demons to enter a herd of pigs? Did Jesus heal one demoniac

(Mark 5:2; Luke 8:27) or two (Matt. 8:28)? Did the swine incident occur in the region of the Gadarenes (Matt. 8:28) or Gerasenes (Mark 5:1; Luke 8:26)? Was one of the demoniacs from Gerasa (Luke 8:26-27, 39) or the Decapolis (Mark 5:20)?

EN 3, p. 307: Did Jesus encounter Jairus immediately after healing the two demoniacs and crossing the lake (Mark 5:21-22; Luke 8:40-41), or later at Matthew's house (Matt. 9:10-18)?

EN 4, p. 308: Was Jairus' daughter dying (Mark 5:23; Luke 8:42) or already dead (Matt. 9:18) when he first approached Jesus with his request?

EN 5, p. 308: Was Jesus rejected at Nazareth once (Matt. 13:54-58; Mark 6:1-6) or twice (Luke 4:16-30)?

EN 6, p. 309: Was Jesus unable to do many miracles at Nazareth (Mark 6:5), or did he choose not to do many (Matt. 13:58)?

EN 7, p. 310: Did Jesus instruct his twelve apostles to take a staff and a pair of sandals on their first missionary journey (Mark 6:8-9) or not (Matt. 10:10; Luke 9:3)?

EN 8, p. 310: When Herod imprisoned John the Baptist, did he want to kill John (Matt. 14:5), or did he fear and protect him (Luke 6:20)?

EN 9, p. 311: Following the feeding of the 5,000, did the disciples leave in a boat to go to Bethsaida (Mark 6:45) or to Capernaum (John 6:17)? Was it before Jesus went up to pray (Matt. 14:22-23) or afterward (John 6:15-17)? Did Jesus walk on the water to approach the disciples (Matt. 14:25) or to pass by them (Mark 6:48)? Did they land at Capernaum (John 6:17) or Gennesaret (Matt. 14:34; Mark 6:53)?

CHAPTER SEVEN: **MINISTRY BEYOND GALILEE**

EN 1, p. 313: Was the woman with the demon-possessed daughter a Canaanite (Matt. 15:22) or a Syrian-Phoenician (Mark 7:26)?

EN 2, p. 313: After Jesus fed the 4,000, did he go to Magadan (Matt. 15:39) or Dalmanutha (Mark 8:10)?

EN 3, p. 314: Did Jesus rise from the dead on the third day

(Matt. 16:21; Luke 9:22), after three days (Mark 8:31), or after three days and three nights (Matt. 12:40)? On what day of the week was Jesus crucified?

EN 4, p. 316: After Jesus first predicted his death, did six days (Matt. 17:1; Mark 9:2) or eight days (Luke 9:28) pass before he and the three apostles ascended the Mount of Transfiguration?

EN 5, p. 317: On the Mount of Transfiguration, did Peter address Jesus as *Lord* (Matt. 17:4), *Rabbi* (Mark 9:5), or *Master* (Luke 9:33)?

EN 6, p. 318: Was John the Baptist Elijah (Matt. 17:12; Mark 9:13) or not (John 1:21)?

CHAPTER EIGHT: LAST FEAST OF TABERNACLES

EN 1, p. 319: Is Luke 9:51–18:14 chronological? Does it include any incidents recorded in the other Gospels?

EN 2, p. 321: How can Matthew dislocate an incident in time yet begin the account with the word *Then* (Matt. 8:23)?

EN 3, p. 322: When and where did Jesus encounter those disciples who had not counted the cost (Matt. 8:18-22; Luke 9:52, 56-62)?

CHAPTER NINE: MORE JUDEAN MINISTRY

EN 1, p. 323: Do the Gospels record that Jesus delivered two "Lord's Prayers" or one (Matt. 6:9-13; Luke 11:2-4)?

EN 2, p. 324: How many times do the Gospels record that Jesus spoke of the sign of Jonah (Matt. 12:38-45; 16:1-4; Luke 11:29-32)?

CHAPTER TEN: PEREAN MINISTRY AND RAISING OF LAZARUS

EN 1, p. 325: Did Jesus lament over Jerusalem once (Luke 13:34-35) or twice (Matt. 23:37-39)?

EN 2, p. 326: Do the Gospels record that Jesus taught the parable of the lost sheep on one or two occasions (Matt. 18:12-14; Luke 15:3-7)?

CHAPTER ELEVEN: LAST TRIP TO JERUSALEM

EN 1, p. 327: Do Mark 10:18 and Luke 18:19 relate the exact

EN 2, p. 328: dialogue between Jesus and the rich young ruler, or does Matthew 19:17?

EN 2, p. 328: Did James and John (Mark 10:35), or did their mother (Matt. 20:20), make the request to Jesus that the two brothers sit on Jesus' immediate right and left hand in his kingdom?

EN 3, p. 328: Did Jesus heal the two blind men on his entry into Jericho (Luke 18:35) or on his departure (Matt. 20:29; Mark 10:46)?

EN 4, p. 330: On his last approach to Jerusalem, did Jesus heal one blind man near Jericho (Mark 10:46; Luke 18:35) or two (Matt. 20:30)?

CHAPTER TWELVE: **LAST JERUSALEM MINISTRY**

EN 1, p. 331: At his Triumphal Entry into Jerusalem, did Jesus have one donkey (Mark 11:7; Luke 19:35; John 12:14) or two (Matt. 21:7)? Did he sit simultaneously on both the donkey and her colt?

EN 2, p. 331: Did Jesus cleanse the temple on Sunday (Matt. 21:1-17; Luke 19:29-46) or Monday (Mark 11:1-17) of Passion Week?

EN 3, p. 332: Did Jesus cleanse the temple by expelling the money changers once (Matt. 21:12; Mark 11:15; Luke 19:45) or twice (John 2:13-16)?

EN 4, p. 333: Did the disciples see the fig tree withered on Monday, the same day Jesus cursed it (Matt. 21:20), or on Tuesday, the day following the curse (Mark 11:20)?

CHAPTER THIRTEEN: **PREDICTING THE FUTURE**

EN 1, p. 335: Do the Gospels account for one, two, or three anointings of Jesus while he was alive (Matt. 26:7; Mark 14:3; Luke 7:38; John 12:3)? If there were two anointings, was the one at Bethany two days before Passover (Matt. 26:2; Mark 14:1) or six days before (John 12:1)?

CHAPTER FOURTEEN: **LAST SUPPER AND GETHSEMANE**

EN 1, p. 339: Did Jesus and his apostles eat the Passover meal (Matt. 26:17-26; Mark 14:12-18; Luke 22:8-19) or not (Luke 22:15-16)?

EN 2, p. 340: Did Jesus and his apostles eat the Passover meal on the Day of Passover (Matt. 26:17; Mark 14:12; Luke 22:7) or the day before (John 18:28; 19:14)?

EN 3, p. 343: When Judas left the Upper Room, did the disciples understand that he would betray Jesus (Matt. 26:20, 25) or not (John 13:27-28)?

EN 4, p. 348: Was Judas present during the institution of the Communion service (Luke 22:17-22; John 13:26-30)?

EN 5, p. 349: When Jesus instituted the Communion service, are his exact words recorded in Matthew 26:26-28 and Mark 14:22-24 or in Luke 22:19-20 and 1 Corinthians 11:24-25?

EN 6, p. 349: Did the disciples' dispute over which of them was the greatest emerge before they ate the Passover or afterward (Luke 22:24)?

EN 7, p. 350: Did Jesus predict Peter's denials before they all left the Upper Room (Luke 22:34-39; John 13:38; 14:31) or afterward (Matt. 26:30-35; Mark 14:26-31)?

EN 8, p. 351: Did Jesus and his apostles leave the Upper Room before his words in John 14–17 or afterward (Matt. 26:30; Mark 14:26; Luke 22:39)? What was the order of events surrounding their departure?

EN 9, p. 352: What were the exact words that Jesus prayed in Gethsemane (Matt. 26:39-44; Mark 14:36-39; Luke 22:42)?

CHAPTER FIFTEEN: TRIALS, DEATH, AND BURIAL

EN 1, p. 354: Who was the *young man* who fled Gethsemane naked, leaving his linen garment behind (Mark 14:51-52)?

EN 2, p. 354: Who was the other disciple who accompanied Peter at Jesus' trials (John 18:15-16)?

EN 3, p. 354: Did Peter make his first denial of Jesus in the courtyard of Annas (John 18:12-15, 24) or of Caiaphas (Matt. 26:57-58)?

EN 4, p. 356: Who was the high priest: Caiaphas (Matt. 26:3, 57; John 11:49; 18:13-14) or Annas (Luke 3:2; Acts 4:6)? Which one examined Jesus while Peter made his first denial (John 18:19-24)?

EN 5, p. 359: Was Peter sitting in the courtyard or standing in the gateway when he made his first and second denials of Jesus (Matt. 26:69-72; Mark 14:66-70; Luke 22:54-58; John 18:17, 25)?

EN 6, p. 360: Who accused Peter at his second denial: the same servant girl as before (Mark 14:66, 69), another girl (Matt. 26:69, 71), or a man (Luke 22:58)?

EN 7, p. 361: Did one person question Peter the third time he denied Jesus (Luke 22:59; John 18:26), or did several people question him (Matt. 26:73; Mark 14:70)?

EN 8, p. 362: How many times did Peter deny Christ?

EN 9, p. 363: When Peter made his third denial, did the cock crow for the first time (Matt. 26:74; Luke 22:60; John 18:27) or the second time (Mark 14:30, 68, 72)?

EN 10, p. 364: Did the Sanhedrin assemble at night, before Peter's denials (Matt. 26:59, 69; Mark 14:55, 68), or at daybreak, after them (Luke 22:57, 66)?

EN 11, p. 365: At Jesus' trial before the Sanhedrin, did the high priest ask the question that led to the charge of blasphemy (Matt. 26:63-65; Mark 14:61-64) or did others (Luke 22:66-70)? What was the form of the question and Jesus' answer to it?

EN 12, p. 366: Did Judas buy the potter's field (Acts 1:18), or did the chief priests buy it (Matt. 27:7)?

EN 13, p. 367: Did Judas hang himself (Matt. 27:5), or did he fall to his death (Acts 1:18)?

EN 14, p. 367: Was the potter's field later called the *Field of Blood* because of the *blood money* (Matt. 27:6-8) or Judas' bloody fall (Acts 1:18-19)?

EN 15, p. 368: How many times was Jesus mocked? Did the soldiers put a robe and a crown of thorns on Jesus once (Luke 23:11; John 19:1-2) or twice (Matt. 27:27-31; Mark 15:16-20)? What was the order of events surrounding the examinations of Jesus by the Roman authorities? Was the robe scarlet (Matt. 27:28) or purple (Mark 15:17; John 19:2)?

EN 16, p. 369: How many trials did Jesus endure?

EN 17, p. 370: Did Jesus carry his own cross (Matt. 27:32; Mark 15:21; Luke 23:26) or did Simon of Cyrene carry it (John 19:17)?

EN 18, p. 371: Was the drink that Jesus refused at Golgotha wine mixed with gall (Matt. 27:34) or wine mixed with myrrh (Mark 15:23)?

EN 19, p. 371: Was Jesus crucified at the third hour (Mark 15:25) or after the sixth hour (John 19:14)?

EN 20, p. 377: Which of the four different inscriptions provided by the Evangelists was written on the sign attached to Jesus' cross (Matt. 27:37; Mark 15:26; Luke 23:38; John 19:19)?

EN 21, p. 378: Did both of the criminals crucified with Jesus insult him (Matt. 27:44; Mark 15:32), or did only one mock him (Luke 23:39)?

EN 22, p. 378: How many times was Jesus offered a drink at Golgotha (Matt. 27:34, 48; Mark 15:23, 36; Luke 23:36; John 19:29-30)?

EN 23, p. 379: What year was Jesus crucified? How old was Jesus when he died?

EN 24, p. 380: Did Mary, the mother of Jesus, and Mary Magdalene stand near the cross (Matt. 27:55; Mark 15:40; Luke 23:49) or watch from a distance (John 19:25)?

EN 25, p. 380: Was Jesus' body wrapped with a single linen cloth (Matt. 27:59; Mark 15:46; Luke 23:53) or with strips of linen (John 19:40)?

CHAPTER SIXTEEN: RESURRECTION, APPEARANCES, AND ASCENSION

EN 1, p. 381: Can the NT accounts of the resurrection of Jesus be harmonized?

EN 2, p. 383: When Mary Magdalene first visited the tomb on Easter morning, was she alone (John 20:1) or with the other women (Matt. 28:1; Mark 16:1; Luke 24:1)? If with others, why did John mention only that Mary Magdalene went to the tomb?

EN 3, p. 383: In order to anoint Jesus' body, did the women buy and prepare spices before the Sabbath (Luke 23:55-56) or afterward (Mark 16:1)?

EN 4, p. 384: If Jesus' body had already been anointed (John 19:39-40), the tomb sealed, and a Roman guard posted there (Matt. 27:66), why did the women visit the tomb to anoint the body (Mark 16:1; Luke 24:1)?

EN 5, p. 385: Did the women leave for the tomb during darkness (John 20:1) or after sunrise (Mark 16:2)?

EN 6, p. 386: Did the women first see the angel(s) outside the tomb (Matt. 28:2) or inside it (Mark 16:4-5; Luke 24:2-4)?

EN 7, p. 387: Was there one man (Mark 16:5) or one angel at the tomb (Matt. 28:2), or were there two men (Luke 24:4) or two angels (Luke 24:23; John 20:12)?

EN 8, p. 388: Were the angels in the tomb sitting (Mark 16:5) or standing (Luke 24:4) when the women first saw them?

EN 9, p. 389: Did the angel conclude his announcement to the women by saying he had told them (Matt. 28:7), or that Jesus had told them (Mark 16:7)?

EN 10, p. 390: Were the women afraid (Mark 16:8) or joyful (Matt. 28:8) when they hurried off to tell the disciples of the empty tomb?

EN 11, p. 391: Did Mary Magdalene enter the tomb and hear the angel's announcement (Mark 16:1-8) on her first visit there Easter morning or not (John 20:1-2)? What is the order of events surrounding Mary Magdalene's two visits to the tomb?

EN 12, p. 393: Who was *the other disciple* (John 20:2, 4, 8) whom Mary Magdalene told about the empty tomb and who outran Peter there?

EN 13, p. 393: How many women visited Jesus' tomb on Easter morning (Matt. 28:1; Mark 16:1; Luke 24:1, 10; John 20:1)? Why does each Evangelist report a different number of women who visited the tomb?

EN 14, p. 394: Did the risen Jesus appear to the other women on their way to tell the apostles of the empty tomb (Matt. 28:9) or afterward (Luke 24:9, 22-23)? What was the order of events on that Easter Sunday?

EN 15, p. 395: Why did Jesus give instructions for his disciples to go to Galilee to meet him (Matt. 28:10), since he met them that evening in Jerusalem (Mark 16:14; Luke 24:36; John 20:19)?

EN 16, p. 397: As the disciples gathered in Jerusalem that first Easter evening, did they believe that Jesus had risen from the dead (Luke 24:34) or not (Luke 24:38; Mark 16:13-14)?

EN 17, p. 399: Did Jesus meet his disciples in and near Jerusalem (Luke 24:13-51) or in Galilee (Matt. 28:16)?

EN 18, p. 400: When Jesus appeared to his gathered disciples that first Easter evening, were there ten (John 20:24) or eleven (Luke 24:33) apostles present?

EN 19, p. 401: When Jesus appeared to the gathered disciples that first Easter evening, were they overjoyed (John 20:20) or doubtful (Luke 24:38)?

EN 20, p. 401: When and where did Jesus appear to the disciples in Galilee (Matt. 28:16)?

EN 21, p. 402: Did Jesus appear to over 500 brethren (1 Cor. 15:6) in Galilee (Matt. 28:16) or on the Mount of Olives (Luke 24:50; Acts 1:12)?

EN 22, p. 403: Do the Gospels record that Jesus gave The Great Commission to his disciples once (Matt. 28:19-20) or twice (Mark 16:15)?

EN 23, p. 403: Did Jesus give instructions for the disciples to go to Galilee (Matt. 28:7, 10; Mark 16:7) or to remain at Jerusalem (Luke 24:49)?

EN 24, p. 404: Did Jesus ascend to heaven from the Mount of Olives (Acts 1:9, 12) or from the vicinity of Bethany (Luke 24:50)?

Abbreviations.

A.D.	*Anno Domini* (in the year of our Lord)
assoc. ed.	associate editor
aug.	augmented by
AV	*Authorized Version = King James Version*
B.C.	Before Christ
ca.	*circa* (about, approximately)
cf.	*confer* (compare)
ch(s).	chapter(s)
comp.	compiler, compiled by
ed. (eds.)	editor(s), edited by, edition
e.g.	*exempli gratia* (for example)
EN	endnote
et al.	*et alii* (and others)
etc.	*et cetera* (and so forth)
f. (ff.)	and following (*pl.* ff.)
gen. ed.	general editor
Ibid.	*ibidem* (in the same work previously cited)
i.e.	*id est* (that is)
KJV = AV	*King James Version = Authorized Version*
lit.	literally
LXX	Septuagint (Greek translation of the Hebrew OT)
MS (MSS)	manuscript(s)
n	note
NASB	*New American Standard Bible*
n.d.	no date
NIV	*New International Version*
NT	New Testament
OT	Old Testament

p., pp.	page, pages
pt.	part
rep.	reprint
rev.	revisor, revised by
rev. ed.	revised edition
RSV	*Revised Standard Version*
TR	*Textus Receptus* (Received Text)
tr.	translator, translated by
v., vv.	verse, verses
viz.	*videlicet* (namely)
vol(s).	volume(s)
[]	Brackets in a quotation either indicate this author's own words, or the English equivalent for a Greek word.

Introduction to Harmonization Endnotes.

Harmonization

Most believers in Jesus Christ accept the four Gospels of the New Testament (NT) as divinely inspired by God and without error in the original autographs. Upon making a comparison of the Gospels for the first time, the faithful are likely to become troubled over certain variations in the accounts, some of them appearing as contradictions. These comparisons are often called *apparent discrepancies*. Discrepancy means an "inconsistency between facts; disagreement." An apparent discrepancy, however, only *appears* to be a contradiction, not that it actually *is* one. Attempts to resolve such difficulties are referred to as *harmonization*. With a few brief exceptions, these endnotes are concerned only with the treatment of harmonizing and chronological difficulties arising from a comparison of the Gospels. Their primary purpose is to acquaint the reader with these apparent discrepancies and present the leading proposals offered by commentators to harmonize them. In these endnotes Gospel differences are pointed out in question form and in each case solutions are presented in the "answer" that follows.

Harmonizing difficulties in the Gospels are of various types. Some are simply variations resulting from two or more writers reporting the same incidents differently. Others may be attributed to one writer presenting additional information not found in the other accounts. Both are phenomena often observed in law court cases involving multiple witnesses. A few problems arise because a later Gospel writer has edited previously written sources for the sake of brevity or explanation. This is the frequent solution to many harmonizing difficulties arising from a comparison of Matthew's Gospel with those of the other Synoptics. (The Synoptic Gospels are those of Matthew, Mark, and Luke.)

History and Necessity of Harmonization

Throughout church history, biblical scholars have devoted considerable attention to harmonization of the Gospels. Augustine, one of the greatest minds to influence Western civilization, produced ca. A.D. 400 the first full-fledged work on harmonization of the four Gospels.[1] It is regarded by scholars as Augustine's most laborious undertaking, yet it receives little recognition compared to his other works. John Calvin authored the first major Protestant work on harmonization of the Synoptic Gospels. He prefaces this three-volume commentary with the following observation:

> It is beyond all dispute, that it is impossible to expound, in a proper and successful manner, any one of the Evangelists, without comparing him with the other two; and, accordingly, faithful and learned commentators spend a very great portion of their labour on reconciling the narratives of the three Evangelists.[2]

From the Reformation until this century, there appeared much work on Gospel harmonization. However, in the past century, attention to harmonization of the Gospels has greatly dwindled among NT scholars. This may be attributed to the following factors:

a. a long history of unwarranted, forced, dogmatic harmonizations by conservative scholars who, in their eagerness to present a solution to every problem, fail to consider the many facets of a harmonizing difficulty[3], and

b. the rise of form criticism, which tends to undermine the historical accuracy of the Gospels and render harmonization irrelevant.

Despite the claims by radical critics that harmonization of the Gospels is impossible and to be forsaken, careful harmonization of the Gospels is a commendable and necessary discipline. D.A. Carson concurs:

---

1. Augustine, *The Harmony of the Gospels*, vol. 6 in *The Nicene and Post-Nicene Fathers (First Series)*, ed. Philip Schaff, 14 vols. (New York: Scribner's, 1888).
2. John Calvin, *Commentary on a Harmony of the Evangelists, Matthew, Mark, and Luke* [1555], tr. Rev. William Pringle (Grand Rapids: Eerdmans, 1956), pp. xxxix-xl.
3. It is only fair here to state that these are often no more unwarranted and dogmatic than those speculative assertions laid down by liberal form critics who try to "get behind the Gospels" to establish oral tradition between the time period of the beginning of the Christian era and the writing of the NT Gospels.

Harmonization . . . currently has a very bad name in NT scholarship.

Harmonization should be avoided where details are obscure, but refusal to attempt harmonization of documents treating the same events is methodologically irresponsible.[4]

Forced, dogmatic harmonizations of the Gospels, however, are a hindrance to the Christian faith, fueling charges by liberal scholars that conservative scholarship is irresponsible. M.B. Riddle provides this assessment:

The dangers attending harmonistic methods are obvious enough, and appeared very early. The tendency has been to create a rigid, verbal uniformity. . . . When uniformity could not be secured by this process, false exegesis was often resorted to, and hermeneutical principles avowed which injured the cause of truth. Evangelical truth cannot be defended with the weapons of error. This vicious method was usually the result of mechanical views of inspiration.

The tendency just referred to brought harmonistic labours into disrepute.[5]

Robert Stein explains:

The terms *harmonize* and *harmonization* have fallen into disrepute. Some of this may be due to the farfetched and unconvincing harmonizations made in the past by certain scholars.

A prejudiced handling of the data for the sake of establishing the harmony of the Gospels (or for establishing a disharmony) is neither commendable nor, in the case of the former, devout.

On occasion the reader may be disappointed that the author has not found a convincing explanation. This should not be construed as a lack of confidence in the Word of God on the part of the author. Rather it should be interpreted as indicating that the Christian in this life can only "know in part" (1 Cor. 13:12).[6]

---

4. D.A. Carson, *Matthew*, gen. ed. Frank E. Gaebelein, *The Expositor's Bible Commentary*, 12 vols. (Grand Rapids: Zondervan, 1984), 8:11, 221.
5. M.B. Riddle, "Introductory Essay" to Augustine's *Harmony in Nicene and Post-Nicene Fathers (First Series)*, Schaff, 6:68.
6. Robert Stein, *Difficult Passages in the Gospels* (Grand Rapids: Baker, 1984), 13-14.

In conclusion, consider the following comments by harmonist A.T. Robertson, who generally rejects dogmatic solutions of the more debated difficulties:

> It is the work of supererogation to proceed to show that this or that explanation is the real solution of the problem.
> The harmonist has done his duty, if he can show a reasonable explanation of the problem before him.[7]

Biblical Criticism

In the last century, biblical scholars entered into a deeper study of the differences in the Gospel accounts by applying what is called *literary criticism*. The first result was a discipline called source criticism. It is based on the conviction that a detailed comparison of the Gospels indicates that some, or all, of the Gospel writers made use of previously written sources in compiling their Gospels. In this century, the disciplines of form and redaction criticism have arisen. Form criticism refers to the supposed forms of oral tradition that developed preceding the written Gospels. Redaction criticism identifies a method of composition in which the Gospel author supposedly editorialized previously written sources. The overall term applied to these three categories is *biblical criticism*.

These terms and their concepts may seem threatening to the devout believer in God's Word. Indeed, liberal scholars have radically applied these disciplines to Scripture, thereby injuring the faith that has been handed down to us by the apostles of Christ. Form criticism is a very speculative discipline which generally rests on weak views of inspiration of Scripture. However, a conservative use of the literary tools of source and redaction criticism are continually being recognized by faithful biblical scholars as a beneficial discipline in biblical studies.

In this century, literary biblical criticism has undergone reaction from the Christian community similar to that toward textual criticism in the last century. NT textual criticism is the science of determining the most accurate Greek text of the NT, the oldest NT MSS being written in Greek.[8] Due to the discovery of many older and more reliable Greek MSS of the NT, such new Greek texts

---

7. John A. Broadus, *A Harmony of the Gospels*, with additional notes by A.T. Robertson (New York: A.C. Armstrong, 1893), 232.
8. New Testament textual criticism is the indispensable science of composing a Greek text of the New Testament from more than 5,000 extant Greek manuscripts. It is from such a Greek text that versions of the New Testament are translated.

provide a definite improvement over *Textus Receptus* (TR = Received Text), from which the Authorized Version (AV = KJV) was translated. The Greek text of Westcott and Hort (WH, 1881), from which the Revised Version (RV) of the English Bible was translated, began the flood of modern versions of the Bible. Although such improved Greek texts compiled from earlier MSS insure greater accuracy of Scripture, for a while there remained considerable opposition. Similar opposition to modern versions of the Bible still continues today by some Fundamentalists who largely ignore the advances of textual criticism.

There continues to exist a need for Gospel harmonization that takes into account recent biblical criticism.[9] This need is at least partially addressed in these endnotes.

The Gospel of Matthew

A predominant number of harmonizing difficulties arise in comparing the Gospel of Matthew with the other Synoptics. Most contemporary biblical scholars, taking source and redaction criticism into account, regard many of these difficulties in the Gospel of Matthew as the result of the author's editorializing of previously written sources. These are some of the distinctives of the Gospel of Matthew compared to the other Synoptics:

a. It is the least chronological of the Gospels, the sections being arranged topically more often than in the other Gospels.

b. Matthew often abbreviates his narratives, presumably to include more events from the life of Jesus on his scroll. (Scrolls generally conformed to a standard length, a maximum of 25 to 35 feet.)

c. If, of the Synoptists, Matthew wrote last, as has been widely accepted by NT scholars for more than a century, he surely followed a practice employed by the Apostle John in his Gospel. Both internal evidence and tradition from the writings of early church fathers confirm that one of John's purposes in writing the last Gospel was to supplement the material of the previously published Synoptic Gospels. Likewise, Matthew supplements his written sources by including additional events; it is further believed that Matthew, in consulting his written sources, frequently editorialized with the aim of interpretation or explanation of what had already been written. When the literary style and method of composition of the Gospel of Matthew are understood and accepted, many harmonizing difficulties disappear.

---

9. Carson, *Matthew*, 8:25-26.

Inspiration of Scripture

No study more greatly affects one's view of the inspiration of the Holy Scriptures than a comparative study of the Gospels. Believers in the NT Gospels accept as their basis of inspiration the following promise of Jesus to his apostles: *The Holy Spirit, whom the Father will send in my name, will teach you all things and will remind you of everything I have said to you* (John 14:26). In applying this statement, many of the faithful restrict it to a mechanical view of inspiration of Scripture: that the Gospel writers acted only in the capacity of stenographers, receiving mental dictation from the Spirit of God when they penned their Gospels. Most believers, however, accept that, along with the inspiration of the Spirit, the individual personality, vocabulary, and writing style of the human authors was not obliterated, being evidenced in their writings. Literary criticism, however, further alleges that these writers borrowed and interpreted from each other, or from other written sources, raising serious implications regarding theories of inspiration of Scripture. Stein remarks:

> If the Christian can accept that the Evangelists were permitted to be inspired interpreters of Jesus' teachings, and were not simply stenographers, numerous difficulties disappear.[10]

Regardless of the degree of legitimacy of his personal use of such literary tools, Robert Gundry well defends source and redaction criticism in the Gospel of Matthew by explaining:

> Doubt that [Matthew] would have used the Gospel of Mark rests on modern antipathy toward literary borrowing. Moderns regard such borrowing as plagiarism or, at best, unworthy dependence. Ancients did not share this antipathy. On the contrary, they strongly believed in literary borrowing as a way of preserving tradition.[11]

Like other sciences, communication skills in writing have advanced in modern times. Modern writers have the advantages of avoiding plagiarism and identifying sources by using quotation marks, parentheses, brackets, and other means of punctuation, footnote references, etc. All of these writing tools were unavailable to

---

10. Stein, *Difficult Passages*, 125.
11. Robert H. Gundry, *Matthew: A Commentary on His Literary and Theological Art* (Grand Rapids: Eerdmans, 1981), 621.

ancient writers. In fact, no punctuation at all was used in Greek until about the fourth century, a fact which arouses curiosity among scholars regarding the later scribal addition of punctuation to Greek NT MSS.

Gundry alleges that those who embrace a mechanical view of inspiration (Spirit dictation only) fail to recognize the editorial style of Matthew. He concludes concerning their observations:

> The differences [between the Gospels] are so acute that [some] suggested harmonizations look pathetic, as in the views (all actually put forward) that Peter denied Jesus not just three times, but four, six, and even eight times.[12]

Ipsissma Vox and Ipsissma Verba

Direct personal quotes in the Gospels, particularly those of Jesus, are of the utmost importance. The first three Gospels often vary in rendering the same quotation. Many scholars identify these numerous variations in quotations as either the *ipsissma vox* or *ipsissma verba.*[13] (See EN 2:2.) The *ipsissma vox* refers to the intent or meaning of the person's voice, which is accurately preserved but in the writer's own words. The *ipsissma verba* means the words actually spoken. Augustine is one early commentator who recognized this difference yet did not regard it as significant. He maintained that "what we have to look to in studying a person's words is nothing else than the intention of the speakers."[14]

The concept of *ipsissma verba* raises another consideration. "It has long been recognized that Jesus' discourses were spoken in Aramaic."[15] The same is presumably true for most quotations of persons in the Gospels. Aramaic was a Semitic language kin to Hebrew. It was spoken by the Jews in Jesus' day. The church at Jerusalem consisted primarily of those of the Aramaic-speaking community (Acts 6:1). A few words in Jesus' sayings are preserved in Aramaic in the Greek MSS. Yet almost all quotations of characters appearing in the Gospels have been preserved only in Greek. Besides the few actual Aramaic words which Greek MSS include, the *ipsissma verba* is generally regarded as including precise translation into Greek. In some instances, the difference in wording of the same quotation by

---

12. Ibid., 626.
13. E.g., see Carson, *Matthew,* 8:110.
14. Augustine, *Harmony,* 6:149.
15. Everett F. Harrison, *A Short Life of Christ* (Grand Rapids: Eerdmans, 1968), 60.

Gospel writers may be attributed to the possibility that an Aramaic word or expression was capable of more than one translation into Greek.

Chronology

A minor purpose of these endnotes is to discuss some chronological difficulties in the Gospels. The chronology of events in *The Gospels Interwoven* is determined by prevailing opinion among leading harmonists, as demonstrated in The Chronological Table. (Also see Principles of Composition.)

Neither the ancient nor the Eastern mindset has been as keenly attuned to chronological historiography as the modern Western has been, oftentimes to the frustration of the latter. The Gospel writers were not always concerned with reporting their facts in chronological order; sometimes it is evident that the author's thematic purpose superseded chronological interests. One of several examples is that Matthew and Luke record the three temptations of Jesus with the second and third in opposite order. Perhaps Matthew records the actual order while on the other hand Luke places the temptation at the temple in Jerusalem last due to his focus upon Jerusalem. (See EN 2:3.)

Some harmonists regard the least variation in wording, as well as any deviation in chronological arrangement, as indicating separate events. Such an approach is predicated on a mechanical view of inspiration. The classic example is Osiander's old and popular *Harmonia Evangelourum* (1537), which represents all four Gospels as written in perfect chronological order. This resulted in his adoption of such views as the following: Jesus raised Jairus' daughter from the dead twice; Jesus was crowned with thorns on two separate occasions; and Peter denied Jesus six times! J.H.A. Ebrard gives the following assessment of Osiander's method:

> His dogmatic assumption was this, that as the Evangelists were inspired, and therefore wrote *truth*, the discourses of Jesus must be reported word for word, and his acts and words must all be narrated in the exact order in which they occurred. This conclusion from the doctrinal notion of inspiration was evidently founded upon a second *philosophical* assumption, viz., that there can be no higher truth than that of chronological sequence and verbal accuracy. Osiander could not see that an author may arrange his materials according to their subjects

rather than their sequence, and yet write with historical fidelity and truth.[16]

In addition, Stein observes that

> Augustine and Calvin believed that a high view of the inspiration and trustworthiness of the Scriptures does not require such a radical view.[17]

For this reason Calvin pronounced quite an unfavorable opinion on Osiander's work.[18]

In contrast to those harmonists just mentioned, form critics tend to regard similar but different incidents as identical. This issues from their weak view of the inspiration of Scripture and speculative conviction that Gospel writers relied heavily on the earlier development of a refined oral tradition, which tradition these scholars believe it is possible to extract from the written Gospels, reshape, and finally recover. For example, form critics generally recognize only one anointing of Jesus with perfume in the Gospels. Harmonists who view the Gospels as written wholly chronologically distinguish three anointings, but most harmonists find two anointings, as herein.[19] This author shuns form criticism but allows for a source-critical view of the formation of the Gospels.

Scanning the Scripture Index and/or The Chronological Table reveals which events have been identified as chronologically displaced by the majority of leading harmonists over the past 325 years. The Gospel of Matthew is indisputably regarded as having been arranged topically more than any of the other Gospels,[20] although it is still far more chronological than it is topical. The entire Gospel of Mark is accepted as chronological in *The Gospels Interwoven*, except for Mark's location of Jesus' prediction of Peter's denials and some of the denials themselves—a total of only fourteen verses.[21] According to the Scripture Index, Luke has topically rearranged only two sections and twelve other verses. John's Gospel is found herein

---

16. Ebrard, *Gospel History*, 49.
17. Stein, *Difficult Passages*, 12.
18. Schaff-Herzog, *New Schaff-Herzog Religious Encyclopedia*, 153.
19. "Herein" is used in the following endnotes to refer to the composite text of *The Gospels Interwoven*.
20. The exceptions would be those few harmonists who claim all four Gospels were written chronologically.
21. Mark's retrogression on John the Baptist's imprisonment in Mark 6:17-18 is, strictly speaking, not a chronological dislocation.

to be chronological throughout except for his dislocation[22] of the anointing at Bethany (John 12:1-11), this author's only noteworthy departure from The Chronological Table.[23]

The meaning of Luke's prologue has been of utmost importance to NT scholars. Not only does it contain a possible hint at Luke's use of written sources for composing his Gospel, but what did Luke mean when he claimed that he wrote *an orderly account*? (Luke 1:3) I. Howard Marshall is probably representative of contemporary scholarship in explaining that the Greek word

> may be taken to imply chronological exactitude or simply an orderly and lucid narrative. Luke's actual procedure may seem to rule out the idea of chronological exactitude, but . . . he is broadly chronological in his treatment.[24]

Early patristic evidence suggests that certain connective words used between events in the synoptics may not indicate the chronological sequence of events that is generally supposed. (See EN 8:2 and EN 14:7.) William L. Lane observes:

> The earliest statement concerning the Gospel of Mark is that of Papias, Bishop of Hierapolis, who wrote a book now lost, *Exegesis of the Lord's Oracles* (ca. A.D. 140), but known to us through quotations made by Eusebius. At one point he cited the testimony of an elder, who was evidently an older contemporary: "And the Elder said this also: 'Mark, having become the interpreter of Peter, wrote down accurately whatever he remembered of the things said and done by the Lord, but not however in order.' For neither did he hear the Lord, nor did he follow him, but afterwards, as I said, Peter, who adapted his teachings to the needs of his hearers, but not as though he were drawing up a connected account of the Lord's oracles."[25]

It seems best, therefore, to regard any sequential arrangement of events of the Gospels, such as found in *The Gospels Interwoven*, with a certain tentativeness. Such imperfection need not disturb the reader

---

22. Herein, the term *dislocations* refers exclusively to incidents that are not chronologically arranged by the Gospel writers, usually arranged topically instead.
23. The other departures from The Chronological Table are as follows: Section 9: The Genealogies of Jesus; Section 196: The Greeks Seek Jesus; Section 197: The Jews Continue in Their Unbelief.
24. I. Howard Marshall, *The Gospel of Luke* (Grand Rapids: Eerdmans, 1978), 43.
25. William L. Lane, *The Gospel According to Mark: The English Text with Introduction, Exposition and Notes* (Grand Rapids: Eerdmans, 1974), 8.

or cause the forsaking of a harmony. The facts are that the Gospel arrangements of events themselves vary chronologically in many places. Although the Gospel writers were not always concerned with chronological exactitude, this did not deter them, or the Spirit of God, from producing these arrangements.

Conclusion

Most Christians remain unaware of the existence of apparent discrepancies, as well as of past efforts to harmonize them. This is due to a lack of comparative study of the Gospels. Some commentators contend that a composite harmony ought to be avoided because it ignores the individual distinctions of the Gospels. Nevertheless, readers of an interwoven harmony may be stimulated to comparative study for the first time in an effort to determine whether they can trust their harmony.

The following serves as an outline for each of the Harmonization Endnotes:
   a. Identification of the problem
   b. A survey of solutions offered by leading commentators
   c. Some discussion of their strengths and/or weaknesses
   d. The prevailing view among these commentators
   e. The author's preference when he has one

Efforts were made to avoid dogmatic assertions regarding those problems much debated by conservative commentators. This approach seeks to maintain intellectual honesty.

Both novice and student can well benefit from the work of Gospel harmonization. It is an apologetic study that supports the integrity of the Gospels and undergirds faith in the Lord Jesus Christ.

:

Harmonization Endnotes:
Help in Understanding Gospel Differences.

CHAPTER ONE
BIRTHS OF JOHN THE BAPTIST AND JESUS

1. Did Joseph know of Mary's pregnancy soon after her virginal conception or only after her condition was discovered?

The angel announced to Mary that she would conceive by the Holy Spirit (Luke 1:35), but Matthew 1:18 suggests that Joseph did not know this until at least three months later, when *she was found to be with child.* Some presume a discrepancy here, supposing that Mary would have told Joseph of the angel's appearance and message. However, Joseph probably did not see Mary from the time of the angel's appearance to her (Luke 1:39) through the first three months of her pregnancy, which time she spent with Elizabeth in Judah (v. 56). On her return home, or soon afterward, Mary's pregnancy became evident. Joseph could have had his dream immediately after Mary's arrival, before she had opportunity to explain to him. On the other hand, she could have explained the matter to Joseph, in which case he did not believe her. Possibly Mary kept these things to herself, as she did on other occasions (e.g., Luke 2:19, 51).

2. Did Joseph have his dream before the birth of John or afterward?

It seems from Luke's arrangement of the facts that Mary returned home before John the Baptist was born. During the sixth month of Elizabeth's pregnancy with John the Baptist, the angel appeared to Mary to announce her conception by the Holy Spirit and the coming birth of Jesus (Luke 1:35). Immediately following the angel's announcement, Mary left Nazareth in Galilee, went approximately 60 miles away to *the hill country of Judah* (v. 39), *stayed with Elizabeth for about three months and then returned home* (v. 56). From these two figures it is concluded that Mary remained with Elizabeth until Elizabeth neared her full term of pregnancy; then Mary returned home. In Luke's account, the birth of John the Baptist immediately follows Mary's return home (Luke 1:56-57).

It seems Joseph did not see Mary for the first three months of her pregnancy. Apparently upon her return home Joseph discovered Mary's pregnancy, for she *was found to be with child* (Matt. 1:18). He considered a private annulment of their engagement, which in ancient custom involved stronger commitment than modern Western engagement. It was at that time that Joseph had his dream. Whether it occurred before or after the birth of John the Baptist cannot be determined with certainty. Herein,[1] Joseph's dream follows John's birth, where the majority of harmonists in The Chronological Table have placed it.

3. What is the correct genealogy of Jesus?

The genealogy of Jesus is only recorded in Matthew 1:1-17 and Luke 3:23-38. These two lists differ in several respects, causing a considerable and complex harmonizing difficulty that has received much attention throughout the history of the church. The primary differences, along with some explanation for them, may be summed up as follows:

a. The genealogies are located differently, have a different starting point and opposite order. Matthew locates his genealogy at the beginning of his Gospel, just prior to the birth of Jesus. He introduces it as *the genealogy of Jesus Christ the son of David, the son of Abraham* (Matt. 1:1), with the descent progressing forward in the time from Abraham to Jesus. As a former Jewish tax collector, Matthew initially wrote his Gospel to what has been historically accepted as a primarily Jewish readership, hence the origin with Abraham.[2] On the other hand, Luke the physician distinguished his Gospel from the others by writing it as a letter addressed to the Gentile name Theophilus (Luke 1:3). That is why Luke's genealogy traces backward beyond Abraham to Adam (Luke 3:38), "probably with the intention of stressing the identification of Jesus with the entire human race."[3] Luke surprisingly places his genealogy after the birth and boyhood of Jesus, between his baptism and three temptations. Apparently, Luke's later location of the genealogy was designed to connect, and possibly contrast, Jesus with Adam. He first establishes that Jesus is the *Son* of God from the

---

1. "Herein" is used in these Endnotes to reference the composite text of *The Gospels Interwoven.*
2. The Jewish title "Son of David" is applied to Jesus more frequently in Matthew's Gospel than in the other Gospels.
3. Walter Liefeld, *Luke* in *The Expositor's Bible Commentary*, gen. ed. Frank E. Gaebelein, 12 vols. (Grand Rapids: Zondervan, 1984), 8:61.

testimony of the *voice . . . from heaven* (v. 22), then introduces the genealogy that culminates in Adam being *the son of God* (v. 38). Additional evidence for such a design is that Luke follows his genealogy with the temptations, in which the devil questions the unique Sonship of Jesus to God (Luke 4:3, 9). Perhaps Luke again intends a subtle contrast of the failure of Adam in temptation with the victory of Christ in temptation.

b. The lists of names are different. This is the most serious problem. In the NIV, the two lists are identical from Abraham to David, having the same 14 names.[4] Thereafter, almost all the names are different. Furthermore, from David to Jesus, Matthew lists only 27 names in contrast to 43 listed by Luke. Comparing these lists with other genealogical lists in the OT (e.g., cf. 1 Chron. 3:11-19 with Matt. 1:9-13) reveals that Matthew omits some names resulting in three symmetrical groups, supposedly designed to enhance memorization. Also, the first two-thirds of Matthew's genealogy exactly follows the Septuagint (LXX: the Greek translation of the OT, published in the third century B.C.).[5]

On the basis of their differences, some critics have questioned the authenticity of Matthew's and Luke's genealogies and even the existence of genealogical records at all at the time of these writings. Yet Josephus, Eusebius, and other historians during the early centuries of the church confirm that Jewish genealogical records existed in Jesus' day, and even after the destruction of Jerusalem in A.D. 70.[6] Josephus mentions the "public registers," official genealogical records of the Jews, and makes several references to such records.[7] In ancient Israel "lineage was important in gaining access to temple worship."[8] The Apostle Paul could trace his ancestry back to the tribe of Benjamin (Phil. 3:5).[9] Genealogical records were kept in the time of Jesus by both priestly and lay families.[10] The probability is that some records traced different lines of descent and that Matthew and Luke appealed to different genealogical records.

Various explanations have been proposed to explain the difference in names between the two lists. Without entering into the many complexities involved, these are the three leading views:

a. Both Matthew and Luke provide a genealogy of Joseph, with Matthew giving the real, physical descent and Luke providing the legal, royal descent. This rather complex view was first proposed in the early part of the third century by Aristides and Julius Africanus, but modern variations of it

---

4. The NIV footnote for Luke 3:33a, however, indicates wide MS variance, some MSS inserting one or two extra names.
5. Carson, *Matthew*, 8:63.
6. Ibid.
7. Josephus, *Life*, 1.
8. Carson, *Matthew*, 8:63.
9. Cited by Stein, *Difficult Passages*, 40.
10. Marshall cites J. Jeremias in *Luke*, 157.

are more widely held. It hinges on the conjecture of levirate marriage; Africanus held there was a double levirate marriage. The Mosaic law of levirate marriage provided that *if a man dies without having children, his brother must marry the widow and have children for him* (Matt. 22:24; see also Deut. 25:5-10). According to this view, Jacob (Matt. 1:16) and Heli (Luke 3:23) were brothers (modern view), or half brothers (Africanus' view), because a levirate marriage took place in which their mother married separately two brothers—Matthat and then Matthan. The real physical father of Jacob, Matthan, was listed by Matthew, and the adoptive but deceased father, Matthat, was listed by Luke, as was also the case with Jacob (physical father) and Heli (adoptive father) with regard to Joseph. For collaboration, Africanus claimed access to information received from the descendants of Jesus' brother James. However, Africanus appears to be ignorant of the two generations immediately preceding Joseph, viz., Levi and Matthat (Luke 3:24), because he skips over them and claims it was Melki, not Matthat, who married his brother's widow. At least Africanus' form of the theory seems flawed due to this omission, probably resulting from his MS copies omitting the two names.[11]

b. Both Matthew and Luke provide a genealogy of Joseph, with Matthew giving the legal descent and Luke the physical descent, just the opposite of the older theory above. This view has received considerable support in modern times. Besides the same conjecture of levirate marriage as above, many object that Matthew's verb "begat" (omitted in the NIV) must be understood as natural descent, making Joseph the real, not adopted, son of Jacob (Matt. 1:16).

c. Matthew gives the genealogy of Joseph, whereas Luke has that of Mary. This is the most popular view, advocated by Luther and others, perhaps because it is the simplest and easiest to understand. Indeed, Matthew would seem to give the legal lineage through Joseph because of his Jewish readership and his themes of the promised son of David and the Messianic kingdom. Conversely, Luke would seem to give the real lineage through Mary because of his considerable attention previously devoted to her, and because he writes his Gospel to the Gentile Theophilus (Luke 1:3). However, this view hinges much on the translation and meaning of Luke 3:23. Here, Luke does not introduce Jesus as the son of Mary but *the son, so it was thought, of Joseph.* Some suppose that Luke has arbitrarily substituted Joseph's name in place of Mary's in her genealogy, either because females were not customarily included in genealogies (Matthew's inclusion of them is extra-genealogical) or because of the uniqueness of the virgin birth. Also, since Heli, Mary's father, presumably had no sons, his son-in-law Joseph stands in as heir. Others take the whole statement *he was*

---

11. Marshall, *Luke*, 158.

the son, so it was thought, of Joseph as parenthetical, making v. 23 declare Jesus as Heli's grandson through Mary. However, such a parenthetical understanding is not included in the major versions because of strong objections by many scholars.[12]

Commentators are much divided among these explanations. It is sometimes claimed that most of the better commentators avoid reconciling these differences.[13] Marshall is one of several excellent scholars who concludes:

> There is in fact no wholly satisfactory method of bringing the two lists into harmony with each other.
>
> It is only right, therefore, to admit that the problem caused by the existence of the two genealogies is insoluble with the evidence presently at our disposal.[14]

Perhaps it is best to regard the difference of names in these genealogies of Jesus as yet unresolved.

4. What is the order of events immediately following the birth of Jesus?

While complete agreement among scholars is lacking, amazingly, all thirteen harmonists in The Chronological Table subscribe to the following order of events:

a. Jesus was circumcised (Luke 2:21).

b. At the completion of Mary's forty days of purification, Joseph and Mary took Jesus to Jerusalem for dedication at the temple (Luke 2:22-39a).

c. After the dedication, they returned to Bethlehem, where the Magi later visited and worshiped the child (Matt. 2:1-12).

d. God warned Joseph in a dream and the family escaped to Egypt (Matt. 2:13-18).

e. They returned from Egypt to Galilee and settled in Nazareth (Matt. 2:19-23; Luke 2:39b).

This order of events necessitates a time gap within Luke 2:39 between the dedication and the return to Nazareth, into which are inserted the events of Matthew 2.

---

12. Carson (*Matthew*, 8:64) asserts that "this is painfully artificial and could not easily be deduced by a reader with a text without punctuation marks or brackets, which is how our NT Greek MSS were first written. Few would guess simply by reading Luke that he is giving Mary's genealogy. The theory stems, not from the text of Luke, but from the need to harmonize the two genealogies." See also Marshall, *Luke*, 158.
13. Robertson, *Harmony*, 261.
14. Marshall, *Luke*, 158-59. See also Stein, *Difficult Passages*, 42.

CHAPTER TWO
PREPARATION FOR MINISTRY

1. Does Mark's *beginning* mean the same as John's *beginning*?

The *beginning* in Mark 1:1 and John 1:1 are not the same, as their contexts indicate. Mark refers to *the beginning of the gospel about Jesus Christ*, which the following verses show to mean either John's baptizing and preaching ministry in general (e.g., see Acts 1:22) or his baptism of Jesus in particular. Mark 1:1 has been taken by many as a title for this Gospel due to the absence of a verb. The Apostle John's *beginning* in his prologue (John 1:3) goes back to Creation, with strong similarity to Genesis 1:1.

2. At Jesus' baptism, what were the exact words of the voice from heaven?

Both Mark 1:11 and Luke 3:22 include the quotation of the voice from heaven addressing Jesus in the second person, as herein: *You are my Son, whom I love; with you I am well pleased.* But Matthew has it in the third person: *This is my Son, whom I love; with him I am well pleased* (Matt. 3:17). Augustine explains the variation in words as the *ipsissma verba* (exact words) versus the *ipsissma vox* (exact meaning), concepts which have wide application throughout the Gospels.

> For the heavenly voice gave utterance only to one of these sentences; but by the form of words thus adopted [by Matthew], namely, "This is my beloved Son," it was the Evangelist's intention to show that the saying was meant to intimate specially to the hearers . . . the fact that he was the Son of God. . . . If you ask which of these different modes represents what was actually expressed by the voice, you may fix on whichever you will, provided only that you understand that those of the writers who have not reproduced the self-same form of speech have still reproduced the identical sense intended to be conveyed.

... that whichever of the Evangelists may have preserved for us the words as they were literally uttered by the heavenly voice, the others have varied the terms only with the object of setting forth the same sense more familiarly.[1]

Mark and Luke likely quote the actual words (though presumably spoken in Aramaic, the mother tongue of the bystanders, rather than Greek), while Matthew changes the words from second to third person as an interpretive method to assure his readers that the spectators heard the heavenly saying. Matthew frequently edits like this in his Gospel, e.g., the Beatitudes.[2] This seems more probable if Matthew uses the earlier Mark as a written source from which he composes his Gospel, as is generally accepted by current scholarship. (See Introduction: *Ipsissma Vox* and *Ipsissma Verba*.)

3. In what order did Jesus' second and third temptations occur?

Only Matthew and Luke list the three temptations with which Satan solicited Jesus. Both record the same temptation first but have the second and third temptations in opposite order. This is no discrepancy because neither Synoptist specifically enumerates the order of the temptations. Matthew's order is generally regarded by commentators as the actual historical order.[3] The primary reasons are as follows:

a. Satan's offer of the kingdoms of the world was surely his most powerful temptation, being directly related to Jesus' mission of obtaining a kingdom (Dan. 7), although by means of the cross. Satan would have likely saved this temptation for last.

b. In Jesus' answer to Satan's offer of the kingdoms of the world, Matthew adds the words *"Away from me, Satan!"* (Matt. 4:10), which only seem appropriate if this is the third and last temptation.[4]

c. Matthew unites the two "Son of God" temptations, which are regarded as an original pair.[5]

If Matthew's order is historical, why has Luke changed the order? The following reasons have been adduced:

---

1. Augustine, *Harmony*, 6:119-20. See also Gundry, *Matthew*, 53.
2. Matthew records the Beatitudes in the third person, e.g., *Blessed are the poor in spirit, for theirs is the kingdom of heaven* (Matt. 5:3). On the other hand, Luke has them in the second person, e.g., *Blessed are you who are poor, for yours is the kingdom of God* (Luke 6:20). (See EN 4:3.)
3. Marshall, *Luke*, 167.
4. John F. Walvoord, *Matthew: Thy Kingdom Come* (Chicago: Moody Press, 1974), 36.
5. Marshall, *Luke*, 167.

a. Luke changes the actual order of Satan's last two temptations of Jesus to parallel the order of Satan's temptations to Eve in the Garden of Eden (Gen. 3:6; cf. 1 John 2:16)[6] and/or to make Jesus' quotations from Deuteronomy conform to the order in that book.[7]

b. Compared to the other Evangelists, Luke reveals a special attachment to Jerusalem and its temple. Jerusalem is mentioned 32 times in Luke's Gospel, compared to 11 times in Mark, 12 in Matthew and 13 in John. From Luke 9:51 onward, Jesus is portrayed as on a journey to Jerusalem. Luke, therefore, chronologically dislocates the last two temptations for thematic purposes, reserving the temple temptation for the climax. However, a missionary theme to the Gentiles is witnessed in the Gospel of Matthew, perhaps making it just as probable that Matthew has placed the offer of the kingdoms of the world last for thematic purposes.

Overall, it appears more probable that Matthew has preserved the actual historical order of the devil's three temptations of Jesus.

---

6. Walvoord, _Matthew_, 35.
7. Marshall, _Luke_, 167.

CHAPTER THREE
GALILEAN MINISTRY

1. Did Jesus begin preaching in the synagogues of Galilee or Judea?

Matthew 4:23 and Mark 1:39 record that Jesus preached throughout *Galilee*, whereas Luke 4:44 reads *synagogues of Judea*. However, the alternate reading for *synagogues of Judea* in Luke 4:44 in the NIV footnote does not conflict: "Or *the land of the Jews*; some manuscripts Galilee." Yet I. Howard Marshall solves the problem by claiming that Luke sometimes uses *Judea* to refer to the whole of Palestine: "[Judea] is used in its wide sense (4:44; 6:17; 23:5; Acts 1:8; et al.) and not in the narrow sense of the southern part of the country around Jerusalem as distinct from Samaria and Galilee (so 1:65; 2:4; 3:1; 5:17; 21:21; Acts 9:31 . . .)."[1]

2. Was Jesus' hometown Nazareth or Capernaum?

Some confusion exists over whether Jesus' hometown was Nazareth or Capernaum. Jesus grew up in Nazareth, where Joseph had resettled when Jesus was a young child (Matt. 2:23; Luke 2:39). Jesus was the *carpenter's son* (Matt. 13:54) and became *the carpenter* (Mark 6:3) of, no doubt, his hometown of Nazareth (John 1:45).

Early in his public ministry Jesus experienced such intense rejection at Nazareth (Luke 4:16-30) that *leaving Nazareth, he went and lived in Capernaum* (Matt. 4:13; cf. Luke 4:31), presumably with his family. Jesus did not actually have his own house, at least not after he began his ministry (Matt. 8:20; Luke 9:58). Sometime after Peter and Andrew began to follow Jesus, their family moved from Bethsaida (John 1:44) to Capernaum as well (Mark 1:29; cf. Mark 1:21). Thereafter, both Nazareth and Capernaum (see Matt. 9:1) are called Jesus' *hometown* in the Gospels. Though he no longer lived in Nazareth, people continued to refer to him as *a Nazarene*, or *of Nazareth* (Matt. 21:11; John 19:19; Luke 24:19, et al.).

---

1. Marshall, *Luke*, 51.

Thus when Mark implies that Jesus was from Nazareth (Mark 1:9) yet later *entered Capernaum*, where *he had come home* (2:1), it must be understood that Mark 2:1 occurred after Matthew 4:13, and that Mark has simply omitted that Jesus had by then moved to Capernaum. When Mark later adds that Jesus visited his *hometown* (Mark 6:1), presumably Nazareth, Mark merely adheres to the common style of referring to Jesus' childhood dwelling place of Nazareth as his hometown.

3. Did the men carrying the paralytic on a mat dig through the roof of the house or only remove the tiles?

Mark 2:4 states that the men *made an opening in the roof above Jesus and, after digging through it, lowered the mat*. Luke 5:19, however, relates that they *lowered him on his mat through the tiles*. Mark's Greek word translated *digging through it* (NIV) has also been translated "made an opening" (RSV), which does not appear to conflict with Luke's account. That Luke has editorially recast the description of the roof for the Gentile Theophilus' comprehension is a view which calls Luke's account into question.[2]

Jewish law at that time included building codes requiring that the top of the roof be paved with brick, stone or some other hard substance. For those who object to the possibility of the bearers of the paralytic digging through this substance, Alfred Edersheim proposes that Jesus did not stand under the main roof of the house, but under a "covered gallery" which would have been easier to dig through.[3] In addition, it may be questioned whether Galileans submitted to such building codes. Walter W. Wessel offers the best solution:

> The roof itself was usually made of wooden beams with thatch and compacted earth in order to shed the rain. Sometimes tiles were laid between the beams and the thatch and earth placed over them.[4]

4. Was one of Jesus' apostles named Matthew or Levi?

Matthew gives the name *Matthew* (Matt. 9:9) while the other synoptics have *Levi* (Mark 2:14; Luke 5:27). Levi may have been his preconversion name and Matthew his postconversion name or perhaps Matthew was of the tribe of Levi.

2. Stein, *Difficult Passages*, 38.
3. Alfred Edersheim, *The Life and Times of Jesus the Messiah* (1883) (Grand Rapids: Eerdmans, 1971), pt. 1, 503.
4. Walter W. Wessel, *Mark* in *The Expositor's Bible Commentary*, gen. ed. Frank E. Gaebelein, 12 vols. (Grand Rapids: Zondervan, 1984), 8:632.

5. Was it John's disciples or those of the Pharisees who questioned Jesus about fasting?

Mark 2:18 only generally identifies Jesus' questioners about fasting as *some people*. Matthew 9:14 refers to them as *John's disciples*, but Luke 5:30 contends they were *the Pharisees and the teachers of the law*. All three Synoptists record that the question itself referred to both John's and the Pharisees' disciples. This suggests that both kinds of disciples were involved in the questioning and that Matthew and Luke simply omitted mention of one party or the other.

6. Did Matthew's banquet and the question on fasting immediately follow his call or was it later?

Here occurs the first notable chronological difficulty in the Gospels. All three Synoptists group together Matthew's call (Matt. 9:9; Mark 2:14; Luke 5:27-28) with Matthew's banquet and the occasion when Jesus was questioned about fasting (Matt. 9:10-17; Mark 2:15-21; Luke 5:29-39). This arrangement makes it appear that the dinner at Matthew's house and the question there on fasting immediately followed Matthew's call. However, no specifically connective words tie the two together in any of the Gospels. Moreover, the language opening the following section in the Gospel of Matthew, *while he was saying this* (Matt. 9:18), appears to bring together the dinner with Jairus' encounter with Jesus. The other two Synoptists place the stories of Jairus' daughter's illness and the woman with the issue of blood later in their Gospels. Have the Synoptists arranged Matthew's call and his banquet together topically, when there was in fact a separation of time between them? The question is not easily answered. Matthew's call, his dinner, and the question on fasting are herein placed together according to a slight majority of harmonists in The Chronological Table.

7. How long was the Lord Jesus' public ministry?

The Gospels do not directly specify the duration of Jesus' public ministry. Historically, the answer has generally been determined by the number of Passover Feasts Jesus attended in Jerusalem following his baptism. The Synoptists mention only one Passover because they primarily relate the latter part of Jesus' career. But John informs us that Jesus attended at least three Passovers (John 2:13; 6:4; 11:55), and possibly four, with John 5:1 being contested as either the Feast of Purim or Passover. If the former number is accepted, then Jesus' public ministry lasted about two and one-half years; if the latter, which is the majority opinion, then three and one-half years.

Perhaps Jesus intimated the length of his public ministry when he taught the Parable of the Fig Tree in Luke 13:6-9, which is not to be confused with a later cursing of a fig tree during Passion Week. In the parable, the owner of a vineyard inspects his fig tree and, to his dismay, finds no fruit on it. He says to his caretaker, _For three years now I've been coming to look for fruit on this fig tree and haven't found any. Cut it down!_ (Luke 13:7) The owner then instructs the caretaker to cut it down the next year if it fails again to produce fruit. Comparing this parable with the later actual event in which Jesus cursed a real fig tree on his way to "cleansing" the temple, it appears his intended meaning in the parable may be this: As the rightful owner/heir of the vineyard, which is Israel, Jesus came to the temple at Jerusalem for three years to look for the fruit of righteousness. Generally speaking, he found none. This may suggest, therefore, that Jesus' public ministry lasted just over three years.

CHAPTER FOUR

CHOOSING THE TWELVE AND SERMON ON THE MOUNT

1. Was the apostle named Thaddaeus the same as Judas son of James?

Apparently *Thaddaeus* (Matt. 10:3; Mark 3:18) was also called *Judas, son of James* (Luke 6:16; Acts 1:13). Thaddaeus may have been his post-conversion name. Since Thaddaeus means "beloved," perhaps he was called "Judas the beloved" to distinguish him from Judas the betrayer, and later his name "Judas" was entirely replaced by "Thaddaeus."[1]

2. Are the Sermon on the Mount and the Sermon on the Plain the same or two separate sermons?

Augustine held that Matthew 5–7 and Luke 6:17-49 were two different sermons. This view prevailed until the Reformation. Calvin, and a majority of commentators since, have regarded these two accounts as reports of one sermon delivered in one place, although some have thought it was given over more than one day. Some more recent scholars allege that these are two collections of detached sayings Jesus expounded on different occasions, evidenced by similar parallels in the other Synoptics. At least two points oppose this latter view:

a. As a busy itinerant preacher, Jesus likely taught the same or similar messages on various occasions.

b. If Matthew's and Luke's introductory and concluding remarks are accepted as historically accurate, this disallows a collection of separate sermons delivered at different times and places (Matt. 7:28-29; 8:1; Luke 7:1).

Despite some minor differences and omissions, Jesus' sermon in Matthew 5–7 and Luke 6 is generally regarded by harmonists as the same event.

---

1. Carson, *Matthew*, 8:239.

The leading objections lodged against the one-sermon view, and their rebuttals, are as follows:[2]

a. The place of the two sermons seems different. Matthew records that Jesus delivered this sermon on a *mountainside* (Matt. 5:1), whereas Luke claims the sermon he records was expounded *on a level place* (Luke 6:17). Augustine distinguished these as The Sermon on the Mount and The Sermon on the Plain. This is supported by the KJV, which has "mountain" and "plain" respectively, Luke seemingly indicating an expansive plain somewhere other than on a mountain. But the NIV's *mountainside* and *level place* are more accurate translations, making it easier to envision Jesus descending from a higher elevation on a mountain to a level place on the mountainside. Regardless, D.A. Carson claims: "There is little difference between Matthew's 'mountain' and Luke's 'plain.' "[3]

b. The places from which Jesus departed to deliver the two sermons seems different. Matthew relates that Jesus *went up . . . and sat down. His disciples came to him* (Matt. 5:1). Luke records that *he went down with them and stood on a level place* (Luke 6:17). A.T. Robertson offers a plausible solution in the following order of events:

> Jesus first went up into the mountain to pray (Luke 6:12) and selected and instructed the Twelve. Afterwards he came down to a level place on the mountainside whither the crowds had gathered, and stood there and wrought miracles (Luke 6:17). He then went up a little higher into the mountain where he could sit down and see and teach the multitudes (Matt. 5:1). Matthew gives the multitudes as the reason for his [Jesus] going up into the mountain. By this arrangement any discrepancy between "sat" in Matthew and "stood" in Luke disappears. . . . Many writers affirm that the tradition mentioned by Jerome, making the Horns of Hattin the place where the Sermon on the Mount was delivered, suits this explanation exactly. There is a level place on it where the crowds could have assembled.[4]

c. The time of delivery of the two sermons seems different. Matthew records the sermon (Matt. 5–7) before the choosing of the twelve apostles (10:1-4), whereas Luke locates the sermon (Luke 6:17-49) after the choosing of the Twelve (Luke 6:12-16). But since "Matthew's arrangement in chaps. 8–13 is not chronological, but topical, it is entirely possible, even likely, that the same arrangement should prevail in chaps. 5–7."[5] Furthermore, it may be questioned whether Matthew's account of the commission-

---

2. Some of the following outline is taken from Robertson's *Harmony*, 273-74.
3. Carson, *Matthew*, 8:129.
4. Robertson, *Harmony*, 274.
5. Ibid., 273.

ing, in Matthew 10:1-4, is the same as Luke's account of the choosing. "Matthew's language suggests that the Twelve became a recognized group somewhat earlier."[6] The choosing occurred just before the sermon. Perhaps the commissioning was some time later, in which case Matthew omits the choosing and Luke omits the later commissioning.

d. The audience which heard each sermon seems different. Some have supposed that Jesus left the crowds to speak the Sermon on the Mount to his disciples (Matt. 5:1), but that he taught the Sermon on the Plain to the crowds (Luke 6:17). However, Jesus was *looking at his disciples* when he delivered the sermon recorded by Luke (Luke 6:20).

e. The recorded content of the two sermons seems different. Very possibly, Matthew includes those portions pertaining to Jews, those to whom he was writing, while Luke omits them because he addresses the Gentile Theophilus (Luke 1:3). D.A. Carson adds: "In any case to insist that a writer must include everything he knows or everything in his sources is poor methodology."[7]

Two additional points indicate that both accounts refer to the same sermon:

a. Both accounts of the sermon are placed in the same chronological scenario, being preceded by the healings of the multitudes and succeeded by the healing of the centurion's servant.

b. Both accounts of the sermon begin with the beatitudes and end with the wise and foolish builders.

While the evidence is by no means conclusive, the one-sermon view seems to this author the most acceptable. A.T. Robertson states concerning the one-sermon view: "There are no objections to this theory that do not admit of a probable explanation."[8]

3. If Matthew and Luke record the same sermon, do Matthew 5:3-11 and Luke 6:20-22 reflect different beatitudes or are they the same, with Matthew as editor?

Luke's first two Beatitudes are similar to Matthew's while conveying a very different idea. Luke 6:20 has *Blessed are you who are poor* and Matt. 5:3 has *Blessed are the poor in spirit.* Luke 6:21 reads *Blessed are you who hunger now* and Matthew 5:6 reads *Blessed are those who hunger and thirst for righteousness.* Calvin, and many contemporary critics, regard the similar beatitudes in Matthew and Luke as the same. Possibly Matthew editorializes what Luke accurately but more generally records. However, it is possible that Jesus

---

6. Carson, *Matthew*, 8:236.
7. Ibid., 8:125.
8. Robertson, *Harmony*, 276.

said both, as herein, and that each writer was inspired to select his material according to different purposes. It is unlikely that each writer knew only what he recorded; at least Matthew was an eyewitness (Luke 6:12-15; cf. v. 17).

Jesus' Beatitudes are perhaps his most famous sayings. The popularity of Matthew's account of this sermon overshadows that of Luke. This may be attributed to the fact that Matthew is placed first in the NT and that he has arranged his material more liturgically, enhancing understanding as well as memorization. Matthew's presentation emphasizes spiritual poverty and repentance while Luke's focus is social injustice, i.e., the economically poor.[9] The lesser-known account of Luke tends to sharpen the social conscience. The two accounts of the Beatitudes of Jesus exemplify how a composite of the Gospels offers a complete and balanced account.

---

9. This pattern continues throughout each Evangelist's account. E.g., Matthew omits the woes against social injustice found in Luke 6:24-26. A paraphrased summary of these Beatitudes would have Luke saying, "Blessed are the physically hungry," but Matthew saying, "Blessed are the spiritually hungry." Other examples are: only Luke relates Mary's song in Luke 1:46-56, which includes *he has filled the hungry with good things but has sent the rich away empty* (v. 53), or *Sell your possessions and give to the poor* (Luke 12:33), which Matthew omits in the indirect parallel in Matthew 6:25-33.

CHAPTER FIVE
MORE GALILEAN MINISTRY AND PARABLES

1. Did the centurion himself approach Jesus to request his servant's healing or did others make the request? Was the healing of the centurion's servant the same as that of the royal official's son?

Matthew appears to say that the centurion himself came to Jesus and conversed with him about his servant (Matt. 8:5-13), yet Luke makes it quite clear that the centurion sent Jewish elders to speak to Jesus on his behalf (Luke 7:1-10). Moreover, while Jesus was on the way to the centurion's house, another group of the man's friends met Jesus with a message from the centurion, saying, *I did not . . . come to you* (Luke 7:7). Due to this difference in accounts, Osiander claimed these were two different miracles, to which Calvin rightly objects:

> Those who believe that Matthew and Luke are telling different stories are making a fuss over nothing. Matthew quite reasonably attributes to him what was done as his request and in his name. In all the circumstances the two Evangelists agree so well, that it would be ridiculous to make two miracles out of the one.[1]

Luke's more detailed account ought not to be regarded as an embellishment, for this would undermine the historical reliability of the author. Compared to the other two Synoptists, Luke's style presents more human interest features of a historical story. Matthew's account demonstrates his characteristic editorial condensing. The centurion, therefore, did not come to Jesus but spoke indirectly to him through his representatives.

An additional problem arises in John 4:46-54, where John records the healing of a royal official's son. Most contemporary scholars regard it as the same healing as that recorded by the Synoptists of the centurion's servant.

---

1. John Calvin, *Calvin's Commentaries: A Harmony of the Gospels Matthew, Mark and Luke* (1555), 3 vol., tr. A.W. Morrison and T.H.L. Parker, eds. David W. Torrance and Thomas F. Torrance (Grand Rapids: Eerdmans, 1972), 1:247.

This is in contrast to those of previous generations who considered John's account to be a different healing, as herein, in accord with The Chronological Table. There are some notable differences indicating that John 4:46-54 is a separate incident from that recorded by the Synoptists:

a. John presents the healing of the official's son as the second miracle Jesus performed after entering Galilee, the first being the changing of water into wine at Cana. Both Matthew and Mark, however, locate the healing of the centurion's servant much later in their Gospels, and therefore in Jesus' public ministry.

b. Jesus rebukes the royal official for needing miraculous signs to believe (John 4:48). The exact opposite occurs with the centurion; Jesus commends him more than anyone in Israel for his faith (Matt. 8:10; Luke 7:9).

c. John describes the sick lad as the official's son; in the Synoptics he is the centurion's servant. There is much dispute on whether the Greek words can refer to the same individual.[2] Some claim the word in Matthew 8:6 can mean either "son" or "servant," and probably the latter. On the other hand, D.A. Carson observes, "But fair examination of NT usage . . . reveals that only one of twenty-four NT occurrences requires 'son,' viz., John 4:51. This further supports the view that John 4 records a different healing on a separate occasion."[3]

d. John has only two sections that are identical with the Synoptics: Section 95: "Jesus Feeds the Five Thousand" and Section 96: "Jesus Walks on the Water." This lack of sections common to John and the Synoptics makes it more probable that John 4:46-54 records a healing separate from that of the centurion's servant.

2. When Jesus' relatives came to get him, did he refer to the *will of my Father in heaven* or *God's will*?

Matthew reports that when Jesus' mother and brothers came to get him, he said to the crowd, *whoever does the will of my Father in heaven is my brother and sister and mother* (Matt. 12:50). In Mark, however, Jesus said, *Whoever does God's will is my brother and sister and mother* (Mark 3:35). Such variations in wording in quotations occur frequently throughout the Gospels. The actual words spoken by Jesus, i.e., the *ipsissma verba*, cannot always be determined, especially considering that the words were spoken in

2. Bauer-Arndt-Gingrich-Danker, Walter Bauer's *A Greek-English Lexicon of the New Testament and Other Early Christian Literature*, tr. William F. Arndt and F. Wilbur Gingrich, 2nd ed. rev. and aug. by F. Wilbur Gingrich and Frederick W. Danker from Walter Bauer's 5th ed., 1958 (Chicago and London: University of Chicago Press, 1979), 604.
3. Carson, *Matthew*, 8:200-01.

Aramaic and translated into Greek, the language of the NT manuscripts. The traditional view is that Matthew wrote his Gospel particularly for Jewish readers and Mark published his Gospel in Rome for Gentiles. It is believed that the Gospel of Matthew, though written last of the Synoptics, preserves Jewish idiom more frequently while Mark adapts his expression to his Gentile readers.[4] Therefore, when Jesus' relatives came to get him, he probably said *the will of my Father in heaven*. However, in such cases, whichever word or phrase is used really makes little or no difference, since they mean the same.

---

4. Comparing Matthew and Mark, the word "God" appears in Matthew and Mark the same number of times. But the word "Father," as used for God, is found in Matthew an astounding 43 times compared to a meager 5 times in Mark. Another example is the kingdom. The phrase "kingdom of heaven" occurs 32 times in Matthew and "kingdom of God" only 4 times, whereas "kingdom of God" appears 13 times in Mark while "kingdom of heaven" is absent. The terms "Father" for God and "kingdom of heaven" are considered Jewish idioms. What can be derived from these statistics? When the same quotations are recorded in both Matthew and Mark, but one has "Father" and the other "God," or one has "kingdom of heaven" and the other "kingdom of God," the *ipsissma verba* is more likely "Father" in the first example and "kingdom of heaven" in the second example. Perhaps the writer who presents the *ipsissma vox* has editorialized by replacing a word or phrase with one more known or understandable to his readers, according with either their Jewish or Gentile backgrounds.

CHAPTER SIX
MINISTRY OF MIRACLES

1. When Jesus finished teaching the many parables, did he remain in the boat and leave the shore or get out and later get back in to leave?

Matthew 8:23 relates that Jesus *got into the boat* as if to cross the lake immediately. However, Mark 4:36 reads *they took him along, just as he was, in the boat*. This event must immediately follow the teaching of the parables recorded in Matthew 13:1-52, Mark 4:1-33 and Luke 8:4-18, according to Mark 4:35. (*One day* in Luke 8:22 corresponds to *that day when evening came* in Mark 4:35—after he finished teaching the parables.) Both Matthew and Mark report that Jesus previously got into a boat in order to teach the parables (Matt. 13:2; Mark 4:1). There are at least two possible resolutions to this confusion:

a. Jesus got out of the boat after his teaching, got back in, and later crossed the lake.

b. More likely, Matthew simply restates in Matthew 13:2 Jesus' initial entry into the boat, mentioned earlier in 8:23, due to his several dislocations of material both before and after these parables. (See the dislocations of Matthean sections in the Outline and Scripture Index.) Accordingly, Jesus got into the boat before teaching the parables; when he finished teaching, the disciples took him along, as he was, in the boat.

2. How many times did Jesus permit demons to enter a herd of pigs? Did Jesus heal one demoniac or two? Did the swine incident occur in the region of the Gadarenes or Gerasenes? Was one of the demoniacs from Gadara, Gerasa, or the Decapolis?

All three Synoptists unquestionably report the same event (Matt. 8:28-34; Mark 5:1-20; Luke 8:26-39). Mark and Luke mention only one demoniac, whereas Matthew mentions two. This difference can be accounted for by any of the following reasons, arranged in decreasing order of probability:

a. One was more notorious for his former savagery, his astounding strength and nakedness (Augustine).

b. Only one went out and testified, becoming the more prominent disciple and therefore a focus of the story.

c. Only one remained for the townspeople to see and thus become the focus of the Evangelists.

d. Mark and Luke only knew of one, whereas Matthew, as an eyewitness, relates the fuller account.

e. A combination of these.

The same pattern occurs in Matthew's account of the two blind men (Matt. 20:30) and two donkeys (Matt. 21:2) compared to only one reported by Mark (Mark 10:46; 11:2) and Luke (Luke 18:35; 19:30).

According to the NIV, Matthew locates this incident in the region of the Gadarenes; Mark and Luke place it in the region of the Gerasenes. Yet, as indicated in the NIV footnotes, considerable manuscript variance exists in all three Synoptics. Gadarenes, Gerasenes, or Gergesenes refer to citizens of three different cities or their regions.

Mark's and Luke's Gerasa (modern Jerash) was located about thirty-five miles southeast of Lake Galilee (Sea of Galilee). It was actually just as close to the Dead Sea as to the Sea of Galilee and, according to the geography of these cities themselves, the least likely to be the correct reading. Matthew's Gadara (modern Um Qeia) was six miles southeast of the southern tip of the Sea of Galilee, 12 miles south of Gergesa. Gergesa (modern Kersa or Koursi), an NIV alternate reading in all three Synoptics, was the only one of the three cities situated on Lake Galilee, slightly north of the mideastern coastline. Many observers have designated an area near Gergesa as the only coastline on the eastern shores of Galilee steep enough to afford the slope for the drowning swine episode.[1] Ancient tombs dot the hillsides where the demoniac(s) may have lived (Mark 5:3, 5; Luke 8:27).[2]

The committee for the United Bible Societies' Greek New Testament (third edition) prefers *Gadarenes* in Matthew 8:28 and *Gerasenes* in both Mark 5:1 and Luke 8:26, 37, as in the NIV. The committee's reasons are as follows:

a. superior MS evidence in each case,

b. the probability that "Gergesenes" is a correction by later scribes, perhaps originally proposed in the third century by Origen, as evidenced in his writings, and

---

1. The Greek does not suggest that the animals plunged over a sharp cliff, a common misconception, but that they rushed down a steep slope.
2. Merrill Tenney, gen. ed., *The Zondervan Pictorial Encyclopedia of the Bible*, 5 vols. (Grand Rapids: Zondervan, 1975), 2:623, 701. See also James Orr, *The International Standard Bible Encyclopedia*, 5 vols. (Grand Rapids: Eerdmans, 1939), 2:1217.

c. the weaker attestation for "Gerasenes" in Matthew is a scribal assimilation to Mark and/or Luke while the same is true of "Gadarenes" in Mark and Luke compared to Matthew.[3]

The most significant fact is that all three Synoptics do not actually identify a city, but a region or country associated with a city. Apparently, such descriptions extended a considerable distance and overlapped unestablished boundaries. Metzger cites that Josephus named "Gadara as possessing territory 'which lay on the frontiers of Tiberias' (the Sea of Galilee). That this territory reached to the Sea may be inferred from the fact that ancient coins bearing the name Gadara often portray a ship."[4]

In conclusion, the exact location of the swine incident remains uncertain, except that it was on the eastern or southeastern coast of Lake Galilee, further substantiated by Luke's additional words *across the lake from Galilee* (Luke 8:26: better translated "opposite Galilee").

Calvin identifies a lesser problem: was the one demon-possessed man from Gadara, Gerasa, or the Decapolis? It is assumed that Mark and Luke refer to the same one of the two demon-possessed men. Luke claims this man was *from the town* (Luke 8:27), presumably Gadara. When Jesus told him to *return home and tell how much God has done for you* (v. 39), Luke says he *told all over town*. Mark, on the other hand, is more specific in quoting Jesus, *Go home to your family and tell them* (Mark 5:19). However, Mark says nothing about the man spreading the news in his nearby hometown but adds that *the man went away and began to tell in the Decapolis how much Jesus had done for him* (v. 20).

The Decapolis designated a wide desert region of ten small Hellenistic cities east and south of the Sea of Galilee. Gadara was one of them. Calvin, appealing to Matthew's *the region of the Gadarenes*, contends that Luke's account does not mean that the man was a citizen of Gadara, but that he met Jesus as the Lord approached that town.[5] This solution fails to account for Mark's additional instruction to the man to tell his family, and for his subsequent spreading the news in the Decapolis rather than in his hometown. A better solution would seem to be that this man returned to his hometown, whether Gadara, Gergesa, or some other place, where he told his family. He did not stop there but continued to spread the news throughout the wider Gentile region of the Decapolis. Mark, therefore, has simply omitted the detail of the man's obedience and gone beyond it; Luke does likewise, omitting the report that the man told his relatives but including that the man *told all over town* (Luke 8:39).

3. For a full account of the leading MS evidence, see Bruce M. Metzger, *A Textual Commentary on the Greek New Testament* (United Bible Societies, 1971), 23-24, 84, 145.
4. Ibid., 23.
5. Calvin, *Harmony/Gospels*, 1:284.

3. Did Jesus encounter Jairus immediately after healing the two demoniacs and crossing the lake, or later, at Matthew's house?

Mark 5:21-22 and Luke 8:41-42 place the meeting with Jairus immediately following Jesus' healing of the demon-possessed men. Mark records it in the following order: Jesus healed the two demoniacs on the east side of the Sea of Galilee; Jesus crossed the lake by boat to Galilee on the western side; *While* [Jesus] *was by the lake* (v. 21), Jairus met Jesus and made his request. On the other hand, Matthew inserts three other events between the healing of the demoniacs (Matt. 8:28-34) and the encounter with Jairus (Matt. 9:18). The titles of these sections in the NIV and *The Gospels Interwoven* are Section 41: "Jesus Heals a Paralytic," Section 42: "The Calling of Levi (Matthew)," and Section 43: "Jesus Questioned about Fasting," all included in Matthew 9:1-17. Matthew, therefore, appears to recount that Jairus made his request while Jesus was in Matthew's house having dinner rather than beside the lake. Some have supposed that Matthew's house was located beside the lake—a possible view, but one not widely received.

The NIV renderings of Mark 5:21-22 and Luke 8:41, which connect the crossing of the lake and Jairus' request, are contested. D.A. Carson contends:

> But the NIV rendering of Mark 5:21-22 links Jesus by the lake with the approach of the synagogue ruler ("While he was by the lake, one of the synagogue rulers . . ."). The Greek does not suggest this; syntactically Jesus' presence by the lake terminates the thought of Mark 5:21: Jesus crossed back after the Gadara episode, a large crowd again gathered, and he was by the lake. Verse 22 then begins a new pericope without a necessary transition.[6]

Neither does the Greek text require the NIV rendering of Luke 8:41, *Then a man*, which closely connects these two incidents. The RSV has, "And there came a man;" the NASB reads, "And behold, there came a man."

The correct order of the above incidents is not easily determined. Harmonists and other commentators seem to be about evenly divided on the sequence of these events. The order herein follows Mark and Luke, as well as the majority of harmonists in The Chronological Table (7 out of 13, with 5 others opting for Matthew's order).

---

6. Carson, *Matthew*, 8:229.

4. Was Jairus' daughter dying or already dead when he first approached Jesus with his request?

Matthew 9:18 narrates that Jairus said, *My daughter has just died.* However, Mark 5:23 and Luke 8:42 assert that she was not yet dead when Jairus first requested Jesus' help. Both Mark and Luke add that while Jesus and the others were on their way to the house, messengers came to inform them that the girl had died and that it was useless for Jesus to come. Thus, the accounts of both Mark and Luke require that she was alive when Jairus first encountered Jesus. Some earlier commentators solve this problem by interpreting that Matthew meant by Jairus' words, "By now she would be dead." In fact, the NIV originally included the alternate reading *daughter is now dying*, but the translation committee for the NIV deleted this alternative in its first revision copyrighted in 1984. Many contemporary commentators maintain that this type of reading represents a forced harmonization, explaining that Greek syntax disallows it.[7]

The best solution, which receives wide support from scholars, is that Matthew's quotation of Jairus reveals his work as a redactor, i.e., editor. Matthew, therefore, does not report verbatim what Jairus first said about his daughter, as Mark likely does, for the following reasons:

a. Matthew omits the detail about the messengers coming from Jairus' house to inform them of the girl's death.

b. Matthew characteristically condenses this section, as compared with Mark and Luke, and combines the words of Jairus and the messengers. In support of this view, Robert Stein quotes Augustine: "But it was Matthew's object to tell the whole story in short compass. He has represented the father as directly expressing in his request what it is certain had been his own real wish." Stein also quotes Calvin, "Matthew . . . set down as occurring at the very beginning, what actually happened with the passing of time."[8]

5. Was Jesus rejected at Nazareth once or twice?

Matthew 13:54-58 and Mark 6:1-6 speak of the same rejection of Jesus at Nazareth. The narratives are very similar, and their location in the text is the same, i.e., following the day of Jesus' teaching many parables. Luke 4:16-30 is similar, yet some notable differences exist:

a. Luke locates the visit to Nazareth at the very beginning of Jesus' ministry, in contrast to Matthew and Mark.

b. Luke's account leaves a strong impression that healings were not

---

7. E.g., Carson, *Matthew*, 8:230.

8. Stein, *Difficult Passages*, 34. See also Carson, *Matthew*, 8:230.

done. Matthew and Mark, however, record that Jesus was astonished at their lack of faith and that he did/could not do many/any miracles except heal a few sick people.

c. Only Luke recounts that Jesus was driven out of town by those intending to throw him off the cliff, and that he escaped (Luke 4:29-30).

If there were only one visit to Nazareth, would Matthew, and especially the earlier Mark, have omitted this striking incident? Yet the Evangelists do not always write what is expected. It seems unlikely, though, that Jesus would return to Nazareth to teach and do any miracles at all after the Nazarenes previously tried to kill him. This argues against there being two visits to Nazareth. *The Gospels Interwoven*, nevertheless, follows The Chronological Table, in which a majority of harmonists include two different visits of Jesus and accompanying rejections of him at his old hometown of Nazareth.

6. Was Jesus unable to do many miracles at Nazareth, or did he choose not to do many?

Matthew 13:58 says Jesus *did not do many miracles there*, i.e., in Nazareth. In contrast, Mark 6:5 relates that he *could not do any miracles there*, adding *except lay his hands on a few sick people and heal them*. Thus Jesus performed only a few minor healings at Nazareth. Certain critics, e.g., B.H. Streeter, allege that Matthew changes what is to him an objectionable wording here in Mark from *could* to *did*.[9] If Matthew changes the wording from Mark as his source, by no means a certainty, the only view possible that remains faithful to the inspiration of Scripture is that Matthew makes the change for the purpose of explanation. Matthew characteristically writes more from the divine viewpoint whereas Mark writes more from the human perspective. Observe that Matthew adds that Jesus *did not do many miracles there because of their lack of faith* (v. 58), which reason seems to explain Mark's *could not*, thus bringing the two into harmony.

Mark's *could not* should not be reckoned as a christological problem. In the Gospel of John, Jesus teaches that he can of his own self do nothing, that he does only what he sees the Father doing (John 5:19, 30). Indeed, throughout his Gospel, John portrays Jesus as teaching his total dependence on the Father. It, therefore, seems safe to conclude that Jesus could not do many miracles at Nazareth because it was not the Father's will, presumably due to their obstinate hearts and therefore lack of faith.

---

9. Burnett Hillman Streeter, *The Four Gospels: A Study of Origins* (London: MacMillan, 1924), 162.

7. Did Jesus instruct his twelve apostles to take a staff and a pair of sandals on their first missionary journey or not?

Matthew 10:10 and Luke 9:3 agree that Jesus instructed the Twelve not to take a staff, whereas Mark 6:8 records Jesus' words, *Take nothing for the journey except a staff*. Likewise, Matthew 10:10 maintains that they were not to take sandals, while Mark has *wear sandals* (Mark 6:9). Some commentators claim Matthew's instruction about sandals forbids only tied-on shoes. Some likewise claim that Mark's word denotes only a simple staff, while Matthew and Luke prohibit a certain type of staff used as a weapon. D.A. Carson explains:

> It may be that Mark's account clarifies what the disciples are permitted to bring, whereas Matthew's assumes that the disciples already have certain things (one cloak, sandals, a walking stick) and forbids them from "procuring" anything more.[10]

Jesus therefore appears to have prohibited them from taking an additional pair of sandals or a staff. These accounts indicate that Jesus' purpose in giving such instructions was that the disciples take no extra burdens to slow their mission, and that their dependence for hospitality would serve as a test of the citizens' worthiness, for which they would be held accountable (Matt. 10:11-15; Luke 9:4-5).

8. When Herod imprisoned John the Baptist, did he want to kill John, or did he fear and protect him?

Both Matthew and Mark recount that Herod imprisoned John because the Baptist spoke out against Herod's illicit marriage to Herodias. Matthew recounts that *Herod wanted to kill John, but he was afraid of the people, because they considered him a prophet* (Matt. 14:5). Mark, however, writes that *Herodias nursed a grudge against John and wanted to kill him. But she was not able to, because Herod feared John and protected him, knowing him to be a righteous and holy man. When Herod heard John, he was greatly puzzled; yet he liked to listen to him* (Mark 6:19-20).

The seeming discrepancy regarding Herod's motives is resolved when the time factor and Herod's change of attitude are considered. It is certain that a considerable amount of time elapsed between John's imprisonment and his death. For after some time in prison, John sent disciples to inquire of Jesus if he were the Christ (Matt. 11:2-3; Luke 7:19-20). (Note Section 28: "John the Baptist Imprisoned," which is located much earlier in *The*

---

10. Carson, *Matthew*, 8:245.

Gospels Interwoven than Section 93: "John the Baptist Beheaded.") At first, both Herod and Herodias wanted to kill John. During John's imprisonment, however, Herod must have summoned the Baptist to listen to him preach, then changed his mind about John. Thus, the accounts of Matthew and Mark do not conflict; Matthew reflects Herod's earlier desire to kill John, and Mark indicates Herod's later motive to protect him.

Matthew's account itself provides evidence that Herod had a change of mind concerning John. When the daughter of Herodias requested the Baptist's head on behalf of her mother, Matthew agrees with Mark (Mark 6:26) that *the king was distressed* (Matt. 14:9). Matthew, therefore, shows that Herod first wanted to kill John but later was distressed when his death was requested.

9. Following the feeding of the 5,000, did the disciples leave in a boat to go to Bethsaida or to Capernaum? Was it before Jesus went up to pray or afterward? Did Jesus walk on the water to approach the disciples or to pass by them? Did they land at Capernaum or Gennesaret?

Matthew and Mark record that immediately following the feeding of the 5,000, Jesus sent his disciples in the boat *to the other side/to Bethsaida* (Matt. 14:22-23; Mark 6:45-46) *before* he went up into the hills to pray into the night. On the other hand, John 6:15-17 discloses that the disciples got into a boat that evening *and set off across the lake for Capernaum* (v. 17), sometime *after* Jesus withdrew to pray. Confusion exists over whether the disciples set off southeast for nearby Bethsaida, or northwest for Capernaum, on the other side of the lake. It is also puzzling whether they left before or after Jesus went up to pray.

The distance from Bethsaida to Capernaum is less than three miles. By boat the disciples would no doubt have hugged the coastline in a fairly straight line. Instead, they were apparently blown widely off course because *the boat was already a considerable distance from land* (Matt. 14:24) and *in the middle of the lake* (Mark 6:47). One solution has been that their original destination was Bethsaida, but that having been blown off course, they eventually went ashore near Capernaum. While this view solves the problem of the two intended destinations, it fails to account for the time relationship of their departure with Jesus' withdrawal to pray.

A better solution would be that Jesus first sent the disciples ahead of him in the boat to Bethsaida, a short distance away, then he retired into the hills to pray into the night. This seems likely, since John 6:17 recounts that *Jesus had not yet joined them*, as if they were expecting him to do so at Bethsaida, to which he could have easily walked. Indeed, Mark 6:45 mentions that

Jesus sent them *ahead of him to Bethsaida*. It was already *late in the day* (Mark 6:35) when Jesus fed the 5,000 (cf. Matt. 14:15: *as evening approached*). Apparently, after waiting into the night for Jesus' arrival at Bethsaida, the disciples set off again in the boat without Jesus, this time for Capernaum. Thus, a side trip to Bethsaida, a late departure from there, and the difficulty in high winds together would account for the disciples' crossing of the lake at such a late hour. Thus, Jesus came walking on the water (Matt. 14:25; Mark 6:48) during *the fourth watch of the night*, i.e., between 3 A.M. to 6 A.M. This view accounts for both intended destinations, as well as the departure of the disciples for Bethsaida before Jesus went up to pray and their departure for Capernaum after Jesus went up to pray. John, therefore, has omitted the detail of the short side trip to Bethsaida.

Another perplexing problem is whether Jesus, while walking on the lake, was approaching his disciples or passing by them. Matthew relates that Jesus *went out to them, walking on the lake* (Matt. 14:25); John says that he was *approaching the boat* (John 6:19); Mark states the same, but adds that *he was about to pass by them* (Mark 6:48). Vincent Taylor discusses the various renderings of Mark's phrase in the English versions and by commentators, opting for the translation, "He was going to pass by them," which does not conflict with the other Evangelists.[11] This is illustrated by William L. Lane's suggestion that Mark's addition corresponds to Exodus 34:6, in which God *passed by* Moses for the purpose of revealing himself.[12] The point is that Mark's theological language similarly depicts Jesus' revelation of himself to his disciples, not that he intended literally to pass by and continue onward.

An additional problem is that Matthew and Mark record, *When they had crossed over, they landed at Gennesaret* (Matt. 14:34; Mark 6:53), while John claims they *set off across the lake for Capernaum* (John 6:17) *and immediately the boat reached the shore where they were heading* (v. 21). Although the small town of Gennesaret lies south of Capernaum, the name Gennesaret also refers to a small, very fertile plain, four miles long from north to south and two miles wide, bordering on the west shore of the Sea of Galilee. It encompassed the land between the towns of Capernaum and Magdala. In fact, the lake itself is sometimes called *Lake of Gennesaret* (e.g., Luke 5:1), the name being derived from the plain.[13] The boat, therefore, apparently landed and anchored on the north end of the plain of Gennesaret, very near Capernaum.

---

11. Vincent Taylor, *The Gospel According to St. Mark* (London: MacMillan, 1952), 329.
12. Lane, *Mark*, 236.
13. Tenney, *Pictorial Encyclopedia*, 2:695-96.

CHAPTER SEVEN
MINISTRY BEYOND GALILEE

1. Was the woman with the demon-possessed daughter a Canaanite or a Syrian-Phoenician?

Matthew 15:22 identifies the mother of the demon-possessed daughter as a *Canaanite woman*, but Mark 7:26 describes her as a *Greek, born in Syrian Phoenicia*. She was of Greek descent, living in the non-Israeli vicinity of Tyre and Sidon, part of ancient Canaan then called Syrian-Phoenicia.

2. After Jesus fed the 4,000, did he go to Magadan or Dalmanutha?

Matthew 15:39 states *vicinity of Magadan*, while Mark 8:10 reads region of Dalmanutha, both of which locations remain uncertain.

> Magadan and Dalmanutha may have been contiguous; Magadan was identical with, or at least included in, Magdala, the home of Mary Magdalene.[1]

Also,

> The textual variants for Dalmanutha in Mark 8:10 are several. ... The variant Magdala may have been the original reading.[2]
> :

On the other hand, Bruce M. Metzger thinks copyists replaced *Dalmanutha* in Mark 8:10 (because its existence was probably unknown to them) with "Magedan" or "Magdala" to conform to Matthew 15:39. Metzger adds that, while *Magadan* is well attested by Greek MSS in Matthew 15:39, in both it and Mark 8:10 "the well-known Semitic word for Tower, in

---

1. Tenney, *Pictorial Encyclopedia*, 4:29-30.
2. Ibid., 2:6.

Greek [Magdala(n)], is read in many manuscripts in place of [Magadan] or [Dalmanoutha]."[3]

3. Did Jesus rise from the dead on the third day, after three days, or after three days and three nights? On what day of the week was Jesus crucified?

Jesus alluded to his death on several occasions, usually through his teaching of parables. At three different times, however, he gave his disciples a clear and direct prediction which included the period of time that would intervene between his death and resurrection. Yet the Synoptists differ slightly among themselves in quoting the time period Jesus predicted. Their terminology is listed as follows:

1st prediction
  Matthew 16:21: *on the third day*
  Mark 8:31: *after three days*
  Luke 9:22: *on the third day*
2nd prediction
  Matthew 17:23: *on the third day*
  Mark 9:31: *after three days*
3rd prediction
  Matthew 20:19: *on the third day*
  Mark 10:34: *three days later* (lit. "after three days")
  Luke 18:33: *on the third day*

In summary, Matthew and Luke consistently use *on the third day*, but Mark writes *after three days*. But Matthew records an earlier allusion by Jesus that he would be *three days and three nights in the heart of the earth* (Matt. 12:40). Do the Synoptists disagree on the predicted time period between Jesus' death and resurrection, or do all these terms signify the same time period, and if so, how long was it?

All the Gospels make it clear that the tomb was empty on Sunday, *the first day of the week* (Matt. 28:1; Mark 16:2; Luke 24:1; John 20:1), so that Jesus probably arose early Sunday morning. The main problem arises from the modern conception that three days equals seventy-two hours. Some popular commentators find it difficult to accept the reliable and widely accepted tradition that the Lord's death occurred on Friday, in which case he would have been in the tomb only about thirty-six hours. Instead, focusing on a seventy-two-hour period, they conclude that Jesus was crucified on Thursday, some even opting for Wednesday.

If Matthew and Luke used Mark as a written source in compiling their

---

3. Metzger, *Textual Commentary*, 41, 97.

Gospels, as is generally accepted among contemporary scholars, they would not have changed Mark's *after three days* to *on the third day* if these terms indicated different time periods. Additional evidence that these terms are used interchangeably is obtained from examining their use within a single Gospel. This internal evidence supports the traditional view that Jesus was crucified on Friday.

What Luke means by *the third day* is made unmistakably clear when Jesus said in another context, *"I will drive out demons and heal people today and tomorrow, and on the third day I will reach my goal"* (Luke 13:32). In Jesus' use of *the third day* here, there are only three days in view. Applied to the resurrection, the first day (like *today* in Luke 13:32) would be the day of crucifixion; the second day (like *tomorrow*) would be the following day, when Jesus was in the tomb; *the third day* would be the day after that, when Jesus arose from the dead. Comparing Jesus' usage here with Luke 9:22; 18:33; 24:7, and v. 21, Luke's *the third day* for the resurrection must mean that Jesus died on Friday.

Mark's *after three days* (Mark 8:31; 9:31) and *three days later* (Mark 10:34: the NIV here translates differently the same Greek words as in Mark 8:31 and 9:31) mean the same as *the third day* and signify crucifixion on the first day, with a second day in the tomb followed by resurrection the next (or *third*) day. This is made clear in his account of the burial and the visit to the empty tomb; Luke gives a parallel account. In both, Jesus was crucified on Friday, confirmed by the fact that the regular Sabbath (Saturday) followed immediately after the burial. Joseph of Arimathea and Nicodemus were hard pressed to complete the burial because *it was Preparation Day, and the Sabbath was about to begin* (Luke 23:54; cf. Mark 15:42). That this Sabbath was the regular Sabbath, i.e., Saturday, is indicated by the facts that the women saw the burial on the day of crucifixion (Mark 15:47; Luke 23:55), *went home and . . . rested on the Sabbath* (Luke 23:56), then *when the Sabbath was over* (Mark 16:1), *on the first day of the week* (Luke 24:1), went to the tomb. Between the day of crucifixion and the day of resurrection, only the one day is in view—the Sabbath (Saturday).

Matthew reveals that the phrases *after three days* and *the third day* mean the same thing: The Pharisees said to Pilate about Jesus, *"We remember that while he was still alive that deceiver said, 'After three days I will rise again.' So give the order for the tomb to be made secure until the third day"* (Matt. 27:63-64). To the Pharisees, therefore, and obviously to Matthew as well, *after three days* equals *the third day*. If the Pharisees had thought three days meant a seventy-two-hour period, they would have insisted that Pilate secure the tomb until the fourth day.

Especially troublesome, however, is Matthew's earliest account of Jesus' allusion to his death and resurrection: *The Son of Man will be three days and three nights in the heart of the earth* (Matt. 12:40). Yet Matthew's account of

Jesus' other three predictions date his resurrection as *the third day* after his death. Assuming Matthew (not to mention Jesus) is consistent, he indicates in Matthew 12:40 that he understands *three days and three nights* to designate the same time period as *the third day* in Matthew 16:21; 17:23; 20:19. Furthermore, if Matthew writes to Jewish readers, as has been widely accepted throughout church history, Jews likely understood *three days and three nights* to mean the same as the *third day*, while Gentiles might find these terms difficult to reconcile. This may indicate why the dialogue in Matthew 12:38-45, which includes the prediction of *three days and three nights*, only appears in Matthew's Gospel, since it is believed that Mark and Luke were written primarily for Gentile readers.

The Jewish meaning of the expression *three days and three nights* thoroughly clears up the matter. D.A. Carson explains:

> In rabbinical thought a day and a night make an *onah*, and a part of an *onah* is as the whole (. . . cf. further 1 Sam. 30:12-13; 2 Chron. 10:5, 12; Es. 4:16; 5:1). Thus according to Jewish tradition, "three days and three nights" need mean no more than "three days" or the combination of any part of three separated days.[4]

In regard to one of these similar references cited by Carson, *three days, night or day* (Es. 4:16) means the same thing as *third day* (Es. 5:1). Therefore, according to Hebrew usage, *third day, three days,* and *three days and three nights* can all mean the same length of time.

In conclusion, all these terms are used interchangeably both between the Gospels and within each Gospel, and according to Hebrew usage mean the same, supporting the early and well-established tradition that Jesus died on Friday afternoon and was raised early Sunday morning.

4. After Jesus first predicted his death, did six or eight days pass before he and the three apostles ascended the Mount of Transfiguration?

Matthew 17:1 and Mark 9:2 relate that *after six days* Jesus led Peter, James, and John up a high mountain, while Luke 9:28 relates that he did so after *about eight days.* Luke's imprecise word *about* obviously makes the eight days indefinite, so that even non-harmonist H.A.W. Meyer thinks this qualifying word enables Luke not to conflict with the other Synoptists.[5] Charles Ryrie presents the traditional view: "Luke's 'some eight days'

---

4. Carson, *Matthew*, 8:296.
5. Heinrich August Wilhelm Meyer, *Critical and Exegetical Hand-Book to the Gospels of Mark and Luke,* tr. Robert Ernest Wallis, rev. and ed. William P. Dickson, (Edinburgh: T. & T. Clark, 1883; Peabody, Mass.: Hendrickson, 1983), 308.

includes the beginning and ending days as well as the interval between."[6] This view, however, has not been well received among contemporary critical scholars, despite the fact that dismissing it weakens their view that Luke appealed to Mark as a written source. Several suggest that Luke, perhaps due to his writing to the hellenistic Christian community, adopted a Greek manner of indicating an eight-day week, similar to our saying "about a week later."[7] Many see in the six days an allusion to Exodus 24:16, with Moses' experience on Mount Sinai regarded as a type of Christ's experience on the Mount of Transfiguration. Moses waited on the mountain six days, God revealed himself to Moses the seventh day, then Moses later descended with his face shining (Ex. 34:29-35).

5. On the Mount of Transfiguration, did Peter address Jesus as *Lord*, *Rabbi*, or *Master*?

According to Matthew 17:4, at the Transfiguration *Peter said to Jesus, "Lord, it is good for us to be here."* The same quotation is recorded in the other Synoptics, except that the word with which Peter addressed Jesus is different: *Rabbi* in Mark 9:5 and *Master* in Luke 9:33. It would be absurd to think that Peter addressed Jesus with all three titles. Peter more likely spoke in Aramaic, but his words have been transmitted in Greek. What is the *ipsissma verba*, i.e., which one did he actually say? D.A. Carson proposes: "Mark is probably original; Luke translates 'Rabbi' by 'Master' for his non-Jewish readers; and Matthew probably uses 'Lord' in its general sense . . . connoting no more respect than 'rabbi.' "[8]

Regardless of the exact word of address employed by Peter, Matthew reveals in Jesus' preaching of the Seven Woes that *Rabbi* and *Master* may be used interchangeably (Matt. 23:8).[9] NT writers themselves are known for their free translation of OT quotations. In fact, the Septuagint (LXX: Greek translation of the OT), quoted by NT writers, frequently translates freely from the Hebrew text. The actual word of address, the *ipsissma verba*,

---

6. Charles Caldwell Ryrie, *The Ryrie Study Bible: New American Standard Translation* (Chicago: Moody Press, 1976), 1475. For a list of some of those earlier commentators who held this view, see Meyer, *Mark and Luke*, 308.

7. E.g., Carson, *Matthew*, 8:384 and Marshall, *Luke*, 382.

8. Carson, *Matthew*, 8:386. For a similar example, see Section 86: "Jesus Calms the Storm," in which Matthew again has *Lord* (Matt. 8:25), Mark has *Teacher* (Mark 4:38), very similar to *Rabbi*, and Luke has *Master* (Luke 8:24). When Mark and Luke record the same quotation but have a different word of address, Mark usually employs "Rabbi" or "Teacher" and Luke uses "Master" (e.g., Mark 9:38; Luke 9:49).

9. For another example of interchangeable words, see *the evil one* in Matt. 13:19, *Satan* in Mark 4:15, and *the devil* in Luke 8:12.

may not really be important so long as the same sense is conveyed. It may, therefore, be noteworthy that those who distinguish a sharp difference between the use of "Rabbi," "Master," and "Lord" in certain texts, in recognition of such passages as Matthew 7:21 and Romans 10:9, may be reading too much into these words.

6. Was John the Baptist Elijah or not?

In the time of Christ, the belief was prevalent, as it continues today in Orthodox Judaism and in many Christian circles, that Elijah will literally return to the earth just before the Messianic kingdom comes (cf. Mal. 4:5-6 with Rev. 11:3). Because of John's message of repentance in preparation for the kingdom, the priests and Levites asked John the Baptist if he were Elijah. The prophet unequivocally denied it (John 1:19-21). Later, as Jesus and his inner core of three disciples were descending the Mount of Transfiguration, they inquired of him about Elijah's coming again before the coming of Messiah. Jesus affirmed that belief and alluded that John the Baptist, indeed, was Elijah (Matt. 17:10-13; Mark 9:11-13).

Since the Apostle John does not record the Transfiguration scene, modern scholarship generally regards that John 1:21 contradicts Matthew's account that John the Baptist was Elijah.[10] However, the apparent contradiction vanishes if John the Baptist answered literally and Jesus, figuratively. On another occasion, Jesus spoke hypothetically to the crowd of Jews about John the Baptist as herald of the kingdom of God. He declared, *If you are willing to accept it, he is the Elijah who was to come* (Matt. 11:14). Jesus meant that if Israel would accept their Messiah and the kingdom he offered, in some sense John the Baptist would serve as Elijah to them.

The angel Gabriel prophesied to Zechariah that his son John would go before the Lord *in the spirit and power of Elijah* (Luke 1:17). Again, following the Transfiguration, Jesus appears to have meant the same thing that the angel announced at John's birth, that figuratively speaking, John was Elijah. All of this taken together indicates that John the Baptist was not actually Elijah, but very much like Elijah in his ministry to Israel.

10. Carson, *Matthew*, 8:269.

CHAPTER EIGHT
LAST FEAST OF TABERNACLES

1. Is Luke 9:51-18:14 chronological? Does it include any incidents recorded in the other Gospels?

A.T. Robertson states concerning Luke's central section, "We now have to deal with the most perplexing question in harmonistic study, the proper disposal of the mass of material furnished by Luke in Luke 9:51-18.14."[1] Some commentators regard the entirety of the Gospel of Luke as chronologically arranged because Luke states in his introduction that he purposed to *write an orderly account* (Luke 1:3). A comparison of the Gospels, however, reveals that this interpretation meets with serious difficulties. Most contemporary scholars do not interpret *orderly account* in Luke 1:3 to necessitate a chronological arrangement. On the contrary, they regard Luke 9:51-18:14 as a collection of nonchronological events, as is indicated by the lack of geographical connections between incidents and seeming contradictions in Jesus' travel itinerary. Indeed, several perplexing problems surface in an examination of Jesus' travels in Luke 9:51-18:14.

Luke 9:51 maintains that *Jesus resolutely set out for Jerusalem*, later presumably visited Bethany, just outside Jerusalem (Luke 10:38-42; cf. John 11:1-2), yet thereafter *went through the towns and villages, teaching as he made his way to Jerusalem* (Luke 13:22). Comparing John with Luke, if the insertion in the composite of the material from John 11:1-54 is correct, Jesus visited Bethany in Luke 10:38 and again in John 11:17-44 to raise Lazarus, after which *he withdrew to a region near the desert, to a village called Ephraim* (John 11:54). Still he did not proceed to Jerusalem. After this he *traveled along the border between Samaria and Galilee* (Luke 17:11), then *went on ahead, going up to Jerusalem* (Luke 19:28).

Calvin said of these difficulties, "It is not clear whether Luke was speaking of only one journey," meaning Jesus' last journey to Jerusalem.[2] I. Howard Marshall goes further:

---

1. Robertson, *Harmony*, 276.
2. Calvin, *Harmony/Gospels*, 2:81.

Luke cannot have been consciously providing a geographical progress from Galilee to Jerusalem. The incidents are not tied to specific locations. . . . Above all, Luke is able to stress that Jerusalem is from now onwards the goal of Jesus.[3]

Walter L. Liefeld adds:

Actually, Luke does not state that Jesus made one journey from north to south but rather suggests that he crisscrossed the area, making perhaps several trips to Jerusalem before his final stay there. . . . while Jesus did not go directly from Galilee to Jerusalem, his mind was definitely set on the impending events he faced in that city. Even at times when he may have traveled north again, his ultimate goal was Jerusalem.[4]

In this "central section," Luke does not explicitly state that Jesus visited Jerusalem during this time period before his Triumphal Entry, but it is assumed that he did so when he twice visited Bethany. Most commentators believe that this Lukan material corresponds to the last months of Jesus' earthly ministry.

It is uncertain whether there are any events in Luke 9:51-18:14 that are recorded in the other Synoptics. Some of the Lukan sections which may be included in the other Synoptics are entitled in *The Gospels Interwoven:* Section 138: "Jesus and Beelzebub Again"; Section 139: "The Sign of Jonah Again"; and Section 157: "Another Parable of the Lost Sheep." (See EN 8:3; EN 9:1, 2; EN 10:1, 2.) Donald Guthrie comments on the tendency of liberal critics to reduce the Gospels to a fewer number of sections than is generally accepted:

One important aspect of the teaching method of Jesus was his practice of repeating his saying. Many source theories have been based on the assumption that this did not happen, and consequently similar sayings were regarded as variant duplicates in the tradition. This method of dealing with the teaching of Jesus is open to criticism on the ground that it does not sufficiently take account of the usual practice of repetition among Jewish teachers (see B. Gerhardsson's *Memory and Manuscript* [1961], which cites evidence of this prevalent procedure).[5]

The sequential arrangement in *The Gospels Interwoven* represents a median

---

3. Marshall, *Luke*, 401.
4. Liefeld, *Luke*, 8:995-96, 932.
5. Guthrie, *A Shorter Life*, 137-38.

position between liberal critics and those few harmonists who regard all the Gospel material as chronological. The least difference between the sections in question is regarded by the latter group as cause to view them as different incidents.

The uncertainty of whether or not Luke 9:51-18:14 is recorded chronologically need not deter the construction of a composite, inasmuch as Calvin has rightly concluded about the Gospels that proper chronology does not always concern the Spirit of God. In conformity to The Chronological Table, Luke 9:51-18:14 is considered chronological in the composite text.

The interweaving of John 7:2–11:54 with Luke 9:51–18:14 found herein follows the majority of harmonists in The Chronological Table. Most harmonists interweave this material because it is regarded to include corresponding journeys back and forth through Judea and Perea. More particularly, many harmonists identify Jesus' region of ministry recorded in the first half of Luke's "central section" (Luke 10:1–13:9 or 13:21) as Judea and the second half (Luke 13:10 or 13:22–17:10) as Perea. These identifications of region of ministry are not certain, however. The second half identification seems likely, but certain passages suggest that Jesus did not minister in Judea during that time period recorded in Luke 10:1–13:9. Harmonists who hold this view usually place John 7:1 before Luke's "central section," as herein. It reads, *After this, Jesus went around in Galilee, purposely staying away from Judea because the Jews there were waiting to take his life.*

Thereafter, it would appear that Jesus did not minister in Judea his last year except while attending the feasts. Furthermore, it would seem that Jesus was in Galilee when he denounced the cities of Korazin, Bethsaida, and Capernaum (Luke 10:13-15), all Galilean towns near or on the Sea of Galilee. In spite of these considerations, since most reliable harmonists so identify this section of Luke, chapter nine is tentatively entitled "More (Judean?) Ministry."

2. How can Matthew dislocate an incident in time yet begin the account with the word *Then?*

According to the chronology in this volume, Matthew 8:19-22 and 11:20-30 are the farthest dislocations in the Gospels. Yet Matthew begins both accounts with the word *Then* (*Then* in Matthew 8:19 is excluded herein). This peculiar style of Matthew's appears to link this and the preceding section chronologically. Other examples are Matthew 8:23, 12:22 and 26:31. D.A. Carson claims the word does not necessarily chronologically connect two incidents:

(*Tote*, "then") is very common in Matthew, occurring ninety times as compared with Mark's six and Luke's fourteen; but in Matthean usage only sometimes does it have temporal force . . . serving more frequently as a loose connective.[6]

The same is true of the phrase *at that time*, which begins dislocated sections at Matthew 12:1 and 14:1. Carson's comment applies to all these verses: "The phrase 'At that time' is very loose . . . and should not be tied to the previous pericope."[7]

3. When and where did Jesus encounter those disciples who had not counted the cost?

Matthew 8:19-22 and Luke 9:57-62 record strikingly similar conversations between Jesus and certain of his disciples. Many harmonists regard them as the same episode even though there are several differences:

a. The location in time of the reports is different. Matthew appears to place the encounter earlier in Jesus' ministry than does Luke.

b. The geography is different. Matthew locates these dialogues beside the Sea of Galilee as Jesus and his disciples prepared to cross the lake by boat (Matt. 8:18). Luke, however, places these encounters *as they were walking along a road*, as if they were going southward from village to village through Samaria (Luke 9:57) toward Jerusalem (v. 51). The Sea of Galilee is north of Samaria, and Jerusalem is south of Samaria. It is unnecessary, therefore, to take Luke 9:51 to mean that Jesus thereafter always traveled southward until reaching Jerusalem. (See EN 8:1.)

c. The arrangement of the dialogue is different. Matthew records Jesus' words *"Follow me"* last, while Luke has them first. Luke also adds an instruction in Luke 9:60 which Matthew omits.

d. The number of disciples is different. Matthew records two inquirers, but Luke adds a third, with an ensuing dialogue.

The chronological and geographical difficulties, of course, are resolved if Matthew and Luke report two separate incidents. Nevertheless, most harmonists, including a majority of those listed in The Chronological Table, regard these accounts as one incident, as herein.

---

6. Carson, *Matthew*, 8:90.
7. Ibid., 8:337.

1. Do the Gospels record that Jesus delivered two "Lord's Prayers" or one?

The form of prayer Jesus taught in the Sermon on the Mount in Matthew 6:9-13 is very similar to that in Luke's record (Luke 11:2-4). A few commentators regard these two accounts as the same incident. The following reasons suggest they are two separate teaching sessions:

a. Matthew and Luke locate the teachings of these two forms for prayer chronologically far apart in each of their scenarios of Jesus' ministry. Furthermore, if Matthew 5–7 and Luke 6 record the same sermon, in which Luke has omitted Jesus' teaching on prayer, this alone would require that the two model prayers were given at separate times.

b. The occasion prompting each instruction is different. In Luke 11:1, after Jesus finished praying *in a certain place*, a disciple said, *"Lord, teach us to pray."* There does not seem to be a multitude present at that time. On the other hand, Matthew locates Jesus' teaching on prayer *on a mountainside* (Matt. 5:1) with his disciples and large crowds present (Matt. 4:25; Luke 6:17-20). This took place during a protracted teaching session (the Sermon on the Mount) and was preceded, not by his praying, as in Luke, but by his contrast of genuine prayer with the ostentatious prayers of the hypocrites.

c. Jesus' itinerant preaching and teaching ministry likely necessitated more than one teaching session on prayer. This view would seem to suggest, though not require, that the disciple who requested teaching on prayer recorded in Luke 11:1 was not one of the Twelve, or anyone else present when Jesus delivered the Sermon on the Mount recorded in Matthew 5–7. Both teachings on prayer are included in the composite. Jesus likely taught on prayer more than once.

2. How many times do the Gospels record that Jesus spoke of the sign of Jonah?

Matthew records two instances when Jesus was approached by Pharisees demanding of him a sign (Matt. 12:38-45; 16:1-4). Both times Jesus said no sign would be given them but the sign of Jonah. In Matthew's first account, Jesus further explained that he would be in the earth *three days and three nights* (Matt. 12:40), just as Jonah was in the huge fish that length of time.

The location of Mark 8:11-13, as well as a similarity of details, indicates it is the same as Matthew's second account. As for Luke's account in Luke 11:29-32, it is located in his "central section," that body of material which finds no *clear* direct parallels with the other Synoptics. Luke's location of Jesus' utterance and the contrast of his details with the other Synoptists suggest that he is reporting another incident when Jesus spoke of the sign of Jonah. Luke reports nothing about Pharisees being present and demanding of him a sign. The similar incident in Matthew 12:38-45 happened before Jesus' mother and brothers came to speak to him (12:4-6), the same day he taught the Parable of the Sower. Luke places both of these episodes together in Luke 8, earlier than and removed from Luke 11:29-32. It therefore seems better to regard Luke 11:29-32 as a third teaching by Jesus regarding the sign of Jonah.

CHAPTER TEN
PEREAN MINISTRY AND RAISING OF LAZARUS

1. Did Jesus lament over Jerusalem once or twice?

The quotation of Jesus' lament over Jerusalem in Luke 13:34-35 is almost verbatim in Matthew 23:37-39. This has caused some commentators to conclude that both authors report the same incident, with Luke displacing Jesus' lament in his Gospel. In Matthew's account the lamentation occurs during Passion Week in Jerusalem, while Luke places it earlier, when Jesus was *teaching as he made his way to Jerusalem* (Luke 13:22). It is difficult to determine whether Jesus spoke these words on two different occasions, as their contexts suggest, or on one occasion. If one, then it appears Luke has displaced the quotation for a thematic reason, i.e., to amplify Jesus' previous remark that *no prophet can die outside Jerusalem* (Luke 13:33). If so, this does not materially impinge on the historical accuracy of Luke's Gospel, since Luke does not directly specify the time that Jesus spoke these words.

Perhaps the last sentence, including the words *Blessed is he who comes in the name of the Lord*, was spoken with different intents on two different occasions, as it has a twofold application. The obvious one is that the citizens of Jerusalem will not see Jesus Christ again until they greet him with quotations from the last of the Hallel Psalm (Ps. 118:26). The context of that psalm vividly portrays Israel's Messianic deliverance from her enemies at the end of the age. This far view, therefore, is that Jesus will soon die, return to heaven, and not be seen by Jerusalem's citizens until his return to earth with his glorious kingdom. However, if Jesus spoke this lament in the time frame where Luke has placed it, Luke's may be the near view that Jerusalem will not see Jesus again until some days later, when he is riding down the Mount of Olives on a donkey with his disciples shouting hosannas, saying, *Blessed is he who comes in the name of the Lord* (Matt. 21:9). It seems best to keep Luke's arrangement intact by regarding the two records of Jesus' lamenting over Jerusalem as spoken on two different occasions, as herein.

2. Do the Gospels record that Jesus taught the parable of the lost sheep on one or two occasions?

Some commentators regard Jesus' teaching about the lost sheep in Matthew 18:12-14 and Luke 15:3-7 as the same event. However, there are many dissimilarities. Matthew has only Jesus' disciples present (Matt. 18:1) and precedes the teaching with the disciples' question about greatness. Calling a little child forward in demonstration, Jesus teaches his disciples the prerequisite of humility for entrance into the kingdom. He next draws a parallel with sheep; i.e., God is like a sheepherder; although a sheep wanders off like a child, *your Father . . . is not willing that any of these little ones should be lost* (Matt. 18:14).

On the other hand, Luke has Jesus telling the sheep parable in the company of the *tax collectors and "sinners"* and of *the Pharisees and the teachers of the law,* who *muttered, "This man welcomes sinners and eats with them"* (Luke 15:1-2). Here, Jesus compares the Pharisees and teachers of the law to the ninety-nine sheep and concludes concerning the one lost sheep, *There will be more rejoicing in heaven over one sinner who repents* (v.7). The lesson derived from the parables in Matthew and Luke are therefore different. In Matthew, Jesus teaches the compassion of God the Father for his children; in Luke, he teaches the need of repentance for the self-righteous, who erroneously regard themselves as belonging to God.

There are other differences. Perhaps the most significant is that there are no other thoroughly convincing direct parallels with the other Synoptics in Luke 9:57–18:14. This is weighty evidence that Jesus, as an itinerant preacher, taught in this sheep country about lost sheep on several occasions.

Similar arguments to those above can be applied to Jesus' teachings about the salt in Mark 9:50 and Luke 14:34, the lamp of the body in Matthew 6:22-23 and Luke 11:34-36, and the narrow gate or door in Matthew 7:13-14 and Luke 13:24. Yet the parables of the mustard seed and yeast in Matthew 13:31-33 and Luke 13:18-21 are more alike. As with the sheep parable, most, if not all, of these teachings were likely given on separate occasions.

:

CHAPTER ELEVEN
LAST TRIP TO JERUSALEM

1. Do Mark and Luke relate the exact dialogue between Jesus and the rich young ruler, or does Matthew?

All three Synoptists record the conversation between Jesus and the rich young ruler (Mark 10:17-21; Luke 18:18-22; Matt. 19:16-21). Mark and Luke relate the same dialogue. Matthew, however, locates the word *good* differently in the wealthy young man's question, with a different response by Jesus. Is the meaning of the conversation as related by Matthew actually different from that of Mark and Luke? Carefully observe the following comparison:

a. Rich man: *Good teacher, what must I do to inherit eternal life* (Mark 10:17; Luke 18:18)?

Jesus: *Why do you call me good? No one is good—except God alone* (Mark 10:18; Luke 18:19).

b. Rich man: *Teacher, what good thing must I do to get eternal life* (Matt. 19:16)?

Jesus: *There is only One who is good* (Matt. 19:17).

Due to doubt by this author as to which of Jesus' responses represents the *ipsissima verba*, both are retained in composite form in the text of *The Gospels Interwoven*. It is possible that the three Synoptists each record only parts of the whole conversation. It appears that the first part of Jesus' response—*Why do you call me good?*—has been omitted by Matthew.

Many contemporary commentators allege that only Mark and Luke render the *ipsissima verba* (exact words). Indeed, as an editor of his written sources, Matthew frequently renders the *ipsissima vox* for further clarification to his readers. The question that concerns most students of the Gospels is this: has the meaning been changed? Not a few scholars assert that either rendering, as well as their comparison, gives rise to a Christological problem as well as a discrepancy. Critic Walter Grundmann, however, concedes that there is no difference in meaning and therefore no serious problem:

It must be admitted that Matthew has altered the tradition maintained in the other two [Synoptics], since the opposite course is inconceivable. Matthew is concerned in his version to avoid the misunderstanding that Jesus is repudiating his own sinlessness or goodness as compared with that of God. Even if he does amend the wording, he surely interprets correctly the intention of Jesus, who is not raising the question of his own sinlessness but rather of the honour of God.[1]

2. Did James and John, or did their mother, make the request to Jesus that the two brothers sit on Jesus' immediate right and left hand in his kingdom?

Matthew 20:20-21 records that the mother of James and John made the request, yet Mark 10:35-37 indicates that the two sons did. A closer examination of Matthew's account shows that, although he has the mother making the request, Jesus answered *to them* (v.22), an addition absent in Mark's account. Matthew therefore implies that Jesus answered the two sons, or all three, but not just the mother. This is further supported by what follows, in which Jesus directed an inquiry to the sons (Matt. 20:22; Mark 10:38). So who made the request that James and John sit at Jesus' side in the kingdom? It was likely both the mother and her sons. Perhaps they approached Jesus together, the sons first requesting a favor, the mother next making the specific request, followed by James' and John's confirmation of her request. Interestingly, Gleason Archer cites 1 Kings 1:11-21, particularly v.14, as a precedent for this request being made first by the mother, then repeated by the sons.[2]

3. Did Jesus heal the two blind men on his entry into Jericho or on his departure?

Luke 18:35 states that Jesus' entourage first met the blind man *as Jesus approached Jericho*. But Matthew 20:29 and Mark 10:46 clearly indicate that

---

1. Gerhard Kittel, ed., *Theological Dictionary of the New Testament*, tr. Geoffrey Bromiley, 10 vols. (Grand Rapids: Eerdmans, 1964-76), 1:15-16. See also Erich Beyreuther, "Good, Beautiful, Kind" in *The New International Dictionary of New Testament Theology* (1967-71), gen. ed. Colin Brown, 3 vols. (Grand Rapids: Zondervan, 1975-78), 2:100. Jesus does not repudiate being called "good," as witnessed in John 10:11, 14, which probably intends a different sense than here (cf. Zech. 11:15-17; 13:7).
2. Gleason Archer, *Encyclopedia of Bible Difficulties* (Grand Rapids: Zondervan, 1982), 332.

Jesus met and healed the sitting blind men/man as he and his disciples *were leaving Jericho/the city*. Here is an example of how variations in the accounts cause some harmonists to view each account as a separate incident. E.g., concerning these passages, Osiander believed Jesus healed four blind men on three separate occasions.

The traditional explanation, advocated by Calvin, is that Jesus first met the blind men as he approached Jericho and later healed them upon exiting the city through the same gate he entered earlier.[3] But the Synoptists portray Jesus as passing through Jericho on his way to Jerusalem, in which case he would have continued in a southwesterly direction on the same road and exited on the other side of the city. Jericho was on one of the main ancient routes to Jerusalem.

A similar view is that the blind men followed Jesus from his entrance into Jericho through the city to his departure on the other side, where he subsequently healed them. It is unlikely that two blind beggars would have walked with the crowd as they followed Jesus for perhaps more than a mile. Matthew and Mark render both of these views unsuitable; they indicate that Jesus and his disciples first met the blind men/man as they were *leaving* Jericho.

The most probable explanation is that Matthew and Mark indicated the Old Testament Jericho, while Luke referred to the new Jericho built by Herod, situated one mile south. The building of a new city of the same name built beside the old one was common in the ancient world.[4] Thus, as Jesus was leaving old Jericho and approaching new Jericho, he met the begging blind men and healed them.[5]

Further evidence that Jesus healed the two blind men between the two Jerichos is found in the next section. Only Luke recounts that after the healing Jesus *entered Jericho and was passing through* when he met Zacchaeus (Luke 19:1-2). While Jesus' travel itinerary in Luke 19:1 does not conflict with Luke 18:35, it does contradict Matthew 20:29 and Mark 10:46 if the traditional explanation of only one Jericho is accepted. It would be most unlikely that Jesus would have first encountered the two blind men on his approach to Jericho, healed them as he was leaving the city, then returned to Jericho to meet Zacchaeus while passing through. again. The two

---

3. Calvin, *Harmony/Gospels*, 2:278.
4. This was frequently done when a city was destroyed by military conquest or fire, so that the new city was built close by, yet the old one often re-emerged. Perhaps the only argument against this view is that evidence is lacking that old Jericho was inhabited at this time. However, there is no proof that it was not. For some, the NIV rendering of *the city* in Mark 10:46 will be misleading, as if it designates an inhabited city thriving at old Jericho. The RSV and NASB correctly render "Jericho," as in the Greek text.
5. See Tenney, *Pictorial Encyclopedia*, 3:451; Lane, *Mark*, 386n.

episodes harmonize if there were two Jerichos, which the combined accounts of the Synoptists indicate.

4. On his last approach to Jerusalem, did Jesus heal one blind man near Jericho or two?

Matthew 20:29-34 mentions two blind men healed by Jesus, while Mark 10:46-52 and Luke 18:35-43 mention only one, with Mark naming him as Bartimaeus. There are several possible explanations for Mark's and Luke's mention of only one blind man, arranged in decreasing order of probability:

    a. Bartimaeus was either the more prominent or more vocal of the two.

    b. Bartimaeus became a well-known disciple of Jesus, while the other did not.

    c. The other blind man died early, moved away, etc.

As the only eyewitness, Matthew adds the detail of the second man. It is typical of Matthew to report two where the other Synoptists report only one. E.g., Mark and Luke both record only one demon-possessed man (Mark 5:2; Luke 8:27) and one donkey (Mark 11:2; Luke 19:30) whereas Matthew reports two demon-possessed men and two donkeys—a colt and its mother (Matt. 8:28; 21:2).

CHAPTER TWELVE
LAST JERUSALEM MINISTRY

1. At his Triumphal Entry into Jerusalem, did Jesus have one donkey or two? Did he sit simultaneously on both the donkey and her colt?

Concerning Jesus' Triumphal Entry into Jerusalem on Palm Sunday, Mark, Luke and John write only that he rode a colt, i.e., a young donkey. Matthew, however, records that Jesus instructed the disciples to bring him both a donkey and her colt, which they did (Matt. 21:2, 7) in fulfillment of Zechariah 9:9. The other three Evangelists simply omit information about the colt's mother, although some liberal critics allege that Matthew fictitiously inserted the second animal into his narrative, as if to fulfill Zechariah's prophecy. However, Matthew, as an eyewitness, here apparently adds details missing from his written source(s), e.g., Mark. (See Introduction: Source Criticism.) It is only Matthew who records *two* demon-possessed men near Lake Galilee and *two* blind men near Jericho (Matt. 8:28; 20:30).

Matthew writes that *they brought the donkey and the colt, placed their cloaks on them, and Jesus sat on them* (v.7). Liberal critics have ridiculed this statement, supposing that Matthew states that Jesus sat on both the donkey and her colt at the same time. The last phrase, *Jesus sat on them*, probably refers to *cloaks* in the previous phrase rather than to the donkeys. It appears the disciples placed garments on both animals, not knowing on which one Jesus intended to sit. He then sat on the cloaks that were on the colt, riding it into Jerusalem with its mother accompanying.

:

2. Did Jesus cleanse the temple on Sunday or Monday of Passion Week?

Matthew and Luke appear to locate Jesus' last cleansing of the temple on Palm Sunday (Matt. 21:1-17; Luke 19:29-46), whereas Mark's more detailed account appears to place it on the following Monday (Mark 11:1-17).

331

Calvin prefers Matthew's and Luke's apparent dating of the cleansing of the temple on Sunday. He considers Mark's account of the cleansing in Mark 11:15-18 a recapitulation of an event which happened on Palm Sunday. However, most contemporary scholars, including ten of thirteen harmonists in The Chronological Table, prefer the more detailed chronology of Mark for the cleansing of the temple on Monday, as herein. It would seem that Jesus inspected the Court of the Gentiles in the temple late Sunday (in partial fulfillment of Mal. 3:1), perhaps the condition of which became reason for his cursing the fig tree the next morning on his way to cleanse the temple.[1]

Calvin adheres to Mark's more detailed chronology regarding Jesus' cursing of the fig tree. He maintained, as herein, that Jesus cursed the fig tree on Monday and that the disciples first viewed the withered fig tree on Tuesday. If Calvin is correct about the temple being cleansed on Sunday, the parabolic lesson of the cursed fig tree as a symbol of judgment before the cleansing of the temple is lost due to the inverted order.

On the difficulty of determining the exact day of the cleansing, Calvin concedes: "But no one who considers how little attention the Evangelists give to noting times will be put off by this kind of difference in narrative."[2]

3. Did Jesus cleanse the temple by expelling the moneychangers once or twice?

Early in his Gospel, John narrates that Jesus cleansed the temple of its ungodly commercialism by expelling the moneychangers with a whip (John 2:13-17). Most contemporary commentators allege that John's account is the same as that of the Synoptists (Matt. 21:12-13; Mark 11:15-18; Luke 19:45-46), so that Jesus cleansed the temple only one time, during Passion Week. However, the following reasons indicate there were two separate cleansings:

a. Several differences exist between John's account and that of the Synoptists, including the application of different OT quotations and the inclusion only in John of Jesus' prophecy about destroying the temple.

b. It seems appropriate that Jesus would denounce merchandising in his Father's house at both the beginning and end of his earthly ministry. If the temple police instituted security measures following the first episode, they probably had relaxed them by this time, about three years later.

c. The omission in the Synoptics of an earlier cleansing may be attributed to their omission of Jesus' early ministry altogether. J.H.A. Ebrard

---

1. Lane, *Mark*, 398.
2. Calvin, *Harmony/Gospels*, 3:10.

believed the Synoptists "only commence their continuous history with the time when Jesus was in Capernaum,"[3] whereas John includes his earlier attendance of feasts at Jerusalem (e.g., John 2:13; 5:1).

d. It is highly improbable that John would place very early in his Gospel an event from the Passion Week, as if it occurred at the beginning of Jesus' public ministry. Except for the possible dislocation of the anointing at Bethany in his twelfth chapter, John arranges his other material chronologically, which substantially favors his doing so here as well. Moreover, there is no precedent anywhere in the Gospels for such an extreme dislocation of an incident.

4. Did the disciples see the fig tree withered on Monday, the same day Jesus cursed it, or on Tuesday, the day following the curse?

Many critics dismiss the possibility that this incident of the fig tree (Matt. 21:18-22; Mark 11:12-14; 20-26), like the purging of the temple the following day, was prefiguring God's future judgment on the city and nation. They allege that the Synoptists created this piece of fiction by borrowing from Jesus' earlier teaching of the parable of the fig tree in Luke 13:6-9. More than just radical critics have rejected the historicity of Jesus' cursing of the fig tree, regarding the incident as out of character for Jesus and inappropriate, since the fruit was supposedly out of season. Surely the cost of the life of a fig tree is not too great for Jesus' purpose. Such critics seem to overlook the cursed fig tree serving a symbolic purpose similar to the millions of sacrificial animals that bore the curse of sin. The assertion of some of these critics, perpetuated even by some conservative commentators, that in the springtime in Jerusalem figs appear before the leaves, is erroneous. Wessel correctly comments, "Fig trees around Jerusalem usually leaf out in March or April, but they do not produce figs till June."[4] The small green figs first appear after the tree has fully leafed out, but do not ripen until June.

Of the three Synoptists' accounts, Mark's is generally preferred over the others for obtaining a clear chronology because he gives the most detailed account of Jesus' cursing of the fig tree. Mark 11:11-21 has the order of events as follows:

a. Jesus made his Triumphal Entry into Jerusalem on Sunday, went to the temple area, and looked around. Perhaps he again witnessed the ungodly and greedy practices of the moneychangers in the Court of the Gentiles that evening, as he had done earlier in his ministry (John 2:13-17).

---

3. Ebrard, *Gospel History*, 379.
4. Wessel, *Mark*, 8:726.

b. Jesus left the temple for Bethany, since it was already late in the day (v.11).

c. On Monday morning, as he was returning to Jerusalem, he cursed the fig tree for being unfruitful (v.12-14).

d. Upon arriving at the temple at Jerusalem, he expelled the money-changers. He left the city again that evening and returned to Bethany (v.19).

e. On Tuesday morning the disciples first observed the fig tree withered (v.20) as they walked back to Jerusalem.

Matthew and Luke seem to compress these events into two days' time instead of three: Jesus both rode into Jerusalem and cleared the temple on Sunday, then he cursed the fig tree and the disciples saw it withered on Monday. This divergence between Mark and the other Synoptists is due to the frequent habit of Matthew (as mentioned many times in these notes), as well as Luke in this case, to condense events, as compared to Mark, in order to include additional material not found in Mark. Not concerned with providing the detailed chronology already published by Mark, Matthew seems to strive to include in his Gospel as many incidents as possible from the life of Jesus. Some think Matthew's penchant for condensation is due to his recognition of the standard maximum length of a scroll (25-35 feet). Matthew and Luke are about the same length, nearly twice as long as Mark and over one-third longer than John.

Mark's chronology is also preferred in that a symbolic meaning of Jesus' cursing of the fig tree better fits his subsequent cleansing of the temple. The fig tree having leaves without fruit represents Israel's hypocrisy—outward acts of prayer, fasting, almsgiving, etc., without the fruit of true righteousness. The merchandising practices in the temple demonstrate how far Israel had departed from true worship. Both the cursing of the fig tree and the cleansing of the temple are precursors of the judgment of God upon Jerusalem, to which Jesus alluded in other prophecies that week (e.g., Matt. 21:43; 24:2). Such symbolism is confirmed by what Jesus said before and after this event, as well as by history. Upon seeing Jerusalem and making his Triumphal Entry the previous day, Jesus wept over the city and predicted its judgment in detail (Luke 19:41-44). Probably afterward, i.e., on Tuesday afternoon, he pronounced seven woes upon Israel's leaders, predicting judgment on the city and nation within a generation (Matt. 23). History reveals that the Romans completed their destruction of Jerusalem in A.D. 70, exactly a generation, or forty years, later.

CHAPTER THIRTEEN
PREDICTING THE FUTURE

1. Do the Gospels account for one, two or three anointings of Jesus while He was alive? If there were two anointings, was the one at Bethany two days before Passover or six days before?

Much attention has been drawn to the differing Gospel accounts of a woman's anointing of Jesus with perfume. Some harmonists think the four Evangelists account for three separate anointings of Jesus: first, at Simon the Pharisee's house, presumably in Galilee, by the sinful woman (Luke 7:36-50); second, at Lazarus' home in Bethany by his sister Mary, six days before Passover (John 12:1-8); and third, at Simon the Leper's house at Bethany by an unknown woman, two days before Passover (Matt. 26:2-13; Mark 14:1-9).

On the other hand, many contemporary scholars think there was only one anointing due to the striking similarities between Luke's account and those of the other Evangelists:

a. Both anointings occurred at the house of a man named Simon (Luke 7:40; Matt. 26:6; Mark 14:3), although this was a fairly common name.

b. It occurred while they were reclining at a table (Luke 7:36; Mark 14:3; John 12:2) and eating (Luke 7:36-37; cf. John 12:2).

c. A woman brought an alabaster jar of perfume (Luke 7:37; Matt. 26:7; Mark 14:3).

d. The woman poured perfume on Jesus' feet and wiped them with her hair (Luke 7:38; John 12:3).

Nevertheless, there are differences indicating Luke's account is separate from that of the other Evangelists, that it records an earlier anointing by another woman:

a. While Luke does not specifically locate this anointing, the context of his account indicates it occurred in Galilee. The other Evangelists clearly locate the anointing in Bethany (Matt. 26:6; Mark 14:3; John 12:1).

b. Luke places the incident considerably earlier in his Gospel and therefore presumably earlier in Jesus' public ministry. The other Evangelists place the anointing late in their Gospels, during Passion Week.

c. Luke identifies the owner of the house as *Simon the Pharisee* (Luke 7:36,39), whereas Matthew and Mark identify the owner of the house as *Simon the Leper* (Matt. 28:6; Mark 14:3). It is improbable that Simon the Leper could have been Simon the Pharisee. Simon the Leper must have been a former leper now healed, probably by Jesus. It is doubtful that a former leper could even become a Pharisee.

d. The observers' response is different. In Luke's account the owner of the house faults Jesus for receiving the anointing from the sinful woman and, on the basis that Jesus must not have known who she was, questions whether he is a prophet (Luke 7:39). In the other two Synoptics, Jesus' disciples (particularly Judas, according to John 12:4), not the owner of the house, criticize the woman for wasting the perfume (Matt. 26:8-9; Mark 14:4-5). The disciples' objection is recorded almost identically by the other Evangelists, in contrast to its omission in Luke.

e. Jesus' response is different. In Luke, Jesus gives a parable, faults Simon, and forgives the woman's sins (Luke 7:40-43, 44-47, 48). In the other accounts, Jesus reprimands the disciples and praises the woman.

f. The women who anointed are different. John identifies the woman as Mary, sister of Lazarus and Martha (John 12:3; cf. 11:1-3), all close friends of Jesus. It does not seem that Mary could have been *a woman who had lived a sinful life in that town* (Luke 7:37) because such a former reputation of Mary of Bethany would surely not have escaped mention in the Gospels. Indeed, some commentators suppose that Mary of Bethany, the sister of Lazarus and Martha, was formerly Mary of Magdala (Mary Magdalene). Those who take this view usually regard Luke's sinful woman who anointed Jesus as Mary Magdalene. It does not seem likely that Matthew and Mark would fail to identify *the woman* as Mary Magdalene, since they name her so soon afterward, more than once, in the account of the death and resurrection of Jesus (Matt. 27:56, 61; 28:1; Mark 15:40, 47; 16:1, 9).

g. The result is different. Matthew and Mark show that the anointing became the final impetus for Judas to betray Jesus by contacting the authorities (Matt. 26:14-16; Mark 14:10-11; cf. John 12:4-6). There is no indication of this in Luke's account.

h. Luke's introduction later in his Gospel of Mary as Martha's sister (Luke 10:38-39) clearly indicates that Mary is a new character not previously mentioned in his Gospel, and therefore not the sinful woman of Luke 7:37.

While some of these differences between Luke and the other Evangelists can be attributed to silence, the overall evidence seems to indicate that Luke has recorded a separate anointing from that of the other three Evangelists.

There remains another view: that John also records a separate anointing from that of Matthew and Mark. The primary evidences for this view are:

a. Matthew and Mark relate that the woman poured the perfume on Jesus' head (Matt. 26:7; Mark 14:3), while John writes that Mary poured the perfume on Jesus' feet (John 12:3; see also Luke 7:38).

b. Matthew and Mark place the anointing at Bethany after the Triumphal Entry, whereas John places it before (John 12:1; cf. v. 12).

c. Matthew and Mark record that Jesus was anointed two days before Passover (Matt. 26:2; Mark 14:1), whereas John appears to place the anointing six days before Passover (John 12:1).

The following points indicate what this author regards as the better view: that John's account of an anointing is the same as that of Matthew and Mark, and that it occurred no more than two days before Passover, i.e., Tuesday, and possibly even the evening before Passover, i.e., Wednesday.[1]

a. Mary very well could have poured the perfume on both Jesus' head and feet, this difference in evidence having only the weak basis of silence.

b. Both Matthew and Mark preface their account of the anointing at Bethany by mentioning that two days before Passover the Jewish authorities plotted to kill Jesus. This arrangement implies that Jesus was anointed either at that time or afterward.

c. Immediately after the anointing, both Synoptists state that *then* Judas Iscariot visited the chief priests to betray Jesus to them. Matthew and Mark, therefore, link the anointing with both the plotting of the authorities to kill Jesus and Judas' departure to the authorities to betray him (Matt. 26:14-16; Mark 14:10-11). John's addition that Judas was the predominant objector to the use of the perfume further ties these three events together. It appears that Jesus' rebuke of Judas at the anointing, coupled perhaps with Jesus' repeated mention of his impending death, moved Judas to go to the authorities to betray the Master. Judas likely would not have betrayed Jesus until after the Triumphal Entry, still hoping for the crown without the cross. It therefore seems more probable that Jesus was anointed after the Triumphal Entry, on the same day as, or soon after, the meeting of the authorities two days before Passover to plot Jesus' death.

d. Those who hold to either one or two anointings, with only one in Bethany, must account for what appears to be a glaring discrepancy between John's *six days* before Passover (John 12:1) and the *two days* before Passover of Matthew and Mark (Matt. 26:2; Mark 14:1). A few critics regard either the Synoptist's *two* or John's *six* as an error.[2] Some commentators (e.g., Calvin and Augustine) maintain that John has the correct time of

1. Nigel Turner, *Grammatical Insights into the New Testament* (Edinburgh: T. and T. Clark, 1965), 66. Turner is one who thinks this anointing occurred on Wednesday.

2. Heinrich August Wilhelm Meyer, *Critical and Exegetical Hand-Book to the Gospel of Matthew*, (Edinburgh: T. and T. Clark, 1883; Peabody, Mass.: Hendrickson, 1983), 453.

the anointing while the two Synoptists have displaced their account for thematic reasons. While this view accounts for the location of the anointing in the Synoptics, it fails to account for the difference of dates.

John, however, does not explicitly state that Jesus was anointed six days before Passover. He recounts that *six days before Passover, Jesus arrived at Bethany* (John 12:1); then, *here a dinner was given in Jesus' honor* (v. 2). The anointing episode follows. Upon finishing the story, John begins the next paragraph with *Meanwhile* (v. 9). This word *Meanwhile*, as well as the absence of connectives beginning vv. 2 and 9, suggests that it is John who chronologically displaces the anointing incident, inserting it here due to the mention of Bethany. A.T. Robertson agrees, locating the Bethany supper and anointing two days or less before Passover.

> John (12:2-8) gives the supper in the house of Simon the leper at this stage, probably because it is the last mention of Bethany in his Gospel. It seems better to follow the order of Mark here in the location of the anointing of Jesus by Mary of Bethany.[3]

e. Jesus explained that Mary anointed him in preparation for his burial, though it seems doubtful that she understood this purpose beforehand. It is unlikely that in the providence of God, Jesus would have been anointed in preparation for burial six days before that event. The two days or less recorded by the Synoptists attaches more significance to Jesus' stated purpose for the anointing.

It seems best to conclude that Jesus arrived at Bethany six days before Passover, that he lodged in Bethany at least the first few nights of Passion Week (Matt. 21:17; Mark 11:11, 19), and that he was anointed by Mary in Simon the Leper's house in Bethany, one or two days before Passover. John has recorded the same event as that of Matthew and Mark, inserting the anointing incident topically, antedating the event. John, the only Evangelist who mentions Jesus' arrival at Bethany before Palm Sunday, apparently chose to do this because it is his last mention of Bethany.

---

3. Robertson, *Harmony*, 152. See also R.C.H. Lenski, *The Interpretation of St. John's Gospel* (Minneapolis: Augsburg, 1942), 834-35 and William Hendriksen, *New Testament Commentary: Exposition of the Gospel According to John*, 2 vols. (Grand Rapids: Baker, 1954), 2:173. In addition, Robinson (1845) and A.T. Robertson (1922), generally recognized as two of the better harmonists (Robertson has the fewest deviations from the majority in The Chronological Table), are the only two harmonists in The Chronological Table who, like Lenski and Hendriksen, locate the supper and anointing two days before Passover, as herein, instead of six. Except for the genealogies (not a chronological event) and John 12:20-50, which are not noteworthy and vary considerably among the harmonists, this is the only section in *The Gospels Interwoven* that is not arranged according to the majority view of harmonists in The Chronological Table.

CHAPTER FOURTEEN
LAST SUPPER AND GETHSEMANE

1. Did Jesus and His apostles eat the Passover meal or not?

At the beginning of the meal in the Upper Room, Jesus expressed both his desire to eat this particular Passover (Luke 22:15: *I have eagerly desired to eat this Passover with you before I suffer*) and what some take as a refusal to eat it (Luke 22:16: *I will not eat it*). In light of the evidence, it is surprising how many expositors, although still a small minority, believe that Jesus avoided partaking of the Passover meal. The following reasons indicate that Jesus ate the Passover:

a. Jesus told the two disciples to go to a man's house to prepare the Passover and say, *the Teacher says: "My appointed time is near. I am going to celebrate the Passover with my disciples at your house"* (Matt. 26:18) and *Where is my guest room, where I may eat the Passover with my disciples* (Mark 14:14)? Jesus would not have so instructed his disciples unless he intended to eat the Passover. The Passover meal is not an accessory to the celebration, but the very essence of it.

b. Both Matthew and Mark attest that *they were eating* (Matt. 26:21, 26; Mark 14:22), which suggests that Jesus was eating too.

c. Jesus indicated his betrayer would be *one who dips bread/has dipped his hand/into the bowl with me* (Mark 14:20; Matt. 26:23), which necessitates Jesus' eating the Passover.

d. Luke does not record that Jesus only said *I will not eat it* but *I will not eat it again*, meaning that he would eat this Passover, but none following, until the Messianic banquet in the consummated kingdom.

A further difficulty arises in the placement of Luke 22:16-18, in which Jesus said *I will not eat* the paschal lamb of Passover or *drink again of the fruit of the vine* (a reference to the wine of feasts) *until the kingdom of God comes*. Luke locates these words prior to the institution of the Eucharist, making it appear that Jesus would not eat the Passover or drink from the cup. But Luke's quotation here must be understood to refer not to that immediate Passover, but to all future celebrations until the wedding supper

339

of the Lamb (Rev. 19:9), which will inaugurate the Messianic kingdom. Matthew and Mark place Jesus' comment about drinking the wine during, not before, his institution of that element in the Eucharist. While there may exist some uncertainty as to when Jesus said these words, there is ample evidence that he did indeed eat and drink at this final Passover celebration just before he suffered. (See EN 2, following.)

2. Did Jesus and his apostles eat the Passover meal on the Day of Passover or the day before?

The Synoptists agree that Jesus and his apostles celebrated the Passover the evening before his crucifixion (Matt. 26:17; Mark 14:12; Luke 22:7). Accepting the traditional day of Friday as the day Jesus was crucified would mean that Jesus and the apostles ate the paschal lamb on Thursday evening after 6 P.M. However, two passages in the Gospel of John seem to indicate otherwise. John relates that Jesus was crucified on *the day of Preparation of Passover Week* (John 19:14), presumably the day before the Jewish religious leaders ate their Passover, so that the Jewish authorities had not yet eaten their Passover by early Friday morning when they delivered Jesus over to Pilate. Pilate accommodated them by coming out to meet them, because *to avoid ceremonial uncleanness the Jews did not enter the palace; they wanted to be able to eat the Passover* (John 18:28). Edersheim observes: "Few expressions have given rise to more earnest controversy than this."[1] The leading solutions for this difficulty are as follows:

a. The author of the fourth Gospel is historically incorrect in dating the Passover. This view is held by some of the more radical critics. Aside from consideration of theories of inspiration of Scripture, it is implausible that John, as the last Gospel writer, would have introduced such an obvious discrepancy.

b. Jesus and his disciples ate a preliminary meal rather than the Passover, since it occurred twenty-four hours before the official Passover meal observed by the religious authorities. (See John 18:28 and 19:14.) This view is impossible to reconcile with the Synoptists, as the following listed Scriptures make plain:

> 1. *On the first day of the Feast of Unleavened Bread* (Mark 14:12), the Passover lamb had to be sacrificed (Luke 22:7). All four Evangelists make it clear that this celebration occurred the evening before Jesus' crucifixion.
>
> 2. *"Go and make preparations for us to eat the Passover"* (Luke 22:8; see also Matt. 26:17; Mark 14:12, 15).

---

1. Edersheim, *Life and Times*, pt. 2, 566.

3. *I am going to celebrate the Passover with my disciples at your house* (Matt. 26:18; see also Mark 14:14; Luke 22:11).

4. *So they prepared the Passover* (Mark 14:16; Luke 22:13; see also Matt. 26:19).

5. *I have eagerly desired to eat this Passover with you* (Luke 22:15).

6. *They were reclining at the table eating* (Mark 14:18; see also Matt. 26:20-21) what had earlier been prepared, i.e., the Passover.

Edersheim points out that some of the disciples thought Judas went out *to buy what was needed for the Feast* (John 13:29). "Had it been on the evening before [Passover], no one could have imagined that Judas had gone out during the night to buy provisions, when there was the whole next day for it."[2]

c. Jesus and the apostles ate the Passover meal, and so did the religious authorities, but on two separate days, i.e., Jesus and his apostles on the night before the Lord was crucified, and the Jewish authorities on the night after. This is based largely on a supposed difference in the observance of the day of Preparation of Passover between Jesus and the authorities, evidenced by the latter's scrupulous care to avoid ceremonial uncleanness in anticipation of celebrating the Passover after Jesus was killed (John 18:28). If Jesus died on Friday, the Synoptics reveal that the two disciples prepared the Passover lamb on Thursday, when *the Passover lamb had to be sacrificed* (Luke 22:7), *when it was customary to sacrifice the Passover lamb* (Mark 14:12), *on the first day of the Feast of Unleavened Bread* (Matt. 26:17; Mark 14:12). Yet John recounts that on the following morning (Friday) Pilate *sat down on the judge's seat . . . on the day of Preparation of Passover Week* (John 19:13-14; see also v. 31). There are several variations of this view, based on different explanations offered for why they ate the Passover on separate days.

1. The Jewish leaders arbitrarily postponed their celebration of Passover a day so that it would fall on the Sabbath. Calvin held this view, suggesting that the reason the authorities changed the day was that "two days on end without work would have seemed too difficult for the people."[3] A slight variation of this view is that the authorities delayed their Passover a day due to the increased priestly workload brought on by the Passover preceding the regular Sabbath. But the precise instructions of Exodus 12:8-11, supported by the historical meaning of Passover, preclude a delay for any reason. They were commanded to eat *that same night . . . in haste.*

2. Ibid., pt. 2, 508.
3. Calvin, *Harmony/Gospels*, 3:126.

2. The Galileans reckoned a day from sunrise to sunrise, while the Judeans observed the day from sunset to sunset, thus allowing for Jesus, a Galilean, to eat the Passover on one day, while the Jews of Jerusalem ate it on the following day. One of several objections to this view is that there is insufficient evidence that the Galileans considered a day as beginning at any other time than that observed by other Jews, i.e., at sunset. A similar view is that Jesus and the Synoptists observed a solar calendar while the Pharisees and John followed a lunar calendar.

3. The Sadducees, who presided over the temple at Jerusalem, observed a different calendar than the Pharisees and were therefore in conflict with them on dating the Passover. The Synoptics are regarded as following the Pharisaic calendar and John, the Sadducean calendar. It is believed that the Sadducees had added an extra day, so that the Sadducean leaders of the Sanhedrin ate the Passover on Friday evening, Nisan 16, while Jesus followed the popular Pharisaic tradition and ate the Passover on Thursday evening, Nisan 15.[4] At least two arguments arise against this view. First, included among the Council who examined and condemned Jesus were scribes, or Pharisaic teachers of the law (Matt. 26:57; Mark 14:53; Luke 22:66). Second, Luke reports concerning the day before Jesus was crucified, *then came the day of Unleavened Bread on which the Passover lamb had to be sacrificed* (Luke 22:7). This statement suggests that it was binding on all Jews, whether Galileans, Judeans, Pharisees, or Sadducees, to celebrate, and therefore eat, the Passover on the same day.

  d. Jesus, his apostles, and the Jewish authorities all ate the Passover meal at the same officially designated time, on Thursday evening. The arguments for this view are as follows:

    1. The Jewish authorities' avoidance of ceremonial uncleanness in John 18:28 does not mean that the Jewish authorities had not yet eaten the Passover by Friday morning. The word *Passover*, there, refers "to the *chagigah*, the feast-offering offered on the morning of the first full paschal day (Num. 28:18-19)."[5]

    2. Edersheim explains about Pilate's palace that "Entrance into a heathen house *did* Levitically render [individuals] impure for that day—that is, till the evening." He continues that this, however, "would *not* have disqualified [them] for eating the Paschal Lamb,

---

4. I. Howard Marshall, *Last Supper and Lord's Supper* (Grand Rapids: Eerdmans, 1980). See this for a full treatment of this view.
5. Carson, *Matthew*, 8:531. For a thorough treatment of this problem see 528-32.

since the meal was partaken of *after* the evening, and when a new day had begun. . . . There would have been no reason to fear 'defilement' on the morning of the first Passover Sacrifice; but entrance into the *Praetorium* on the morning of the first Passover day would have rendered it impossible for them to offer the *Chagigah*."[6]

3. *The day of Preparation of Passover Week* (John 19:14; see also v. 31) does not indicate that the Paschal Lamb the Jewish authorities were to eat had not by then been prepared (Friday morning) or that they had not yet eaten the Passover. Instead, this is a technical phrase referring to the day of preparation for the ensuing regular Sabbath (Saturday).

In summation, this view advocates that Jesus and the religious authorities ate the Passover on Thursday evening. To avoid uncleanness, the leaders did not enter Pilate's palace so they could eat the chagigah that Friday morning, and *the day of Preparation* in John 19:14 and v. 31 refers to preparation that Friday for the Sabbath on Saturday, a special Sabbath because Passover fell that year on Friday. This last view seems to this author the most appealing.

Regardless of the correct interpretation of John 18:28; 19:14 and v. 31, and how these are to be reconciled with the Synoptics, Jesus and his apostles likely followed popular and acceptable custom in eating the Passover on Thursday evening, the night before the Savior suffered.

3. When Judas left the Upper Room, did the disciples understand that he would betray Jesus or not?

In the midst of what was certainly a joyous occasion (Luke 22:15), Jesus became *troubled in spirit* (John 13:21) and announced during the Passover meal that one of those present would betray him (Matt. 26:21; Mark 14:18; Luke 22:21; John 13:21). At first the disciples *stared at one another, at a loss to know which of them he meant* (John 13:22). *They were saddened, and one by one they said to him, Surely not I?* (Mark 14:19; see also Matt. 26:22) About this time, Judas also asked him, *"Surely not I, Rabbi?" Jesus answered, "Yes, it is you"* (Matt. 26:25). In addition, Peter motioned to John and said, *"Ask him which one he means"* (John 13:24). John did so and Jesus answered, *"It is the one to whom I will give this piece of bread when I have dipped it in the dish"* (v. 26; cf. Matt. 26:23; Mark 14:20). When Jesus gave the bread to Judas, he took it and Jesus said, *"What you are about to do, do quickly"* (John 13:27). Judas then left the room to betray Jesus. Yet John recounts:

6. Edersheim, *Life and Times*, pt. 2, 566-68.

No one at the meal understood why Jesus said this to him. Since Judas had charge of the money, some thought Jesus was telling him to buy what was needed for the Feast, or to give something to the poor (vv. 28-29).

Did the disciples not understand from Jesus' disclosures that Judas would betray him? Jesus seemed to have made this clear at two different times during the supper: first, by Jesus' affirmative answer to Judas that he was the betrayer, and second, by the clue Jesus gave by giving the dipped bread (sop) to Judas.

It becomes necessary at this point to understand the Passover celebration, as well as Mideastern eating customs. The head of the family was responsible for preparation of the Passover meal (Ex. 12:3; Matt. 26:17-19; Mark 14:12-16; Luke 22:7-13). As Master of his chosen apostles, Jesus represented the head and host of his company as they reclined (Matt. 26:20; Mark 14:18) for the Passover meal that evening. (In many Eastern cultures, people still sit with their legs crossed or lie on the floor before a low table to eat their meals.)[7] It was customary for right-handed people to recline on the left side while eating, leaning on the left elbow and cushioned by a low couch. Thus the right hand was free to reach the food placed on a very low table. Only if the Lord and John were reclining in this way, and if John were positioned immediately to the right of him, does it seem possible that *leaning back against Jesus, he asked him, "Lord, who is it?"* (John 13:25)[8] If the Apostle John were therefore on Jesus' right, who was on the left of the Master?

The identity of the person reclining on Jesus' immediate left could be crucial to comprehending why the disciples failed to understand that evening that Judas would be the betrayer. At Passover, the immediate left side of the head of the family was reserved as a place of honor. The Evangelists are silent as to who occupied that place; scholars are divided in their speculation about his identity. Some reckon it was Peter,[9] on account of his being the leading spokesman for the apostles and member of the inner core of three disciples. Also, the fact that Jesus sent only Peter and John to prepare the Passover (Luke 22:8) further suggests the possibility that they sat adjacent to the Lord during the meal. The following reasons, however, indicate that Judas, rather than Peter, occupied the place of honor on Jesus' immediate left side during the Passover meal:

a. Peter would not have told John to ask Jesus to identify the betrayer;

---

7. The root Greek word *anakeimai*, here translated *reclining*, can mean either to "be at table" or "recline at table" (Bauer-Arndt-Gingrich-Danker, *Lexicon*, 55).

8. The NIV omits translating *stethos*, which means "chest" or "breast." The AV and NASB have "Jesus' breast;" the RSV has "breast of Jesus."

9. E.g., B.F. Westcott, *The Gospel According to St John: The Authorized Version with Introduction and Notes* [1881] (rep. Grand Rapids: Eerdmans, 1962), 194.

being also next to Jesus, he would have asked the Lord himself. He only told John to do it because Peter was some distance away from Jesus, while John occupied the nearest place to the Lord.

b. John recounts that Peter *motioned to this disciple* (John 13:24) to ask, strongly suggesting that Peter was on the opposite side of the table motioning John to get his attention.

c. With John being on Jesus' right side and leaning on his left side at the time Peter motioned, John's back would have been toward both Jesus and the person on Jesus' left. Thus John could not have seen Peter motioning him if Peter reclined on Jesus' immediate left.

d. The previous footwashing scene seems to locate Peter some distance away from Jesus at the table (John 13:5-6).

e. Judas was respected enough by the others to be trusted with the money bag (John 13:18; Ps. 41:9). "As treasurer (John 12:6) he may have warranted a (or even *the*) place of honor among the disciples."[10] When Jesus revealed that one of them would betray him, none of the disciples suspected Judas. In fact, each one questioned himself, having no suspicion of Judas.

Interestingly, only a few days earlier, Jesus had warned that it is the hypocrites who love the place of honor at banquets (Matt. 23:6; see also Mark 12:39; Luke 20:46), further solidifying Judas' place at Jesus' left. Indeed, in betraying the Lord, Judas became the greatest hypocrite throughout human history.

Thus Judas is the most likely candidate for occupying the place of honor on Jesus' immediate left. Judas' nearness to Jesus would explain how the other disciples might not have heard Jesus' response to Judas, *"Yes, it is you"* (Matt. 26:25).[11] Many have assumed that during a hushed silence each disciple one by one inquired of Jesus, *"Surely not I?,"* until Judas at last spoke up to avoid being the obvious culprit. Yet Luke adds that *they began to question among themselves which of them it might be who would do this* (Luke 22:23). Apparently, several conversations proceeded among them as to who it was, easily causing Jesus' answer to Judas to go undetected by the others.

There remains another view of Matthew's recorded dialogue between Jesus and Judas which does not depend on Jesus' answer having gone unheard by the others, one that has received little attention by commenta-

---

10. Ibid., 574.
11. The same Greek words, *su eipas*, appear later in Matt. 26:64, which the NIV translates differently. The more literal translation for both, and one that captures the meaning more clearly is, "you said it" or "it is as you say." In addition, the NIV reads that *Jesus answered* Judas (v. 25). The Greek words translated "answered" are *legei auto*, meaning "says to him," which may indicate that the utterance was heard only by the person addressed (J.H. Bernard, *A Critical and Exegetical Commentary on the Gospel According to John*, 2 vols. [Edinburgh: T. and T. Clark, 1928], 2:473), i.e., Judas. Furthermore, Matthew gives no indication that the others heard this exchange.

tors. In a footnote the NIV provide a more literal alternate reading for Jesus' answer to Judas (Matt. 26:25: "You yourself have said it"), which comes closer to the original Greek. Also, the same Greek words, *su eipas*, appear later in Matthew 26:64, where the NIV translates them, "*Yes, it is as you say.*" (See EN 15:11.) In both passages, the rendering that comes closest to *su eipas* is "you have said it" or "it is as you say" (RSV: "You have said so"; NASB: "You have said it yourself"). "Yes" is not in the Greek text. Many scholars admit to a certain ambiguity in the words *su eipas*, which arouses much discussion regarding Jesus' answer to Caiaphas and the Sanhedrin. Concerning Jesus' reply to Caiaphas in Matthew 26:64, grammarian Nigel Turner remarks, "Simple, yet ambiguous and non-committal, the answer recalls what he replied to Judas Iscariot's inquiry before the Last Supper, 'Master, is it I?' and Jesus answered, 'You have said.'" Turner maintains that the Greek disallows the answer "Yes."[12] Accordingly, even if the disciples heard Jesus' answer to Judas, it was not an unequivocal yes answer, and probably ambiguous enough for them to fail to grasp its meaning. This was certainly not the case before the Sanhedrin, however, due to Jesus' further identification of himself as the victorious Messiah by his application to himself of a composite of Psalm 110:1 and Daniel 7:13.

John's interchange with Jesus appears to have been a private dialogue. When he leaned back against Jesus, John probably asked him in a soft voice, perhaps a whisper not heard by the others, "*Lord, who is it?*" (John 13:25). *Jesus answered, "It is the one to whom I will give this piece of bread when I have dipped it in the dish*" (v. 26). The fact that Peter signaled John to ask Jesus who was the betrayer (v. 24) further suggests that conversations ensued which might have drowned out Jesus' reply to all except to John, and perhaps Judas (v. 26; see also Matt. 26:23; Mark 14:20).

It was customary for the Passover host to give an honored guest a piece of bread wrapped around accompaniments to the meal and dipped in a bowl of sauce. This guest would appropriately be the one who occupied that place of honor on the immediate left side of the host. Dipping the piece of bread, Jesus presumably was able to hand it to Judas (John 13:26-27) without standing up to walk over to him.[13] Therefore his position at Jesus' left fits the giving of the sop to Judas. Giving the sop to Judas was Jesus' indirect answer to John's question. Yet it is not certain that John or any one else understood that when Jesus gave Judas the sop, it meant that he was the one.

In contrast to what might have been quiet responses to both Judas and John, all heard Jesus' final words to Judas, "*What you are about to do, do quickly*" (John 13:27). Knowing the evil intention of Judas' heart, Jesus was

12. Turner, *Insights*, 72-73. See also Bauer-Arndt-Gingrich-Danker, *Lexicon*, 226.
13. Raymond E. Brown, *The Gospel According to John (xiii-xxi)* (Garden City, N.Y.: Doubleday, 1970), 574.

telling him to hurry and proceed with his plan. The Redeemer was feeling distressed, wanting to finish his imminent baptism of suffering and death (Luke 12:50). *But no one at the meal understood why Jesus said this to him* (John 13:28).

It seems astonishing that neither the beloved disciple himself nor any of the other disciples would understand Jesus' revelations about his betrayer. C.K. Barrett has received much criticism from other scholars for his statement about John's apparent failure to comprehend Judas as the betrayer: "To say that he [John] failed to grasp the meaning of the sign is to make him an imbecile. His subsequent inactivity is incomprehensible, and . . . casts doubt on John's narrative."[14] Commentators are divided on whether John or any of the others understood that Judas would be the betrayer. Bernard thinks "it does not appear that John identified the traitor even when this clue was provided."[15] Some have thought that John, and perhaps Peter, understood but they kept this knowledge to themselves, not suspecting that the betrayal was imminent. This view does not square with the nature of either of these apostles. Surely it is unnecessary to establish the impetuous nature of Peter. But what about the Apostle John, whom his writings reveal in his older age to be the "apostle of love"? When Jesus chose John and his brother James (who became the first martyred apostle) as apostles, he surnamed them *sons of Thunder* (Mark 3:17). And when the Samaritans did not welcome Jesus, James and John asked, "*Lord, do you want us to call fire down from heaven to destroy them?*" (Luke 9:54) Furthermore, when Judas later led the band to approach Jesus in the Garden of Gethsemane, every indication is that all of the disciples were caught unawares, not suspecting Judas as the betrayer. Moreover, had any of the disciples understood at the Supper that Judas would be the betrayer, it is unlikely that this would have escaped mention by at least one of the Evangelists in his Gospel.

Yet there is precedent for the disciples' lack of understanding. Despite Jesus' repeated predictions about his impending death and resurrection, the disciples continually failed to understand them. Concerning the last and most detailed of these predictions, Luke relates, *The disciples did not understand any of this. Its meaning was hidden from them, and they did not know what he was talking about* (Luke 18:34; see also Luke 9:45). Why then would John and the others be any less perceptive for not understanding this lesser disclosure?

In conclusion, it is uncertain whether any of the apostles knew from Jesus' revelations at the Supper that Judas would be the betrayer; the probability is that they all failed to understand. But it is certain that they

---

14. C.K. Barrett, *The Gospel According to St. John: An Introduction with Commentary and Notes on the Greek Text*, 2nd ed. (Philadelphia: Westminster, 1955), 447.
15. Bernard, *John*, 2:473.

did not understand by Jesus' words to Judas, *What you are about to do, do quickly*, that Judas immediately went out into the night to betray the Master, and thereby seal his doom to eternal darkness.

4. Was Judas present during the institution of the Communion service?

Judas was certainly present at the beginning of the Passover Feast: *The one who has dipped his hand into the bowl with me will betray me* (Matt. 26:23; see also Mark 14:20). John writes: *As soon as Judas had taken the bread, he went out* (John 13:30). Although neither Matthew nor Mark relates Judas' exit from the meal, it is generally assumed to have taken place immediately following Matthew 26:25 and Mark 14:21. Judas, therefore, did not remain to celebrate the entire Passover meal. However, Luke 22:21-22 places Jesus' prediction of Judas' betrayal *after* the institution of the Eucharist, as though Judas were present during the entire meal, including Jesus' institution of Communion.[16] Nearly the same words in v. 22 appear in Matthew 26:24 and Mark 14:21 before Jesus instituted the Eucharist.

The Jews celebrated the traditional Passover meal according to a prescribed sequence of courses, liturgical prayers and singing of hymns. The meal was structured around the drinking of four cups of diluted wine. The Passover lamb was only eaten between the drinking of the second and third cup. It was between the first and second cup, when a kind of hors d'oeuvres were served, that Jesus' offer of the sop to Judas best fits the proceedings.[17] After taking the sop, Judas immediately made his exit.

It is generally believed that Jesus instituted Communion with the third of the four traditional cups of wine at Passover. Called "the cup of blessing," it is alluded to by the Apostle Paul in 1 Corinthians 10:16.[18] "According to the Jewish ritual, *the third Cup* was filled at the close of the Supper."[19] Since Judas left the room immediately after receiving the sop, he would not likely have been present for the eating of the Passover lamb, and certainly not for the later drinking of the traditional third cup. Accordingly, Luke 22:21-23 is chronologically displaced. Perhaps Luke did this to link thematically the betrayal with what he records next: the dispute that later broke out among the Eleven.

In addition, the significance of the Eucharist would seem to preclude

---

16. This interpretation is advocated by A.R. Fausset's "Harmony of the Gospels" in *The Ryrie Study Bible: New American Standard Translation*, p. 1930.

17. Pierre Benoit, *Jesus and the Gospel: Volume 1* (New York: Seabury, 1973), 100. Edersheim (*Life and Times*, pt. 2, 506) thinks the sop commenced the meal.

18. Edersheim, *Life And Times*, pt. 2, 511; Lane, *Mark*, 506; Carson, *Matthew*, 8:536. See 1 Cor. 10:16 in AV, RSV, and NASB.

19. Edersheim, *Life and Times*, pt. 2, 511. See also Wessel, *Mark*, 8:761.

Judas' presence, since it commemorates the Lord's death for the partici-
pants' sins and acknowledges the Lord's forgiveness.

5. What were Jesus' exact words when he instituted the Communion service?

Both Matthew and Mark record that Jesus instituted the communion
service with the words, *This is my blood of the covenant* (Matt. 26:28; Mark
14:24), with some manuscripts having the *new covenant*. Both Luke and
Paul, however, have recorded a different arrangement of words: *This cup is
the new covenant in my blood* (Luke 22:20; 1 Cor. 11:25). The former
language alludes to the blood sacrifice of Exodus 24:8 and Zechariah 9:11,
while the latter refers to *the new covenant* of Jeremiah 31:31-34. Contemporary scholarship generally regards as uncertain the actual words Jesus spoke
at this first Eucharist, while maintaining that Paul's and Luke's quotation
dates back closer to the oral tradition of what Jesus said. Luke, as a
companion of the Apostle Paul on his missionary journeys, is regarded by
some commentators to have adopted Paul's record of Jesus' words when
instituting Communion. Many commentators think neither the Matthew/
Mark nor Luke/Paul records designate the *ipsissma verba*.

Jesus' offer of both the bread and the cup may have been more personal
than is generally thought; the elements may not have been passed from one
to the other. Instead, Jesus may have personally distributed the bread by
breaking off a piece and handing it to each disciple, one at a time.[20] If so, it
would be quite natural for the Lord to say different things, varying
somewhat in his words to different individuals about the bread, and
perhaps about the cup as well. This would conveniently account for more
than one saying about the cup, as herein. Regardless of the method of
distribution, Jesus most likely taught more than is recorded by any one of
the Evangelists about this memorial ritual.

6. Did the disciples' dispute over which of them was the greatest emerge before they ate the Passover or afterward?

In addition to regarding Luke 22:21-23 as chronologically displaced (see
EN 14:3), a few commentators claim the same for Luke 22:24-30. They
maintain that this dispute, which exposed the disciples' pride, connects
with Jesus' act of washing their feet as a lesson in humility and service and
therefore must immediately precede it. There is nothing in the texts to
support this. A strong case can be made that the dispute in Luke 22:24-30

---

20. Carson, *Matthew*, 8:536.

fits well with what follows in Luke's account, viz., Jesus' prediction of Peter's denials (vv. 31-34). Moreover, the dispute may have even been prompted by Jesus' announcement that one of them would betray him. None of the Eleven seems to have understood at the Supper that Jesus identified Judas as the betrayer (John 13:27-29). It therefore seems better to regard that the dispute happened after Judas' exit, as herein.

7. Did Jesus predict Peter's denials before they all left the Upper Room or afterward?

Matthew 26:30-35 and Mark 14:26-31 place Jesus' prediction of Peter's denials after Jesus and the disciples left the Upper Room. On the other hand, Luke locates the prediction before their exit (Luke 22:31-39). In addition, John makes it quite clear that Jesus predicted Peter's denials soon after Judas' departure from the meal (John 13:30-38), before Jesus and the Eleven left the Upper Room (14:31b).

Mark does not begin the prediction (v. 27) with a word that connects it to the previous exit (v. 26). Matthew does use the connective *Then* following the exit (v. 31). Matthew, however, characteristically uses this connective loosely, so that it does not necessarily require a chronological connection with what immediately precedes. As cited earlier, D.A. Carson comments:

> (*tote*, "then") is common in Matthew, occurring ninety times as compared with Mark's six and Luke's fourteen; but in Matthean usage only sometimes does it have temporal force . . . serving more frequently as a loose connective.[21]

Following John's account (the chronologically clearest of all four Gospels), Jesus predicted Peter's denials in the Upper Room before their departure. Matthew and Mark, therefore, have chronologically displaced the prediction of Peter's denials apparently for emphasis,[22] as if to connect them with the following scene at Gethsemane. There, a sign of Peter's imminent defection, as well as that of the other two members of the inner core of disciples, will emerge. The flesh is weak; Peter and the other two disciples will not stay awake and pray even for a few minutes, leading to the falling away of all the disciples, more particularly the spokesman for them all—Simon Peter. Further support for such a chronological displacement by Matthew and Mark is that they have done the same with Peter's denials themselves, placing them together following Caiaphas' crucial question to

21. Ibid., 8:90.
22. Ibid., 8:540.

Jesus. Perhaps they have done this for the sake of clarity and memory, which they judged in this case more important than chronological order.

8. When did Jesus and his apostles leave the Upper Room? What was the order of events surrounding their departure?

Only John recounts Jesus' discourse and high priestly prayer in John 14-17. That Matthew 26:30 and Mark 14:26 preclude the possibility that Jesus spoke any of these words after leaving the Upper Room is a view based only on the Synoptists' silence. Comparing John with the Synoptics, when Jesus said, *Come now; let us leave* (John 14:31), it appears they sang a hymn and left the Upper Room.[23] Somewhere between the Upper Room and the Mount of Olives Jesus spoke the words of John 15-17. A.T. Robertson concurs:

> The Synoptic Gospels . . . represent Jesus as going forth to Gethsem-
> ane after the institution of the supper. . . . The time was probably not
> long and they apparently sang the hymn (probably one of the Psalms)
> as they rose to leave the Upper Room (John 14:31). Hence the
> passage in John 15 to 17 comes in between singing the hymn and
> reaching Gethsemane.[24]

The fact that Jesus *looked toward heaven and prayed* (John 17:1) is evidence that by then they had left the house and were outdoors. There are only two other occasions in the Gospels when Jesus looked up and prayed to the Father. These were at the feeding of the 5,000 (Matt. 14:19; Mark 6:41; Luke 9:16) and the raising of Lazarus (John 11:41), both outdoors.

Alfred Edersheim proposes what seems to be the likely order of events surrounding the close of the supper and the exit from the Upper Room:

> The new institution of the Lord's Supper did not finally close what
> passed at that Paschal Table. According to the Jewish Ritual, the Cup
> is filled a fourth time, and the remaining part of the *Hallel* repeated.
> Then follow, besides Ps. 136, a number of prayers and hymns, of
> which the comparatively late origin is not doubtful. The same remark
> applies even more strongly to what follows after the fourth Cup. But,
> so far as we can judge, the Institution of the Holy Supper was

23. According to tradition, the hymn, the second part of the Hallel (Ps. 115-118), was sung antiphonally at the close of the Passover celebration, immediately follow-ing the drinking of the fourth cup. The first part of the Hallel (Ps. 113-114) was sung earlier.
24. Robertson, *Harmony*, 201. See also Carson, *Matthew*, 8:86-87.

followed by the Discourse recorded in St. John 14. Then the concluding Psalms of the *Hallel* were sung, after which the Master left the 'Upper Chamber.' The Discourse of Christ recorded in St. John 16, and his prayer, were certainly uttered after they had risen from the Supper, and before they crossed the brook Kidron. In all probability they were, however, spoken before the Saviour left the house. We can scarcely imagine such a Discourse, and still less such a Prayer, to have been uttered while traversing the narrow streets of Jerusalem on the way to Kidron.[25]

It is possible that Jesus and his disciples lingered in an open courtyard of the house. Perhaps the surroundings included grapevines, used as an object lesson in Jesus' sermon (John 15:1-8). Many courtyards of the day had gardens, sometimes with grapevines. William Temple, however, offers the interesting suggestion that Jesus delivered his discourse on the vine as he escorted his disciples out toward Gethsemane, and as they passed by, or through, the temple where a golden vine (signifying Israel from Isa. 5:1-7) trailed over Solomon's porch.[26]

9. What were the exact words that Jesus prayed in Gethsemane?

Only the Synoptists record that in the Garden of Gethsemane Jesus prayed to the Father about his imminent suffering and death. Luke quotes only one prayer (Luke 22:42), as if there were no others, whereas Matthew and Mark reveal that he went *a little farther* (Matt. 26:39; Mark 14:35), prayed, and returned to the three disciples on three different occasions (Matt. 26:39-45; Mark 14:35-41). Like Luke, Mark quotes one prayer but adds that Jesus *prayed the same thing* at the second prayer (Mark 14:39). Matthew quotes Jesus' first two prayers. Like Mark, he adds that Jesus *prayed the third time, saying the same thing* (Matt. 26:44). However, a comparison of these prayers reveals some variations in words, even slight differences in meaning. For the first prayer, Matthew 26:39 has *if it is possible*, Mark 14:36 has the quotation *everything is possible for you*, and Luke 22:42, *if you are willing*. Mark's retention in 14:36 of *Abba, Father* is a reminder that the actual words, i.e., the *ipsissma verba*, that Jesus prayed were in Aramaic but have been transmitted in Greek. Since Luke mentions only one prayer, he renders a summary quotation of all three prayers. It must be concluded that there can be no certainty of the exact words of these first two prayers, but their general meaning is clear.

25. Edersheim, *Life and Times*, pt. 2, 513.
26. William Temple, *Readings in St. John's Gospel* (1939-40), 2 vols. in 1 (London: MacMillan, 1959), 250-51.

Matthew and Mark quote Jesus saying to the three apostles following his first prayer, *Could you* men *not keep watch . . . for one hour?* (Matt. 26:40; Mark 14:37) Each time all three disciples fell asleep, perhaps partly due to the meal and certainly to their exhaustion from sorrow (Luke 22:45). Luke writes that Jesus' location was quite near, only *about a stone's throw beyond them* (Luke 22:41). The total time required to do and say everything the Synoptists record of Jesus' prayer experience in Gethsemane could have been less than 15 minutes. The fact that the disciples had time to fall asleep three times indicates that the Lord must have prayed considerably more at each prayer session than is recorded by the Synoptists; they recorded but a small portion, perhaps a condensed summary, of what Jesus actually prayed. This demonstrates that it may sometimes be the overall meaning, and not the actual words, which the Evangelists quote. Some commentators would add that none of the Apostles were present to hear the actual words, although in his resurrection appearances it is conceivable that Jesus told them these summaries.

A comparison of the Synoptists' quotations of Jesus' prayers in Gethsemane indicates that, rather than a contradiction, there may have been a progression of thought from prayer to prayer. Perhaps in the first prayer Jesus requested removal of the suffering and affirmed God's ability to do anything. In possibly the second prayer, Jesus indicated it might not be possible for the Father to remove his imminent suffering, in light of his plan of salvation. In both of these prayers, all three Synoptists affirm Jesus' persistent, expressed desire to do the Father's will above his own. No doubt it was in his final prayer that Jesus revealed his full acceptance of his imminent suffering as the Father's will.

CHAPTER FIFTEEN
TRIALS, DEATH, AND BURIAL

1. Who was the young man who fled Gethsemane naked, leaving his linen garment behind?

It is generally held that the *young man* in Mark 14:51 was John Mark, the author of the Gospel of Mark, who used a modest writer's technique to avoid reference to himself. Mark's presence at Jesus' arrest is further supported by the tradition that the house (Upper Room) where Jesus and the disciples ate the Passover was owned by John Mark's father.

2. Who was the other disciple who accompanied Peter at Jesus' trials?

The Apostle John's reference to *another disciple* in his Gospel (John 18:15) is a modest writer's technique used to avoid reference to himself.[1]

3. Did Peter make his first denial of Jesus in the courtyard of Annas or of Caiaphas?

Some commentators regard the Gospel accounts of Peter's denials, and the circumstances surrounding them, as the most difficult harmonizing problem in the Gospels. Nonharmonist H.A.W. Meyer identifies the problem areas regarding Peter's denials by asserting:

> The Synoptists agree neither with John nor with one another as to certain points of detail connected with the three different scenes in question, and more particularly with reference to the localities in which they are alleged to have taken place, and the persons by whom the apostle was interrogated.[2]

---

1. E.g., see Turner, *Insights*, 135-38.
2. Meyer, *Matthew*, 486.

Some of the difficulties concerning Peter's three denials arise due to a lack of information, a possible reversal of order of Peter's first two denials between John's account and that of the Synoptists, a translation difficulty in John 18:24, and a failure to allow for more than one interrogator at the last denial and perhaps the second as well. While there may remain some unanswered questions, there is insufficient evidence to discredit the Gospel accounts of Peter's denials, their diversity being one more example of reliable independent reporting.

The first problem encountered respecting Peter's denials is the place where Jesus was examined, near which was the courtyard Peter entered and made his first denial. John, as an eyewitness, introduces details not contained in the Synoptics. One detail is that following his capture, Jesus was first taken to Annas (John 18:12-13). John relates in v. 15 that he and Peter followed Jesus, entering the high priest's courtyard, where Peter made his first denial. Yet John does not specify in v. 15 where Jesus was taken, or to whom the courtyard belonged.

Consequently, most commentators assume this to be a retrogression, in which it is inferred that Peter and John entered the courtyard of Annas, where Peter made his first denial (v. 17) while Jesus was interrogated by Annas, in vv. 19-23. On the other hand, the Synoptists report only that Jesus was taken to the house of Caiaphas, the high priest (cf. Matt. 26:3 with vv. 57-58; Mark 14:53-54; Luke 22:54-55), in whose courtyard Peter seems to have made all three denials.

The traditional harmonizing solution for this apparent contradiction has been that Annas and Caiaphas lived in the same house, or adjoining quarters, that shared the same courtyard. If so, all four Evangelists agree on the place of Peter's first denial: the courtyard of both Annas and Caiaphas. However, many contemporary scholars regard this view of a shared courtyard as a forced harmony, some expecting that in that case the word "priest" in *the high priest's courtyard* would occur in the plural instead of the singular (John 18:15).

There is no seeming discrepancy if the NIV footnote for John 18:24 is the correct reading, as herein: (*Now Annas had sent him, still bound, to Caiaphas the high priest*). In that case, v. 15 is not a retrogression, though v. 24 obviously is; thus John implies that Annas sent Jesus to Caiaphas *before* Peter's first denial, which follows in v. 17. It may be argued that John omits specifically mentioning in v. 15 that Jesus was taken from Annas and delivered to Caiaphas because his delivery to Caiaphas had already been well established by all three Synoptists. (For further discussion see EN 15:4.)

The following other factors indicate that in v. 15 Jesus was taken from Annas' custody to Caiaphas, that the courtyard in v. 15 therefore belonged to Caiaphas, and that the interrogator in vv. 19-23 was Caiaphas:[3]

a. After stating that the soldiers first brought Jesus to Annas in vv. 12-13, John turns his attention to Caiaphas in vv. 13-14, continuing to have Caiaphas in view as the high priest (vv. 15, 16, 19, 22) to whom the courtyard belonged (v. 15).

b. John continues throughout this narrative to mention the high priest a surprising total of nine times (vv. 10, 13, twice in 15, 16, 19, 22, 24, 26). In two of these instances John reiterates that the high priest is Caiaphas (vv. 13, 24), whom he first identified in 11:49, in agreement with Matthew (Matt. 26:3, 57). This strongly suggests that the high priest's courtyard refers to Caiaphas' courtyard.

c. If Annas was the high priest to whom belonged the courtyard in v. 15, and Annas was Jesus' interrogator in vv. 19-23 as well, it is incredible that John would mention an interrogation of Jesus by Annas but none by Caiaphas, when all three Synoptists mention the interrogation by Caiaphas and Peter's three denials there in his courtyard but do not mention Annas. It is therefore safer to regard John as the only Evangelist who records Annas' preliminary custody of Jesus in v. 13 (according to this view, there is no indication that Annas even questioned Jesus), before the beginning of the Sanhedrin's investigation led by Caiaphas in vv. 19-23.

Accordingly, the only courtyard of the high priest mentioned in the Gospels belonged to Caiaphas, where Peter made all three denials.

4. Who was the high priest: Annas or Caiaphas? Which one examined Jesus while Peter made his first denial?

The Jews traditionally had one "high priest," who presided over the chief priests in the religious life of Israel. At least three times in his Gospel, John identifies Caiaphas as the high priest at that time (John 11:49; 18:13: *that year;* v. 24), in agreement with Matthew (Matt. 26:3, 57). Yet John also *seems* to call Annas the high priest (John 18:19), in agreement with Luke, who recognized *the high priesthood of Annas and Caiaphas* (Luke 3:2), and again, *Annas the high priest* (Acts 4:6).

The elderly Annas was the former high priest and father-in-law of Caiaphas. He apparently continued to exercise considerable influence, indicated by the authorities' first bringing Jesus to Annas. Edersheim relates that "he had held the Pontificate for only six or seven years; but it was filled

---

3. Some problems in respect to Peter's denials and separated in these endnotes are so linked (e.g., to whom belonged the courtyard where Peter made his first denial and who was the interrogator of Jesus at that time), that it is difficult to avoid some overlapping in the comments.

by not fewer than five of his sons, by his son-in-law Caiaphas, and by a grandson."[4] It was customary for a former high priest to continue to be addressed by that title,[5] just as many Americans incorrectly refer to a former President with the title "President." D.A. Carson sheds further light:

> There is no real conflict. Annas was deposed by the secular authorities in A.D. 15 and replaced by Caiaphas, who lived and ruled till his death in A.D. 36. But since according to the OT the high priest was not to be replaced till after his death, the transfer of power was illegal. Doubtless some continued to call either man "high priest." Certainly Annas, Caiaphas' father-in-law (John 18:13), continued to exercise great authority behind the scenes.[6]

It would appear that Annas was sometimes called the high priest, though at this time he officially was not.

Matthew is the only Synoptist who identifies Caiaphas as the high priest who examined Jesus. Mark and Luke seem to agree with Matthew because they account for no change in the chief interrogator. None of the Synoptists mention Annas' involvement in the proceedings. According to their arrangement of Peter's denials, in apparent contrast to John's Gospel, they imply that Peter made his first denial while Jesus was examined by Caiaphas in his house.

Many expositors think John identifies both Annas and Caiaphas as the high priest, and that Annas was the interrogator of Jesus only during Peter's first denial. Despite Luke's reference to a shared high priesthood of Caiaphas and Annas, it seems quite unlikely that John would clearly identify Caiaphas as the high priest three times in his Gospel (John 11:49; 18:13, 24), again refer to this high priest without naming him (v. 10), then without making a distinction, change his reference to Annas as *the high priest* four times (vv. 15, 16, 19, 22). Moreover, John more explicitly identifies Caiaphas as high priest *that year* (v. 13). Thus, all references that follow v. 13 about the high priest must be regarded as applying to Caiaphas and not Annas. B.F. Westcott concurs by first admitting that "it is very difficult to decide who is here spoken of under the title [high priest]," and adding, "it is difficult to suppose that the title is abruptly used, without any explanation, to describe Annas." Westcott concludes that vv. 15-23 depict Caiaphas.[7]

Luther agreed with some early fathers who alleged that a copyist misplaced John 18:24, where *Annas sent him, still bound, to Caiphas the high*

4. Edersheim, *Life and Times*, pt. 2, 547.
5. Meyer, *Mark and Luke*, 294.
6. Carson, *Matthew*, 8:524.
7. Westcott, *John: Authorized Version*, 255.

priest. They reinsert it to follow v. 14, as well as rearrange other verses in vv. 13-24. Such arrangements are textually supported only by a bare few late MSS.[8] If so, v. 19 does not identify Annas as the high priest or examiner of Jesus in vv. 19-23, but Caiaphas, so that Peter's first denial occurred while Christ was before Caiaphas, not Annas.

A more preferable view than that of Luther and some patristic fathers is one that accomplishes the same results without rearranging verses in the Greek text. It is to regard the alternate reading in the footnote of the NIV for John 18:24 as the correct one, as herein. The KJV similarly reads, "Now Annas had sent him bound unto Caiaphas the high priest." This reading harmonizes with the point stated above, that those verses following the identification of the high priest in v. 13 unequivocally identify the high priest as Caiaphas. In v. 24, therefore, John retraces by adding a detail he had previously omitted: Jesus had been delivered to Caiaphas (between vv. 14 and 15), during which trial Peter made his first denial. Edersheim agrees, positing the following two points:

> First, the preceding reference to Peter's denial must be located in the house of Caiaphas. Secondly, if vv. 19-23 refer to an examination by Annas, then St. John has left us absolutely no account of anything that had passed before Caiaphas—which, in view of the narrative of the Synoptists, would seem incredible.[9]

Furthermore, this view of v. 24 avoids an abruptness between vv. 23 and 24. It offers a smoother-flowing narrative in which John makes a commentary on what precedes by referring back to v. 22, when Jesus was struck, perhaps implying this act was against Jewish jurisprudence. This connection with the previous verses is lost in the main reading of the NIV text. It must be noted, however, that most contemporary NT scholars do not accept this NIV alternate reading for John 18:24.[10]

If the NIV alternate reading for John 18:24 is correct, Jesus appeared

---

8. Metzger, *Textual Commentary*, 251-52. For further discussion against this transposition of verses, see Bernard, *John*, 1:xxvi-xxviii and Raymond E. Brown, *The Gospel According to John (xiii-xxi)* (Garden City, New York: Doubleday, 1970), 821.

9. Edersheim, *Life and Times*, pt. 2, 548.

10. See, e.g., Meyer, *John*, 484-85; Brown, *John (xiii-xxi)*, 827. Benoit (*Jesus and the Gospel*, 155) includes extensive lists of those scholars who take the verb as pluperfect, and those who relocate verses. Benoit's (p. 126) primary argument for Annas being Jesus' examiner in vv. 19-23 is the absence in John of events recorded in the Synoptics before Caiaphas. The retort to this is that John seldom repeats what the first three Evangelists have already written (and his readers apparently already know) but supplements them. Surprisingly, Benoit next offers this same argument for why (according to his view) John omits relating anything about the trial before Caiaphas.

briefly before Annas, the details about which are not related.[11] Perhaps the presumably brief stopover at Annas' house was for the purpose of alerting the several authorities to assemble at Caiaphas' house before their captive was ushered in. Verse 15 and following concerns Jesus' appearance before Caiaphas. This solves the problem of whose courtyard they entered in John 18:15, as well as other problems.

This is the only place in *The Gospels Interwoven* where the alternate reading, supplied in a footnote of the NIV, has been substituted in place of the main NIV text. This alternate reading provides the following scenario:

a. Jesus was first brought to Annas (v. 13).

b. Then he was taken to Caiaphas (v. 15), whom John calls the high priest (vv. 15b, 19 and 22).

c. Peter made his first denial in Caiaphas' courtyard (v. 15; cf. v. 19).

d. Caiaphas began to examine Jesus while Peter made his first denial. Accordingly, John is in full harmony with the Synoptists. Excepting John's retrogression in v. 24, Annas is no longer in view following v. 13.

5. Was Peter sitting in the courtyard or standing in the gateway when he made his first and second denials of Jesus?

All three Synoptists agree that Peter was in the courtyard when he was questioned by a servant girl and denied the Lord Jesus the first time. During this first denial, Matthew has Peter sitting in the courtyard (Matt. 26:69) and Mark has him by the fire warming himself (Mark 14:66). Luke brings both facts together, so that Peter was sitting in the courtyard by the fire warming himself when he was first questioned (Luke 22:55). John, however, relates more specifically that it was the girl who attended the door (gate) who questioned him (John 18:16-17). John seems to imply that she questioned him when he was first entering the courtyard through the door. On the other hand, it is quite possible that John does not mean that Peter and the girl were at the doorway when she questioned him and he made his first denial. John's account allows that Peter could have entered the doorway and been sitting at the fire when the doorkeeper came by and questioned him.

Both Matthew 26:71 and Mark 14:68 are clear that following his first denial, Peter went out to the gateway, where he seems to have been challenged again and to have committed his second denial. On the other hand, John records what appears to be a glaring discrepancy compared to the Synoptists—he is silent about Peter's exit and alleges that Peter *stood warming himself* at his second denial (John 18:25). Where did Peter warm himself at his second denial, according to John? It would seem to be at the

11. Edersheim, *Life And Times*, pt. 2, 548.

fire in the courtyard. So John seems to locate Peter at the gateway for his first denial and at the fire for his second denial, just the opposite order of that of the Synoptists.

The most formidable difficulty concerning Peter's denials, then, may be whether all four Evangelists present them in chronological order. Many commentators conclude that either the Synoptists have the order of Peter's first two denials reversed from the historical order, or John does. If so, one might mathematically calculate that John has reversed the order, i.e., three against one. Yet John's more precise narrative of Peter's denials and of the examinations of Jesus reveals an eyewitness account, Peter and John being the only apostolic eyewitnesses. The possibility of there being a reverse order in the Evangelists' reports of Peter's denials may be disturbing to some readers. However, there is precedence for reverse order in the Gospels. As previously noted, Matthew and Luke, the only two Evangelists who describe Jesus' three temptations, list the last two in opposite order.

On the other hand, Augustine was of the opinion that Peter had returned from the gateway to the fire when he denied Jesus the second time, so that John and the Synoptists have arranged Peter's denials in the same chronological order.[12] If so, Matthew and Mark omit mention of Peter's return from the gateway to the courtyard in Matthew 26:71 and between Mark 14:68 and v. 69. In support, the NIV's *there* in Mark 14:69 is not in the Greek text. Augustine's view, however, has not been well accepted.

A similar view, held by some, is that there were two fires, so that Peter also stood at another fire at the gateway during his second denial, as herein. Or Peter and the girl may have both abandoned the entryway for the courtyard fire. Either solution affirms that all four Evangelists have recorded the denials in chronological order.

In conclusion, due to the scanty details, it is difficult to determine whether the Synoptists and John relate the same historical order of Peter's first two denials, and if not, who has reversed the order, and for what reason(s). If the order is reversed, this is another example that chronology was not the concern to Gospel writers that it is to modern readers.

6. Who accused Peter at his second denial: the same servant girl as before, another girl, or a man?

Assuming all four Evangelists have arranged Peter's three denials in their actual order, Peter's accuser(s) who prompted his second denial are as follows:

Matthew 26:71 *another girl*
Mark 14:69 *the servant girl . . . said again*

---

12. Augustine, *Harmony*, 6:187-88.

Luke 22:58 *someone else*
John 18:25 *he was asked*[13]

Mark claims the same servant girl accused Peter at both his first two denials, whereas Matthew and Luke introduce another accuser. Mark relates that there were other servant girls on duty (Mark 14:66), providing the possibility that two girls accused Peter. This was Augustine's conclusion.[14]

Luke's Gospel presents special problems in the Greek text. The NIV's *someone else*, in Luke 22:58, translates the Greek word *heteros*. Commentators disagree on whether its masculine gender restricts it to a male interrogator or only designates "otherness." Regarding Peter's first denial, only Luke quotes Peter's address of his accuser as *Woman* (v. 57), using the Greek word strictly depicting a female. In contrast, Luke's word of address for Peter during his second denial is *Man* (v. 58, also v. 60), which appears to conflict with Matthew's and Mark's *girl*. However, Luke's Greek word for *Man* is *anthrope*, a generic word for mankind; like the word "friend," it does not designate only the male sex. Thus Luke's account of Peter's second accuser may not preclude the person's being a girl.[15]

Matthew and Mark recount that the girl accused Peter to *the people there/those standing around* (Matt. 26:71; Mark 14:69). *He was asked,* in John 18:25, derives from the Greek word *eipon*, which indicates a plurality of accusers (RSV: "They said to him"; NASB: "They said therefore to him"). Consequently, John presumably adds that the bystanders, viz., *the servants and officials* in verse 18, questioned Peter also.[16] Calvin suggests that

> it is likely, that one girl's remark went round them all [maids], the first pointing him out to many over and over again, the others going up to find out for sure and spreading the discovery further still.[17]

Peter's second denial is a formidable difficulty. It is uncertain whether Peter was then questioned by one or two servant girls, or if others nearby joined in the interrogation, as herein, a view which certainly resolves the difficulty.

7. Did one person question Peter the third time he denied Jesus, or did several people question him?

Matthew reports that Peter was provoked to make his third denial when

---

13. Raymond E. Brown (*John* [xiii-xxi], 838-39) provides a complete table comparing Gospel details of Peter's three denials.
14. Augustine, *Harmony*, 6:187. I. Howard Marshall (Luke, 842-43) assents that this is probably the correct view.
15. Bauer-Arndt-Gingrich-Danker, *Lexicon*, 68.
16. Barrett, *John*, 529; R.E. Brown, John (xiii-xxi), 828.
17. Calvin, *Harmony/Gospels*, 3:171. See also Frederick Louis Godet, *Commentary on the Gospel of Luke* (1870), 2 vols. in 1 (Grand Rapids: Zondervan, n.d.), 315.

those standing there went up to Peter and said, "Surely you are one of them, for your accent gives you away" (Matt. 26:73). Mark and Luke support this by adding that *those standing near,* or, *another,* accused Peter of being *a Galilean* (Mark 14:70; Luke 22:59). John, however, claims *a relative of the man whose ear Peter had cut off, challenged him, "Didn't I see you with him in the olive grove?"* (John 18:26) These quotations do not conflict when it is understood that there was more than one accuser of Peter at his third denial.

8. How many times did Peter deny Christ?

In comparing the Gospels, some commentators find four denials by Peter: a few find more, even as many as eight and nine.[18] Such suppositions arise out of mechanical views of the inspiration of Scripture, resulting in failure to recognize the editorializing style of some or all of the Evangelists, or from failure to recognize a plurality of interrogators possibly at Peter's second denial, and certainly at his third denial. Despite the variations in the four Gospel accounts, the following facts militate against there being more than three times that Peter denied Jesus:

a. All four writers record that Jesus predicted Peter would deny him three times (Matt. 26:34; Mark 14:30; Luke 22:34; John 13:38).

b. Each Synoptist records three denials.

c. Each Synoptist concludes his account of Peter's three denials by reporting that just as Peter committed his third denial, the rooster crowed, *then Peter remembered the word* Jesus *had spoken* (Matt. 26:75; Mark 14:72; cf. Luke 22:61), again confirming that there were no more than the three predicted denials.

d. It would be the most incredible contradiction for those Evangelists writing later to narrate denials additional to the three already established by previous writers.

Although there exists some uncertainty regarding the order of Peter's first two denials due to his location, the number of interrogators in the last two denials, and whether some statements have been editorialized by the Evangelists, the complex subject of Peter's denials becomes an outstanding example of the usefulness of a composite of the Gospels in presenting the most complete scenario possible.

---

18. Some commentators find at least four denials, e.g, Thomas and Gundry (*Harmony*, 229). Johnston M. Cheney (*The Life of Christ in Stereo*, 190-92, 258) claims six. For as many as eight, see the citations by Meyer (*Matthew*, 486) and Robert Gundry (*Matthew*, 626). Raymond E. Brown (*John [xiii-xxi]*, 837) alleges that "some literal-minded interpreters have concluded that there must have been three sets of three denials, thus making Peter guilty nine times!"

9. When Peter made his third denial, did the cock crow for the first time or the second time?

Matthew, Luke, and John relate that in Jesus' prediction of Peter's denials, as well as in the denials themselves, there is mention of a cock's crowing when Peter denies Jesus the third time. Mark's parallel passages in Mark 14:30, 68 (NIV alternate reading) and v. 72 account for two cock crowings. However, it should be noted that Mark's two cock crowings do not actually conflict with the other Evangelists. In other words, though the others mention a single cock crowing, they do not restrict their accounts to only one.

As may be observed in the NIV footnotes, all three passages in Mark have some manuscript variance. The United Bible Societies' third edition of the *The Greek New Testament* leads the field in Greek texts appealed to by translators of the NT.[19] Its editorial committee assigns ratings for 1,440 selected manuscript variants in the NT. A companion volume was prepared by one of the committee members, Bruce M. Metzger, and approved by the committee to provide further explanation of the more prominent variants.[20] The conclusions of the committee are as follows:

a. In Mark 14:30, the committee assigns a C rating ("a considerable degree of doubt") for the word *twice*. Some MSS of Mark 14:30, however, omit *twice*, regarding which Metzger explains: "It is probable that the omission of [twice] arose from scribal assimilation to the parallel accounts (Matt. 26:34; Luke 22:34; John 13:38)," i.e., a scribe's misguided effort to harmonize Mark's texts with the other Gospels.[21]

b. In Mark 14:68, the committee assigns a D rating ("a very high degree of doubt") for the NIV alternate reading *and the rooster crowed*. Metzger adds: "It is very difficult to decide whether these words were added or omitted from the original text."[22]

c. In Mark 14:72, the committee assigns a C rating for the words *the second time* and a B rating ("some degree of doubt") for the entire quotation, *Before the rooster crows twice you yourself will disown me three times* (Mark 14:30).

Despite the varying degrees of doubt about these phrases, there remains sufficient MS evidence for the NIV readings in at least Mark 14:30 and 72. Earlier MSS of Mark's Gospel presumably included these phrases; later scribes omitted them in an attempt to harmonize their copies of Mark's Gospel with those of Matthew and Luke. It is likely that Jesus did predict two cock crowings and that two cock crowings occurred.

19. Kurt Aland, Matthew Black, Carlo M. Martini, Bruce M. Metzger, and Allen Wikgren, eds., *The Greek New Testament* (London: United Bible Societies, 1975).
20. Metzger, *Textual Commentary.*
21. Ibid., 114.
22. Ibid., 115.

A few scholars do not interpret a literal cock crowing in Mark but regard the expression as an idiom for "the third watch." The Romans gave the name "cock-crow" to the third watch, that period of time from midnight to 3 A.M.[23] (Also see Mark 13:35.) However, in embracing such a view, it is not necessary to abandon a literal interpretation of a cock crowing in Mark.[24] William Lane cites the following interesting study documented in the *Annual of the Swedish Theological Institute*:

> It was the peculiar habit of the cock crowing, with comparative regularity, at three times during the period between midnight and 3:00 A.M. that accounts for the designation of the third watch of the night as 'cock-crow.' . . . Observation over a period of twelve years in Jerusalem has confirmed that the cock crows at three distinct times, first about a half hour after midnight, a second time about an hour later, and a third time an hour after the second. Each crowing lasts from 3-5 minutes, after which all is quiet again.[25]

It is conceivable that Peter denied the Lord all three times between midnight and 3 A.M., since it was apparently late in the night. Luke reveals that *about an hour* separated the second and third denials (Luke 22:59).

10. Did the Sanhedrin assemble at night, before Peter's denials or at daybreak, after them?

Matthew and Mark relate that during the night, before Peter's denials, the chief priests, teachers of the law, and elders, i.e., the whole Sanhedrin, assembled (Matt. 26:57, 59; Mark 14:53, 55) at the house of Caiaphas the high priest (Matt. 26:57; Luke 22:54).[26] Luke, however, does not mention the assembly of the Council and its interrogation until after Peter's denials,

23. David Hill, *The Gospel of Matthew* (Greenwood, S.C.: Attic Press, 1972), 341.
24. Meyer (*Matthew*, 471) affirms both.
25. Lane, *Mark*, 543.
26. The Council of the Sanhedrin was composed of 70 members and was comprised of the chief priests of the leading tribal families, elders, and teachers of the law. The high priest served as chairman and the 71st member. To make official judgments, it was only necessary for a quorum of 23 members to be present. Some commentators think that not all the members of the Sanhedrin were present for the initial interrogations during the night vigil, but that others joined early the next morning to pass final judgment. They regard *the whole Sanhedrin* in Matt. 26:59 and Mark 14:55 as meaning the quorum. All the members had to be in Jerusalem for Passover. Joseph and Nicodemus, who laid Jesus' body in the tomb, were members of the Council (Mark 15:43; Luke 23:50; John 3:1). Yet Joseph, if present as it appears, and surely Nicodemus also, *had not consented to their decision and action* (Luke 23:51).

when *at daybreak* they *met together*. They apparently met to make the final decision (Luke 22:66), which Matthew and Mark describe in their second account of the Council's proceedings (Matt. 27:1; Mark 15:1). Many commentators therefore suppose that the Sanhedrin assembled twice, reconvening early in the morning at the nearby temple to pass formal judgment in the exercise of proper legal jurisprudence. A few commentators propose that Luke's *the council of the elders of the people* (Luke 22:66) refers to the smaller, political Sanhedrin that joined the regathering at the temple in the morning. Regardless of the details, it seems clear that the larger religious council of the Sanhedrin convened in the night and tried Jesus. During this time Peter made his three denials. The final sentence of the death penalty was pronounced early the next morning.

11. At Jesus' trial before the Sanhedrin, did the high priest ask the question that led to the charge of blasphemy or did others? What was the form of the question and Jesus' answer to it?

There are significant differences among the Synoptists concerning the questions and answers at Jesus' trial before the Sanhedrin:

a. Matthew 26:63 and Mark 14:61 reveal that Caiaphas, the high priest, demanded that Jesus tell if he were *the Christ, the Son of God/the Blessed One*. Matthew has *God* in place of Mark's *the Blessed One*. Perhaps Mark has the *ipsissma verba* and Matthew has the *ipsissma vox* as an explanation of his source. Caiaphas' use of the words the *Blessed One* may indicate the Jews' superstitious practice of avoiding pronunciation of the divine name, but more likely the high priest reveals his familiarity with the repeated OT phrase, "Blessed be the LORD God." D.A. Carson states, "The two titles are formally equivalent and both may have been used at various points in the trial (cf. John 19:7)."[27]

b. Unlike the other Synoptists, Luke has the query split into two separate questions (Luke 22:67-70). He does not specify that the questions were delivered by the high priest. It appears that several officials participated in the questioning process. Finally, Caiaphas charged Jesus under oath to respond to the full two-part question (Matt. 26:63; Mark 14:61).

c. After the challenge, *If you are the Christ . . . tell us* (Luke 22:67), Luke inserts Jesus' answer referring to Psalm 110:1 about being *seated at the right hand of the Mighty God* (Luke 22:69). Then Luke records the question of whether Jesus is *the Son of God* (v. 70). In Jesus' response Luke omits the words *coming on the clouds of heaven* (Matt. 26:64; Mark 14:62; cf. Dan. 7:13-14). Matthew and Mark join together the two-part question, placing Jesus' entire answer after it.

---

27. Carson, *Matthew*, 8:554.

d. Luke reports Jesus' answer differently than do the other Synoptists. Matthew has, "*Yes, it is as you say*" (Matt. 24:64); Mark gives a brief, "*I am*" (Mark 14:62). Luke provides a composite of the two, "*You are right in saying I am*" (Luke 22:70), which probably represents the *ipsissima verba*. The NIV renderings of Matthew's and Luke's quotation are more accurately translated "You say it" and "You say that I am," respectively.[28] (See EN 14:3.) Many scholars admit to some ambiguity in Jesus' answer, in which Jesus emphasizes the word "you" to point out that the words proceeded from the other person, as if he is the witness, rather than Jesus himself (cf. John 5:31). Also, Luke records Jesus' answer of the OT quotation as if he referred only to his future sitting ("session") at the right hand of God following his ascension into heaven, whereas Matthew's and Mark's quotation represents a composite of Psalm 110:1 and Daniel 7:13, which concern only his second coming. It is possible that Jesus referred to both his session and second coming, as herein.

In conclusion, some uncertainty exists regarding the exact wording and chronological order of statements in this part of Jesus' trial. Although some ambiguity exists in Jesus' answer to the high priest, his quotations from the OT unequivocally identified himself to the Sanhedrin as the Messiah, the Son of God, for which his accusers charged him with blasphemy and condemned him to death.

12. Did Judas buy the potter's field, or did the chief priests buy it?

Matthew reports that the chief priests took Judas' thirty pieces of silver and *decided to use the money to buy the potter's field* (Matt. 27:7). But Luke writes that *with the reward he got for his wickedness, Judas bought a field* (Acts 1:18-19). These are reconciled by understanding that Luke means Judas bought the field only in the sense that it was his money. According to Jewish law, money unlawfully gained could not be accepted into the temple treasury (Matt. 27:6); it was to be returned to the donor. So the chief priests

28. The NIV's *Yes* for Jesus' answer in Matthew 26:64 is not in the Greek text: Matthew 26:64 has literally "You say it," Mark 14:62 has "I am," and Luke 22:70 (as herein) represents a fusion of the readings in Matthew and Mark, "You say that I am." (See EN 14:3.) It is worth noting that due to some textual variance for "*I am*" in Mark 14:62, Nigel Turner (*Insights*, 72-73) cites eminent third-century father Origen and moderate form critics B.H. Streeter and Vincent Taylor who accept the longer reading for Mark 14:62 which is the same as Luke 22:70: "You say that I am.") A similar thing occurs in the NIV when Pilate questioned Jesus whether he was a king. The NIV's *Yes, it is as you say* in Matthew 27:11; Mark 15:2; and Luke 23:3 is literally, "You say it"; "Yes" is not in the Greek text. In John 18:37, the apostle may provide the *ipsissima verba* with the words *You are right in saying I am a king* (actually, "You say that I am a king," similar to Luke 22:70), since he elaborates more fully.

picked up the coins and decided to use them to buy the field on Judas' behalf (Matt. 27:7).[29] Whether it was purchased before or after Judas' death is not stated. Moreover, it is not necessary to translate Luke's word *ektesato* as "bought." The word means "procure for oneself, acquire, get."[30] The NASB translates it: "Now this man acquired a field," i.e., by proxy.

13. Did Judas hang himself, or did he fall to his death?

Matthew says Judas *hanged himself* (Matt. 27:5), but Luke states that *he fell headlong, his body burst open and all his intestines spilled out* (Acts 1:18). Judas first hung himself. He probably did not bring a rope. Edersheim provides an interesting supposition that "slowly and deliberately he unwound the long girdle that held his garment. It was the girdle in which he had carried those thirty pieces of silver."[31] Whatever his equipment, Judas presumably hung himself on a tree limb that either hung or swayed over some precipice. For some reason his body fell below. Perhaps the article with which he hung himself broke, or the knot came loose, or the branch broke, the latter being a church tradition. At the moment Jesus died, *the earth shook and the rocks split* (Matt. 27:51). Some have proposed that the hanging might have occurred near this time and that the earthquake caused the tree limb to break, or the whole tree to be uprooted. Whether Judas was alive or dead when his body fell, or what caused the fall, is not reported and may not have been known, but *everyone in Jerusalem heard about* Judas' fall and death (Acts 1:19).

14. Was the potter's field later called the *Field of Blood* because of the *blood money* or Judas' bloody fall?

Matthew relates that the place was called the *Field of Blood* because of the blood money with which it was purchased (Matt. 27:6-8). Luke reports it was so-called because Judas' body burst open there (Acts 1:18-19). The religious authorities of Jerusalem may have connected the name with the blood money for Jesus' capture. Perhaps the common people connected it more with the bloody fall of Judas' body. Both could be true.

---

29. J.A. Motyer, "Akeldama," Brown, *Dictionary of New Testament Theology*, 1:93.
30. Bauer-Arndt-Gingrich-Danker, *Lexicon*, 455.
31. Edersheim, *Life and Times*, pt. 2, 575.

15. How many times was Jesus mocked? Did the soldiers put a robe and a crown of thorns on Jesus once or twice? What was the order of events surrounding the examinations of Jesus by the Roman authorities? Was the robe scarlet or purple?

Together, the Gospels record that Jesus was mocked on four separate occasions: by the Sanhedrin and their guards during the first trial (Matt. 26:67-68; Mark 14:65; Luke 22:63-65); by Herod and his soldiers (Luke 23:11); by Pilate's soldiers (Matt. 27:27-31; Mark 15:16-20; John 19:2-3); by onlookers while he hung on the cross (Matt. 27:39-44; Mark 15:29-32; Luke 23:35-37).

Luke writes that Jesus was first ridiculed, mocked and dressed *in an elegant robe* (Luke 23:11: the Greek word translated "robe" means only "clothing"[32]) by Herod's soldiers. John relates a scornful robing (may or may not be the same clothing as in Luke) and crowning of thorns incident *later*, during Pilate's last examination of Jesus and his dialogues with the Jews (John 19:1-2). Matthew and Mark locate the robe and crown incident *after* Pilate handed him over to be crucified (Matt. 27:26-31; Mark 15:15-20). At first glance it appears that a robe was put on Jesus a total of three times, and a crown of thorns on him twice. Augustine explains that John

> makes it evident that Matthew and Mark have reported this incident in the way of recapitulation, and that it did not actually take place after Pilate had delivered him up to be crucified. For John informs us distinctly enough that these things took place when he yet was with Pilate.[33]

This is a likely solution, providing two robings of Jesus and one crown of thorns episode. Accordingly, the material in John 19:4-15 is additional to that of the Synoptics, fitting chronologically between Matthew 27:30 and v. 31; Mark 15:19 and v. 20; Luke 23:25 and v. 26. The order of events would have been as follows:

a. The Jewish Council (Sanhedrin) took Jesus to Pilate (Mark 15:1; Luke 23:1; John 18:28).

b. Pilate sent Jesus to Herod (Luke 23:7).

c Herod and his soldiers mocked Jesus, dressed him in a purple robe and sent him back to Pilate (Luke 23:11).

d. Pilate released Barabbas (Matt. 27:26a; Mark 15:15a; Luke 23:25a; presumably between John 18:40 and 19:1).

e. Pilate had Jesus flogged (Matt. 27:26b; Mark 15:15b; John 19:1).

f. Pilate's soldiers placed the robe and crown of thorns on Jesus and mocked him (Matt. 27:27-31; Mark 15:16-20; John 19:2-3).

---

32. Bauer-Arndt-Gingrich-Danker, *Lexicon*, 312.
33. Augustine, *Harmony*, 6:197.

g. Pilate conducted his final dialogue with the Jews and made his official judgment (John 19:4-15).

h. Pilate *handed him over to them to be crucified* (John 19:16).

i. The soldiers took the robe off Jesus, put his own clothes back on him, and led him away to be crucified (Matt. 27:31; Mark 15:20).

In conclusion, Herod's soldiers first dressed Jesus in a purple robe and mocked him. Later, Pilate's soldiers put the same(?) robe back on Jesus, placed a twisted crown of thorns on his head, and mocked him again.

As for the color of the robe, Matthew 27:28 has *scarlet* while Mark 15:17 and John 19:2 have *purple*. Speaking of his own Roman culture, Augustine observed, "There is also a certain red-coloured purple which resembles scarlet very closely."[34] Carson comments, "The ancients did not discriminate among colors as closely as we do."[35]

16. How many trials did Jesus endure?

There were two official trials of Jesus: religious and political.[36] The former was before the Jewish religious authorities, the Sanhedrin; the latter was before the Gentile authority, the Roman governor (prefect) of Judea, Pontius Pilate. Both trials issued in the condemnation of Jesus to death. Of course, the religious trial ending in the condemnation of death was not binding, since Israel remained under the jurisdiction of the Roman Empire. These trials and their accompanying investigations were held by the authorities in the following order:

a. Examination(?) by Annas at night (John 18:12-13)[37]

b. Examination by Caiaphas in the night and early morning (Matt. 26:57-68; Mark 14:53-65; Luke 22:54; John 18:19-23)

c. Trial before the Sanhedrin, *very early in the morning, at daybreak* (Matt. 27:1; Mark 15:1; Luke 22:66-71)

d. Examination before Pilate at *early morning* (Matt. 27:2, 11-23; Mark 15:1-15a; Luke 23:2-6, 13-22; John 18:28–19:12)

---

34. Ibid.

35. Carson, *Matthew*, 8:573. The more particular Greek word for *robe* in Matthew 27:28 is *chlamuda*, meaning "cloak." Many scholars maintain that the cloak placed on Jesus was an official Roman soldier's coat, which would most likely be described as red, but possibly also as scarlet or purple. See Bauer-Arndt-Gingrich-Danker, *Lexicon*, 440, 312, 694, 882.

36. For a legal perspective of the trials of Jesus, see the outstanding Harvard law professor Simon Greenleaf's *The Testimony of the Evangelists Examined by the Rules of Evidence Administered in Courts of Justice* (New York: Cockcroft, 1874; Grand Rapids: Baker, 1965).

37. It is possible that Annas questioned Jesus, though John does not explicitly say so. The recorded examination in John 18:19-23, however, probably occurred before Caiaphas, with John 18:24 being a retrogression. (See EN 15:4.)

e. Examination by Herod (Luke 23:7-11)
f. Trial by Pilate (John 19:13-16)

17. Did Jesus carry his own cross or did Simon of Cyrene carry it?

Only John relates that Jesus carried his own cross, omitting that Simon of Cyrene assisted (John 19:17). In contrast, none of the three Synoptists include that Jesus carried his own cross but report that Simon of Cyrene was pressed into this service (Matt. 27:32; Mark 15:21; Luke 23:26). A few liberal critics have questioned the Synoptists' accounts on grounds that it was not customary to substitute another person to carry the condemned man's burden. Even if so, extenuating circumstances were probably cause for altering custom.

It was indeed customary for a criminal condemned to be crucified to carry his own crossbeam to the common place of execution just outside the city wall, where centerposts for crosses remained implanted. The crossbeam was laid across the shoulders of the condemned man, whose arms were stretched out and tied to it. Hence, Jesus was forced to carry his own cross, i.e., crossbeam. The wooden plank weighed approximately forty pounds. Part way to Golgotha—many think at a main road at the city gate (Matt. 27:32: *going out* of the city)—the procession apparently slowed as Jesus tired quickly. This is reasonable, since he undoubtedly suffered from lack of sleep and weakness occasioned by the Roman soldiers' flogging with the whip and thongs.[38] C.E.B. Cranfield observes:

> Presumably Jesus had carried [the crossbeam] for awhile, but had been physically unable to carry it further. . . . It is reasonable to connect it (and perhaps also the fact that Jesus died more quickly than was usual (cf. xv. 44)) with the unique character of his sufferings.[39]

In addition, the Jewish authorities may have been eager to complete the crucifixion before the Sabbath began that evening, or perhaps in time for the eating of the chagigah near noon that Friday. On this account they may have persuaded the Roman soldiers to hasten the procession, prompting them to seize Simon of Cyrene as he was passing that way and force him to carry Jesus' cross the remainder of the distance to Golgotha (Luke 23:26).

---

38. It was not customary to flog the criminal before he carried his cross, although sometimes he was flogged after the sentence was pronounced, or on the way to be crucified. Pilate had Jesus flogged before he pronounced judgment, apparently in an effort to appease the Jews' wrath and avoid the execution of Jesus.
39. C.E.B. Cranfield, *The Gospel According to Saint Mark* (Cambridge: University Press, 1959), 454.

18. Was the drink that Jesus refused at Golgotha wine mixed with gall or wine mixed with myrrh?

Matthew reveals that the soldiers offered Jesus *wine to drink, mixed with gall; but after tasting it, he refused to drink it* (Matt. 27:34). Yet Mark describes this same drink as wine mixed with myrrh (Mark 15:23). Gall and myrrh refer to the same substance. Gall is a general word that refers to a bitter substance; myrrh likely refers to frankincense that was added to a drink. D.A. Carson explains, "Mark keeps the word 'myrrh' to describe the content, and Matthew uses 'gall' to describe the taste and to provide a link with Psalm 69:21."[40] Scholars debate whether this was a bitter narcotic in the drink, making it a merciful act intended to deaden pain,[41] or a bitter substance used only to make it undrinkable, and therefore offered in mockery. Matthew and Mark indicate that this was the drink Jesus refused. It was the first offer of a drink to Jesus because it happened upon their arrival at Golgotha, before the crucifixion (Matt. 27:34-35; Mark 15:23-24).

19. Was Jesus crucified at the third hour or after the sixth hour?

Mark maintains concerning Jesus that *it was the third hour when they crucified him,* or 9 A.M. (Mark 15.25). On the other hand, John claims that Pilate officially judged Jesus and handed him over to be crucified *about the sixth hour* (John 19:14). Commentators are quite divided on this apparent contradiction; it seems more solutions have been offered for it than for any other problem in the Gospels:

a. In some ancient languages, including Greek, letters were occasionally used to represent certain numerals. Early church historian Eusebius and many others since have alleged that an early copyist confused the Greek letter representing a three (capital "F" in English) for that which stands for a six (an "F" without the middle bar).[42] Like others, Gleason Archer points out that "this does not really solve the problem at all, because John 19:14 does not indicate the time Christ was crucified but only the time of his appearance before Pilate's judgment seat."[43] So this view fails to allow for the necessary time required for the procession to travel from Herod's Palace

---

40. Carson, *Matthew*, 8:575.
41. Edersheim, *Life and Times*, pt. 2, 589-90.
42. A few Greek MSS of the Gospel of John have the word *third* and only a few MSS of the Gospel of Mark have the word *six*. Bruce M. Metzger (*Textual Commentary*, 118, 252) asserts that these variant readings in both Mark and John represent scribal glosses, i.e., misguided attempts to harmonize the two passages. Nearly all scholars concur. Metzger cites the evidence and concludes there is overwhelming support for *sixth hour* in John and *third hour* in Mark.
43. Archer, *Bible Difficulties*, 364.

(modern view) in the southwest of the city to Golgotha, outside the northwest wall of the city, and for preparations to be made there to crucify the three condemned men. Moreover, Stein observes that "the best Greek manuscripts all have 'third' (Mark) and 'sixth' (John) and they also have the numbers spelled out rather than in letter equivalents."[44]

b. Mark's *third* is a scribal gloss inserted by an early copyist. The reasons adduced for this are as follows:

1. If original, *third hour* in Mark would have been attached to v. 24 rather than appear as an afterthought in v. 25.[45] Yet the same could be said of the two robbers in v. 27. Much Gospel material would be altered if such minor retrogressions were regarded as glosses.

2. The absence of the time of Jesus' crucifixion in Matthew and Luke, who usually follow Mark as a written source, is evidence that their copy of Mark did not contain v. 25. However, it is *very* atypical of scribes to add a gloss that creates an apparent contradiction with other Gospels, as this does with John 19:14, unless the gloss were penned before the other Gospels were circulated enough to be known to that scribe. In addition, other important examples can be cited where the other Synoptists do not follow Mark, thereby resulting in harmonizing difficulties (e.g. the "cock crow" of Mark 14:30, 68, and 72).

c. John's *sixth hour* was meant to be a correction of Mark's *third hour*.[46] This view is advocated by leading moderate form critic Vincent Taylor and others. It must be dismissed as founded upon too weak a view of the inspiration of Scripture.

d. By using *about the sixth hour*, John allegorically connects the judgment and the crucifixion of the Lamb of God (John 1:29), our Passover (see 1 Cor. 5:7), with the slaying of the paschal lambs. In preparation for Passover, the slaying of perhaps over 10,000 paschal lambs at the temple began just after noon, as soon as the sun began its descent.[47] Nothing in the text suggests an allegorical interpretation, which calls into question the historicity of John's account. Furthermore, it requires the questionable supposition that Jesus and the Jewish authorities ate the Passover on separate days.

e. The third and sixth hours reflect the writers' inexact manner of identifying the same general time period. The Hebrews and other ancients reckoned time by quarters. For the Jews, the new day began at 6 P.M. There

---

44. Stein, *Difficult Passages*, 60.
45. Lane, *Mark*, 567.
46. Taylor, *Mark*, 590.
47. Cranfield, *Mark*, 455-56.

were four quarters (called "watches") in the night and four quarters in the daytime. The first quarter represented the first three hours, the second quarter referred to the fourth through sixth hours, etc. Accordingly, they frequently (seldom in John, e.g., John 1:39; 4:52) designated time by the third, sixth, or ninth hour of a twelve-hour day (e.g., Matt. 20:1-12; John 11:9). Calvin supposes that Mark's *third hour* means the last part of the quarter that begins at the third hour, i.e., Christ was crucified toward the end of the period between 9 A.M. and noon, possibly 11:30 A.M.[48] This makes Mark's time of the crucifixion more harmonious with John's *about the sixth hour* (about noon) for Pilate's judgment. However, a preponderance of commentators agree that there is no indication of computing time in this manner elsewhere in the Gospels, making this view a desperate and arbitrary attempt at harmonization. Instead, a time between the quarter hours would have been rounded off to the nearest quarter, e.g., 11 A.M. would be rounded off to noon (the sixth hour), rather than to 9 A.M. (the third hour). Moreover, this view only serves to minimize, rather than harmonize, the time difference, still failing to solve the problem of Jesus' crucifixion preceding Pilate's time of judgment in John. As to John's being inexact, it may be argued that he calculated time even more particularly than the Synoptists by identifying hours next to quarter hours without rounding them off (e.g., John 1:39: *the tenth hour;* John 4:52: *the seventh hour*).

Those who adopt this view (conservative expositors included) often make light of the time difference, suggesting that the ancients were not careful timekeepers because they did not have clocks and watches.[49] Such assertions have caused critics like Marxsen to allege:

> The conclusion is inescapable: a synchronizing harmony of the different accounts [is] to be impossible. Anyone who persists in the attempt must alter the texts and declare the differences to be trivialities.[50]

f. Mark regards *the third hour when they crucified him* (Mark 15:25) as beginning with the earlier flogging,[51] since he and Matthew unite the scourging and crucifixion: Pilate *had Jesus flogged, and handed him over to be*

---

48. John Calvin, *Calvin's Commentaries: The Gospel According to St John 11-21* (1553), tr. T.H.L. Parker, eds. David W. Torrance and Thomas F. Torrance (Grand Rapids: Eerdmans, 1961), 176.
49. E.g., Leon Morris, *The Gospel According to John* (Grand Rapids: Eerdmans, 1971), 801.
50. Willie Marxsen, *The Resurrection of Jesus of Nazareth*, tr. Margaret Kohl (Philadelphia: Fortress Press, 1970), 74.
51. Frederick Louis Godet, *Commentary on the Gospel of John* (1886), 2 vols. (Grand Rapids: Zondervan, n.d.), 2:380.

crucified (Matt. 27:26; Mark 15:15). According to this view, the scenario is as follows: Jesus was flogged about 9-10 A.M., officially judged about 11 A.M., and crucified at 12 noon, after which occurred the three hours of darkness from 12 to 3 P.M. The Apostle John, however, more acutely separates these events in time.

This view appears to be another forced harmonization, receiving scant attention from scholars since being proposed by Lange and Godet in the last century. It seems very unlikely that anyone would describe the flogging in Pilate's palace as the beginning of the crucifixion event, the two being separated by both time and space. The following facts further preclude tnis view:

    1. Mark locates the hour of crucifixion after the scourging, the journey to Golgotha, and the offer of the narcotic drink.
    2. The exact time is given for when Jesus was crucified.

    g. Augustine, applying his penchant for the allegorical method of interpretation, rather tenuously, and inconsistently, suggests that "the Lord was crucified at the third hour by the tongues of the Jews, at the sixth hour by the hands of the soldiers." He means that Mark indicates it was the third hour that the Jews shouted to Pilate, *Crucify him* (cf. Mark 15:13 with v. 25).

    h. Admitting this to be a difficult problem, Augustine halted between the above opinion and one other allegorizing interpretation: that John's *sixth hour* refers to the last hour of the time of preparation of the Paschal Lamb, Jesus Christ, rather than the literal sixth hour of the day, similar to another view presented above (d). This means that the examinations of Jesus by the Jews and Pilate-Herod-Pilate lasted six hours, from 3 A.M. to 9 A.M.[52] Both this and Augustine's above proposal lack the support of other commentators.

    i. John used Roman time, which began at midnight, while Mark employed Jewish time, which for daytime began at 6 A.M. Accordingly, John's *sixth hour* was 6 A.M. and Mark's *third hour* was 9 A.M. Pilate therefore officially judged Jesus about 6 A.M. and Jesus was crucified at 9 A.M. This view allows ample time for the procession to Golgotha.

It is supposed that John employed this Roman time system in consideration of his Gentile readers. Strong patristic evidence does indeed establish that John penned his Gospel toward the end of the century in Ephesus, the capital of a Roman province. This hotly debated view has been the leading position maintained by most conservative scholars, though rejected by some of them. While this popular view of a difference in time systems

---

52. Augustine, *Harmony*, 6:428.

appears most attractive, it is well to be aware that many commentators advance notable arguments against it.

1. It was *early in the morning* (Matt. 27:1; Mark 15:1), *at daybreak* (Luke 22:66), when the Sanhedrin condemned Jesus and delivered him to Pilate. Sunrise occurs about 6 A.M. in Palestine during Passover. If the Sanhedrin turned Jesus over to Pilate at daybreak, yet Pilate sentenced Jesus about 6 A.M. (*the sixth hour*), there was insufficient time for Pilate's two examinations of Jesus and accompanying dialogues with the Jews, the appearance before Herod, and the mockings and flogging, all of which occurred before Pilate's sentencing. Some think this would have taken as much as three hours.[53] A.T. Robertson smoothes over the difficulty by supposing a slightly earlier sunrise than 6 A.M., so that "all the events, moreover, narrated by the Evangelists, could have occurred between dawn (John 18:27) and six or seven."[54] Nevertheless, William Hendriksen, agreeing with Robertson, adopts this midnight starting point in John and admits, "It is difficult for us to understand how the trial before Pilate (in reality the Pilate-Herod-Pilate trial) was so speedy, how everything transpired so rapidly."[55]

2. It is questionable whether Pilate or Herod would have received Jesus at such an early hour, or that a considerable crowd of Jews would have gathered before Pilate by 6 A.M. or earlier to demand Jesus' crucifixion.

3. There is a lack of historical evidence to support the Romans' beginning their civil day at midnight. Leon Morris cites four historical sources from this generation in support of the Romans beginning their day at sunrise, including additional evidence that the Romans "marked noon on their sundials with VI not XII."[56] Nevertheless, a surprising amount of disagreement continues among scholars on this point. Delitzsch, B.F. Westcott, and McClelland offer ancient references to support the Romans beginning their day at midnight. A.T. Robertson dogmatically asserts:

> For a long time it was doubted whether the Romans ever used this method of computing time for civil days. Farrar vehemently opposes this idea. But Plutarch, Pliny, Aulus Gellius, and Macrobius expressly say that the Roman civil day was reckoned

53. Meyer, *Matthew*, 509.
54. Robertson, *Harmony*, 285.
55. Hendriksen, *John*, 2:421.
56. Morris, *John*, 158. Morris adopts the view of imprecise calculation of time by ancients.

from midnight to midnight. So the question of fact may be considered as settled.[57]

More recently, F.F. Bruce disagrees, while attempting no solution.

Despite Westcott's arguments, no evidence is forthcoming that at this time, whether among Romans, Greeks or Jews, hours were ever reckoned otherwise than from sunrise.[58]

However, historians, with the support of legal documents, land leases, etc., agree that the Roman legal day began at midnight. The disagreement concerns the beginning of the Roman civil day. Leon Morris quotes the disputed words of the ancient historian Pliny:

The actual period of a day has been differently kept by different people: the Babylonians count the period between two sunrises, the Athenians that between two sunsets . . ., the common people everywhere from dawn to dark, the Roman priests and the authorities who fixed the official day, and also the Egyptians and Hipparchus, the period from midnight to midnight.[59]

Pliny appears to say that both the Roman civil and legal day began at midnight. Robertson adds what appears to be a weighty argument:

He [John] wrote the Gospel late in the century, probably in Asia Minor, long after the destruction of Jerusalem, when the Jewish method would not likely be preserved.[60]

4. John's other designations of hours (*sixth* in 4.6; *seventh* in 4.52; *tenth* in 1.39) indicate he reckons the day beginning at 6 A.M.[61] Yet other scholars argue just as strenuously for the opposite, that these hours in John indicate a midnight and noon time system. C.K. Barrett concludes: "It is impossible to settle with complete certainty the method of enumerating the hours employed by John."[62]

57. Robertson, *Harmony*, 285-86.
58. F.F. Bruce, *The Gospel of John* (Grand Rapids: Eerdmans, 1983), 364.
59. Morris, *John*, 801.
60. Robertson, *Harmony*, 286.
61. E.g., see Brown, *John (i-xii)*, 75, 169 and *John (xiii-xxi)*, 882-83. The Samaritan woman drew water *about the sixth hour* (John 4:6). Rather than noon, during the heat of the day, Genesis 24:11 designates the time ancient Hebrew women drew water as about 6 P.M.: *it was toward evening, the time the women go out to draw water*. Furthermore, they probably walked all day from Judea (John 3:22 and 4:3) to Sychar (4:5), a distance of perhaps 25-30 miles. It is, therefore, more likely that Jesus grew *tired as he was from the journey* (v. 6) at 6 P.M. rather than noon.
62. Barrett, *John*, 194.

This apparent discrepancy between Mark's *third hour* and John's *sixth hour* may be the most difficult harmonizing problem in the Gospels. Some excellent commentators conclude that due to the scanty information available, no satisfactory solution has yet been proposed. Of all the solutions offered, the preferred, though uncertain, one is that Mark and John employed two different time systems.

20. Which of the four different inscriptions provided by the Evangelists was written on the sign attached to Jesus' cross?

When a condemned criminal was to be crucified by the Romans, someone was designated to carry a signboard and lead the procession to the place of crucifixion. The victim followed next, carrying his cross. The sign was usually painted white, with either red or black letters stating the name of the condemned and the charge against him. This board was eventually attached to the cross, usually above the criminal's head on the centerpost.

All four Evangelists record different wordings for what Pilate had written on the sign fastened to Jesus' cross (Matt. 27:37; Mark 15:26; Luke 23:38; John 19:19). John explains the seeming contradiction: Pilate had the inscriptions on the sign *written in Aramaic, Latin and Greek* (John 19:20). Edersheim did not think that John listed the three languages in John 19:20 in their order of arrangement on the sign from top to bottom. He proposed that Matthew translated the official Latin inscription which Pilate placed at the top of the sign, Mark's words were the actual Greek which was in the middle, and John translated the Aramaic title located at the bottom of the sign.[63] On the other hand, Gleason Archer, whose view appears more convincing, retains John's order of the languages for the sign but thinks Matthew probably contains the Aramaic wording, since Papias claimed that Matthew wrote his Gospel in Hebrew (Aramaic?); Mark has the Latin title, since his Gospel is believed to have been published in Rome; Luke reads almost the same as Mark; John retains the Greek form due to his settled ministry in Ephesus.[64]

One cannot be certain that John lists the languages according to the order in which the inscriptions were arranged, or from what language two of the Gospel writers translated his title. One thing is clear: THE KING OF THE JEWS was written in Aramaic, Latin, and Greek. The titles are arranged in *The Gospels Interwoven* merely for their symmetrical appearance in English.

---

63. Edersheim, *Life and Times*, pt. 2, 590-91.
64. Archer, *Bible Difficulties*, 346.

21. Did both of the criminals crucified with Jesus insult him, or did only one mock him?

Matthew 27:44 and Mark 15:32 reveal that both of the criminals crucified with Jesus *heaped insults on him.* Thereafter, both Synoptists remain silent about the crucified robbers. However, Luke 23:39 reads that only *one of the criminals who hung there hurled insults at him.* Luke quotes the criminal's insult, then becomes the only Gospel writer to record the conversion experience of the other criminal (Luke 23:39-43). Both Matthew and Mark have located the insults of the robbers (Matt. 27:44; Mark 15:32) *before* the second drink offered to Jesus (Matt. 27:48; Mark 15:36). Luke's mention of the offer of wine vinegar (Luke 23:36) appears to be identical to the second drink offered in the other Synoptics. Therefore, Luke's mention of the penitent criminals' response toward Jesus occurs *after* the second drink offer, later in the crucifixion event than that recorded by the other Synoptists. Accordingly, it is generally assumed that early during their crucifixion the two criminals insulted Jesus; later, one had a change of heart, rebuked the other, and was converted.

22. How many times was Jesus offered a drink at Golgotha?

Matthew and Mark account for two drinks offered to Jesus at Golgotha. The first drink was clearly offered upon Jesus' arrival at Golgotha, immediately before the crucifixion (Matt. 27:34; Mark 15:23). This drink Jesus refused. The other drink recorded by Matthew and Mark was offered after the crucifixion, immediately following the three hours of darkness and near the time of Christ's death. A man offered him wine vinegar from a sponge lifted up on a stick (Matt. 27:48; Mark 15:36). Although the two Synoptists do not specify, circumstances seem to indicate that Jesus accepted this drink. John leaves no doubt. In reporting what must be this same drink, he adds that it was offered in response to Jesus' words, *I am thirsty* (John 19:28). They soaked the sponge in a *jar of wine vinegar . . . and lifted it to Jesus' lips. When he had received the drink . . . he bowed his head and gave up his spirit* (vv. 29-30).

The Greek word used by Matthew, Mark, and John for this later drink is *oxous,* literally meaning vinegar. It consisted of vinegar mixed with wine, a sour drink which retarded thirst. Wine vinegar was drunk by soldiers and ordinary people.[65] It was customary for the soldiers guarding the crucified to maintain provisions for themselves, i.e., food and drink. The wine vinegar was contained in a large jar nearby (John 19:29).

Like John, Luke reports only one drink offered to Jesus at Golgotha

---

65. Marshall, *Luke,* 870.

(Luke 23:36). It is the same wine vinegar (*oxous*) as the second drink reported by Matthew and Mark to have been offered to the Lord as he hung on the cross. The mocking that accompanies Luke's account of this drink corresponds to that of the later drink recorded by the other Synoptists (Matt. 27:49; Mark 15:36; Luke 23:36-37). If identical with it, Jesus was offered a total of two drinks at Golgotha, one immediately before the cross, which was refused, and one on the cross after the three hours of darkness, which was drunk. However, while Luke also locates this drink incident after the crucifixion, in contrast to the other Synoptists he places it before the three hours of darkness, well before Jesus' death. Luke's placement of this drink offer makes it difficult to tell whether Jesus was offered two or three drinks at Golgotha, the latter appearing in *The Gospels Interwoven*. If two, Luke's account represents a chronological dislocation in which Luke has thematically connected the drink offer with the earlier taunts of the rulers and soldiers (Luke 23:35-37). If three, there is no indication that Jesus received this second drink, which may have been an ungenuine offer due to the associated taunts. Otherwise, it was necessary for someone to lift a soaked sponge up on a stick, as in John 19:29.[66]

In conclusion, whether Jesus was offered two or three drinks at Golgotha, surely he drank only one drink, the wine vinegar offered to him as he hung on the cross immediately before he died.

23. What year was Jesus crucified? How old was Jesus when he died?

The Scriptures do not specify Jesus' age at his death. Following the Lord's baptism by John, Luke 3:23 declares, *Now Jesus himself was about thirty years old when he began his ministry.* Jesus' age at his death, therefore, has been calculated by adding the supposed length of time of his public ministry to Luke's figure of thirty years. The length of Jesus' public ministry has traditionally been determined by the number of Passovers, as recorded in John's Gospel, which Jesus attended at Jerusalem following his baptism. Some commentators believe that John records three Passovers, with John 5:1 referring not to a Passover but either a Feast of Dedication or of Purim. Jesus' public ministry, then, would have lasted about two and a half years, making Jesus about 32½ years of age when he died. However, the prevailing view among scholars has always been that John 5:1 was a Passover, which would make Jesus about 33½ years old when he died. This fits with a birthdate between 5 and 4 B.C. if Jesus died in A.D. 30.

It has been well established from a comparison of Roman records and the Gospels that Jesus was born between 6 and 4 B.C. Without going into detail, it has been somewhat established from astronomy, secular history

---

66. Meyer (*Mark and Luke*, 566) thinks so.

and the Gospels that Jesus died in A.D. 30. However, there continues to exist some diversity of opinion, a few scholars opting for A.D. 33.[67]

24. Did Mary, the mother of Jesus, and Mary Magdalene stand near the cross or watch from a distance?

Matthew 27:55, Mark 15:40, and Luke 23:49 show that the women who were disciples of Jesus, among them Mary Magdalene, watched the crucifixion *from a distance.* But John 19:25 says that Mary Magdalene stood *near the cross* with Mary, Jesus' mother, when Jesus spoke from the cross to his mother and the Apostle John. Augustine proposed the logical solution that since the Synoptists mention the women after Jesus died, they had by then somewhat removed themselves from the gruesome sight.[68] Tradition maintains that soon after Jesus spoke to John about his mother's care, John escorted Mary to a house, perhaps his own. If so, Jesus' mother did not remain with the other women in the vicinity of the cross after Jesus died.

25. Was Jesus' body wrapped with a single linen cloth or with strips of linen?

Matthew seems to indicate that Jesus' body was wrapped in a single clean linen cloth (Matt. 27:59), yet John 19:40 reads *strips of linen.* Mark simply relates *some linen cloth* (Mark 15:46) while Luke is even less specific with *linen cloth* (Luke 23:53). G.E. Ladd cites Edersheim as representing the traditional view, then amplifies:

> The traditional harmonization is that the body was first wrapped in a shroud after being taken down from the cross; but before being left in the tomb, the shroud was torn into strips which were used to bind the body, limb by limb, between layers of myrrh and aloes. Possibly the body was first wrapped in a shroud and then strips of cloth were wound around the shrouded body.[69]

It is certain that the body was wrapped in strips of linen with myrrh and aloes, the latter weighing *about seventy-five pounds* (John 19:39). Such a large amount of spices must have required a considerable amount of linen cloth, suggesting that Edersheim's addition to the traditional solution is the correct one: Jesus' body was first wrapped in a large linen cloth, after which many linen strips were soaked with the spices and wound about the corpse.

---

67. For the minority view that Jesus was crucified in A.D. 33 rather than A.D. 30, see Harold Hoehner, *Herod Antipas* (Cambridge: University Press, 1967).
68. Augustine, *Harmony*, 6:207.
69. George Eldon Ladd, *I Believe in the Resurrection of Jesus* (Grand Rapids: Eerdmans, 1975), 85.

CHAPTER SIXTEEN
RESURRECTION, APPEARANCES, AND ASCENSION

1. Can the NT accounts of the resurrection of Jesus be harmonized?

Several twentieth-century biblical scholars claim that the resurrection accounts of Jesus in the Gospels cannot be reconciled. E. Brunner asserts, "The sources contradict one another, and only a harmonizing process which is not too much concerned about the truth, could patch up a fairly connected account of the events."[1] F.C. Burkitt affirms the bodily resurrection of Jesus, yet comments, "There are many variations and discrepancies, but all the Gospels agree in the main facts."[2] H.A.W. Meyer agrees, while stating it more boldly,

> In no section of evangelical history have harmonists, with their artificial mosaic work, been compelled to expend more labour, and with less success, than in the section on the resurrection. The adjustment of the differences between John and the Synoptics, as also between the latter amongst themselves, is impossible, but the grand fact itself and the chief traits of the history stand all the more firmly.[3]

The purpose of these resurrection notes is to acquaint the reader with the apparent discrepancies and to offer possible solutions, especially those proposed by leading biblical commentators. The author's position is that the Gospel accounts of the resurrection of Jesus Christ do not conflict and can be harmonized by God, but that men and women may lack sufficient information or insight to be able to do so. Unwarranted, forced harmonizations of the resurrection accounts do more harm than good for the testimony of Jesus. Thus, it behooves the student of the resurrection of Christ to exercise caution in making dogmatic harmonizations.

---

1. Cited by Wenham, *Easter Enigma*, 10.
2. Cited by Orr, *The Resurrection of Jesus* (London: Stoughton & Hodder, 1908), 59.
3. Meyer, *John*, 523.

Three things were well accepted by biblical scholars until the last century: (1) the resurrection of Jesus, (2) the historicity of the Gospel accounts of his resurrection, and (3) the necessity of faith in the resurrection of Jesus for salvation. James Orr observes that "the Resurrection of Jesus was regarded as an immovable cornerstone of Christianity," adding that it was only challenged from outside the faith, but recently has been eroded from within.[4] Leading Anglican scholar, Bishop J.A.T. Robinson, is an example of those who regard the resurrection of Jesus as unimportant. Rudolf Bultmann has been the leading biblical form critic, as well as the most influential theologian, in this century. He flatly asserts, "A historical fact which involves a resurrection from the dead is utterly inconceivable."[5]

Historic Christianity has always maintained that belief in the bodily resurrection of Jesus is an absolute necessity for salvation. The Apostle Paul clearly states the Gospel in 1 Corinthians 15:2-5:

> By this gospel you are saved, . . . that Christ died for our sins according to the Scriptures, that he was buried, that he was raised on the third day according to the Scriptures, and that he appeared to [many].

The faith of Jesus Christ stands or falls on his bodily resurrection:

> And if Christ has not been raised, our preaching is useless and so is your faith. . . . And if Christ has not been raised, your faith is futile; you are still in your sins. . . . But Christ has indeed been raised from the dead (1 Cor. 15:14, 17, 20).

It behooves every student of the Bible to examine carefully the most crucial testimony of the Christian faith—the events surrounding the resurrection of Jesus. The primary evidences are the empty tomb and the resurrection appearances of Jesus. A superficial comparison of the Gospels leaves the impression of many discrepancies. However, several of these differences exemplify a common feature of independent reporting, and provide evidence of the absence of collusion. In some cases one record supplements others. Several differences can be attributed to each writer's unique purpose in that portion of his narrative. Some questions cannot be answered with certainty due to a lack of information. But it will become evident that *if any one chooses to do God's will, he will find out whether my* [Jesus'] *teaching comes from God* or not (John 7:17). This includes Jesus' predictions about his resurrection, as well as the records of his post-resurrection appearances. *And without faith it is impossible to please God*

---

4. Orr, *Resurrection*, 9.
5. Cited in Orr, *Resurrection*, 11.

(Heb. 11:6). Admittedly, there were no human witnesses of Jesus' resurrection itself.[6] It must be accepted by faith. Yet faith in the resurrection of Jesus rests on substantial historical evidence, to which we now turn.

2. When Mary Magdalene first visited the tomb on Easter morning, was she alone or with the other women? If with others, why did John mention only that Mary Magdalene went to the tomb?

John mentions only Mary Magdalene as going to the tomb early Sunday morning (John 20:1). Since John does not mention any other women who visited the tomb, some commentators maintain that Mary Magdalene went there alone, most of them proposing that she visited the tomb before the other women did. The following evidence reveals that Mary Magdalene accompanied others on her first visit to the tomb that resurrection morning.

a. It is unlikely that a woman would go alone in the darkness of morning to a grave outside the city wall.

b. John relates that Mary Magdalene ran to tell Peter and John the news, saying, *We don't know where they have put him* (v. 2). By saying *we*, she indicates others accompanied her during her first visit to the tomb.

c. The Synoptists agree that one or more women accompanied Mary Magdalene to the tomb early that morning (Matt. 28:1; Mark 16:1; Luke 24:1, 10).

John does not state that Mary Magdalene attended the tomb alone her first time Sunday morning, nor does his account preclude the possibility of others accompanying her. Many commentators agree that John omits mention of the other women because it does not relate to his narrative that follows. B.F. Westcott no doubt correctly assesses that John recounts from his own experience just those incidents which relate to him personally and omits several details contained in the earlier written Synoptics, already known to his readers.[7]

3. In order to anoint Jesus' body, did the women buy and prepare spices before the Sabbath or afterward?

Luke relates that the women *saw the tomb and how his body was laid in it. Then they went home and prepared spices and perfumes. But they rested on the*

---

6. Contemporary scholars often remark that no one witnessed the Resurrection (e.g., Ladd, *Resurrection*, 94). Though usually not stated, this comment presumably refers only to human beings. Though some would consider the point irrelevant, perhaps the two angels witnessed the resurrection; Cranfield (*Mark*, 466) unequivocally maintains that they did.

7. Westcott, *John: Authorized Version*, 287.

Sabbath (Luke 23:55-56). Mark, however, claims that *when the Sabbath was over* the women *bought spices so that they might go to anoint Jesus' body* (Mark 16:1). The women went home and quickly prepared the spices and perfumes they already had on hand in order to begin the Sabbath rest at 6 P.M. Friday evening. Apparently, soon after the Sabbath, i.e., after 6 P.M. Saturday, they bought more spices to add to what they had already prepared. They took them on their way to the tomb Sunday morning to anoint the body of Jesus. Some commentators, however, suppose that the women bought the additional spices on their way to the tomb Sunday morning. The following reasons indicate otherwise:

a. Mark's order of events is: *When the Sabbath was over the women bought spices and very early on the first day of the week . . . they were on their way to the tomb* (Mark 16:1-2). This suggests that they bought the spices Saturday evening, soon after the completion of the Sabbath at 6 P.M.[8] If they bought them Sunday morning, Mark surely would have placed their buying of the spices after their departure for the tomb, not before.

b. After purchasing the additional spices, the women would have needed to prepare them at home. They probably would not have done this if they were already on their way to the tomb.

c. It is unlikely that shops selling spices would be open at 6 A.M. or earlier.

4. If Jesus' body had already been anointed, the tomb sealed and a Roman guard posted there, why did the women visit the tomb to anoint the body?

The Synoptists record that the women saw how Joseph and Nicodemus wrapped the body of Jesus in linen and laid it in the tomb (Matt. 27:61; Mark 15:47; Luke 23:55). John adds that the men wrapped it with myrrh and aloes in strips of linen (John 19:39-40). While the women presumably saw this too, they bought and prepared *spices and perfumes*, i.e., aromatic oils (Mark 16:1; Luke 23:56–24:1) with which to anoint the body as an addition to the Jewish burial customs performed by Joseph and Nicodemus. They saw Joseph roll the stone in place (Matt. 27:60). He no doubt had Nicodemus' assistance for this too, or the several women would not have later been concerned about their inability to remove a stone placed by one man.

On the way to the tomb Easter morning, the women questioned among themselves who would roll away the stone (Mark 16:3). Apparently they were unaware that the day after the burial, the grave had been sealed and a

---

8. B.F. Westcott, *The Gospel According to St. John: The Greek Text with Introduction and Notes*, 2 vols. (rep. Grand Rapids: Eerdmans, 1954), 2:335.

Roman guard posted there. Tampering with sealed graves was a serious offense. The following are some reasons that may be adduced for the women's visit to the tomb that Easter morning:

a. They went to complete the previously hurried and partially completed burial, ignorant of the sealed tomb and Roman guard.

b. It was Jewish custom. Matthew writes only that they *went to look at the tomb* (Matt. 28:1). D.A. Carson suggests Matthew's brief account "may reflect an ancient Jewish tradition that says Jews visited the tomb of the deceased till the third day to ensure that the party was truly dead."⁹ This was due to the common, though false belief, that the spirit of the body hovered above it for three days before departing. It was believed that Jewish burial customs prevented bodily corruption for three days, since on the fourth day the body began to stink (e.g., see John 11:39). The corruption would not have been accelerated by hot weather as some have supposed, since *it was cold* when Peter stood warming himself before the fire while he denied the Lord (John 18:18).¹⁰

c. It was also an ancient custom for friends and relatives of the deceased to visit the gravesite to mourn and weep (Gen. 50:3-4; John 11:31-35), which is what John reports that Mary Magdalene did when she visited the tomb the second time that day (John 20:11). Some evidence exists from Jewish writings of the third century that "mourning was at its height on the third day," which may have been the reason the women went to the tomb that day.¹¹

d. It was a demonstration of piety. Their purpose for anointing the body "is not incredible, since love often prompts people to do what from a practical point of view is useless."¹²

5. Did the women leave for the tomb during darkness or after sunrise?

John records that *while it was still dark, Mary Magdalene went to the tomb* (John 20:1). However, Mark claims that *just after sunrise* the women *were on their way to the tomb* (Mark 16:2). It is at this time that Mark quotes their question about removing the stone, asked just before they arrived at the tomb to see the stone already removed. What John and Mark together indicate is that at least one of the women, Mary Magdalene, started for the tomb during darkness, but that the sun had already risen by the time the women approached the tomb.

Ample evidence indicates that at least some of the women walked a

9. Carson, *Matthew*, 8:588.
10. Brown, *John (xiii-xxi)*, 982. Brown states, "It can be quite cool in mountainous Jerusalem in early spring."
11. Ibid.
12. Cranfield, *Mark*, 464.

considerable distance from their place of lodging to the tomb. It is generally believed that some started from Bethany, that town where Jesus had lodged at least some of his nights during Passion Week. *Bethany was less than two miles from Jerusalem* (John 11:18), to the southeast. The majority of scholars now accept the location of Jesus' tomb at or near the present Church of the Holy Sepulchre, located on the north side of the Old City of Jerusalem, outside what was at that time the outer wall of the city. The direct road from Bethany to the tomb was about two and one-third miles long, requiring at least a 45-minute walk. John Wenham proposes that *Mary Magdalene and the other Mary* (Matt. 28:1) started from Bethany but did not go directly to the tomb. They circled back around the south side of the city wall to the Apostle John's house in Jerusalem, where they were joined by John's mother, Salome, then proceeded to the tomb.[13] If so, this adds approximately another mile or more to their trip—a total of between three and four miles. This lengthy distance required for some of the women to travel to the tomb further enhances the possibility that they started during darkness and neared the tomb after sunrise.

6. Did the women first see the angel(s) outside or inside the tomb?

Matthew explains that *an angel of the Lord came down from heaven and, going to the tomb, rolled back the stone and sat on it* (Matt. 28:2).[14] When Matthew resumes the narrative with the angel and the women, some assume that their initial meeting was outside the tomb with the angel sitting on the tombstone. However, Mark states that when the women first arrived at the tomb, *they saw that the stone, which was very large, had been rolled away. As they entered the tomb, they saw a young man dressed in a white robe* (Mark 16:4-5). He is assumed to be one of the two angels mentioned by Luke and John. Mark and Luke (Luke 24:2-4) assure us that the women did not see an angel sitting on the gravestone, or any other angel, until they entered the tomb. Matthew therefore has passed over what transpired from the time of the angel's sitting on the stone to his initial appearance to the women inside the tomb. The four Evangelists supplement each others' accounts, and Matthew is no exception. Only Matthew reports the posting of the guard at the tomb (Matt. 27:62-66), the guards' later fainting at the sight of the angel, their departure to tell the authorities, and their being bribed to

13. Wenham, *Easter Enigma*, 82. Tradition has it that Zebedee and Salome, the parents of the Apostles James and John, by now lived in Capernaum but owned a second house in Jerusalem. Wenham supposes that it was kept because of Zebedee's need to market fish in Jerusalem.
14. The angel could not have sat on a tombstone that was in the shape of a wheel, as some have assumed, since it would have been rolled along a groove, adjacent to the outer wall or a cut inside the wall. Wheel gravestones were very uncommon.

spread the false rumor of the stolen body (Matt. 28:4, 11-15). Matthew's mention of the guards' departure (Matt. 28:11) after his account of the departure of the women is probably a chronological dislocation, recapitulating what happened before the women arrived.

Had the women first encountered the angel(s) outside the tomb, they might have been frightened away and not entered to discover the missing body.[15] Matthew's angel said to the women, *Come and see the place where he lay* (v. 6). Mark thus clarifies that it was from inside the tomb that the angel so directed the women, who were also by then inside (Mark 16:5-6). It must be concluded that Matthew does not contradict what the other Gospels affirm: the other women entered the tomb, where they first encountered the angels.

Matthew has omitted certain details, e.g., the arrival of the women, their entry into the tomb, and their first sight of the angel(s), perhaps for his characteristic purpose of brevity. Because Matthew has omitted details regarding the guards, one might suppose that the unconscious guards lay prostrate before the entrance to the tomb as the women approached. Instead, the guards must have already awakened and left before the women arrived. Had the guards been present, it would surely have been reported by the Evangelists. The point has often been made that each Evangelist's omission of certain details provided by others is evidence for a lack of collaboration between the writers, further establishing the historical accuracy of their Gospels.

The scenario of events early that Sunday morning at the tomb would appear to be as follows:

a. *There was a violent earthquake* (Matt. 28:2).

b. *An angel . . . came down from heaven . . . and rolled back the stone and sat on it* (v. 2).

c. The guards saw him, shook, and fainted (vv. 3-4).

d. The guards awoke and went to tell the authorities (v. 11).

e. The women, including Mary Magdalene, arrived and entered the tomb (Luke 24:3). Mary Magdalene probably left before hearing the angels' message. (See EN 16:11.)

f. The women searched the tomb (Luke 24:3), saw, and heard the angels (Mark 16:5-6).

7. Was there one man or one angel at the tomb, or were there two men or two angels?

Matthew 28:2 mentions only one *angel of the Lord*, which presumably was

---

15. Wenham, *Easter Enigma*, 86. Wenham also suggests that at first the angel sat on the stone to frighten away the guards.

the same angel as Mark's *a young man dressed in a white robe* (Mark 16:5). Angels often appeared as men (cf. Gen. 18:2 with 19:1) and were often dressed in white that sometimes shone brightly (cf. Luke 24:4 and John 20:12 with Acts 1:10). It appears that the guards saw the angel sitting on the stone, whereas the women later saw him inside the tomb. The mention of one angel by Matthew and Mark in no way excludes the possibility of another angel having been present.[16] Luke maintains that there were *two men in clothes that gleamed like lightning* (Luke 24:4). He later unequivocably identifies the men as angels (v. 23), presumably including the angel mentioned by Matthew and Mark. Luke's two angels were likely the same *two angels* to whom Mary Magdalene later spoke on her second visit to the tomb that day (John 20:12). The difference in number of angels reported by the Evangelists can be accounted for by any one of the following reasons, listed in descending order of probability:

a. One angel was the primary spokesman for the two. This is the most likely reason two Synoptists mention only one angel.

b. Luke credits to the angels additional statements not found in the other Synoptics. It is therefore possible that one of the angels spoke the words recorded by Matthew and Mark, while the other angel spoke the additional words recorded by Luke, a possible reason Luke includes mention of both angels, whereas Matthew and Mark do not.

c. If Matthew and Mark make use of written or oral reports (e.g., from the women), perhaps these reports mentioned only one angel.

8. Were the angels in the tomb sitting or standing when the women first saw them?

Mark 16:5 relates that when the women *entered the tomb, they saw a young man dressed in a white robe sitting on the right side*. Mark's *young man* gave the same message to the women as Matthew's angel, thus identifying the *young man* as an angel. According to Luke 24:3-4, when the women entered the tomb *they did not find the body of the Lord Jesus. While they were wondering about this, suddenly two men in clothes that gleamed like lightning stood beside them*. Mark says the angel was *sitting* and Luke claims the *two men* (*angels* in Luke 24:23) were standing. John Wenham attempts to resolve the difficulty by appealing to a different meaning for the Greek word, here translated *stood* in Luke:

---

16. Similar omissions have already occurred in the Gospels, as when Matthew mentions two demoniacs at Gadara (Matt. 8:28), two blind men at Jericho (Matt. 20:30), and two donkeys on Palm Sunday (Matt. 21:2), whereas the other two Synoptists write of only one.

The translation "stood by," which would bring Luke into contradiction with Mark's "sitting," cannot be insisted on. The word is frequently used meaning "to appear to," often implying suddenness.[17]

On the other hand, if the angels were standing, it is not inconceivable that this can be reconciled with Mark's account of one angel sitting. Mark relates that soon after entering the tomb, the women saw an angel sitting. Perhaps he was sitting at one end (Mark 16:5: *the right side*) of a ledge hewn in the wall of the limestone cave where Jesus' body was laid. When Mary Magdalene later visited the tomb a second time that day, she *saw two angels in white, seated where Jesus' body had been, one at the head and the other at the foot* (John 20:11-12). Probably these two angels recorded by John were seated in the same places earlier, when the other women first entered the tomb to search for the body. It was very dark, and many tombs in Israel had more than one chamber. It is possible that some of the women saw the sitting angel while others had their backs turned. As soon as one or more of the women saw the sitting angel, he may have risen as the others turned to see. In a matter of seconds, all the women could have then seen the two angels, who *gleamed like lightning* (Luke 24:4), standing beside them. More particularly, the order of events may have been as follows:

a. The women entered the tomb, did not find the body, and stood pondering the circumstances.

b. The first angel became visible to some of the women. He was *sitting on the right side* (Mark 16:5), probably next to where Jesus' body had lain.

c. The angel stood up to invite the women to take a closer look at the place where the body had lain (Matt. 28:6; Mark 16:6).

d. As he stood up, the other standing angel appeared. This too could have taken only a few seconds. Thus, Luke's account of the two angels seeming to appear at the same time would be acceptably accurate reporting.

9. Did the angel conclude his announcement to the women by saying he had told them, or that Jesus had told them?

Matthew 28:7c states that the angel concluded his message to the women by saying, *Now I have told you.* But Mark 16:7c relates that the angel's message concluded with a reminder of what Jesus had earlier said, or *just as he told you.* Matthew's Greek word for *I have told* is *eipon*; Mark's Greek word for *he told* is *eipen.* Due to a difference of only one letter between the two words, and these two letters being similar in appearance in Greek, a few commentators believe that Matthew's word is a scribal error. If so, the NIV rendering would likely be, "Now he told you," which would not make

---

17. Wenham, *Easter Enigma*, 85-86.

sense. The Greek word translated *Now* in Matthew, however, is "Behold" in the NASB.[18] If Matthew has a scribal error, using the "Behold" in the NASB renders the sensible reading, "Behold, he told you."

Ascribing an apparent discrepancy to a scribal error, however, is the easy way out of a harmonizing difficulty, and almost surely the incorrect one here. Both readings are included in *The Gospels Interwoven*. Calvin supports the inclusion of both in his following explanation of the angel's words, *I have told you*: "But it does not come from himself as if he were the first author, but he underlines Christ's promise. So in Mark's account he simply recalls Christ's words to their minds."[19] Mark's phrase, *"just as he told you,"* therefore recalls Jesus' repeated prediction to his disciples of his death and resurrection, especially his later addition that *I will go ahead of you into Galilee* (Matt. 26:32; Mark 14:28; see also Luke's addition about Galilee in Luke 24:6; cf. 9:44 with Matt. 17:22-23 and Mark 9:30-31). Therefore the angel's words *just as he told you* were intended to remind the disciples of what Jesus had previously told them about his death and resurrection. The angel said *Now I have told you* to acknowledge to the women that he had accomplished his mission in explaining to them the empty tomb and delivering the message about meeting Jesus in Galilee.

10. Were the women afraid or joyful when they hurried off to tell the disciples of the empty tomb?

After the angelic announcement inside the tomb, Mark 16:8 relates, *Trembling and bewildered, the women went out and fled from the tomb. They said nothing to anyone, because they were afraid.* On the other hand, Matthew 28:8 reads, *So the women hurried away from the tomb, afraid yet filled with joy, and ran to tell his disciples.* Both Synoptists claim that the women left the tomb afraid. The fact that only Matthew records that they were also filled with joy cannot seriously be considered a discrepancy. It is conceivable that the women could have experienced fear and joy simultaneously. H.A.W. Meyer quotes Euthymius Zigabenus: "With fear, because of the incredible things which they saw; with joy, because of the good news which they heard."[20]

---

18. Bauer-Arndt-Gingrich-Danker, *Lexicon*, 371. The Greek word *idou* can be variously translated, e.g., "now," "behold," "remember." It is rendered "Lo" in the RSV.
19. Calvin, *Harmony/Gospels*, 3:225.
20. Meyer, *Matthew*, 522.

11. Did Mary Magdalene enter the tomb and hear the angel's announcement on her first visit there Easter morning or not? What is the order of events surrounding Mary Magdalene's two visits to the tomb?

All three Synoptists appear to indicate that on her first visit to the tomb Easter morning, Mary Magdalene entered with the other women, saw the angel(s) and heard their announcement that Jesus was risen (cf. Matt. 28:1 with vv. 5-7; cf. Mark 16:1 with vv. 5-7; cf. Luke 24:10 with vv. 3-7). Luke relates that Mary Magdalene and the other women returned and *told all these things to the Eleven and to all the others . . . but they did not believe the women* (Luke 24:10-11). Yet John quotes Mary Magdalene as first telling Peter and himself, *"They have taken the Lord out of the tomb, and we don't know where they have put him"* (John 20:2), as if she never heard the angels' announcement. It is possible that Mary Magdalene failed to believe the announcement of the angels, though previously entering the tomb to see and hear them. Perhaps this is indicated by the report of the two disciples returning from Emmaus. They recounted that their women *had seen a vision of angels* (Luke 24:23). This may indicate that the women, including Mary Magdalene, were uncertain whether their experience was a vision or an actual angelic encounter, as the Synoptists clearly present. If so, this suggests that they too were slow to believe what the angels announced.

On the other hand, John records only that *Mary Magdalene went to the tomb and saw that the stone had been removed from the entrance. So she came running to Simon Peter* (John 20:1-2). Many commentators conclude that Mary Magdalene left the tomb without entering it with the others to see the angels and hear their announcement. B.F. Westcott claims that from John's Gospel alone "it is clear that she had no vision of angels before she returned, and received no message" from the angels.[21] That she saw no angels on her first visit to the tomb that morning is indicated by what appears to be her first sight of them on her second visit (John 20:12-13). According to John's account, therefore, Mary Magdalene seems to have left the vicinity of the tomb immediately after she saw the removed tombstone, or after the women, stooping to peer into the tomb or maybe even entering it, discovered the body was missing. She certainly had left before the angels appeared and made their announcement.

Some expositors presume that upon initially seeing the removed tombstone, and before entering the tomb, the women discussed among themselves which one of them should run to tell Peter and John, and that Mary Magdelene was chosen because of her youth. But this is only conjecture.

But what of the Synoptists' accounts? Westcott singles out Matthew and explains, "The main difficulties are due to the extreme compression of St. Matthew's narrative, in which there is no clear distinction of points of

---

21. Westcott, *John: Greek Text*, 2:336.

time."[22] As for Luke, perhaps he only intends Luke 24:9-10 to identify those women who returned from the tomb to tell the disciples, with Mary Magdalene not included among those who saw and heard the angels (vv. 1-7).[23] In more apparent conflict with John, Mark seems to include Mary Magdalene among those women who *entered the tomb* (Mark 16:5), saw, and heard the angel(s).

The author of these notes does not know how this difficulty is to be resolved, i.e., whether Mary Magdalene actually saw and heard the angels on her first visit to the tomb or not. The order of events surrounding Mary Magdalene's two visits to the tomb that first Sunday morning appears to have been as follows, though tentatively offered concerning her first visit:

a. Mary Magdalene, apparently accompanied by Mary the mother of James (Matt. 28:1; Mark 16:1), left Bethany and started for the tomb.

b. The other women (Mark 16:1; Luke 24:1, 10) either joined the two Marys along the way or met them at the tomb, making a total of at least five women and perhaps more.

c. The women saw that the stone was removed (Mark 16:4; Luke 24:2; John 20:1).

d. Mary Magdalene either left the tomb at this time only knowing that the body was missing (John 20:2) or remained to enter with the others and see and hear the angels' announcement that Jesus was risen.

e. The women entered the tomb, searched for the missing body, saw and heard the angels (Mark 16:5-7; Luke 24:3-7).

f. The women fled from the tomb.

g. Mary Magdalene arrived first to tell Peter and John of the missing body (John 20:2).

h. The women arrived and *told all these things to the Eleven and to all the others* (Luke 24:9), but the men *did not believe the women* (v. 11).

i. Peter and John ran to the tomb to discover the missing body (Luke 24:12; John 20:3-4), with Mary Magdalene apparently following them from well behind (John 20:10-11).

j. Mary Magdalene arrived at the tomb for the second time that morning (v. 11) after Peter and John left for their homes (v. 10).

k. Mary Magdalene looked into the tomb and spoke with the two angels (John 20:11-13).

l. Mary Magdalene saw and spoke with Jesus (John 20:14-17). This was Jesus' first resurrection appearance if Mark 16:9 is authentic.[24]

---

22. Ibid., 2:337.
23. The claim of the two disciples from Emmaus need not be understood *by our women* (Luke 24:22-23) to include the presumably unmarried Mary Magdalene, but probably the wives of these two disciples and perhaps other women as well.
24. Mark 16:9-20 is omitted in the most reliable MSS, as indicated by the note in the NIV text.

m. Mary Magdalene went to tell the disciples she had seen the Lord and what he had said (Mark 16:10; John 20:18).

12. Who was the other disciple whom Mary Magdalene told about the empty tomb and who outran Peter there?

The other disciple (John 20:2, 4, 8) was the Apostle John, who uses a modest writer's technique to avoid reference to himself.

13. How many women visited Jesus' tomb on Easter morning? Why does each Evangelist report a different number of women who visited the tomb?

John names only one woman who visited the tomb on Easter morning: *Mary Magdalene* (John 20:1). Matthew mentions two women, adding *and the other Mary*, i.e., *the mother of James and Joseph* (cf. Matt. 27:56 with 28:1). To these two, Mark adds *Salome* (Mark 16:1), who was probably the mother of the Apostles James and John (cf. Matt. 27:56 with Mark 15:40 and 16:1). If Salome is included, Luke indicates that there were a minimum of five: *Mary Magdalene, Joanna, Mary the mother of James, and the others with them* (Luke 24:10). The Evangelists do not give the exact number of women that visited the tomb together Easter morning. The following points suggest why the Evangelists vary in recounting the number of women who visited the tomb:

a. Matthew probably mentions only the two Marys because he previously names only them as witnesses of the burial performed Friday evening by Joseph and Nicodemus (Matt. 27:61). Yet Matthew also identifies Salome, *the mother of Zebedee's sons* (cf. Matt. 27:56 with Mark 15:40 and 16:1), as among those women from Galilee who witnessed Jesus' crucifixion. Why would he exclude Salome, despite the fact that Mark includes Salome among those who watched the burial and accompanied the two Marys to the tomb Sunday? If Wenham is correct, that only these two Marys (cf. Matt. 28:1 with Mark 16:1) left from Bethany *while it was still dark* (John 20:1),[25] this would explain why Matthew excludes mention of Salome and others. In identifying the travelers, Matthew takes up with the beginning of the trip to the tomb (Matt. 28:1: *at dawn*) while Mark mentions only a later part of the trip, i.e., *just after sunrise, they were on their way to the tomb* (Mark 16:2). Thus the others joined the two Marys later in the trip and Matthew does not identify these later additions to the group.

---

25. Wenham, *Easter Enigma*, 81-83.

b. Mark names three women because it was they who bought spices Saturday night and, *just after sunrise, . . . were on their way to the tomb* (Mark 16:2).

c. Each writer is not exclusive in his identification of those women who attended the tomb. In identifying only Mary Magdalene, John does not say that she first visited the tomb alone. For John to quote Mary Magdalene as saying *we* (John 20:2) proves that other women accompanied her that first visit. (See EN 16:2.)

In summary, no writer claims to give a comprehensive list of the women.

14. Did the risen Jesus appear to the other women on their way to tell the apostles of the empty tomb or afterwards? What was the order of events on that Easter Sunday?

Only Matthew 28:9 records that Jesus *met them,* i.e., the women, following their visit to the tomb Sunday morning. If Matthew means to include Mary Magdalene among these women whom Jesus met, this would conflict with John's account that Jesus appeared to her alone on her second visit to the tomb that day (John 20:11-18), as well as with the disputed ending of Mark. (Mark 16:9-20 has questionable MS authority.) The opening verse, Mark 16:9, states that Jesus *appeared first to Mary Magdalene.*[26] Though considered by some critics as a harmonizing expedient, it is generally regarded by harmonists that Mary Magdalene was no longer present with these women when Jesus met them, since she had fled the tomb alone to find and tell Peter of the missing body. If so, Matthew's *them* would not include Mary Magdalene among the women in Matthew 28:9, thereby indicating that other women were present together at the tomb besides the two Marys mentioned in Matthew 28:1.

Perhaps the more formidable problem raised by Matthew 28:9 is that Matthew seems to indicate that Jesus appeared to the women soon following their exit from the tomb early that Sunday morning while they were on their way to tell the disciples of the empty tomb. But Luke 24:9 reads, *When they came back from the tomb, they told all these things to the Eleven,* indicating that the women first told the disciples only of the empty tomb and the angel's announcement (vv. 4-8), not that they had seen the Lord Jesus. This is further corroborated by the two disciples walking to Emmaus, when they told Jesus that *some of our women amazed us. They went to the tomb early this morning but didn't find his body. They came and told us that they*

---

26. Some commentators (e.g., Ladd, *Resurrection,* 91-93) maintain that Matthew indicates the other women saw Jesus first, before Mary Magdalene, suggesting that the problem emerging from Mark 16:9 is evidence that Mark's long ending (Mark 16:9-20) is noncanonical.

had seen a vision of angels, who said he was alive (Luke 24:22-23). Had the women seen Jesus before their initial return to the disciples that morning, these two disciples would not have failed to report this most important event. Here is conclusive evidence that the women did not see Jesus until after they first reported the empty tomb to the disciples. Furthermore, Luke includes Mary Magdalene among the women who told the disciples of the empty tomb (v. 10). If Jesus had already appeared to her with the other women, Mary's failure to recognize him at the later appearance to her alone that day (John 20:10-18) would be inexplicable.

Therefore, it is certain that a time gap exists between Matthew 28:8 and v. 9, into which are inserted certain events recorded in the other Gospels. The scenario of events on that Easter Sunday would be as follows:

a. The women saw the removed stone and first looked into the empty tomb (Matt. 28:1; Luke 24:3).

b. Mary Magdalene rushed off to tell Peter and John of the empty tomb, apparently before any of them entered it to see and hear the angels, or at least before the angels' appearance (John 20:1-2).

c. The other women who remained, entered the tomb, saw, and heard the angels, who announced that Jesus was risen and instructed them to go tell the disciples (Matt. 28:5-7; Mark 16:5-7; Luke 24:4-7).

d. The women went to tell the disciples (Matt. 28:8).

e. Mary Magdalene arrived first to tell Peter and John of the empty tomb (John 20:2).

f. The other women arrived and told the other disciples of the empty tomb and of the angels' announcement that Jesus was risen and would meet his disciples in Galilee (Luke 24:9), all of which they did not believe (Luke 24:11, 25).

g. Peter and John ran to the tomb to discover the body missing, then returned to their homes (John 20:3-10).

h. Mary Magdalene arrived at the tomb a second time that day. Here, Jesus made his first appearance, which was to Mary Magdalene alone (Mark 16:9; John 20:11-16).

i. He appeared to the other women (Matt. 28:9).

j. He appeared to Peter (Luke 24:34; 1 Cor. 15:5).

k. He appeared to the two disciples on the road to Emmaus (Mark 16:12; Luke 24:13-35).

The order of these last three appearances (i, j, and k) is uncertain.

l. Finally he appeared to the gathering of the disciples at Jerusalem that first Sunday evening (Mark 16:14; Luke 24:36-43; John 20:19-23).

15. Why did Jesus give instructions for his disciples to go to Galilee to meet him since he met them that evening in Jerusalem?

Matthew records the instruction for the disciples to go to Galilee to meet

Jesus (Mark 28:10). The only resurrection appearance to *the eleven disciples* that Matthew records is in Galilee (Matt. 28:16-17). From Matthew's account alone, it seems that Jesus first appeared to his gathered disciples in Galilee. Yet the other three Evangelists record that Jesus appeared to *the Eleven* in Jerusalem on that first Easter evening (Mark 16:14; Luke 24:33, 36; John 20:19).

A surprising number of commentators find difficulty with the instruction to go to Galilee. Calvin thought the disciples should have "set out immediately for Galilee, on the same day as he commanded," as if they did not follow his instructions soon enough.[27] Jesus could not have meant for the disciples to go immediately to Galilee that first Sunday. If the Lord intended to meet them that evening, as he in fact did in Jerusalem, there was insufficient time for them to travel over sixty miles to Galilee, about a two- or three-day journey.

Although only Jesus himself actually commanded the disciples to go to Galilee (Matt. 28:10), the angels at the tomb told the women that his disciples would see him in Galilee (Mark 16:7), which some commentators also consider as an instruction to go. T.W. Manson supposes that the women failed to deliver the message about going to Galilee due to fear. "To return to Galilee would be fatal, with [Herod] Antipas waiting there to liquidate the remnant of the Nazarene movement."[28] However, it is unlikely that the women would have pondered such thoughts. Most, if not all, of the disciples were residents of Galilee. Moreover, such fears would not have led them to be disobedient to a commission from the angels and the risen Jesus. Besides, Luke 24:9 states that the women told the Eleven and all the others *all these things,* which surely included the message to go to Galilee.

Some commentators have difficulty reconciling the instruction for the disciples to go home to Galilee with their long stay in Jerusalem before returning home.[29] This results from failure to understand these events from the Jewish perspective. It would be unthinkable for pious Jewish pilgrims to abort the remaining six days of the Feast of Unleavened Bread and return home. It may be safely assumed that it was unnecessary for Jesus or the angels to explain to the disciples to go to Galilee *after* the feast was completed; that would naturally have been assumed by all. So the meeting in Galilee could not have occurred until after the Feast of Unleavened Bread was completed,[30] two or three days after the appearance of Jesus in Jerusalem on the second Sunday, the day following the feast (John 20:26).

The following points explain why Jesus did not wait to give this instruc-

---

27. Calvin, *Harmony/Gospels*, 3:248.
28. T.W. Manson, *The Servant-Messiah: A Study of the Public Ministry of Jesus* (Cambridge: University Press, 1953; Grand Rapids: Baker, 1977), 95.
29. E.g., see Brown, *John (xiii-xxi)*, 972.
30. Ebrard, *Gospel History*, 457-58.

tion to the disciples that evening in Jerusalem and why an emphasis was placed on the meeting in Galilee.

a. The message about the meeting in Galilee was not intended just for the Eleven. It was for the wider circle of Galilean disciples[31] staying in and around Jerusalem for the feast. That is why the angel and Jesus told the women about it rather than waiting until Jesus' Jerusalem appearance to the Eleven that evening. The women were not specifically told to go and tell the eleven apostles, but the disciples, which suggests the wider company (Matt. 28:7, 10: *brothers;* Mark 16:7).[32] In relating that *they told all these things to the Eleven and to all the others* (Luke 24:9), Luke distinguishes between the apostles and other disciples, most or all of whom accompanied Jesus from Galilee. Moreover, Jesus' resurrection appearances in Jerusalem the first eight days were to only a few disciples, consisting mostly of the inner circle of apostles and a few others, including some of the women. Calvin claims the instruction to go to Galilee was in order for Christ to show himself to more people.[33] Further indication of this is that it was probably at this predicted meeting in Galilee where Jesus appeared to over 500 brethren at one time.

b. Galilee was the disciples' home, where Jesus had done most of his miraculous works. Galilee represented hope and encouragement to them. In Galilee, the Lord would gather together his many scattered sheep (Mark 14:27-28).

c. Jesus wanted to direct their attention to their future mission. Their Great Commission to evangelize and make disciples in all nations (Matt. 28:19-20) would begin at Jerusalem (Acts 1:8), where they would first be empowered. But the Commission itself would first be delivered to them in "Galilee of the Gentiles" (Isa. 9:1). " 'Galilee of the Gentiles' (or, foreigners) as we read in 1 [Maccabees] 5:15—seems to be regarded as the land of salvation."[34]

16. As the disciples gathered in Jerusalem that first Easter evening, did they believe that Jesus had risen from the dead or not?

The two disciples returned from Emmaus to Jerusalem that resurrection Sunday and reported to the disciples gathered in the Upper Room that they

---

31. There is much evidence that most of Jesus' disciples were Galileans. The primary way in which those at Jerusalem recognized Jesus' disciples was by their Galilean accent. (See Matt. 26:73; Mark 14:70; Luke 22:59; Acts 1:11; 2:7.) "Eleven of Jesus' twelve apostles were Galileans" (Tenney, *Pictorial Encyclopedia*, 2:643).

32. Carson, *Matthew*, 8:589.

33. Calvin, *Harmony/Gospels*, 3:225.

34. R.H. Lightfoot, *St. John's Gospel: A Commentary*, ed. G.F. Evans (Oxford: Clarendon, 1956), 36.

had seen the risen Lord. The women had already told these disciples of the empty tomb, the angels' message that Jesus was risen, and probably later that day that they had seen Jesus as well. Concerning the apostles' reception of the message by the two disciples from Emmaus, Mark reveals that *they did not believe them either* (Mark 16:13). Then *Jesus appeared to the Eleven as they were eating* (Mark 16:14) and *still talking about this* (Luke 24:36). Mark adds that Jesus *rebuked them for their lack of faith and their stubborn refusal to believe those who had seen him after he had risen* (Mark 16:14).

Luke, however, reports a different response by the gathered apostles to this message. He contends that the Eleven and those with them were saying, *It is true! The Lord has risen and has appeared to Simon* (Luke 24:34). By that time John and Peter had surely believed (see John 20:8 and 1 Cor. 15:5). But what about the other disciples in attendance? Augustine and other commentators contend that the word *saying* in Luke 24:34 does not require that the words which follow, *The Lord has risen*, represent the response of all those disciples in attendance.[35] In support, Luke adds that Jesus addressed them, *Peace be with you*, adding, *Why are you troubled, and why do doubts rise in your minds?* (Luke 24:36, 38) Wenham surmises, "The truth must surely be that the ten apostles present were in various states of part-belief and part-unbelief."[36]

Nonharmonist H.A.W. Meyer considers the above solution a piece of fanciful harmonization, asserting that logically the text does not allow it.[37] But must Luke 24:34 be understood as representing every disciple in attendance? None of the apostles believed the women earlier that day. What actually changed their minds so quickly? Thomas was likely not the only one who remained troubled with doubts.[38] Earlier that day at the tomb, John reports that he believed but implies that Peter had not yet believed (cf. John 20:8 with Luke 24:12). If Peter now believed only because he saw the Lord sometime that Sunday afternoon (1 Cor. 15:5), what about the other disciples who had not yet seen him? This was the case even when Jesus appeared to the larger gathering of disciples on the mountain in Galilee where, *when they saw him, they worshiped him; but some doubted* (Matt. 28:17). Furthermore, there were other disciples gathered with the Eleven on that first Sunday evening (Luke 24:33). Despite confirmation of Jesus' resurrection by Peter and John, some of these probably held lingering doubts.

Thus, Luke 24:34 may not indicate that every disciple present believed.

---

35. Cited by Meyer, *Mark and Luke*, 203.
36. Wenham, *Easter Enigma*, 104.
37. Meyer, *Mark and Luke*, 203.
38. It was apparently typical of Thomas' nature to voice boldly the pessimism others held silently (see John 11:16).

Of course, the entire problem vanishes if Mark's longer ending is regarded as noncanonical.[39]

17. Did Jesus meet his disciples in and near Jerusalem or in Galilee?

Both Matthew and Mark twice record verbatim the same prediction by Jesus, that after his resurrection he would *go ahead of* his disciples *into Galilee* (Matt. 26:32; cf. 28:7; Mark 14:28; cf. 16:7). In addition, Matthew's focus in his post-resurrection narrative is Galilee. Regarding the women, he reports that on Easter Sunday *Jesus met them,* instructing them to *go and tell my brothers to go to Galilee; there they will see me* (Matt. 28:9-10). Matthew's only other record of a resurrection appearance is a fulfillment of the message to the women: *the eleven disciples went to Galilee,* where they saw Jesus (v. 16). Matthew, therefore, conveys the impression that Jesus first appeared to a gathering of his disciples in Galilee.

The other three Evangelists clearly locate the first resurrection appearances in Jerusalem. Only John records appearances of Jesus in both Jerusalem and Galilee. Accordingly, Ladd states, "The most foreboding problem is that of the locale of the appearances of the resurrected Jesus to his disciples."[40]

A major theme in Luke's post-resurrection narrative, as well as throughout his Gospel, is Jerusalem.[41] Luke's report of the angels' message omits the announcement about the meeting in Galilee because it is not his purpose to record Jesus' appearances there, but only those in and near Jerusalem.[42] He quotes the angel as mentioning Galilee, but only to remind the women that it was there that Jesus first predicted his crucifixion and resurrection (cf. Luke 24:6-8 with 9:22, 44).

On the other hand, a primary theme in the Gospel of Matthew is that the kingdom of God will come to the Gentiles. Matthew relates The Great Commission given in Galilee without reporting any of the resurrection appearances in Jerusalem or the ascension near there. Although the Gospel

---

39. Some commentators regard Mark 16:11 and v. 13 as evidence that Mark 16:9-20 is noncanonical, since it is the only resurrection narrative in which Jesus rebukes the disciples for their unbelief, and since it seems to contradict Luke 24:36. These notes are written as if Mark 16:9-20 is canonical, whether a later addition or not.
40. Ladd, *Resurrection*, 86.
41. In Luke, the word "Jerusalem" occurs 30 times, more than twice as many as in any other Gospel. This, together with Luke's travel narrative of Jesus' journey beginning at Luke 9:51, indicates Luke's emphasis upon Jerusalem.
42. The appearance on the road to Emmaus was only a few miles from Jerusalem, Emmaus itself being *about seven miles from Jerusalem* (Luke 24:13). The location of Emmaus remains uncertain, but it is thought to have been west of Jerusalem on or near the road to Joppa.

must first be preached in Jerusalem (Acts 1:8), "Galilee of the Gentiles" (Isa. 9:1) becomes the gateway for the evangelization of the world (Matt. 28:16-20).

Liberal critics have had a heyday supposing a contradiction exists between the post-resurrection appearances recorded by Matthew and Luke concerning Galilee and Jerusalem, respectively. This discrepancy reflects merely thematic differences, and each writer's silence proves nothing. A composite of Matthew and Luke make it clear: Jesus appeared to his disciples first in Jerusalem, then in Galilee.

18. When Jesus appeared to his gathered disciples that first Easter evening, were there ten or eleven apostles present?

Luke 24:33 relates that on that first Easter evening Jesus appeared to *the Eleven,* Judas being absent. However, John reports that Thomas was also absent (John 20:24), leaving ten apostles, not eleven. The same problem occurs in 1 Corinthians 15:5, where Paul says that Jesus *appeared to Peter, and then to the Twelve,* despite the absence of Judas. The latter appearance presumably refers to the second Sunday evening. A popular explanation has been that these terms, *the Eleven* and *the Twelve,* refer to the original apostles as a company but are not to be taken as numerically literal following the defection of Judas.

Perhaps a better solution relates to the apostles' replacement for Judas following Jesus' ascension, as recorded by Luke in Acts 1:20-26. Though Judas' replacement was not yet named, Matthias, who was eventually chosen, was probably present at these first two appearances to the gathered disciples on the first two Sundays. Luke writes that not only the Eleven were gathered together on that first Easter Sunday, but also *those with them* (Luke 24:33), suggesting that other disciples (e.g., see John 21:2: *Nathanael*) were in attendance with the apostles, possibly including Matthias. In fact, in choosing Judas' replacement, Peter laid down that he must be *a witness with us of his resurrection* (Acts 1:22), suggesting that Matthias was present at the two Sunday evening appearances. Luke and Paul, therefore, use an anachronism in counting Matthias as one of the twelve apostles before he was so officially. Matthias was eventually chosen by lot and *added to the eleven apostles* (Acts 1:26). Thereafter, Matthias was officially and literally reckoned among *the Twelve* (Acts 2:14; 6:2).[43]

---

43. The view that the eleven apostles, under Peter's leadership, acted apart from the will of God in choosing Matthias to replace Judas, and that God later chose the Apostle Paul as the twelfth apostle, is erroneous. A simple check of a Bible concordance reveals that the Apostle Paul was one of many apostles later added to the church, albeit outstanding among all the apostles he was (2 Cor. 11:5).

In conclusion, it is certain that after Matthias was chosen to take Judas' apostleship, he was included as one of *the Twelve*. Likely he was present at both of Jesus' resurrection appearances the first two Sunday evenings and therefore regarded by Luke as one of *the Eleven* on the first Sunday and by Paul as one of *the Twelve* on the second Sunday.

19. When Jesus appeared to the gathered disciples that first Easter evening, were they overjoyed or doubtful?

John recounts that when Jesus appeared to the gathered disciples that first Sunday evening, *the disciples were overjoyed when they saw the Lord* (John 20:20). Luke, however, quotes Jesus as saying to them, *Why are you troubled, and why do doubts rise in your minds?* (Luke 24:38) These two reports of the disciples' experience cannot be regarded as a discrepancy, since Luke adds: *When . . . he showed them his hands and feet. . . . they still did not believe it because of joy and amazement* (Luke 24:40-41). This is similar to what the women who attended the tomb that morning experienced: being both fearful and joyful. (See EN 16:10.)

20. When and where did Jesus appear to the disciples in Galilee?

On Easter morning the disciples were told to go to Galilee, where Jesus would meet them (Matt. 28:10; cf. Mark 16:7). Due to the ensuing Feast of Unleavened Bread, however, the apostles and other Galilean disciples would not have returned home until the feast days were completed in Jerusalem. The earliest they could have left would have been the day after the second Sunday, the evening Jesus appeared to the apostles in Jerusalem, with Thomas present. (See EN 16:15.) Assuming all the Galilean disciples left the next day, it would likely have been Tuesday or Wednesday, about ten days after Jesus' resurrection, before they arrived home in Galilee.

Jesus did not immediately appear to the wider circle of disciples upon their arrival in Galilee. Instead, he first appeared to seven of the disciples while they were fishing on the Sea of Galilee. John relates that *this was now the third time Jesus appeared to his disciples after he was raised from the dead* (John 21:14). John does not mean to include the appearances to the women or the two disciples on the road to Emmaus, but speaks only of gatherings of several apostles. The predicted meeting in Galilee had not yet occurred. Neither had Jesus yet appeared to the gathering of over 500 brethren (1 Cor. 15:6).

The Evangelists do not record that Jesus or the angel informed the women of the exact location where he would meet the wider company of disciples in Galilee. If the apostles had known the location before this appearance at the Sea of Galilee, they probably would have gone there immediately upon arriving at home and not have gone fishing. Perhaps it was at this appearance to the seven at the Sea of Galilee that Jesus gave the necessary instructions about where the apostles were to gather the many Galilean disciples to meet him.

Matthew records that eventually *the eleven disciples went to Galilee, to the mountain where Jesus had told them to go* (Matt. 28:16). Because of the emphasis placed on this meeting, its being the only predicted post-resurrection appearance, and because it was intended for the wider circle of Galilean disciples, it seems that this appearance of Jesus on a mountain in Galilee was the one reported by Paul as to more than 500 brethren. The mountain, however, is unknown.

21. Did Jesus appear to over 500 brethren in Galilee or on the Mount of Olives?

Some commentators speculate that Jesus appeared to more than 500 disciples on the Mount of Olives, where he ascended into heaven. Several reasons indicate otherwise:

a. A public gathering of over 500 brethren would probably not occur in Jerusalem for fear of the Jews (see John 20:19, 26). It is more likely that sometime after returning home from the Feast of Unleavened Bread, the more than 500 disciples gathered somewhere in Galilee, where they could assemble without fear of the Jews.

b. The most likely place for Jesus Christ to give The Great Commission was no doubt to the largest gathering of disciples. The Commission was given on the mountain in Galilee (Matt. 28:16-20), the most suitable place for the Lord to appear to more than 500 disciples at one time. Most of Jesus' disciples were Galileans, and Jesus himself was a Galilean.

c. Only a few days after Jesus' ascension, *a group numbering about a hundred and twenty* (Acts 1:15) gathered in Jerusalem and Matthias was chosen to take Judas' place. This smaller number would seem to more closely represent the number of people who gathered at the ascension on Mt. Olivet. Gleason Archer adds:

> If there were over 500 assembled at Olivet on Ascension Day, it is unlikely that 380 of them would have disregarded Christ's solemn instructions and would have failed to tarry for the specified ten days until Pentecost (Luke 24:49; Acts 1:4), when the Spirit would descend from heaven on them.[44]

---

44. Archer, *Bible Difficulties*, 356.

Thus it appears more likely that the 500 brethren saw the resurrected Lord Jesus on a mountain in Galilee rather than on the Mount of Olives at his ascension.

22. Do the Gospels record that Jesus gave The Great Commission to his disciples once or twice?

If the "longer ending" of Mark (i.e., Mark 16:9-20) is noncanonical, the answer to the above question is, once. Accepting Mark's ending as canonical, the similarity of the opening lines in the message of Matthew 28:18-20 and Mark 16:15-18, called The Great Commission, has led many harmonists to assume that they were offered at the same time and place. Mark does not locate where this message was delivered, but Matthew does: a mountain in Galilee (Matt. 28:16). However, Mark seems to introduce v. 15 as if it is connected to the preceding narrative, which would require that Jesus delivered the message of vv. 15-18 in the Upper Room at Jerusalem on the first Easter night. If so, this is the only evidence that Jesus gave The Great Commission before the meeting in Galilee. On the other hand, if no break in the narrative is intended between vv. 18 and 19, this passage implies that Jesus spoke vv. 15-18 on Mt. Olivet as his farewell address immediately before ascending to heaven. Either way, he would have delivered The Great Commission twice. It seems better to assume that Jesus did not give The Great Commission until his appearance on a mountain in Galilee to more than 500 brethren due to the importance attached to that meeting, as well as due to the symbolism of "Galilee of the Gentiles." Most harmonists regard Matthew 28:16-20 and Mark 16:15-18 as the same message, so that Jesus delivered The Great Commission one time, on a mountain in Galilee, as herein.

23. Did Jesus give instructions for the disciples to go to Galilee or to remain at Jerusalem?

Jesus instructed the women to tell the disciples to go to Galilee, where he would meet them (Matt. 28:7, 10), yet Luke reports the first appearance of Jesus to his gathered disciples in Jerusalem on Easter evening (Luke 24:36-49). Near the end of Jesus' message, as written by Luke, he commanded the disciples to remain in Jerusalem until they were empowered with the Holy Spirit (v. 49; Acts 1:4). Were they to remain at Jerusalem at that time or go to Galilee?

Calvin contends that the whole message of Luke 24:36-44 is one unit, and was delivered at the one appearance on Easter evening, offering the following explanation:

The command to stay at Jerusalem should be understood as applying after they had returned from Galilee. For . . . although he gave them a sight of himself at Jerusalem, he did not change his original instruction about Galilee.[45]

I. Howard Marshall presents the more plausible view held by many contemporary commentators concerning Luke 24:36-49. "It is probable that he [Luke] is here summarizing what Jesus said to his disciples over the period of the resurrection appearances."[46]

Most harmonists maintain that Luke joins two of Jesus' messages, delivered at two separate appearances, into one, without any explanation by Luke and apparently for the sake of brevity. The break in the narrative is usually placed between vv. 43 and 44, as herein, so that the episode of vv. 36-43 occurred in Jerusalem on Easter evening, while the quotation in vv. 44-49 was spoken later, probably again at Jerusalem. Luke's preoccupation with Jerusalem and his silence regarding appearances of Jesus in Galilee make it likely that this supposed second message was also delivered in Jerusalem, probably just before Jesus' ascension, due to what immediately follows in Luke, i.e., *stay in the city* (v. 49).

24. Did Jesus ascend to heaven from the Mount of Olives or from the vicinity of Bethany?

Luke discloses in Luke 24:50 that Jesus ascended to heaven after he led the disciples out *to the vicinity of Bethany*. In Acts 1:9 and v. 12, however, Luke implies the traditional view that Jesus ascended from *the Mount of Olives*, although he says only that the disciples returned from there following the ascension, not specifically that it took place there. The Greek word in Luke 24:50, translated in the NIV *to the vicinity of*, is *pros*, meaning "toward," which does not require that Jesus ascended from the vicinity of Bethany. Instead, it suggests that Jesus led the disciples out toward Bethany by way of the Mount of Olives. From the temple area in Jerusalem, the usual route to Bethany, which was located southeast of Jerusalem, was over the Mount of Olives. Thus the well-established tradition is no doubt correct—Jesus ascended to heaven from the Mount of Olives.

---

45. Calvin, *Harmony/Gospels*, 3:248.
46. Marshall, *Luke*, 904.

Explanation of
The Chronological Table.

The Chronological Table was composed as a guide to this author for determining the chronological arrangement of sections in *The Gospels Interwoven*. In 1871 John M'Clintock and James Strong (author of *Strong's Exhaustive Concordance of the Bible*) published a helpful "Comparative Table of Different Harmonies" in *Cyclopaedia of Biblical, Theological, and Ecclesiastical Literature*. It is a comparison of the chronological arrangements of Gospel sections in nine leading parallel-column harmonies produced between 1655 and 1851. This author has augmented their table by adding the arrangements of four twentieth-century harmonists. Thus the chronology of events in *The Gospels Interwoven* was achieved by appealing to the majority view of thirteen leading harmonies of the four Gospels appearing over 325 years, 1655–1980.

The "Section" column lists events in the life of Christ. They are numbered in the adjacent left-hand column. Under each harmonist's name is a number indicating his placement of that event in his harmony. Numbers appearing on lines without titles indicate where one or more authors have located that section.

The column entitled "Strong's Order" corresponds to the order of events in James Strong's *Harmony*. Note that there are only 149 sections in M'Clintock and Strong's table, whereas *The Gospels Interwoven* contains 250 sections. For the sake of brevity, M'Clintock and Strong have sometimes joined several undisputed events under one title.

The "Total Harmonists" column totals the harmonists who arrange that section to follow the preceding section. Parallel lines appearing to the left of numbers in this column indicate little or no dispute among harmonists regarding the placement of that section, revealing that harmonists agree on the chronology of events in the Gospels far more than they disagree. All 13 agree on the sequential order of 98 of the 149 events, and 12 of 13 agree on 116 events.

A "Y" signifying "Yes" appears in the column titled "Majority of Harmonists" when the majority agree with Strong's suggested order; when the majority disagree an "N" signifying "No" appears. When an "N" appears, by scanning this column the reader may note that a number in bold print indicates where the majority have placed that numbered event in their arrangements. A zero for "Luke's Preface" means it is omitted in *The Gospels Interwoven*.

The Gospels Interwoven adheres to the majority's arrangement of sections according to The Chronological Table except for three sections, marked by an asterisk in the far left column: "The Genealogies of Jesus" (9), not a chronological event, is placed later to allow a more interesting beginning in the composite Gospel; "Interview with the Greeks" (122) reveals the lack of a clear majority; "Feast at Bethany" (111) is the one clear departure from The Chronological Table due to the author's conviction that Jesus was anointed one or likely two days before Passover. (See EN 13:1.)

The Chronological Table

Majority of Harmonists	Total Harmonists	Strong's Order	SECTION	Lightfoot	Doddridge	MacKnight	Newcome	Townsend	Greswell	Jarvis	Robinson	Tischendorf	Stevens & Burton	Robertson	Wieand	Thomas & Gundry
	3	..	2	..	..	..	..	..	..	2	..	2	2	..	..	..
0	13	‖ 1	Luke's Preface	1	1	1	1	1	1	1	1	1	1	1	1	1
Y	8	2	John's Introduction	2	2	2	2	2	..	..	..	..	..	2	2	2
*9	5	..	9	..	..	..	..	..	..	..	..	9	9	9	9	9
Y	13	‖ 3	John's birth predicted	3	3	3	3	3	3	3	3	3	3	3	3	3
Y	13	‖ 4	Annunciation to Mary	4	4	4	4	4	4	4	4	4	4	4	4	4
Y	12	5	Mary visits Elizabeth	5	5	5	5	5	5	5	5	5	..	5	5	5
..	1	..	9	9	..	..	..	..	..	..	..	..	..	..	..	..
..	4	..	7	7	..	..	..	..	7	..	..	..	7	..	7	..
..	1	..	5	..	..	..	..	..	..	..	..	..	5	..	..	..
Y	13	‖ 6	Birth of John	6	6	6	6	6	6	6	6	6	6	6	6	6
..	1	..	9	..	..	9	..	..	..	..	..	..	..	..	..	..
Y	9	7	Joseph's vision	..	7	7	7	7	..	7	7	7	..	7	..	7
..	1	..	9	..	..	9	..	..	..	..	..	..	..	..	..	..
Y	13	‖ 8	Nativity of Jesus	8	8	8	8	8	8	8	8	8	8	8	8	8
N	3	9	Genealogies	..	..	..	9	9	..	9	..	..	..	..	..	..
Y	13	‖10	The shepherds' vision	10	10	10	10	10	10	10	10	10	10	10	10	10
Y	13	‖11	Circumcision of Jesus	11	11	11	11	·11	11	11	11	11	11	11	11	11
..	1	..	9	..	..	..	..	..	..	9	..	..	..	..	..	..
Y	13	‖12	Presentation in the Temple	12	12	12	12	12	12	12	12	12	12	12	12	12
Y	13	‖13	Visit of the Magi	13	13	13	13	13	13	13	13	13	13	13	13	13
Y	13	‖14	Flight into Egypt	14	14	14	14	14	14	14	14	14	14	14	14	14
Y	13	‖15	Bethlehemite massacre	15	15	15	15	15	15	15	15	15	15	15	15	15
Y	13	‖16	Return from Egypt	16	16	16	16	16	16	16	16	16	16	16	16	16
Y	13	‖17	Boyhood of Jesus	17	17	17	17	17	17	17	17	17	17	17	17	17
..	1	..	2	..	..	..	..	..	..	2	..	..	..	..	..	..
..	1	..	9	..	..	..	..	..	..	..	..	9	..	..	..	..
Y	13	‖18	Mission of John	18	18	18	18	18	18	18	18	18	18	18	18	18
Y	13	‖19	Baptism of Jesus	19	19	19	19	19	19	19	19	19	19	19	19	19
Y	13	‖20	Temptation of Christ	20	20	20	20	20	20	20	20	20	20	20	20	20
..	1	..	2	..	..	..	..	..	..	..	..	2	..	..	..	..
Y	13	‖21	John's testimony	21	21	21	21	21	21	21	21	21	21	21	21	21
Y	13	‖22	Christ's first disciples	22	22	22	22	22	22	22	22	22	22	22	22	22
Y	13	‖23	Water changed to wine	23	23	23	23	23	23	23	23	23	23	23	23	23
Y	13	‖24	Visit at Capernaum	24	24	24	24	24	24	24	24	24	24	24	24	24
Y	13	‖25	Traders expelled	25	25	25	25	25	25	25	25	25	25	25	25	25

Majority of Harmonists	Total Harmonists	Strong's Order	SECTION	Lightfoot	Doddridge	MacKnight	Newcome	Townsend	Greswell	Jarvis	Robinson	Tischendorf	Stevens & Burton	Robertson	Wieand	Thomas & Gundry
Y	13	‖26	Visit of Nicodemus	26	26	26	26	26	26	26	26	26	26	26	26	26
Y	13	‖27	Further testimony of John	27	27	27	27	27	27	27	27	27	27	27	27	27
Y	11	28	John imprisoned	28	28	..	28	28	..	28	28	28	28	28	28	28
Y	13	‖29	Samaritan woman	29	29	29	29	29	29	29	29	29	29	29	29	29
..	2	..	28	..	..	28	..	..	28	..	..	..	..	..	..	..
Y	13	‖30	Teaching in Galilee	30	30	30	30	30	30	30	30	30	30	30	30	30
Y	13	‖31	Nobleman's son	31	31	31	31	31	31	31	31	31	31	31	31	31
..	1	..	40	..	..	..	..	..	..	..	..	40	..	..	..	..
Y	13	‖32	Rejection at Nazareth	32	32	32	32	32	32	32	32	32	32	32	32	32
Y	13	‖33	Draught of fishes	33	33	33	33	33	33	33	33	33	33	33	33	33
..	1	..	36	..	..	36	..	..	..	..	..	..	..	..	..	..
..	1	..	45	..	..	45	..	..	..	..	..	..	..	..	..	..
..	1	..	37	..	..	37	..	..	..	..	..	..	..	..	..	..
Y	13	‖34	Demoniac cured	34	34	34	34	34	34	34	34	34	34	34	34	34
Y	13	‖35	Peter's mother-in-law	35	35	35	35	35	35	35	35	35	35	35	35	35
Y	12	36	First tour in Galilee	36	36	..	36	36	36	36	36	36	36	36	36	36
..	2	..	45	..	45	..	..	..	45	..	..	..	..	..	..	..
Y	12	37	Leper cured	37	37	..	37	37	37	37	37	37	37	37	37	37
..	1	..	55	..	..	55	..	..	..	..	..	..	..	..	..	..
..	1	..	56	..	..	56	..	..	..	..	..	..	..	..	..	..
Y	13	‖38	Paralytic cured	38	38	38	38	38	38	38	38	38	38	38	38	38
Y	13	‖39	Call of Matthew	39	39	39	39	39	39	39	39	39	39	39	39	39
57	7	..	57	..	..	..	..	..	57	57	..	57	57	57	57	57
Y	11	40	Impotent man cured	40	40	..	40	40	40	40	40	..	40	40	40	40
Y	12	41	Ears of corn plucked	41	41	..	41	41	41	41	41	41	41	41	41	41
..	1	..	57	..	..	57	..	..	..	..	..	..	..	..	..	..
..	1	..	58	..	..	58	..	..	..	..	..	..	..	..	..	..
..	1	..	59	..	..	59	..	..	..	..	..	..	..	..	..	..
Y	12	42	Withered hand cured	42	42	..	42	42	42	42	42	42	42	42	42	42
Y	12	43	Multitudes cured	43	43	..	43	43	43	43	43	43	43	43	43	43
Y	13	‖44	Apostles chosen	44	44	44	44	44	44	44	44	44	44	44	44	44
Y	10	45	Sermon on the Mount	45	..	..	45	45	..	45	45	45	45	45	45	45
Y	13	‖46	Centurion's servant cured	46	46	46	46	46	46	46	46	46	46	46	46	46
Y	13	‖47	Widow's son raised	47	48	47	47	47	47	47	47	47	47	47	48	47
Y	13	‖48	John's message	48	48	48	48	48	48	48	48	48	48	48	48	48
Y	13	‖49	Kind offices of a woman	49	49	49	49	49	49	49	49	49	49	49	49	49
Y	13	‖50	Second tour of Galilee	50	50	50	50	50	50	50	50	50	50	50	50	50
..	1	..	40	..	..	40	..	..	..	..	..	..	..	..	..	..
..	1	..	41	..	..	41	..	..	..	..	..	..	..	..	..	..
..	1	..	42	..	..	42	..	..	..	..	..	..	..	..	..	..
Y	13	‖51	Demoniac cured	51	51	51	51	51	51	51	51	51	51	51	51	51
Y	7	52	Discourse on providence	52	..	..	..	..	..	..	..	52	..	52	52	52
Y	13	‖53	The sower, tares, etc.	53	53	53	53	53	53	53	53	53	53	53	53	53
Y	13	‖54	Parables explained	54	54	54	54	54	54	54	54	54	54	54	54	54
Y	12	55	Crossing the lake	55	55	..	55	55	55	55	55	55	55	55	55	55
Y	12	56	Demoniacs cured	56	56	..	56	56	56	56	56	56	56	56	56	56
N	5	57	Matthew's feast	57	57	..	57	57	..	57	..	..	..	..	..	..
Y	12	58	Jairus' daughter raised	58	58	..	58	58	58	58	58	58	58	58	58	58
Y	11	59	Blind men, etc., cured	59	59	..	59	59	59	59	59	..	59	59	59	59
Y	13	‖60	Second rejection at Nazareth.	60	60	60	60	60	60	60	60	60	60	60	60	60
Y	13	‖61	Mission of the apostles	61	61	61	61	61	61	61	61	61	61	61	61	61
Y	13	‖62	John beheaded	62	62	62	62	62	62	62	62	62	62	62	62	62
Y	13	‖63	Five thousand fed	63	63	63	63	63	63	63	63	63	63	63	63	63
Y	13	‖64	Walking on the water	64	64	64	64	64	64	64	64	64	64	64	64	64
Y	13	‖65	Discussion in the synagogue.	65	65	65	65	65	65	65	65	65	65	65	65	65
..	1	..	67	..	67	..	..	..	..	..	..	..	..	..	..	..

Majority of Harmonists	Total Harmonists	Strong's Order	SECTION	Lightfoot	Doddridge	MacKnight	Newcome	Townsend	Greswell	Jarvis	Robinson	Tischendorf	Stevens & Burton	Robertson	Wieand	Thomas & Gundry
Y	11	66	Third passover	66	66	66	66	66	..	66	66	..	66	66	66	66
Y	12	67	Pharisees confuted	67	..	67	67	67	67	67	67	67	67	67	67	67
Y	13	‖ 68	Syrophoenician woman	68	68	68	68	68	68	68	68	68	68	68	68	68
Y	13	‖ 69	Four thousand fed	69	69	69	69	69	69	69	69	69	69	69	69	69
Y	13	‖ 70	A sign demanded	70	70	70	70	70	70	70	70	70	70	70	70	70
Y	13	‖ 71	Blind man cured	71	71	71	71	71	71	71	71	71	71	71	71	71
Y	13	‖ 72	Passion predicted	72	72	72	72	72	72	72	72	72	72	72	72	72
Y	13	73	Transfiguration	73	73	73	73	73	73	73	73	73	73	73	73	73
Y	13	‖ 74	Demoniac cured	74	74	74	74	74	74	74	74	74	74	74	74	74
Y	13	‖ 75	Passion again predicted	75	75	75	75	75	75	75	75	75	75	75	75	75
Y	13	‖ 76	Tax-money provided	76	76	76	76	76	76	76	76	76	76	76	76	76
Y	13	‖ 77	Exhortations to kindness	77	77	77	77	77	77	77	77	77	77	77	77	77
..	1	..	79	79	..	..	..	..	..	..	..	..	..	..	..	..
N	6	78	Mission of the seventy	78	78	..	78	78	..	78	78	..	..	..	..	..
Y	5	79	Departure from Galilee	..	..	..	..	..	..	..	79	79	79	..	79	79
..	1	..	93	..	..	93	..	..	..	..	..	..	..	..	..	..
Y	12	80	Festival of tabernacles	80	80	80	80	80	80	..	80	80	80	80	80	80
Y	12	81	Adulteress pardoned	81	81	81	81	81	81	..	81	81	81	81	81	81
Y	12	82	Violence offered to Christ	82	82	82	82	82	82	..	82	82	82	82	82	82
87	5	..	87	..	..	87	87	..	87	..	..	..	87	87	..	..
88	5	..	88	..	..	88	88	..	88	..	..	..	88	88	..	..
..	2	..	79	..	..	79	..	..	..	..	..	79	..	..	..	..
78	6	..	78	..	..	78	..	..	..	..	..	78	78	78	78	78
Y	9	83	Return of the seventy	83	83	83	83	83	..	..	..	83	83	..	83	83
Y	12	84	Love to one's neighbor	84	84	84	84	84	..	84	84	84	84	84	84	84
Y	11	85	Visit at Bethany	85	85	85	..	85	..	85	85	85	85	85	85	85
Y	10	86	The Lord's Prayer	86	86	..	86	86	..	86	86	86	..	86	86	86
..	1	..	59	..	..	..	..	..	..	..	..	59	..	..	..	..
..	1	..	94	..	..	..	..	..	..	..	..	..	..	..	94	..
..	2	..	83	..	..	..	..	..	..	..	83	..	..	..	83	..
N	4	87	Blind man cured	87	..	..	..	..	87	..	87	..	87	..	..	..
N	4	88	Investigation by the Sanhedrin	88	..	..	..	..	88	..	88	..	88	..	..	..
N	6	89	Festival of dedication	89	..	89	..	..	89	..	89	..	89	..	89	..
Y	5	90	Teaching at the Jordan	..	..	90	..	..	90	..	90	..	90	..	90	..
N	2	91	Lazarus raised	..	..	..	..	..	91	..	91	..	..	..	..	..
N	2	92	Resolution of the Sanhedrin	..	..	..	..	..	92	..	92	..	..	..	..	..
N	2	93	Teaching at Ephraim, etc.	..	..	..	..	..	93	..	93	..	..	..	..	..
..	2	..	86	..	..	86	..	..	..	..	..	..	86	..	..	..
..	5	..	52	..	52	52	..	52	..	52	..	52	..	..	..	..
Y	11	94	Infirm woman cured	94	94	94	94	94	..	94	94	94	94	94	..	94
..	1	..	79	..	..	..	..	..	79	..	..	..	..	..	..	..
..	1	..	89	..	..	..	..	..	89	..	..	..	..	..	..	..
..	2	..	87	..	..	..	..	..	87	..	..	..	..	..	..	87
..	2	..	88	..	..	..	..	..	88	..	..	..	..	..	..	88
..	3	..	89	..	..	..	..	..	..	..	..	..	89	..	89	89
..	4	..	90	..	..	..	..	..	90	..	..	..	90	..	90	90
Y	10	95	Sets out for Jerusalem	..	95	95	95	..	95	..	95	95	95	95	95	95
..	1	..	78	..	..	..	..	..	78	..	..	..	..	..	..	..
..	2	..	83	..	..	..	..	..	83	83	..	..	..	..	..	..
..	1	..	84	..	..	..	..	..	84	..	..	..	..	..	..	..
..	1	..	85	..	..	..	..	..	85	..	..	..	..	..	..	..
..	1	..	86	..	..	..	..	..	86	..	..	..	..	..	..	..
Y	11	96	Warning against Herod	96	96	96	96	..	..	96	96	96	96	96	96	96
..	1	..	93	93	..	..	..	..	..	..	..	..	..	..	..	..
Y	13	‖ 97	Discourse at a Pharisee's	97	97	97	97	97	97	97	97	97	97	97	97	97
..	1	..	52	..	..	..	..	..	52	..	..	..	..	..	..	..

Majority of Harmonists	Total Harmonists	Strong's Order	SECTION	Lightfoot	Doddridge	MacKnight	Newcome	Townsend	Greswell	Jarvis	Robinson	Tischendorf	Stevens & Burton	Robertson	Wieand	Thomas & Gundry
..	1	..	94	..	..	..	..	..	94	..	..	..	..	..	..	..
..	1	..	96	..	..	..	..	..	96	..	..	..	..	..	..	..
Y	13	‖ 98	Tower built, war made, etc	98	98	98	98	98	98	98	98	98	98	98	98	98
Y	13	‖ 99	The prodigal son, etc.	99	99	99	99	99	99	99	99	99	99	99	99	99
Y	13	‖100	The faithless steward	100	100	100	100	100	100	100	100	100	100	100	100	100
..	1	..	104	..	..	..	..	104	..	..	..	..	..	..	..	..
..	1	..	105	..	..	..	..	105	..	..	..	..	..	..	..	..
Y	13	‖101	Dives and Lazarus	101	101	101	101	101	101	101	101	101	101	101	101	101
..	4	..	79	..	79	..	79	..	79	..	..	..	..	..	..	..
..	1	..	80	..	..	..	..	..	..	80	..	..	..	..	..	..
..	1	..	81	..	..	..	..	..	..	81	..	..	..	..	..	..
..	1	..	82	..	..	..	..	..	..	82	..	..	..	..	..	..
..	1	..	87	..	..	..	..	..	..	87	..	..	..	..	..	..
..	1	..	88	..	..	..	..	..	..	88	..	..	..	..	..	..
91	6	..	91	..	..	91	..	..	..	..	..	91	91	91	91	91
92	6	..	92	..	..	92	..	..	..	..	..	92	92	92	92	92
93	5	..	93	..	..	..	..	..	..	..	..	93	93	93	93	93
..	2	..	95	95	..	..	..	95	..	..	..	..	..	..	..	..
..	1	..	96	..	..	..	..	96	..	..	..	..	..	..	..	..
Y	13	‖102	Messiah already come	102	102	102	102	102	102	102	102	102	102	102	102	102
Y	13	‖103	Unjust judge, publican	103	103	103	103	103	103	103	103	103	103	103	103	103
..	1	..	85	..	..	..	85	..	..	..	..	..	..	..	..	..
..	2	..	89	..	89	..	89	..	..	..	..	..	..	..	..	..
..	1	..	87	..	87	..	..	..	..	..	..	..	..	..	..	..
..	1	..	88	..	88	..	..	..	..	..	..	..	..	..	..	..
..	3	..	90	90	90	..	90	..	..	..	..	..	..	..	..	..
..	1	..	91	..	..	..	91	..	..	..	..	..	..	..	..	..
..	1	..	92	..	..	..	92	..	..	..	..	..	..	..	..	..
..	1	..	93	..	..	..	93	..	..	..	..	..	..	..	..	..
Y	12	104	Doctrine of divorce	104	104	104	104	..	104	104	104	104	104	104	104	104
Y	12	105	Children received	105	105	105	105	..	105	105	105	105	105	105	105	105
Y	13	‖106	Rich young man	106	106	106	106	106	106	106	106	106	106	106	106	106
..	1	..	91	..	91	..	..	..	..	..	..	..	..	..	..	..
..	1	..	92	..	92	..	..	..	..	..	..	..	..	..	..	..
..	1	..	93	..	93	..	..	..	..	..	..	..	..	..	..	..
..	1	..	95	..	..	..	..	..	..	..	95	..	..	..	..	..
Y	13	‖107	Passion again predicted	107	107	107	107	107	107	107	107	107	107	107	107	107
Y	13	‖108	Ambition of James and John	108	108	108	108	108	108	108	108	108	108	108	108	108
Y	13	‖109	Bartimaeus cured	109	109	109	109	109	109	109	109	109	109	109	109	109
Y	13	‖110	Visit with Zacchaeus	110	110	110	110	110	110	110	110	110	110	110	110	110
..	1	..	89	..	..	..	..	..	..	89	..	..	..	..	..	..
..	1	..	90	..	..	..	..	..	..	90	..	..	..	..	..	..
..	3	..	91	91	..	..	..	91	..	91	..	..	..	..	..	..
..	3	..	92	92	..	..	..	92	..	92	..	..	..	..	..	..
..	2	..	93	..	..	..	..	93	..	93	..	..	..	..	..	..
*Y	10	111	Feast at Bethany	111	111	111	..	111	111	111	..	111	111	..	111	111
Y	13	‖112	Entrance into Jerusalem	112	112	112	112	112	112	112	112	112	112	112	112	112
..	4	..	122	122	..	..	122	..	122	122	..	..	..	..	..	..
114	10	..	114	114	..	114	114	..	114	..	114	114	114	114	114	114
Y	13	‖113	Traders again expelled	113	113	113	113	113	113	113	113	113	113	113	113	113
*122	5	..	122	..	122	122	..	122	..	..	..	..	..	122	..	122
N	3	114	The barren fig tree cursed	..	114	..	..	114	..	114	..	..	..	..	..	..
Y	13	‖115	His authority demanded	115	115	115	115	115	115	115	115	115	115	115	115	115
Y	13	‖116	The tribute question	116	116	116	116	116	116	116	116	116	116	116	116	116
Y	13	‖117	The resurrection question	117	117	117	117	117	117	117	117	117	117	117	117	117
Y	13	‖118	The greatest commandment	118	118	118	118	118	118	118	118	118	118	118	118	118

Majority of Harmonists	Total Harmonists	Strong's Order	SECTION	Lightfoot	Doddridge	MacKnight	Newcome	Townsend	Greswell	Jarvis	Robinson	Tischendorf	Stevens & Burton	Robertson	Wieand	Thomas & Gundry
Y	13	||119	Messiah's paternity	119	119	119	119	119	119	119	119	119	119	119	119	119
Y	13	||120	Hierarchy denounced	120	120	120	120	120	120	120	120	120	120	120	120	120
Y	13	||121	The widow's gift	121	121	121	121	121	121	121	121	121	121	121	121	121
N	4	122	Interview with the Greeks	..	..	..	..	..	..	..	122	122	122	..	122	..
Y	13	||123	Destruction of Jerusalem, etc.	123	123	123	123	123	123	123	123	123	123	123	123	123
Y	13	||124	Plots against Jesus	124	124	124	124	124	124	124	124	124	124	124	124	124
..	3	..	111	..	..	..	111	..	..	..	111	..	..	111	..	..
Y	13	||125	Preparation for Passover	125	125	125	125	125	125	125	125	125	125	125	125	125
Y	13	||126	Incidents of the meal	126	126	126	126	126	126	126	126	126	126	126	126	126
Y	13	||127	Agony, etc., in Gethsemane	127	127	127	127	127	127	127	127	127	127	127	127	127
Y	10	128	Examination before Annas	128	..	..	128	..	128	128	128	128	128	128	128	128
Y	13	||129	Before the Sanhedrin	129	129	129	129	129	129	129	129	129	129	129	129	129
133	8	..	133	133	..	..	..	133	133	..	..	133	133	133	133	133
Y	13	||130	Accusation before Pilate	130	130	130	130	130	130	130	130	130	130	130	130	130
..	1	..	133	..	..	133	..	..	..	..	..	..	..	..	..	..
Y	13	||131	Taken before Herod	131	131	131	131	131	131	131	131	131	131	131	131	131
Y	13	||132	Sentence from Pilate	132	132	132	132	132	132	132	132	132	132	132	132	132
N	3	133	Suicide of Judas	..	..	..	..	133	..	..	133	133	..	..	..	..
Y	13	||134	Crucifixion incidents	134	134	134	134	134	134	134	134	134	134	134	134	134
Y	13	||135	Burial of Jesus	135	135	135	135	135	135	135	135	135	135	135	135	135
..	1	..	133	..	133	..	..	..	..	..	..	..	..	..	..	..
..	2	..	137	..	..	137	..	..	..	..	..	..	..	..	137	..
Y	13	||136	Sepulchre guarded	136	136	136	136	136	136	136	136	136	136	136	136	136
Y	11	137	Preparation for embalming	137	137	..	137	137	137	137	137	137	137	137	..	137
Y	13	||138	Release from the bomb	138	138	138	138	138	138	138	138	138	138	138	138	138
141	9	..	141	..	..	141	141	141	..	141	..	141	141	141	141	141
142	12	..	142	142	142	142	142	142	142	142	..	142	142	142	142	142
..	2	..	141	141	141	..	..	..	..	..	..	..	..	..	..	..
..	1	..	140	..	..	..	..	140	..	..	..	..	..	..	..	..
Y	13	||139	Appearance to the women	139	139	139	139	139	139	139	139	139	139	139	139	139
..	1	..	141	..	..	..	..	..	..	..	141	..	..	..	..	..
..	1	..	142	..	..	..	..	..	..	..	142	..	..	..	..	..
Y	12	140	Report of the watch	140	140	140	140	..	140	140	140	140	140	140	140	140
N	1	141	Peter and John at the tomb	..	..	..	..	..	141	..	..	..	..	..	..	..
N	0	142	Appearance to Mary	..	..	..	..	..	..	..	..	..	..	..	..	..
Y	13	||143	Appearance at Emmaus.	143	143	143	143	143	143	143	143	143	143	143	143	143
Y	13	||144	Seen by ten apostles	144	144	144	144	144	144	144	144	144	144	144	144	144
Y	13	||145	Seen by eleven apostles	145	145	145	145	145	145	145	145	145	145	145	145	145
Y	13	||146	Seen by seven apostles	146	146	146	146	146	146	146	146	146	146	146	146	146
Y	13	||147	Appearance to all the disciples	147	147	147	147	147	147	147	147	147	147	147	147	147
Y	13	||148	Ascension	148	148	148	148	148	148	148	148	148	148	148	148	148
Y	11	||149	Conclusion	149	149	149	149	149	149	149	149	149	149	..	..	149

Author Index

413

414